BARTH RECEPTION II

BARTH RECEPTION
IN BRITAIN

D. Densil Morgan

t & t clark

Published by T&T Clark International
A Continuum imprint
The Tower Building   80 Maiden Lane
11 York Road   Suite 704
London SE1 7NX   New York NY 10038

www.continuumbooks.com

First published 2010
Paperback edition first published 2012

D. Densil Morgan has asserted his right under the Copyright, Designs and Patents Act, 1988, to be identified as the Author of this work.

British Library Cataloguing-in-Publication Data
A catalogue record for this book is available from the British Library

ISBN: 978-0-5670-3186-0 (Hardback)
ISBN: 978-0-5675-2710-3 (Paperback)

Typeset by Newgen Imaging Systems Pvt Ltd, Chennai, India
Printed and bound in Great Britain

CONTENTS

CONTENTS

CONTENTS

ACKNOWLEDGEMENTS

The following study is an exercise in Bangor theology. It evolved from my ongoing researches in nineteenth and twentieth century Welsh religious history in its European context. Theology and biblical studies have been part of the remit of what was the University College of North Wales, latterly Bangor University, from its inception in the 1880s. Given the soundly biblical character of Bangor theology and its Calvinistic background, it is hardly surprising that Karl Barth's thought resonated here early. Lewis Valentine and Ivor Oswy Davies were Bangor graduates while J. E. Daniel taught Christian doctrine to Bangor ordinands for two decades and more. As a BD student my own teachers, J. Alwyn Charles and E. Stanley John, encouraged me to take Barth's theology with the seriousness that it deserved. It is a privilege to have inherited such a rich tradition.

Research for the volume began in 2008 with a residential term in Regent's Park College, Oxford, and was concluded with my membership of the Center for Theological Inquiry in Princeton, New Jersey, during the latter part of the year. I would like to register my thanks the principal and fellows of Regent's Park College, and to the director, staff and colleagues at CTI for support, facilities and stimulating companionship during my time in residence. Library staff at Regent's Park, the Bodleian, Pusey House and the Theology Faculty Library in Oxford showed me much kindness, as did colleagues in Princeton. Dr Clifford Anderson and Kenneth Henke at Princeton Theological Seminary's Barth Center were especially helpful. Thanks are due too to Dr Iain Torrance, president of PTS. Here in the United Kingdom, Professor David Fergusson of New College, Edinburgh, and Professor John Webster of the University of Aberdeen have shown interest in this project and given encouragement throughout. Thomas Kraft and Anna Turton at Continuum have provided great support while P. Muralidharan has been a pattern of conscientiousness in the production of the text. Robert and Helen Roberts entrusted me with the papers of Helen's late father, the Revd Ivor Oswy Davies, which are now deposited in the Bangor University archive.

I would like to register once more the support of my students and colleagues here in the School of Theology and Religious Studies, not least Dr Robert Pope. He has spent time in reading the manuscript and I have benefited, as always, from his wisdom, erudition and friendship. All weaknesses, it hardly needs to be said, are my own. On the occasion of the 125th anniversary of the establishment of the university, the volume is dedicated to theology at Bangor.

INTRODUCTION

Despite some early studies,[1] it was not until a decade following his death that the beginnings of a measured scholarly assessment of Karl Barth's impact on British theology began to emerge. Commencing with S. W. Sykes's 1979 essay 'The study of Barth',[2] a number of chapters and articles describing his influence and accounting for his significance began to appear. If Richard H. Roberts' 'The reception of the theology of Karl Barth in the Anglo-Saxon world: history, typology and prospect'[3] was the most wide-ranging and substantial, other contributions, most notably Geoffrey W. Bromiley's 'The abiding significance of Karl Barth'[4] and 'The influence of Barth after World War II',[5] had already marked out the bounds of the study and suggested that Barth's fullest effect was yet to come. The first book length study of British Barth reception, Anne-Kathrin Finke's *Karl Barth in Grossbritannien*, an excellent summary of Barth's impact on English and Scottish religion between the 1920s and the 1980s was published in 1995. Written for a German readership, it contains a perceptive analysis of the early context and the way in which P. T. Forsyth, especially,

[1] John McConnachie, 'Karl Barth in Great Britain', *Union Seminary Review* 46 (1935), 302–7; idem., 'Der Einfluss Karl Barths in Schottland und England', in Ernst Wolf (ed.), *Theologische Auftsätze Karl Barth zum 50. Geburstag* (München: Chr. Kaiser Verlag, 1936), pp.559–70.

[2] S. W. Sykes, 'The study of Barth', in idem (ed.), *Karl Barth: studies of his theological method* (Oxford: Clarendon Press, 1979), pp.1–16.

[3] Richard H. Roberts, 'The reception of the theology of Karl Barth in the Anglo-Saxon world: history, typology and prospect' in S. W. Sykes (ed.), *Karl Barth: centenary essays* (Cambridge: Cambridge University Press, 1989), pp.115–71.

[4] Geoffrey W. Bromiley, 'The abiding significance of Karl Barth', in John Thompson (ed.), *Theology Beyond Christendom: essays on the centenary of the birth of Karl Barth* (Allison Park, PA: Pickwick Publications, 1986), pp.331–50.

[5] Geoffrey W. Bromiley, 'The influence of Barth after World War II', in Nigel Biggar (ed.), *Reckoning with Barth: essays in commemoration of the centenary of Karl Barth's birth* (Oxford: Mowbray, 1988), pp.9–24.

paved the way for a positive assessment of Barth, and how T. F. Torrance became the Swiss theologian's most influential British interpreter.[6] With Alister E. McGrath's impressive intellectual biography of Torrance published in 1999, the magnitude of Barth's reputation was, after decades of disparagement, afforded its due: 'Karl Barth is widely acknowledged to be one of the greatest theological luminaries of all times'.[7] Torrance, for his part, was deemed essential in the process of evaluation, appropriation and assimilation of Barth's theology within the English-speaking world.

If the present study follows Finke in mapping out chronology, it approximates McGrath in noting that regional, indeed national differences have been elemental for the reception of Barth's theology in the British Isles. The mechanics of Barth reception, it is claimed, demanded a workable translation into English of key texts including, ultimately, the whole of the *Church Dogmatics*; a reputable journal, namely the *Scottish Journal of Theology*, in which Barth's theology was taken seriously and not marginalized; in T & T Clark a company willing to take on the publishing venture as a whole; and in the faculty of divinity in New College, Edinburgh, a powerful institutional base in which creative theology in Barth could be carried out and perpetuated.[8] This occurred, as it happens, not in England but in Scotland where a Reformed tradition, European in sympathy and moulded by Genevan standards, was already open to Barth's insights. Within the divinity faculties of the Scottish universities, Christian dogmatics, where theology *per se* rather than phenomenology, the philosophy of religion or patristic studies of a historical nature, had been the staple fare since the days of John Knox, meant that Barth's views, even when queried, could never be sidelined or ignored.

It could also be argued that the Augustinianism of Scottish Enlightenment thought, illustrated by the work of the philosopher Norman Kemp Smith and others, was also highly conducive to the acceptance of Barth's theology. Smith, his younger contemporary John Anderson and, more recently, the ethicist Alasdair MacIntyre, all challenged the easy optimism of the reigning progressive liberal or Marxist orthodoxies in order to restate a classical epistemology radically at odds with prevailing trends. Kemp Smith's 'secular Calvinism' and its derivatives signalled 'a theoretical moment which has both a secular and a theological dimension',[9] and served to characterize

[6] Anne-Kathrin Finke, *Karl Barth in Grossbritannien: rezeption und wirkungsgeschichte* (Neukirchen-Vluyn: Neukirchener Verlag, 1995).

[7] Alister E. McGrath, *T. F. Torrance: an intellectual biography* (Edinburgh: T & T Clark, 1999), p.113.

[8] Ibid., pp.113–33.

[9] Craig Beveridge and Ronnie Turnbull, *Scotland after Enlightenment* (Edinburgh: Polygon, 1997), p.121; see their whole discussion in chapter 7, 'The Augustinian Moment', pp.111–34.

Scottish intellectual history in a way which was not replicated elsewhere. The fact is that during his lifetime Barth's reputation was persistently higher in Scotland than south of the river Tweed.

If this was true of Scotland, English theology was dominated by an established religion of a very different kind. Doctrinally the Church of England was minimalist, its mores were insular rather than European, and its key doctrine, since the *Lux Mundi* synthesis of 1889 at least, was that of the incarnation. It eschewed antipathies between nature and grace, philosophy and revelation, and due to its massive institutional presence and indissoluble link with the power of the state, it would instinctively trivialize all alternative theological constructs and ecclesiastical traditions. Along with Roman Catholicism, this was particularly true of Protestant Dissent. It was hardly surprising, therefore, that 'the practice of theology deriving from the English tradition of interpretation disallows challenges that . . . Barth offer[s]. Meanwhile, theology is carried on by experts whose norms are drawn from elsewhere'.[10] According to Daniel W. Hardy's analysis, the English tradition was dominated by epistemological pragmatism, moralism and an aversion to claims of revelation which could not be verified according to rationalistic norms. It was also beholden to a class based social structure organized under monarch and bishops: 'English theologians live and work in a unified English culture that has its own largely hidden standards of value'.[11] There was little wonder, therefore, that Barth, whose programme existed to subvert radically such a scheme, could hardly be understood by English theology during much of the twentieth century, much less embraced.

Even in England this was not the whole story. Anglicanism itself possessed a dissident tradition of Anglo-Catholic Biblicism, represented by Edwyn C. Hoskyns, which reminded the national church that it should not be in thrall to the state and that the gospel existed to judge the people as well as to redeem them. More potent still was Protestant Dissent which, in its churchly, Genevan form, provided the most effective bridgehead for Barthian influence outside Scotland and Wales prior to the work of T. F. Torrance and others. If the *Scottish Journal of Theology* served as a forum where Barth's thought could be debated seriously from the 1950s on, that function had been fulfilled by *The Presbyter* during the 1940s, and if New College, Edinburgh, provided an institutional base for Barthian influence during the post-war decades, the Congregationalists' Mansfield College, Oxford, had performed that purpose during the 1930s and beyond. Like Scottish Presbyterianism, Genevan high church Dissent, replete with

---

[10] Daniel W. Hardy, 'The English tradition of interpretation and the reception of Schleiermacher and Barth in England', in James O. Duke and Robert F. Streetman (eds), *Barth and Schleiermacher: beyond the impasse?* (Philadelphia: Fortress Press, 1988), pp.138–62 [161].

[11] Ibid., p.142.

its alternative vision of the link between gospel, church and state,[12] had been remarkably open to Barth's contribution, not least during the German Church Conflict and the Second World War.

Then, of course, there was Wales. Intellectually Wales has been mostly invisible to the rest of the world. It has certainly been ignored by its neighbour to the east. Yet Barth's theology registered forcefully in Wales at a very early juncture, his work was known through translation in Welsh even earlier than in English, while the standard of Welsh language discussion of Barth has been uniformly high. In the influential Bangor theologian J. E. Daniel, during the 1930s and 1940s Barth found an advocate second to none.[13] The reasons for this receptivity are not hard to find. Barth was, after all, not a hierarchical German Lutheran but a democratic Swiss from a minor European country overshadowed by its neighbours whose principal ecclesiastical tradition was Reformed. Welsh Nonconformity was Calvinistic in creed and put a huge premium on the value of the preached Word. The early Barth was known as a preacher and an exponent of preaching. A vital theology of the Word of God was bound to attract.[14]

'Barth reception', according to McGrath, 'is a developing and contested discipline, in which a "settled" or "received" view is subject to change and modification'.[15] The following assessment is aimed as a modest contribution to that ongoing debate.

---

[12] Cf. Daniel T. Jenkins, *The British: their identity and their religion* (London: SCM, 1975), pp.96–113.

[13] D. Densil Morgan, *The Span of the Cross: Christian religion and society in Wales, 1914–2000* (Cardiff: University of Wales Press, 1999), pp.133–6.

[14] See D. Densil Morgan, *Wales and the Word: historical perspectives on Welsh identity and religion* (Cardiff: University of Wales Press, 2008), pp.120–41 and below.

[15] McGrath, *T. F. Torrance: an intellectual biography*, p.114.

1

ADOLF KELLER AND THE CONTINENTAL INTRODUCTION TO KARL BARTH IN BRITAIN, 1925–30

Barth and his work, 1914–25

On 11 November 1918 the guns of the Great War were finally silenced and an armistice was signed. For four long and bloody years Germany and Britain and their allies had been at war and the whole of Europe as far east as Turkey had been convulsed. From his Alpine parish of Safenwil in neutral Switzerland the 32-year-old Reformed pastor Karl Barth had been following the progress of the conflict from the beginning. If the unconditional truths of the gospel had been suspended in early September 1914 when 93 German intellectuals, including the great Marburg theologians Martin Rade and Wilhelm Herrmann, had signed a statement supporting the Kaiser's policy: 'It is truly sad! Marburg and German civilisation have lost something in my eyes by this breakdown, and indeed forever',[1] on armistice day Barth was correcting the proofs of a commentary on St Paul's epistle to the Romans on which he had been working since the summer of 1916. Although his main concerns throughout the war had been with his parish, from the economic conditions of the few hundred industrial workers who lived in Safenwil to the preacher's problem of finding an adequate theology in which to convey the gospel message to his congregation Sunday by Sunday,[2] he was

---

[1] James D. Smart (ed.), *Revolutionary Theology in the Making: Barth–Thurneysen correspondence, 1914–25* (London: Epworth Press, 1964), p.26; cf. Karl Barth, *The Humanity of God* (London: Collins, 1961), pp.12–13.

[2] Eberhart Busch, *Karl Barth: his life from letters and autobiographical texts* (London: SCM, 1976), pp.60–125.

nevertheless perpetually engaged with what was happening in the world round about. In his almost daily correspondence with his friend and ministerial colleague Eduard Thurneysen in the nearby village of Leitwil, he affirmed what had now become a solid conviction, that a truer theology would have equipped them to respond more effectively to the cataclysmic clash that had taken place: 'If only we had been converted to the Bible *earlier* so that we would now have solid ground under our feet! One broods alternately over the newspapers and the New Testament and actually sees fearfully little of the organic connection between the two worlds'.[3] More an attempt to get to grips anew with the ever-pertinent thought of the apostle than an elucidation of the connection between the biblical world and the present, the commentary at least had a cathartic effect on its author. He had written in his diary, with a sense of relief, on 16 August: 'Romans finished!'[4] Although the Berne publisher had printed the year 1919 on the title page, the volume's print run of a thousand copies had reached the bookshops by December 1918. No-one, its writer least of all, realized the extent of the effect that it was about to have.

Between the publication of the first edition of the Romans commentary and the first impact that his work would have on the English-speaking public both in Britain and elsewhere, Barth had left parish work for a professorship in Reformed theology in the German university of Göttingen. In October 1921 he became the sole Reformed member in a staunchly Lutheran faculty and, without an earned doctorate of his own, he had been obliged to work hard to master not only key reformation texts but a whole body of patristic and medieval teaching. His earliest lecture series, on the Heidelberg Catechism (1921–22), Calvin (1922), Zwingli (1922–23) and the Reformed Confessions (1923) as well as a highly perceptive course delivered during the winter semester of 1923–24 on Schleiermacher, the father of liberal theology (whom he found that he had to challenge at every turn),[5] built up in him sufficient confidence to begin expounding a doctrinal scheme of his own. His first attempt at a systematic theology, a course entitled 'Instruction in the Christian Religion', purposely echoing Calvin's own *Institutio*, was given over two semesters, the summer of 1924 and the winter of 1924–25, the first part treating revelation and the doctrine of God[6] and the second the doctrine of reconciliation. This would become the

---

[3] Smart (ed.), *Revolutionary Theology in the Making*, p.45.

[4] Busch, *Karl Barth: his life from letters*, p.105.

[5] Karl Barth, *The Theology of Calvin* (Grand Rapids: Eerdmans, 1995); idem, *The Theology of the Reformed Confessions* (Louisville: John Knox Press, 2002); idem, *The Theology of Schleiermacher* (Edinburgh: T & T Clark, 1982).

[6] Karl Barth, *The Göttingen Dogmatics: instruction in the Christian religion* (Edinburgh: T & T Clark, 1991).

basis for his first published volume of dogmatics, *Die christliche Dogmatik im Entwurf: Die Lehr vom Worte Gottes* (1927) 'Christian Dogmatics in Outline: The Doctrine of the Word of God'. He also gave regular expository lectures on such biblical texts as the Epistle of James, the First Epistle of John, Paul's letters to the Ephesians and the Philippians and the Sermon on the Mount.

If the small band of Reformed students and ministerial candidates at Göttingen knew something of the detail of his developing thought, from 1923 the German and Swiss public knew Barth through his growing reputation as a lecturer at religious gatherings, from the pages of a new theological publication *Zwischen den Zeiten* ('Between the Times') and a highly contentious, if courteous, controversy with one of the most learned exponents of contemporary liberal theology, the church historian Adolf von Harnack from Berlin. From its first number in January 1923 *Zwischen den Zeiten* became the mouthpiece of the new school of 'dialectical theologians' including Barth, Thurneysen, Emil Brunner soon to be elected to the chair of theology in Zürich, Friedrich Gogarten, Rudolf Bultmann and others. They were all young, hardly identical in their emphases, but all disenchanted with the prevailing liberalism and seeking a new beginning for the evangelical pulpit and for Protestant theology generally. Also in January 1923 on the pages of the Protestant periodical *Die Christliche Welt* ('The Christian World') Barth crossed swords with Harnack, his senior by more than three decades and among the most revered of his former teachers. Whereas Harnack held out for 'scientific' theology, meaning ostensibly objective Christian theology which took the presuppositions of the Enlightenment as its starting point and sought common ground with secular academic disciplines, Barth was adamant that the object of Christian theology was God and therefore it could never accept naturalistic assumptions as being axiomatic. For Harnack, the younger man was nothing less than 'a despiser of academic theology' whereas for Barth, the great Berlin professor had radically secularized the whole Christian scheme. Although they retained respect for one another, there was no doubt that the abyss which had come to separate them was vast.[7]

Neither was there any doubt of the terrific support that Barth was gleaning, and that the younger generation of theological students and post-war ministers felt that a new phase in European religious life had dawned. 1924 saw the publication of three works by Barth, a theological exposition of 1 Corinthians *Die Auferstehen der Toten* ('The Resurrection of the Dead') centring especially on chapter 15,[8] a collection of essays and lectures

---

[7] H. Martin Rumscheidt, *Revelation and Theology: an analysis of the Barth–Harnack correspondence of 1923* (Cambridge: Cambridge University Press, 1972).

[8] Karl Barth, *The Resurrection of the Dead* (London: Hodder and Stoughton, 1933).

entitled *Das Wort Gottes und die Theologie* ('The Word of God and Theology'),[9] and a volume of sermons written jointly by him and Eduard Thurneysen, *Komm, Schöpfer Geist!* ('Come, Holy Spirit!').[10] None of these works conveyed the range of Barth's dogmatic interests or the nature of his reappraisal of the Protestant tradition, but they did serve to show that his work could not be ignored and that new life was being breathed into the evangelical faith from a group of extraordinarily gifted young theologians. After four hectic and exceptionally fruitful years, in October 1925 Barth and his family moved once more, this time to take up an appointment as professor of theology in the University of Münster, Westphalia.

Adolf Keller and 'The Theology of Crisis'

Among those who could not help taking a lively interest in Barth and his companions and in changes in the religious situation generally was a fellow Swiss Adolf Keller (1872–1963). Both men knew one another well, in fact between 1904 and 1909 Keller had been senior pastor of the Swiss Reformed Church in Geneva when Barth, who was 14 years his junior, had begun his ministerial apprenticeship as curate serving the church's German congregation. During succeeding decades Keller would become a leading ecumenical figure and interpreter of continental thought to the churches of Britain and America. His student career had taken him to the universities of Basel, Geneva and Berlin before ordination and 3 years service in Cairo as assistant pastor of the city's Protestant parish as well as teaching in the international school there. From Egypt he had done research at the monastery of St Catherine on Mount Sinai as part of a team collating the Greek text which James Moffatt would use as a basis for his English translation of the New Testament, and later joined an expedition studying archaeological remains in the Coptic monasteries of the Western Desert. Having returned to take up the Geneva pastorate, he had been called in 1909 to the church of St Peter's in Zürich. He became secretary to the Swiss Church Federation in 1920 and throughout the political and financial crisis which had hit post-Versailles Germany he served as secretary to the European Central Bureau for Inter-Church Aid. This led, in turn, to his work with the World Alliance for International Friendship through the Churches. 'The soul of the enterprise was Adolf Keller, a pastor from German Switzerland', recalled Marc Boegner, a leader in the French Reformed Church, 'a man with uncommon capacity for hard work . . . He had the ability to focus attention on the most striking

---

[9] Karl Barth, *The Word of God and the Word of Man* (New York: Harper and Row, 1928).

[10] Karl Barth and Eduard Thurneysen, *Come Holy Spirit* (Edinburgh: T & T Clark, 1934).

aspects of the often unhappy lives of the churches which the committee felt itself obliged to support by financial assistance'.[11] The much-travelled and urbane Keller was soundly Reformed in his faith. Barth was fortunate to find in him such a knowledgeable, well-connected and sympathetic interpreter of his early work.

In a two-part essay entitled 'The Theology of Crisis' in *The Expositor*, the journal edited by James Moffatt, for March and April 1925, Keller described the new theological mood and put Barth's still evolving thought into context. 'Overnight, so to speak, continental theology, at least in Germany and Switzerland', he wrote, 'was found to be in a new position, since Karl Barth has thrown his *Römerbrief* into the field of theological discussion'.[12] The book had caused huge excitement and unprecedented discussion with animated responses by Harnack, Jülicher, Gogarten, Tillich and a host of others. Barth's second edition of the Romans commentary of 1922 had strengthened his position, while his early volume of sermons *Suchet Gott, so werdet ihr leben* ('Seek God and You Will Live'), written jointly with Eduard Thurneysen and published in 1917, and his later publications, *Das Wort Gottes und die Theologie* and *Komm, Shöpfer Geist!* as well as the essays in *Zwischen den Zeiten* had made his position known. Keller provided his readers with biographical information mentioning the Safenwil pastorate and the Reformed professorship in Lutheran Göttingen: 'The new professor attracted at once unusual interest, and started, especially among the students and younger theologians, a movement which fertilized theological interests over the whole field'.[13] Neither Barth nor his colleagues claimed to belong to a new theological school: 'The whole group would rather consider its work as a necessary criticism of every theology, as a critical footnote to be put under all theological and ecclesiastical activity, or as a bit of cinnamon strewn on every theological dish which present day Protestantism is enjoying'.[14] Their precursors were Blumhart, Overbeck, Luther, Zwingli and Calvin but especially St Paul. As for the tradition embodied in Schleiermacher, Harnack and Troeltsch: 'In the eyes of Barth and his friends the tendency represented by this latter group of modern theologians . . . is a deplorable deviation from the truth underlying the Christian religion, a kind of theological fall for which they should do penance in sackcloth and ashes'.[15]

---

[11] Marc Boegner, *The Long Road to Unity* (London: Collins, 1970), p.74; cf. Ruth Rouse and Stephen C. Neill, *A History of the Ecumenical Movement, 1517–1948* (London: SPCK, 1967), pp.554–8.

[12] Adolf Keller, 'The Theology of Crisis', *The Expositor*, 9th series 3 (1925), 164–75, 245–60.

[13] Ibid., 165.

[14] Ibid., 166.

[15] Ibid., 166.

According to Keller, Barth's theology began with the inevitable crisis which occurs when men and women encounter the living God: '*Crisis* is the only word which depicts adequately this situation'.[16] It is the discovery that God is radically different from that which human religiosity or logic had perceived God to be. Humans desire to know, possess or contact God but have to realize that God is uncontactable, 'that there is no way from man to God, that no human thinking, not even the highest moral or religious vision, can get hold of Him . . . Barth blames the whole of modern theology for laying too much emphasis on the immanence of God and for suppressing thereby the distance between God and men'.[17] Orthodoxy and mysticism no less than liberalism had taken for granted that God could be known, while Barth challenged forcibly the blasé nature of their assumptions. In their pious hubris even sound orthodoxy and supernaturalism had forgotten that God was God, the Unknown, who cannot be possessed, domesticated or lived with in a comfortable way. It was Barth's 10-year experience as a parish minister which forced this conviction upon him: 'The preacher who realises the depth of this crisis can no more preach. He is unable to take God's Word on his lips'.[18] God is inaccessible in his sovereignty, a fact that modern theology had blithely ignored. It had based a huge structure of natural theology on what was, in fact, an erroneous supposition: 'It is *hubris* to build a theology . . . on the religious data which are to be found in human souls, on a religious self-consciousness or experience which is fallacious and unable to throw a bridge to the unknown world of God'.[19]

For Barth even revelation was indirect: 'As soon as Christians pretend to express his being in specific concepts or to represent his action in visible forms or in symbols, He disappears, wraps himself in clouds of an unapproachable mystery, till only a questionable human image remains in man's soul'.[20] God certainly exists, and he exists within creation, but he does so in his hiddenness, as the *Deus absconditus* in all earthly forms including that of the human soul, *finitum non est capax infiniti*: 'What men mean when they speak of the God they feel present or immanent in their feelings, in their subjectivity, is not God but an idol'.[21] The error of much current academic theology, and that which was popular in the churches, was the easy belief that God's ways could be known through the historical process: 'It is a specific mistake of the school of Ritschl to pretend to find God in history'.[22] Neither could there be a synthesis between God and spirit as

---

[16] Ibid., 166.
[17] Ibid., 167.
[18] Ibid., 168.
[19] Ibid., 168.
[20] Ibid., 168.
[21] Ibid., 169.
[22] Ibid., 169.

in mysticism: 'Mystical theology is quite the same utter impossibility as natural theology. God is not within human reach'.[23] God, therefore, is only known as the unknown or, in crisis, as the God who is against us: 'A terrible wrathful "No!", condemning the world and men as they are, is the only direct way by which his presence is made known to the human heart and conscience'.[24] On the basis of Keller's exposition, it was difficult to know whether the crisis theologians were condemning human beings for their creatureliness or their sinfulness, a common criticism of the early Barth, but he continued: 'If God transcends all human cognition, then the only positive element in our knowledge of him lies in negation'.[25] Religion, for its part, presupposes not a negation but an affirmation of the genius of human spirituality and as such was false: 'The church tries to transform the impossible God into a possible, intelligible deity'.[26] For Barth and his friends this trivialized the whole process, and they felt that they had scriptural warrant for their view: 'All the woes which Jesus spoke against the synagogue are applied by Barth to the Christian church'.[27] Yet despite everything the church is inevitable and necessary: 'An everlasting "No!" is thrown by God into the face and ears of all men who claim to know him, to do his work, to work for his kingdom, to possess his Spirit'.[28] In the face of the divine crisis, all that people can do is despair of their own righteousness and turn in humble submission to God.

The gospel, moreover, is good news and not a matter for despair. Into this crisis comes Christ, the unique revelation of the transcendent God though as such he is only obliquely apparent: 'Even in the historic life of Christ God touches the human soul only as a tangent touches a circle . . . In so far as the life of Christ forms a part of history, it is quite as problematic as everything else in history'.[29] On the cross Christ places himself at the disposal of the crisis and God breaks through in the resurrection. This is the supreme negation leading to a new reality. Even then its reality is indirect: 'We cannot see, know, prove or feel that Jesus is the Christ, that God is in him as the killing and vivifying power of supreme life. All that we see on the cross is . . . the outstretched finger pointing towards something which is hidden and which can only be *believed*'.[30] All is oblique, contradictory, tangential and indirect. Even faith itself is mysterious and paradoxical: 'Faith is faith only in so far as it does not pretend to yield any historic or

---

[23] Ibid., 169.
[24] Ibid., 169.
[25] Ibid., 169–70.
[26] Ibid., 170.
[27] Ibid., 170.
[28] Ibid., 171.
[29] Ibid., 171–2.
[30] Ibid., 173.

psychological realities, but exclusively the hidden reality of God'.[31] It submits to that which is never its own possession. It is a human impossibility and belongs to the category of the divine.

In his pioneering article, Keller tried to give a feel for Barth in Barth's own words. The Swiss theologian's use of dialectic would have been unfamiliar to his readers: 'A too direct statement concerning the transcendent world has at once to be corrected or annulled by its opposite, containing as much truth as the positive utterance'.[32] Barth's whole scheme was dynamic, not rigid: 'Neither the affirmation alone nor the negation alone expresses the truth'.[33] But was this just another philosophy like Hegel's or Schelling's? Were the dialectic to become a formal method of elucidating truth, that may have been the case, but Barth's point was that divine truth could only be glimpsed rather than commandeered: 'The source of any understanding of God's intention for man lies not in any human method, not even in the dialectic one, but in Jesus Christ exclusively'.[34] What the dialectic method could do was to witness to the transcendent Christ who, in the freedom of revelation, retained his absolute sovereignty: 'With Jesus the new *aeon* appears vertically from heaven, miraculously placed amidst us by God's will'.[35] In direct contradiction to liberalism which had domesticated God, and distinct from orthodoxy which, through the soundness of its formulae, had mastered God, the real God breaks in from beyond: 'A new creation has begun, the reign of grace has replaced the reign of sin, Christ has revealed it as the *Kurios*, as the Son of God'.[36] This Christ cannot be known after the flesh, the scholarly consensus of secular history and profane rationality but can only be known through the miracle of revelation. The same was true of the resurrection. Although Christ's resurrection occurred within history, it could not be comprehended according to the canons of history, 'it is not a miracle in the sense of an exceptional case in the world'.[37] Barth's scheme was wholly eschatological: 'The day of the kingdom, of the resurrection, is the last day of man and therefore not to be found in the relativity of time'.[38] True Christian faith was transcendent, miraculous, having to do with eternal realities not bound by time, though manifested, paradoxically, within both space and time. For Barth, the evangelical preacher, the greatest miracle was the forgiveness of sin, that in Christ God recreated humankind

---

[31] Ibid., 174.
[32] Ibid., 246.
[33] Ibid., 246.
[34] Ibid., 247.
[35] Ibid., 248.
[36] Ibid., 249.
[37] Ibid., 251.
[38] Ibid., 251.

in the midst of sin: 'Barth thus revives in its entirety the Reformation doctrine of justification by faith'.[39]

In bringing his description to a close, Keller repeated the fact that the crisis theology was sweeping much of the younger European world before it, and that there was much more to come. If Barth was the movement's exegete, Brunner was its systematic theologian, Gogarten its philosopher and Thurneysen its pastoral theologian, and during its short life its effect had been salutary and bracing. In fact it was engendering more excitement than any religious movement in recent times. There were, however, questions to be asked and for Keller they had exclusively to do with the matter of ethics. 'Only a constant watchfulness and a very strong sense of responsibility will preserve this exclusion of the human will from a fatal consequence', he claimed, 'namely, a paralysis of the ethical effort'.[40]

For Adolf Keller, the most detailed and perceptive interpreter of Barth's work in Britain during its earliest stage, the most significant aspect of the new Swiss theology was its spirited challenge to a doctrinal status quo that had become jaded and self-satisfied. The older liberal establishment was in denial over the part it had played in the tragedy which had beset Europe during the preceding decade. In Germany the post-war crisis was deepening and the attitude of its traumatized people was ambivalent and difficult to discern. The galloping inflation of the winter of 1922 had added to the already ruinous economic situation and the sullen, suppressed anger over the French invasion of the Ruhr in 1923 exacerbated circumstances which were already dire. Keller would do much to convey the implications of the unfolding tragedy to the British and American churches during the next two decades, and have the invidious task of explaining before long who Adolf Hitler was and what the Nazi Party stood for. Yet however real the context of the mid-1920s was, the new theological movement could not be accounted for glibly as though it were only the product of its milieu; it was, rather, a genuine renewal of Protestant faith. Its weakness, however, was in its apparently unstable ethical base: 'Indeed the ethical problem is the weak point of the whole system'.[41] The movement's protest against historicism, psychologism and the general secularization of the Christian mind was timely and valid. Neither was its critique of a moral law which was based on extra-theological criteria wholly misplaced. Its challenge was to work out an ethics of grace founded on revelation and the doctrine of the Word. A perusal of Barth's essays in *Das Wort Gottes und die Theologie*, notably 'The Christian's Place in Society' (1919) and 'The Problem of Ethics Today' (1922),[42] should have alerted him to that fact that a confession of God's

[39] Ibid., 252.
[40] Ibid., 257.
[41] Ibid., 259.
[42] Barth, *The Word of God and the Word of Man*, pp.272–327, 136–82.

sovereignty did not eradicate morality or inhibit personal or collective responsibility in any way. This is something which he would work out with enormous skill and innovativeness in his lecture course on theological ethics at Münster in 1928 and 1929.[43] Keller, however, still needed to be assured: 'We may expect that the whole group will still have to show how an ethic is possible on such a basis'.[44]

The Anglo-German Theological Conferences

It was the context rather than the content of Barth's scheme which was the subject of a second paper assessing the state of contemporary Europe which followed Keller's initial essay. Writing in the *Church Quarterly Review* in October 1926, Willy Schuster, a theologian from Leipzig, described in breathless terms the sharp reaction against Weimar nihilism which he saw happening around him. 'Since the Reformation', he claimed, 'we in Germany have never experienced a time when religion was so sympathetically received as it is today'.[45] Although in many of the *Landeskirchen* Protestantism was the state religion supported by taxes, since the nineteenth century the intellectual classes had turned their back on Christianity believing it to be discredited while the bulk of the workers had absented themselves from their parish churches and affirmed a materialistic creed instead. By the latter part of the war even the middle classes were in open revolt. As recently as 1923 as many as 111,866 had withdrawn from church membership stating that they were atheists. Since then the tide was on the turn. The shallowness of Enlightenment materialism and emptiness of cosmopolitan hedonism had now been exposed, and people were taking both God and church seriously once more: 'There is a widespread conviction that a new epoch is dawning for the Church'.[46] Shuster's essay appeared at the same time as the young Prussian church leader Otto Dibelius's popular volume *Das Jahrhunder der Kirche* ('The Century of the Church') was making its mark. The instability, anarchy and moral vacuum of the ideologically secular Weimar republic provoked a vigorous counter reaction spearheaded by Dibelius and others: 'Truly it is high time that someone seized the helm with a strong hand, applied the criterion of an absolute morality to the new conditions and restored humanity to an awareness of what is good and what is evil.

---

[43] Karl Barth, *Ethics: lectures at Münster and Bonn* (Edinburgh: T & T Clark, 1981); cf. John Webster, *Barth's Moral Theology: human action in Barth's thought* (Edinburgh: T & T Clark, 1998), pp.41–64.

[44] Keller, 'The Theology of Crisis', 259.

[45] Willy Schuster, 'Present day religious movements in Germany', *Church Quarterly Review* 103 (1926–27), 135–63 [135].

[46] Ibid., 135.

Who can do it if the Church does not?'[47] According to Schuster, 'A new interest in the Church is being awakened everywhere . . . indifference is being thrust out and new life is emerging. It is a joy today to be a theologian. Above all, one has the impression that the world is expecting something from us'.[48]

In describing this scenario, the Leipzig theologian listed the somewhat inchoate religious groupings that had been garnering support. There was the liturgical or High Church movement, a romanticized reaction to the cerebralism and word-centredness of the orthodox Lutheran Church; the followers of the charismatic Christoph Blumhart and his healing mission at Bad Boll; the utopian Christian socialism of the Swiss leaders Leonhard Ragaz and Hermann Kutter; Rudolf Steiner's esoteric anthroposophy, and, in more sinister vein, the 'German Christian' or *Volk* movement. 'The patriotism which has been awakened afresh by the youth movement has led in some instances to a desire to revive the old German mythologies based as they are on a deep reverence for nature'.[49] This recrudescence of paganism was pointedly anti-Christian, despite retaining the title of Christian, and disturbingly anti-Semitic: 'Bitter hatred of modern Judaism has led to a passionate rejection of the Old Testament and does not stop short of the Person of the Lord Jesus'.[50] This crude aberration, however, was hardly significant. What was noteworthy was the vibrant renewal of evangelical Christianity that the Barthian movement was bringing about. 'The Baptist's call to "Repent" is heard in the new theology. It started in what is generally known as the "Dialectical Theology" of Karl Barth in Münster, Friedrich Gogarten at Jena, Emil Brunner at Zürich', and through it 'the rediscovery of the gospel has in fact begun'.[51] For Willy Schuster, a new day was dawning for the German Protestant Church: 'It is in the theology of the present day that the new religious force in German Protestantism is revealing its spiritual character most clearly', he claimed. 'Theology would seem to have realized once again her own particular nature. The conception of God has become again the centre of her thought. Indeed, a new discovery of the gospel would seem to be making itself known'.[52] By 1926, therefore, the British religious public was being clearly informed of the startling changes that were occurring in the field of continental religious thought.

---

[47] Quoted in Klaus Scholder, *The Churches and the Third Reich*, Vol 1, *The Time of Illusions, 1918–34* (London: SCM, 1987), p.35; cf. Otto Dibelius, *In the Service of the Lord: the autobiography of Bishop Otto Dibelius* (London: Faber and Faber, 1964).

[48] Schuster, 'Present day religious movements in Germany', 140.

[49] Ibid., 151.

[50] Ibid., 151.

[51] Ibid., 159–60.

[52] Ibid., 159.

Perhaps the most detailed description of both Europe's malaise and its undoubted signs of theological renewal was Adolf Keller's *Protestant Europe, its Crisis and Outlook*, a panoramic assessment of continental church life which appeared in 1927. 'In fourteen countries', he stated, 'due to an accumulation of calamities, the Protestant Church is fighting for its life'.[53] Like Schuster, Keller referred graphically to the moral degeneracy which had come to the surface in Weimar Germany. 'Drunken men and prostitutes reeled down the avenues in the night life of capitals which have been the watchwords of culture and beauty in the human spirit'.[54] The Swiss ecumenist was more high-minded than prurient, realizing that 'the mad saturnalia of the dance halls and cafes'[55] was an inevitable aspect of a deep spiritual turmoil which commanded sympathy rather than censoriousness. Yet by 1927 there were modest signs that the situation was set to improve. A new idealism was emerging: 'It is slowly eliminating the poison of that deadly relativism and scepticism which undermined culture and society. A new realism or objectivity, including all relative values, is rising in philosophy and theology as well as in literature',[56] while a consensus was forming in favour of international co-operation and brotherhood. Like Willy Schuster, he mentioned the romanticism and nature mysticism of the popular *Volk* groups: 'The Christian experience of sin is void of meaning for the larger part of these self-conscious groups, and pantheism is much nearer their hearts than Christian theism'.[57] Much more significant was the renewal of evangelical life. It was an evangelicalism, however, which diverged radically from the comfortable nineteenth-century norm. The notes of harmony, immanence and synthesis were yielding to something more jarring and confrontational. If for the liberals 'human reason is easily understood as the expression of the creative universal Spirit, as a part and function of divinity, and the laws of reason are taken as laws of divine truth',[58] the new theologians rejected this as indolence and intellectual complacency at best and, at worst, a betrayal of the gospel: 'A Christian humanism is the natural consequence of this philosophical conception . . . The supernatural elements in religious history have been more or less eliminated by liberal theology and the moral element emphasized in the Christian message'.[59] The new 'Crisis Theology', which was undoubtedly

---

[53] Adolf Keller and George Stewart, *Protestant Europe: its crisis and outlook* (London: Hodder and Stoughton, 1927), p.19.

[54] Ibid., p.20.

[55] Ibid., p.20.

[56] Ibid., p.55.

[57] Ibid., p.69.

[58] Ibid., pp.142–3.

[59] Ibid., p.143.

the most exciting development on the contemporary scene, had challenged this conception at its source:

> This movement of thought sprang up in Switzerland and Germany and is spreading like wildfire throughout the continent. It is of immediate importance because of the power and influence it is having especially over large sections of the idealistic youth who feel frustrated by the devastating effects of the war. In it, the aversion of the present generation from the spirit which led to war, becomes a genuine spiritual revolution.[60]

'Barth is the leader of the movement', Keller continued, repeating his contention that 'a large number of the younger theologians of central Europe are under the spell of this new dialectic theology'.[61]

Keller's volume was part of the campaign which had been launched immediately following the Great War to inform the British and American public of the situation abroad. Despite dispiriting odds, much was being done to alleviate hardship and bind the wounds in the Body of Christ which had been caused by the still recent conflict. The committee of the World Alliance for Promoting International Friendship through the Churches had taken the bold step of calling a meeting at Oud Wassenaar in Holland less than three months after the signing of the Versailles Treaty in order to begin a process of reconciliation and reconstruction. For the first time since the advent of the hostilities churchmen from Germany had come face to face with their co-believers from France, Britain, Belgium and the United States. The meeting was not devoid of tension, especially between the German delegation and the French, but it afforded the opportunity for Christian leaders who would play a key role in inter-war collaboration to meet one another and begin making their plans. Its key personnel were the Swedish Lutheran Nathan Söderblom, archbishop of Uppsala, the Berlin New Testament scholar Adolf Deissmann, George Bell, dean of Canterbury and chaplain to the Archbishop who would, in 1929, be elevated to the see of Chichester, and others. Adolf Keller was present representing the Swiss Reformed Church. It was from this gathering that a vision arose for an international conference of the churches to exhibit their solidarity in Christ and try to ensure that a calamity like 1914–18 would not happen again. Its result was the 1925 Stockholm conference of the Christian Council for Life and Work, the first great ecumenical gathering of the post-war era. Archbishop Söderblom set the scene: 'In the region of moral and social

---

[60] Ibid., p.147.
[61] Ibid., p.150.

questions we desire all Christians to begin at once to act together as if they were one body in one visible fellowship. This could be done by all alike without injury to theological principle'.[62] The theological question could not be so easily avoided, especially as the friction between English pragmatism, American activism and the eschatological nature of the Kingdom of God as revealed in Schweitzer's *Quest of the Historical Jesus* (1910) manifested itself tenaciously if in the conference's debates.[63]

The need for theological enlightenment if not wholesale consensus came to the fore in the series of remarkable Anglo-German theological conferences convened by Bell and Deissmann between April 1927 and March 1931.[64] Among the delegates were, on the English side, the Anglo-Catholic biblical theologian Edwyn C. Hoskyns who was even then being drawn towards the theology of Karl Barth, the Congregationalist C. H. Dodd, professor of New Testament at Mansfield College, Oxford, A. E. J. Rawlinson, canon of Durham, E. G. Selwyn, editor of the volume *Essays Catholic and Critical* (1926) and J. K. Mozeley, a large-hearted Anglo-Catholic theologian much indebted to the great Nonconformist P. T. Forsyth. Among the Germans were Karl Ludwig Schmidt, Gerhart Kittel, New Testament professor at Tübingen, Wilhelm Vollrath from Erlangen, Heinrich Frick, a systematician based in Marburg, Paul Althaus, professor of dogmatics from Erlangen and Wilhelm Stählin, professor of dogmatics at Münster. The theme chosen for discussion at the first consultation, at Canterbury in April 1927, was the Kingdom of God not least because of the diametrically opposed ways in which optimistic, evolutionary Anglo-Saxon liberalism and conservative, two-kingdom Lutheranism had tended to treat the subject. '[The Kingdom of God] cannot represent a kingdom which can be established by a natural development of worldly circumstances or by human exertions', stated Karl Ludwig Schmidt bluntly, 'but only by the interference of God from heaven . . . The Kingdom of God is beyond all ethics, a cosmic catastrophe, which is caused by God'.[65] When many Britons were putting their faith in the League of Nations and investing it with a quazi-religious aura, Paul Althaus reminded his co-delegates that the eschatological kingdom

---

[62] Quoted in W. A. Visser't Hooft, *Memoirs* (London: SCM, 1973), p.25.

[63] Ibid., pp.23–8; Kenneth C. Barnes, *Nazism, Liberalism and Christianity: Protestant social thought in Germany and Great Britain, 1925–37* (Louisville: University of Kentucky Press, 1991), pp.40–70.

[64] See Anon, 'Conference of German and English theologians', *Theology* 16 (1927), 247–95, 17 (1928), 183–260; G. K. A. Bell and Adolf Deissmann (eds), *Mysterium Christi: Christological studies by British and German theologians* (London: Longmans Green & Co, 1930), introduction.

[65] Karl Ludwig Schmidt, 'The other-worldly kingdom of God in Our Lord's teaching', Theology 9 (1927), 255–8 [256].

could never be equated with any human or churchly attempt to build or even advance the Kingdom of God on earth:

> The service of the church cannot . . . mean the transformation of world organizations into the Kingdom of God. The church knows the difference between any possible world order or form of civilization and the coming of the Kingdom of God . . . Therefore she does not forget the narrow bounds against which any Christian activity actively runs up.[66]

Yet even in Britain, the divide between the older liberalism and the newer biblical theology was becoming stark. 'A learned and pious professor of divinity has recently defined the immediate task of Christian theologians to be the expression of Christian faith in terms of evolution', stated Edwyn Hoskyns. 'But to those who regard the beliefs of the primitive Christians as in any degree normative for Christian theology, it would appear that the task of Christian theology is rather to preserve the Christian conception of God from the corrupting influence of the dogma of evolution, at least as that dogma is commonly understood'.[67] The tragedy was that the bifurcation between a this-worldly, gradualist, works-based concept of the Kingdom and a traditional Lutheran two-kingdoms dualism could justify not only pietistic inactivity but political pragmatism and, before long, the grotesque enormities of Hitler's policies. Both Kittel and Althaus would become keen supporters of the Nazi Party and, much to the disgust of many of their colleagues, theological apologists for the Third Reich.[68]

Such was the stimulation provoked by this conference that in August 1928 a second gathering was called at Eisenach, in the historic castle of the Wartburg where Luther had translated the Bible into German in 1530. The company was joined this time by the Swedish theologian Gustav Aulén, the English Congregationalist Nathaniel Micklem, then teaching in Queen's University, Ontario, Canada, and Archbishop Söderblom, the leading figure in Life and Work. The theme this time was the doctrine of the Person of Christ. Whereas the German contingent saw Christology in the context of soteriology and brought the discussion back repeatedly to the concept of justification by faith alone, the English were more beholden of the patristic witness and the Chalcedonian formula of the unity of the two natures

---

[66] Paul Althaus, 'The Kingdom of God and the Church', *Theology* 9 (1927), 290–2 [292].
[67] Edwyn C. Hoskyns, 'The other-worldly Kingdom of God in the New Testament', *Theology* 9 (1927), 249–55 [253].
[68] See Robert P. Eriksen, *Theologians under Hitler: Gerhart Kittel, Paul Althaus and Emanuel Hirsch* (New Haven: Yale University Press, 1985).

of Christ. The one British theologian who was least enamoured of the traditional formulae was, ironically, Nathaniel Micklem. 'If today we proclaim
the divinity of Jesus it must be not in virtue of omnipotence or omniscience
or other supposed metaphysical attribute of deity', he claimed, 'but in virtue
of that perfection of his soul which his teaching and life make known to
us and which we ourselves recognize as divine'.[69] Such unreconstructed
liberalism would hardly characterize Micklem after his return to the United
Kingdom in 1931 when he would champion the cause of Chlacedonian
orthodoxy and Genevan churchmanship among the English Congregationalists. But he could still claim, in 1928, that '[Jesus] did not repudiate the
term Messiah but there is reason to think that He was not himself the
subject of his preaching'.[70] The Anglicans were much more soundly orthodox in their claims. They would have nothing to do with the humanistic
suppositions of liberal Protestantism. 'Christology is evacuated of its true
content', stated Mozeley, 'when the relation between Jesus and God is
regarded as typical or illustrative of a general fundamental relation between
man and God'.[71] Hoskyns was even more incisive. On the basis of the
synoptic material including the parables, the sayings and the miracle stories,
there was no doubt that 'Jesus is completely distinct and unique not in
degree but in kind'.[72] Whereas liberal Protestantism had sought to cast
Paul in the role of the one who had deified the simple rabbi of Nazareth,
for Hoskyns Christ's deity was soundly rooted in the synoptic material:
'The death of Jesus is not primarily the death of a martyr in the cause of
reform, but a redemptive, voluntary and liberating act'.[73]

> The student of the synoptic gospels cannot and must not use the
> language of orthodoxy at the moment he is interpreting the New
> Testament. He cannot move easily with such terms as the deity of
> Christ, his human and divine nature, his pre-existence, but this does
> not mean that they are not necessary for bringing out what is latent
> in the synoptic gospels.[74]

It was the patient, scholarly and careful elucidation of the synoptic texts
he insisted, which led to claim that '[the] figure of Jesus is not an epiphany
of the Son of God, but neither is it an ascending deification of a man'.[75]

---

[69] Nathaniel Micklem, 'Jesus as Prophet and Teacher', *Theology* 17 (1928), 208–11 [209].
[70] Ibid., 209.
[71] J. K. Mozeley, 'What is Christology?', *Theology* 17 (1928), 188–90 [189].
[72] Edwyn C. Hoskyns, 'Jesus Christ, Son of God, Saviour', *Theology* 17 (1928), 215–7
[216].
[73] Ibid., 216.
[74] Ibid., 217.
[75] Ibid., 217.

It was left to Heinrich Frich to describe the change of emphasis which was being felt everywhere on the content in the wake of the Barthian movement. The post-war generation had reacted ferociously against the optimistic and leisurely theology of Schleiermacher, Ritschl and Herrmann. Rather than being objective and uninvolved, the call now was for repentance, commitment and obedient faith. 'The human hearer is involved not in *investigare*, but to listen faithfully' to the Word from beyond. That Word was none other than Christ himself, the divine saviour, therefore '[t]heology *is* Christology, and vice versa'.[76] Theology was no longer a speculative science but an existential, eschatological and salvific reality which manifested itself through the crisis of revelation: 'Speaking of God means speaking of Christ, that is, of the saving *historia*'.[77] Such was the impact of Barth, Gogarten, Bultmann and their school that these were the categories which had captured the imagination of the bulk of the younger theologians.

A third and final symposium took place at Chichester in March 1931 by which time the substantial volume *Mysterium Christi: Christological Studies by British and German Theologians* (1930), edited by Adolf Deissmann and George Bell, had been published. It showed the older liberalism to have been largely superseded, among a younger generation of English and German scholars at least. Barth was not named, but the influence of his ideas was readily apparent. Theology was no longer speculative but biblical; its principal categories had become revelation, intrusion, the miraculous, mystery and crisis; synthesis had yielded to antithesis; the iron laws of human rationality were no longer the touchstone for the divine. Over a decade later the aftershock of Barth's 'bomb which had exploded on the playground of the theologians', namely his 1919 Romans commentary, was still being felt and its crater was highly visible to all.

Adolf Keller and 'The Dialectical Theology'

Keller's final contribution to the British reception of Barth's theology during its earliest phase came in January 1928 with an extended essay in the *Congregational Quarterly* entitled 'The Dialectical Theology: a survey of the movement of Karl Barth and his friends'. It was, in essence, an updated version of his 1925 article 'The Theology of Crisis' from the *The Expositor* and a recapitulation of the pertinent chapter from his volume of the previous year. By now the movement's main characteristics were becoming easier to clarify: its still violently expressed break with liberalism: 'The theology of Karl Barth is a frontal attack on the whole line of the theology

[76] Heinrich Frich, 'Christology in contemporary German theology', *Theology* 17 (1928), 193–200 [195].
[77] Ibid., 195.

of consciousness and against all the "historicism" and "psychologism" it implies'.[78] 'Barth and his friends', he continued, 'are directing a furious attack against a theology of immanence professed by the neo-Protestantism of *Kulturprotestantismus* as well as against a theology of experience or any mystical theology, which is considered as the most dangerous self-illusion;'[79] that any valid theology must begin with God's sovereign transcendence and self-revelation in his Word: 'If man can speak of God, it is because He has spoken first;'[80] that the crisis of grace begins with the church and its specific object is 'religion'; and that the way in which that crisis manifests itself is through dialectic: 'Barth attacks the false security of those who are flying into the sure port of *one* fact, *one* word, without knowing that a clandestine dialectic is dominating all human words by which we try to express [the] divine'.[81] The divine Word is broken, antithetic, dialectic, which leads to an existential aspect to Barth's work: 'This dialectic theology means, in fact, the refusal to accept the ordinary theory of knowledge for theological thinking'.[82] Although the Word became flesh within the ambiguities of human history, it remains authoritative even though it is only indirectly perceptible: 'In so far as it is God's hidden Word, although revealed in human relativity, it has supreme authority by placing before us the eternal God'.[83]

The advantage that Keller now had was that Barth himself had published his *Christliche Dogmatik* (1927) and observers did not have to depend on gleaning his thoughts from the Romans commentary and the occasional writings of earlier years. Barth the *enfant terrible* had now become Professor Barth, a constructive theologian in his own right. '[It is] clear that, in his main positions, he is reproducing the ancient orthodox doctrine of the incarnation as the revelation of God in the descent from heaven of the Logos, the eternal Son, who *descendit de caelo et verbum caro factum est*',[84] though he had his own take on this truth, namely, that Christ had taken upon himself sinful humanity which was, by definition, under judgement; that the revealed Christ remained hidden and veiled: 'We could not stand a real direct revelation of God's sovereignty: the miracle of it consists of the veiling of the revealed God in the flesh of sin, in deepest humiliation;'[85] and, echoing both Lutheran and Reformed convictions, that the believer was forced to respond to revelation in the crisis of justifying faith and

---

[78] Adolf Keller, 'The Dialectical Theology: a survey of the movement of Karl Barth and his friends', *The Congregational Quarterly* 6 (1928), 56–68 [61].

[79] Ibid., 61.

[80] Ibid., 61.

[81] Ibid., 65.

[82] Ibid., 65.

[83] Ibid., 66.

[84] Ibid., 62.

[85] Ibid., 62.

through radical costly obedience. 'The movement which he started is indeed sweeping like a whirlwind over a large part of the younger generation of theologians, especially in Switzerland, where it originated, and in Germany where Karl Barth is now teaching in the theological faculty of the University of Münster'.[86] What was remarkable, according to Keller, was the excitement which this new movement had caused, and that its practitioners, Barth, Brunner and Thurneysen who were Swiss Reformed, and the Lutherans Gogarten, Karl Ludwig Schmidt and Rudolf Bultmann, were an exceedingly able group of people. 'The movement has brought up fresh problems and inspired dogmatic theology with a new interest, a new earnestness and new life, to such an extent that the older schools and many of the great leaders of past decades are really bewildered and cannot quite understand whence the new wind came so suddenly'.[87] There were criticisms a plenty. Exegetes like Jülicher faulted Barth for not taking critical minutiae seriously; church historians like Harnack blamed him for not taking history with the seriousness it deserved; the *Religiongeschichte* school thought that he slighted the whole phenomena of religion, cultic activities and human spirituality; 'Orthodox theology . . . is not thoroughly satisfied with this son of the old theology, who has Esau's hands but Jacob's voice'.[88] For liberal theology Barth's view, to which it is 'the sworn enemy', is a grave regression, 'a simple representation of an old supernaturalism and an outworn biblicism'.[89] The main anxiety was that the dialectical method made all this unsure: 'a dialectical theology, it is said, is undermining and basis of ultimate truth by opposing a contra-verity to any truth which has been discovered'.[90]

By 1930 Barth's work was known in the British Isles, with a particularly positive response having occurred in Scotland, Wales and within a section of English Congregationalism. The more muted impact on Anglican theology, chiefly through the mediation of J. K. Mozley and Edwyn C. Hoskyns, would emerge after 1933. In Adolf Keller British readers were especially fortunate in having such a well-informed, insightful and astute interpreter, rooted in Barth's own Swiss Reformed faith. Although these were still early days, before the Barmen Synod, the German Church Conflict and the clash with Hitler, and preceding the publication of the fundamentally significant *Church Dogmatics* (1932–67), Keller's work helped English readers to make an informed judgement on Barth's early work. According to another report on continental theology, by the Anglican Frank Gavin in November 1929: 'Barth's supporters have developed an ardent partisanship, and friends and

---

[86] Ibid., 56.
[87] Ibid., 57–8.
[88] Ibid., 67.
[89] Ibid., 67.
[90] Ibid., 67.

foes alike speak of him with intense feeling'.[91] For Gavin, Barth's work was a timely and wholesome corrective to the subjectivism of much German piety: 'The iterated affirmation of the three-ness and transcendence of God, the insignificance of man apart from correspondence with his will, and the fresh study . . . of Holy Scripture all come as unique contributions to the present religious thought of Germany'.[92] It was through Keller, however, that the door had first been opened and the interest of the British religious public had been initially engaged.

[91] F. Gavin, 'Contemporary religion in Germany', *Theology* 19 (1929), 272–82 [279].
[92] Ibid., 279.

2

HUGH ROSS MACKINTOSH, JOHN McCONNACHIE AND THE RECEPTION OF KARL BARTH IN SCOTLAND, 1925–33

The earliest response to Barth: H. R. Mackintosh

In their significant compendium of the state of European Protestantism during the mid-1920s, Adolf Keller and George Stewart wrote of Scotland: 'Intellectual fearlessness and spirituality have characterized all sections of the Scottish church. Her theologians, historians and preachers have made large contributions to contemporary Protestantism, having also done much to interpret continental theology to American evangelicalism'.[1] Even as they were writing, the two largest Presbyterian bodies, the Church of Scotland with a membership of 756,000 and the United Free Church and its complement of half a million communicants, were in the process of amalgamating to create a unified national church. Both bodies were Presbyterian in polity, Reformed in character and held to the establishment ideal. Since the late Victorian era, even the Free Church had allowed latitude in the interpretation of biblical authority and an increasingly open attitude to the doctrines of the Westminster Confession of Faith.[2] The doctrinal consensus had evolved from a rigid Calvinism to a disciplined liberal evangelicalism, exemplified at the turn of the century by such scholars as George Adam Smith and Marcus Dods in biblical studies and James Denney in theology. Scottish religion was churchly, serious minded and still widely influential, and with the passing of

---

[1] Adolf Keller and George Stewart, *Protestant Europe: its crisis and outlook* (London: Hodder and Stoughton, 1927), p.244.
[2] A. C. Cheyne, *The Transforming of the Kirk: Victorian Scotland's religious revolution* (Edinburgh: St Andrew's Press, 1983), pp.60–87.

the parliamentary motion in October 1929, the long cherished ideal of an effective national church, witnessing to the ideals of a godly commonwealth, had come about: 'The united Church of Scotland was a national church, with control over its endowments, with a territorial organization intended to bring the gospel to every inhabitant, and with its spiritual independence guaranteed by parliamentary act'.[3]

The new situation, though praised by many, was not devoid of ambiguities. Although ideally a church of the people, the industrialized populace of the cities, especially Glasgow and Dundee, had been progressively alienated from organized Protestantism for some time while the many Irish Catholic immigrants were treated with disdain.[4] Although free to witness to the values of the godly commonwealth, the new church excluded, of necessity, Roman Catholics while the labouring classes would be relegated to the role of a permanent proletariat in a hierarchical social order. 'The Presbyterian church sought to portray the union of 1929 as a great event in the nation's history', according to the social historian Callum Brown, 'and it was attended by much pageantry. But it had been hitched to a socially conservative, racist, anti-labour manifesto whilst the leaders of the church washed their hands of the really big issue of the 1930s – unemployment'.[5] Whatever its weaknesses however, the united church did retain the loyalty and in many cases the affection of a still substantial number of the Scottish people and was an undoubted power in the land. It attracted men of enormous talent into its ministry who were faithful to the gospel and served the people with distinction. It was hardly surprising that it was two men from within their ranks, namely Hugh Ross Mackintosh, professor of divinity at New College, Edinburgh, and John McConnachie, United Free Church minister in Dundee, who became the first to alert readers in the United Kingdom that a new and important theological movement was about to break.

In the November 1924 issue of *The Expository Times*, six months before Keller's first articles in *The Expositor*, H. R. Mackintosh published a short essay entitled 'The Swiss group'. This was a brief assessment of Emil Brunner's 1923 work *Erlebnis, Erkenntnis und Glaube* ('Experience, Knowledge and Belief') and his more potent *Die Mistik und Das Wort* ('Mysticism and the Word') which had just appeared from the press. 'Professor Brunner holds the chair of theology in Zürich, and is probably the ablest of the Swiss group including Kutter, Barth and Gogarten, whose

---

[3] Stewart J. Brown, 'The social vision of Scottish Presbyterianism and the union of 1929', *Records of the Scottish Church History Society* 24 (1990), 77–96 [95]; cf. Augustus Muir, *John White* (London: Hodder and Stoughton, 1958), pp.191–267.

[4] See Stewart J. Brown, '"Outside the covenant": the Scottish Presbyterian churches and Irish immigration, 1922–38', *The Innes Review* 42 (1991), 19–46.

[5] Callum G. Brown, *Religion and Society in Scotland since 1707* (Edinburgh: Edinburgh University Press, 1997), p.141.

provocative work is arousing so much interest on the continent'.[6] In a very prescient comment Mackintosh continued: 'It may well be that we are witnessing the first beginnings of a new movement, the counterpart . . . of the Ritschlian school, dating from fifty years since'.[7] Albrecht Ritschl, whose teaching had done much to bring critical theology back to the historical Jesus of the gospels and, above else, to the centrality of the concept of the Kingdom of God, had been a dominating influence on British theologians, mostly in the Nonconformist or non-Anglican churches. 'Ritschl's interpretation of the Kingdom in ethical terms appealed strongly to the activist and progressivist temper of the age . . . It created a widespread popular conviction that Jesus had taught the fatherhood of God and the brotherhood of man and a better way of life which was steadily advancing'.[8]

Hugh Ross Mackintosh (1870–1936) was the son of a Gaelic-speaking Free Church minister in Paisley near Glasgow who had graduated in divinity from New College, Edinburgh in 1896. He was typical of his generation in accepting totally the validity of biblical criticism and the subordinate rather than absolute value of the Westminster tradition. That he was a pronounced liberal evangelical was confirmed by the fact that apart from family piety, the prime influence upon him during undergraduate days was the missionary fervour of Henry Drummond, professor of natural sciences at the Glasgow Free Church College and author of the phenomenally popular *Natural Law in the Spiritual World* (1883) which combined Darwinian evolution with a Moody and Sankey-like evangelicalism,[9] and the 'mediating theology' of Alexander Martin, minister of the Morningside United Free Church, Edinburgh, and part architect of the union between that body and the Church of Scotland in 1929.[10] This enlightened liberalism was confirmed by his New College teachers among whom were A. B. Davidson in Old Testament and Marcus Dods in the New. Following a semester at Marburg, Mackintosh became wholly enthralled by German theology. He became the co-translator of the third volume of Ritschl's *Justification and Reconciliation* (1900) and, along with James S. Stewart, of Scheiermacher's magisterial *The Christian Faith* (1928). Following pastoral charges in Dundee and Aberdeen, he was called in 1904 to the chair of Christian dogmatics in what was now the United Free Church's New College, Edinburgh, where he

---

[6] H. R. Mackintosh, 'The Swiss group', *The Expository Times* 26 (1924–5), 73–5 [73].

[7] Ibid., 73.

[8] Andrew L. Drummond and James Bulloch, *The Church in Late Victorian Scotland, 1874–1900* (Edinburgh: St Andrew's Press, 1978), p.279.

[9] Cf. A. C. Cheyne, 'The religious world of Henry Drummond', in *Studies in Scottish Church History* (Edinburgh: T & T Clark, 1999), pp.185–98.

[10] See Robert R. Redman Jr., *Reformulating Reformed Theology: Jesus Christ in the theology of Hugh Ross Mackintosh* (Lanham PA: University Press of America, 1997), pp.9–26.

stayed, exerting a salutary influence of generations on United Free and thereafter Church of Scotland ministers, until his death in 1936. He was called to the moderatorship of the General Assembly of the reunited Church of Scotland in 1932.

Along with a prolific output of academic articles and more popular books, Mackintosh's doctrinal stance was evidenced by two volumes which attained the status of classics during his own lifetime *The Doctrine of the Person of Jesus Christ* (1912) and *The Christian Experience of Forgiveness* (1928). Despite his liberal temper, his basic evangelical orthodoxy had never been in doubt. He was, however, becoming uneasy with the by now glib anti-supernaturalism of much continental theology, that it was vitiating experiential religion and sat so lightly upon the concerns of the church. The protest of the 'Swiss group', consequently, resonated strongly with him. According to their scheme, 'God confronts us in the majesty of the gospel rather than dwells inarticulately within the arcanum of the soul'.[11] Unlike the abstraction of so much current religious writing, Brunner's prose was earnest as was 'the sheer religious power of his argument'.[12] Even his exaggerations were stimulating. 'The malady of present day theology work is that it starts with man and turns God into an inference from our own experience, because it is much keener on harmonizing with culture than in listening obediently to the divine Word'.[13] The second of Brunner's books *Die Mistik und Das Wort* was a swingeing attack on Schleiermacher, the father of liberal theology and the most brilliant Reformed theologian since Calvin. 'With the conscientiousness of being on a crusade, [Brunner] has composed what is unquestionably the most serious indictment of Schleiermacher's thought that has been written for long [*sic*]'.[14] Subjectivism, immanentism and romanticism alike were taken to task. For the great German master 'continuity is the watchword throughout; the crises of saving grace are ignored'.[15] In Mackintosh's opinion, however, Schleiermacher was not as one-sided as the young Swiss professor contended: 'It may be that Brunner felt he could only get a hearing for certain truths by uttering them at the top of his voice'.[16] Brunner's main points, though, were unassailable: the objective realities of faith had succumbed to spiritual relativism while God, Christ and the gospel had been eclipsed by preconceptions which were alien to the Christian faith: 'By this absorbing and

---

[11] Mackintosh, 'The Swiss group', 74.
[12] Ibid., 74.
[13] Ibid., 74.
[14] Ibid., 74.
[15] Ibid., 75.
[16] Ibid., 75.

formidable book [Brunner] has made a deep mark on a discussion that has lasted a hundred years and is far from dying down'.[17]

This, it seems, was the first occasion that the theological revolution which had emanated in Barth's Safenwil parish and had by then consolidated around Brunner, Thurneysen and Gogarten was mentioned in a British periodical. Although the subject was Brunner more than Barth, and despite the fact that Mackintosh wrote from the heart of the Scottish theological world, a wide English-speaking readership had now been alerted to the changes which were on the way. It would be another decade before Mackintosh would seemingly commit himself to the Barthian scheme,[18] but Barth's name was at least being mentioned as one of the instigators of a new theological trend.

The earliest response to Barth: John McConnachie

John McConnachie (1875–1948) was not a professor but a parish minister who, amid the working class's deepening alienation from the churches following the Scottish religious establishment's debacle at the General Strike,[19] registered that he, too, had been drawn to the theological excitement which was being felt abroad. 'Within the last few years', he wrote in *The Hibbert Journal* in May 1927, 'a small but active group of younger theologians in Switzerland and Germany has been by means of books, lectures, and a very effective magazine *Zwischen den Zeiten*, promoting a new positive movement in theology. Already their influence is being felt in Holland and in Hungary'.[20] McConnachie had graduated from the University Aberdeen in 1896 before proceeding to New College, Edinburgh, to study divinity where he had won the prestigious Cunningham Fellowship. This, in turn, took him to Marburg. 'I was . . . trained in the school of Ritschl, as interpreted by Herrmann, being one of the Scottish "caravan" of students . . . who travelled yearly to sit at the feet of the master'.[21]

---

[17] Ibid., 75.
[18] See Thomas F. Torrance, 'H. R. Mackintosh: Theologian of the Cross', *Scottish Bulletin of Evangelical Theology* 5 (1987), 170–83, but cf. John Lewis McPake, 'H. R. Mackintosh, T. F. Torrance and the reception of the theology of Karl Barth in Scotland', unpublished Edinburgh University PhD, 1994, who is sceptical that Mackintosh either repudiated the liberalism of Ritschl and Herrmann or wholly accepted Barth's views.
[19] See Stewart J. Brown, '"A Victory for God": the Scottish Presbyterian churches and the General Strike of 1926', *Journal of Ecclesiastical History* 42 (1991), 596–617.
[20] John McConnachie, 'The teaching of Karl Barth: a new positive movement in German theology', *The Hibbert Journal* 25 (1926–7), 385–400 [385].
[21] John McConnachie, *The Barthian Theology and the Man of Today* (London: Hodder and Stoughton, 1933), p.34.

Ordained into the United Free Church in 1902, he had served two rural charges before transferring to the parish of St John's Dundee in 1911 where he would remain for the rest of his career.[22] Although his concerns were pastoral rather than academic, he had kept his theological interests intact and remained a keen student of German thought. 'Their interest is more than purely theological', he continued. 'They believe that Protestantism is experiencing today one of the critical hours of its history brought about by its own unfaithfulness to the Word of God and that it must either recover its true nature, as conceived by the Reformers, or perish'.[23] It was here that McConnachie quoted the words of the Karl Adam, from the Catholic journal *Hochland* of a year previously, that the Romans commentary 'fell like a bomb on the playground of the theologians'. It was here, also, that Barth was first likened to the London-based Scottish theologian P. T. Forsyth.

The article itself was a workmanlike description of those aspects of Barth's theology which were apparent at the time: that his basic method was dialectical, that he was overtly critical of the phenomenon of religion, and that his most positive contribution was on the divine transcendence and the deity of Christ.

> Barth's whole outlook on the world and on man, as well as his view of scripture, is ruled by his doctrine of God . . . Neither in nature nor in history nor in human experience is God to be found. Our only knowledge of God comes through revelation . . . The distinctive feature of the Bible is not its history, nor its ethics, nor its religion but the new world that meets us there.[24]

McConnachie, like virtually all his fellow Scottish clergy, had rejected the scholastic doctrine of inerrancy that was being upheld vigorously only in Princeton at the time, yet was convinced that the liberal evangelicalism which had become *de rigueur* among his contemporaries was vulnerable to the accusation of subjectivism in its doctrine of scripture. The fact that Barth had found a way of both preserving the critic's freedom and of upholding the Reformer's insistence on the objective norm of the Word of God was attractive in the extreme. For Barth, the believer 'will find the foundation of faith not in the historical documents, which are uncertain as are all things

---

[22] See John McPake, 'John McConnachie as the original advocate of the theology of Karl Barth in Scotland: the primacy of revelation', *Scottish Bulletin of Evangelical Theology* 14 (1996), 101–14.

[23] McConnachie, 'The teaching of Karl Barth', 385.

[24] Ibid., 391.

human, nor yet on the psychological experiences of religion, which are problematical, but on the revelation where the divine breaks through and the glimpse of the new world is seen'.[25] Accordingly, 'Barth would restore the Reformed valuation of the Bible with its indissoluble correlation between Word and Spirit'.[26]

For McConnachie the fact that Barth was reinstating vigorously some of the key emphases of the Protestant Reformation was most welcome. The rejuvenation of mainstream Scottish Presbyterianism which would occur, it was hoped, in 1929 with the creation of a reunited national church was a lively restatement of the Reformation ideal. Churchmanship and a renewed national establishment needed, however, to be complemented by evangelical revival and the equipping of church members with a vital personal faith. 'Barth', he stated, 'revives in its completeness the Reformation doctrine of justification by faith'.[27] Faith should never be a psychological assent or a matter of pious feelings but rather an existential affirmation of what God had achieved in Christ.

> When a man, not from a religious height, but direct from the sinful world, not with the mark of piety but in his naked creatureliness, broken and in his last distress, standing on the edge of a precipice dares to spring into the uncertain, the bottomless, and there swinging over the gulf, is taken hold of by the hand of God – that is faith.[28]

More Luther and Kierkegaard than Calvin and John Knox, the fact that Barth was taking Reformation realities seriously was as invigorating as it was unexpected. 'He is and remains a son of the Reformation who is prepared to pursue its principles to the last consequence, even beyond Luther and Calvin, in the interest of an absolute theology'.[29]

What is significant about this article apart from its sense of discovery and excitement, is the fact that its author had mastered many of the primary sources. He includes 17 quotations from the fourth edition of the *Römerbrief* (1924), twelve references to the compilation of essays *Das Wort Gottes* (1924) and a handful from the volume of sermons which Barth and his colleague Eduard Thurneysen had published together under the title *Komm, Schöpfer Geist!* (1924). Of the Romans commentary he says: '[It is] an erratic block among commentaries, solitary, old-fashioned among its

---

[25] Ibid., 392.
[26] Ibid., 392.
[27] Ibid., 396.
[28] Ibid., 397.
[29] Ibid., 392.

contemporaries, modelled on the commentaries of Calvin, of that which fills the ordinary commentary there is scarcely a trace'.[30] He was obviously drawn not only by Barth's work but by the man himself:

> He is a dynamic personality, with the prophetic fire, and a sturdy fighter for what he considers the truth. Gay, bold, challenging, unconventional in speech and dress, he is a man of the mountains, a theological mountaineer carrying us to heights where the air is thin.[31]

It was not that the Scot was uncritical of this Alpine wanderer, 9 years his junior. On perusing his work he could find no place for ethics within his scheme, a critique which came naturally to liberal Protestants who had been nurtured on the gradualist kingdom theology of Ritschl and the late-Victorian theologians of the Scottish church. 'A still more dubious feature of this theology is the absence of all verification of faith in experience',[32] he claimed. McConnachie had obviously drawn heavily from the wells of Wilhelm Herrmann, his – and Barth's – revered teacher of old. 'Barth fails also to work out satisfactorily the relation between the historical Jesus and the risen Christ'.[33] Even if a true theology needed to reinstate the objective transcendence of the resurrected Lord, there was something about Barth's writing which seemed obscure and oblique: was he, in fact, a docetist or a spiritualist even? Before the work of the Swiss-German movement could be approved, its protagonists would need to provide a guarantee that its insights were sound:

> The whole attempt of Barth and his school to find a basis of faith that will deliver it from the uncertainties of the historical and the psychological is praiseworthy, but in the end must prove impossible. We cannot dispense with these because they represent the world we know . . . But because Barth rejects this way, his Christ becomes to us too much of a *deus ex machina*, out of relation to our own known world, rather than the divine Son of Man.[34]

Yet the seed had been sown. 'This theology [both] attracts and repels us',[35] he claimed. The time was hardly ripe to reach a verdict, but there was something about the new movement which was salutary and refreshing: 'They

---

[30] Ibid., 386.
[31] Ibid., 386.
[32] Ibid., 399.
[33] Ibid., 399.
[34] Ibid., 400.
[35] Ibid., 400.

have restored the category of revelation to a place of honour, and called Christian thought anew to reverence the Word of God'.[36]

Deepening engagement

Between 1925 and the end of the decade, the British response to Barth's theology would occur most vigorously in Scotland, Wales and among English Congregationalists. Yet in September 1928 Scotland again would take the lead. As part of a series on leaders of current theological thought in *The Expository Times*, H. R. Mackintosh took Barth as his subject. By now the mild interest which he showed previously had turned into obvious engagement. 'The present-day movement in theology which evokes the deepest interest alike in friend and foe is incontestably that associated with the name of Professor Karl Barth. Especially in Germany the controversy is acute'.[37] Mackintosh's earlier essay had given Brunner precedence, yet in a later reference in March 1926 he had put Brunner and Barth on a par. 'The recent uprising of definite Calvinism in continental theology is one of the most interesting and suggestive phenomena of our day. Barth of Göttingen and E. Brunner of Zürich are perhaps the best known leaders of the movement'.[38] His latest essay, however, was on Barth alone. Like McConnachie's treatment, it was more a description of the Barthian standpoint than an assessment of its virtues or ills. God, for Barth, was transcendent and the Bible was the Word of God: 'We have to submit our minds, as theologians, to the essential voice of the Bible, where in his Word God reveals in a final authority before which we can only kneel in the dust'.[39] Whereas Protestant theology since Schleiermacher had sought to find unity, analogy and coherence between humankind and God, for Barth there was a radical disjunction: 'Our one duty as we read [the Bible] is to confess that God is right and we men are always in the wrong'.[40] The *Römerbrief*, stated Mackintosh, was a commentary like no other: 'It exhibits not a trace of purely historical interest or philosophical precision'.[41] The God to whom the text bears witness existed in such a different sphere from humankind that his self-revelation could only be perceived partially, through

---

[36] Ibid., 400.
[37] H. R. Mackintosh, 'Leaders of theological thought: Karl Barth', *Expository Times* 29 (1927–28), 536–40.
[38] H. R. Mackintosh, 'Recent foreign theology', *Expository Times* 27 (1925–26), 282–3 [282].
[39] Mackintosh, 'Leaders of theological thought: Karl Barth', 536.
[40] Ibid., 537.
[41] Ibid., 537.

a radical dialectic. Revelation would remain humanly ambiguous for God was radically different from anything that men and women could naturally absorb. There was no continuum between what we know as reality, whether in history, morals, experience or conscience, and God's unique revelation of himself. Yet the paradox or contradiction was essential in order to do justice to the case: 'We need this broken, mobile, many-dimensional thinking . . . if we are to bear witness to the truth'.[42] Barth's protest was against the harmonizing of the divine, apart from and outside of his holy and incarnate Word, with that which belonged to the sphere of the created. 'If theology is to recover its health, it must cast loose from preoccupation with the subjective phenomena of piety and take its bearings from God, the Holy and the Almighty'.[43]

Virtually all of Barth's early commentators portrayed him as being the prophet of the transcendent. By using the only categories which were to hand, usually those of traditional Calvinistic orthodoxy or those of current liberal evangelicalism, the tendency was to see his thought as being a corrective, a protest at best or a regression at worst. Not even Mackintosh fully realized the significance of what would become Barth's real contribution to modern theology, that God, in Christ, had chosen effectively to turn towards humankind in a mighty covenant relationship which was radically open to the world and called forth from the whole of creation both obedience and joy. Barth's Christ, for Mackintosh, was not the Jesus of history, neither Ritschl's nor Harnack's version of the Galilean prophet, nor Herrmann's saviour figure whose divinity was proved through his ability to compel trust in those who believed in God through him. Christ remained enigmatic, the intruder from the beyond. In him, 'the utterly strange yet absolutely gracious God has . . . by sheer miracle broken into fallen temporality, declaring his sovereign righteousness, disclosing the identity of his wrathful holiness and his pardoning compassion'.[44] 'No Barthian', he concluded, 'will ever admit that his views can be stated by an outsider without caricature, but it is to be hoped that in the foregoing account some approach to justice has been made'.[45] By now 'the Swiss group', the 'crisis theologians', or 'the theologians of the Word' had coalesced around a single figure who, although still a relatively young man, had the potential to be a theologian of immense stature. 'The theology of Barth, whatever else, is the theology of a great, a volcanic soul, that has trembled at the Word of God'.[46]

By 1929, the year of the unification of the United Free Church with the Church of Scotland and, more critically for the economic fate of the west,

---

[42] Ibid., 537.
[43] Ibid., 538.
[44] Ibid., 538.
[45] Ibid., 539.
[46] Ibid., 539.

the year of the Wall Street Crash, Barth's thought was graduating from being an interesting curiosity to becoming an indisputable factor on the British religious scene. The American Congregationalist Douglas Horton's translation of *Das Wort Gottes und die Theologie* (1924) as *The Word of God and the Word of Man* appeared simultaneously in the United Kingdom and the United States in 1928 which meant that pastors, church leaders and lay-people could gain access to Barth's work for themselves for the first time. Between then and 1932 as many as 11 book-length studies, along with Emil Brunner's swashbuckling *The Theology of Crisis* (1929), would be published on either side of the Atlantic both describing and responding to Barthian thought.

McConnachie's initial volume

Between McConnachie's *Hibbert Journal* article of May 1927 and his lengthy study of 1931, Barth himself had moved on while the Scotsman had made it his job to know more about his object's thought. As it happens Barth's first British student was another Scotsman, Norman Porteous who had studied at Münster in 1928 and following ordination into parish work would be appointed to the Aberdeen Old Testament chair. In March 1930 Barth had himself moved to the chair of systematic theology in Bonn, his third professorship within a decade, marking what would become a golden era in the history of the Protestant faculty of the university there.[47] His first visit to Britain occurred in June 1930 where he stayed in the London home of J. H. Oldham, General Secretary of the International Missionary Council, a contact that would prove important during the German Church Struggle later in the decade.[48] After meeting with English theologians and churchmen, he proceeded to Scotland where Glasgow University awarded him an honorary DD. He received tremendous applause at the graduation ceremony and '[i]t was quite apparent', reported *The British Weekly*, 'that he was regarded as one of the outstanding personalities of the occasion'.[49] He had met with theologians in Edinburgh the day before though the only opportunity to speak with H. R. Mackintosh had been on the platform of Waverley station. Thereafter he visited St Andrews and was impressed by its ancient atmosphere of learning and remarkable location.[50]

---

[47] Eberhard Busch, *Karl Barth: his life from letters and autobiographical texts* (London: SCM, 1976), pp.199–262.
[48] Keith Clements, *Faith on the Frontier: a life of J. H. Oldham* (Edinburgh: T & T Clark, 1999), p.272.
[49] Anon, 'Professor Karl Barth in Scotland', *The British Weekly*, 26 June 1930, 257.
[50] Busch, *Karl Barth: his life from letters*, pp.204–5.

McConnachie may have been among those who heard him during his Scottish tour. What we certainly know is that he visited Germany in the autumn of 1930 and sat in on part of Barth's lecture course on ethics and became disabused of his previous idea that the Swiss theologian had an inadequate ethical scheme.[51]

> To sit in his classroom, as the writer has done, and see and hear him among the students who hang upon his lips, to be with him in the more intimate surroundings of his seminars and at the open evenings in his own home, where he lets himself go, is to recognize that he is not only a great theological teacher but one of the spiritual forces of the day.[52]

It was apparent that much of the book was written between McConnachie's time in Münster and the following Christmas. He had forwarded a typescript to Barth himself along with a covering letter dated 4 January 1931. 'It is not meant to be a scientific treatment of your theology but rather your message to the preacher', he explained. 'So much of our preaching is of the subjective psychological type and there is a sense of dissatisfaction and a desire for something objective and authoritative'.[53] He implored Barth to write a foreword, something that the Swiss declined to do, stating that he did not want English or Scottish theologians merely to repeat his own theological formulae but rather to do their own wrestling with scripture in the context of their own particularities and needs: 'This is my own situation, not to produce a new form of security but to raise new questions and searchings which is so much needed in Germany today'.[54] He was, however, very appreciative of McConnachie's earlier essays and was confident that the Scotsman was a true and reliable interpreter of his work.

McConnachie's study, when it appeared, had breadth as well as length, and was based not only on the *Römerbrief* and *Das Wort Gottes* but on the Swiss's more recent publications including his 1926 student Bible studies since translated by J. Strathearn McNab as *The Christian Life* (1930), the *Christliche Dogmatik* of 1927, the Philippians commentary (1928) and the composite volume of essays *Die Theologie und die Kirche* of the same

---

[51] Karl Barth *Ethics: lectures at Münster and Bonn* (Edinburgh: T & T Clark, 1981).

[52] John McConnichie, *The Significance of Karl Barth* (London: Hodder and Stoughton, 1931), p.60; subsequent page numbers will be included in the text.

[53] John McConnichie to Karl Barth, 1 January 1931, *Karl Barth Gesamtausgabe*, Vol. 5: *Offene Briefe 1909–35*, Diether Koch (ed.), (Zürich: Theologischer Verlag, 2001), pp.147–9 [147].

[54] Karl Barth to John McConnachie, 9 January 1931, *Karl Barth Gesamtausgabe*, Vol. 5, pp.149–51 [150].

year. As before McConnachie quoted liberally from the dialectic group's magazine *Zwischen den Zeiten*. The feel of the book was much the same as the *Hibbert* article, clear, well expressed and positive. The reservations which he had expressed in 1927 were now, for the most part, withdrawn. The first chapter was descriptive, placing Barth and the other 'theologians of the Word' in their context, either within Swiss Calvinism in the case of Barth, Thurneysen and Brunner, or German Lutheranism as with Gogarten and Bultmann, while the second chapter provided a perceptive précis of Barth's intellectual development as witnessed by the successive editions of the Roman commentary. The note of novelty, discovery and sheer exhilaration was struck from the first: 'The most interesting event in the post-war religious world has been the phenomenal suddenness with which the word of Karl Barth has captured the ear of Europe, and transformed within a few years the whole outlook of continental theology, in Germany, Switzerland, Holland, Denmark and elsewhere' (p.13).

The fact that such staid middle-aged clerics as Mackintosh and McConnachie – McConnachie was 56 by now – could show such zeal and excitement was a clear indication that the liberal evangelicalism which had exuded so much freshness, energy and daring a generation earlier had now run its course. A. C. Cheyne's comment that in Scotland '[i]n the aftermath of the First World War, liberal evangelicalism continued as a living tradition, though probably with less exuberance and productivity',[55] rather understates the point. In fact it was tired, jaded and well past its prime. As for the new movement, 'what has won for it an instant hearing has been its earnestness, almost its austerity, and its union of intellect and spiritual power, bound up with a deep knowledge of the modern soul' (p.17). It was, patently 'a theology that is in deadly earnest' (p.73). All Barth's dialectical paradoxes and uncompromising axioms were rehearsed: the sovereignty of God, the discontinuity between human religiosity and the divine Word, the radical nature of saving faith and the disconcerting otherness of God's revelation in Christ. 'The biggest thing which Barth has done is that he has once more given to the thought of God its greatness, its tremendous power, its overwhelming earnestness, that he has set the sentence "God is God" once again in the middle point of theology and of religious life' (p.139).

The bulk of the book, chapters three to seven, attempt a descriptive assessment of the terminology which was causing so much difficulty for those reared in philosophical idealism to understand, theology's character as witness to the Word, the nature of the Bible and the office of the preacher, as well as Barth's concept of ethics and living the Christian life. Explaining Barth's concept of dialectic and his revelation-grounded idea of history

---

[55] Cheyne, *The Transforming of the Kirk*, p.207.

was no easy thing, but on the whole McConnachie succeeded in conveying adequately the matter in hand.

> Dialectical thinking, thinking in question and answer so that the answer contains again and again a question, is . . . the only thinking open to us in dealing with the revelation of God to man . . . Because of the contradiction in man, on which the Word of God strikes and gets broken as in a prism, we can only get witness to him in this fragmentary, dialectic manner . . . We are not to think of the Yes and No balanced over against each other in a condition of equilibrium, each, as it were, in its own right. The Yes is always primary. But the truth lies ultimately neither in the Yes nor in the No, but in the beyond where both Yes and No take their rise. (pp.79–80)

Unlike the Hegelians, both Ritschl and Herrmann were clear that there was no salvation apart from history, and McConnachie, true to his legacy in nineteenth century historicism, had no desire either to downgrade the dependability of the gospel narratives nor, for his part, the reality of the empty tomb. He found confirmation for these convictions in Barth's scheme, yet the whole concept of revelation belonged to a different category than that of history as commonly defined: 'Historical science simply cannot cope with revelation', (p.113) he claimed. 'The word, spoken in history, [is yet] on the border of history, to which Barth gives the designation *Urgeschichte*' (p.101). '*Urgeschishte* is a historical event, but has God's Word in it for us. As such it is miracle, and as a miracle is distinct from other historical events' (p.103).

This was heady stuff and McConnachie realized that in order to understand Barth, those who had been raised in the conventional pieties of either evangelicalism or modernism would have to think hard. He was, consequently, at pains to humanize his subject and assure his readers that the great theologian need not intimidate them at all:

> Barth has a healthy mind in a healthy body and a happy home life and many friends. He encourages much opposition but he loves the trumpet call to battle, and never gets 'rattled' but is quiet and patient with his opponents, yet never gives in. His humility and his humour are his saving qualities. (pp.32–3)

Although McConnachie's volume succeeded in conveying much of the essence of Barth's early work, including his reworking of what had become, for the liberals, the problematic if not wholly redundant doctrine of the Trinity, like H. R. Mackintosh he had not yet fully grasped the radical implications of God's decision to turn towards humankind in a covenant relation in Christ. Although this was already plain in the *Christliche Dogmatik* of 1927, as was his revolutionary reformulation of the doctrine of election, little of this comes to the fore. The Scotsman mentions the doctrine of election only once and then in conventional terms of God's election of individuals to service, and not referring to Christ at all (pp.240–1). Yet along with R. Birch Hoyle's *The Teaching of Karl Barth* (1930), McConnachie's book did more than anything else to enlighten the British public as to Barth's contribution by the early 1930s: 'Barth is Reformed to his very bones . . . He is the first outstanding Reformed theologian in Germany for the last 150 years' (p.268).

The volume made an immediate impact. 'Unless I am altogether at fault in my reading of man in these days, or of my own soul', wrote John Hutton in a striking leader based on the book in *The British Weekly*, Britain's premier Nonconformist newspaper of the day,

> we shall hear much of Karl Barth, and may witness even a wholesale return to a prouder, more humble, more difficult, more necessary, more personal but more holy faith . . . We in the Christian churches have been busy in many things. We have, in fact, been tempted to live by our wits. We have failed. Karl Barth, it will be wise for us to believe, has been raised by God to make that clear and to dispose us, in deep contrition, to seek for ourselves and for our age the lost sense of God.[56]

Between 1929 and 1933, the energies of Scottish Presbyterianism went into the largely ineffective church extension scheme and the consolidation of the gains which followed the reunification of the established church.[57] Theology, on the whole, still moved along in its liberal evangelical groove, indeed the liberal tradition still succeeded in drawing into its ranks substantial theologians like John and Donald Baillie who would make a lasting contribution not only to Scottish religion but to wider church life.[58] Not all, however, were comfortable with its stance. Conservative churchmen yearned for a return to the objective certainties of an older creed while the 'Scotto-Catholics' or high churchmen of the Scottish Church Society insisted that the historic faith of the Kirk could never be maintained according to the

---

[56] 'The significance of Karl Barth', *The British Weekly*, 7 May 1931, 1–2 [2].

[57] Muir, *John White*, pp.285–314; J. H. S. Burleigh, *A Church History of Scotland* (Oxford: Oxford University Press, 1960), pp.409–21; Callum G. Brown, *Religion and Society in Scotland since 1707*, pp.142–57.

[58] See David Fergusson (ed.), *Christ, Church and Society: essays on John Baillie and Donald Baillie* (Edinburgh: T & T Clark, 1993); George Newlands, *John and Donald Baillie: transatlantic theology* (New York: Peter Lang, 2002).

presuppositions of undogmatic Protestant liberalism. 'These men', exemplified by Charles Warr, minister of St Giles, Edinburgh, Nevil Davidson of Glasgow Cathedral, and Ronald Selby Wright of Canongate, Edinburgh, 'tended to be strongly conservative in politics, and in theology they came to have a good deal in common with the neo-orthodoxy of the Barthian school'.[59] These dignified liturgists remained, however, in a minority. Yet by the early 1930s central churchmanship and liberal evangelicalism was beginning to look somewhat passé. 'As the twenties gave way to the thirties and the storm-clouds of an even more terrible conflict began to darken the sky, new influences from the continent of Europe gradually transformed the theological scene'.[60] The synthesis between a temperate biblical criticism and the smooth reasonableness of a moderate faith which had become the Scottish Presbyterian norm since the late Victorian age came increasingly under strain. From the early 1930s not synthesis but antithesis would be the watchword, not evolution and continuity but an awe-inducing crisis of faith. 'Dogmatic rather than apologetic, it started not from man – his predicament, his virtues, his self-consciousness – but from God and the divine Word of Judgement',[61] and was linked with the name of Karl Barth. Along with sections of Welsh Nonconformity and English Dissent, Scotland was the place where the change registered the most.

The continuing early impact

A series of five articles on 'The Barthian school' in *The Expository Times* between April and September 1932 showed where the emphasis was now to lie. Of the five, three were written by Scotsmen. In an introductory paper entitled 'An appreciation', J. H. Morrison from Aberdeen described the characteristics of 'the Barthian school'. 'The Barthian school consists of a group of Protestant theologians on the continent whose acknowledged leader is Karl Barth, and who are in general agreement in expounding a system of Christian thought commonly known as "the theology of crisis" or "the dialectic theology"'.[62] Subsequent essays treated the contribution of Friedrich Gogarten, Rudolf Bultmann, Emil Brunner as well as that of Barth himself. In Britain and America Brunner was by far the best known, having spent the academic year 1913–14 in England where he immersed himself in the activities of the Christian labour movement, G. D. H. Coles's guild socialism and the work of the SCM. Thereafter came a fellowship at

---

[59] Cheyne, *The Transforming of the Kirk*, p.196.

[60] Ibid., p.207.

[61] Ibid., p.207.

[62] J. H. Morrison, 'The Barthian school I: an appreciation', *The Expository Times* 43 (1931–32), 314–7 [314].

Union Theological Seminary, New York.[63] More accessible than Barth with an immense fluency in English, he had earlier been thought of holding views identical to those of Barth, an opinion which was, even at the time, far from being the case.[64] 'Brunner', commented Morrison, 'is inclined to push his dialectic through to a clear cut issue. This makes him greatly more readable than Barth, yet it is universally felt that Barth . . . is the real leader of the group'.[65] The 45-year-old Barth was displaying more inventiveness, originality and genius than the rest: 'It cannot be doubted . . . that he is a man with a vital message, and the advent of his school has been hailed as holding the promise of the rebirth of Protestantism'.[66]

In the succeeding number of the series in May, Norman Porteous presented a perceptive assessment of his former teacher's work. Having encouraged his readers first to consult the books by R. Birch Hoyle and John McConnachie, he began with the famous quotation from the introduction to the second edition of the *Römerbrief*: 'If I have a system it is limited to a recognition of what Kierkegaard called the "infinite qualitative distinction" between time and eternity . . . "God is in heaven, and thou art on earth"'. This, however, was only a clue to Barth's work and possibly a misleading one at that. The diastases between created reality and the divine was certainly pivotal in Barth's scheme as was the concept of revelation as a communication not so much as theological information but of God himself. Neither was there any doubt that sin had radically impaired human beings' ability to apprehend the divine revelation which had been actualized and fulfilled in Christ. 'The real question at issue', however,

> between Barth and those theologians who have really understood him . . . relates to the difference which Barth supposes sin to have made in the relations between God and man. Barth maintains not that the human mind has become completely incapacitated for all apprehension of the divine will, from understanding the divine nature, but that it has through sin become an untrustworthy guide.[67]

That there was a valid revelation in nature, within the realm of the creaturely, was not in doubt. Barth's question was whether it had any

---

[63] See 'Intellectual Autobiography' in Charles Kegley (ed.), *The Theology of Emil Brunner* (New York: Macmillan, 1962), pp.3–20; cf. Emil Brunner, *The Theology of Crisis* (New York: Scribners, 1929); idem. *The Word and the World* (London: SCM, 1931).

[64] See John W. Hart, *Karl Barth versus Emil Brunner: the formation and dissolution of a theological alliance, 1916–36* (New York: Peter Lang, 2001).

[65] Morrison, 'The Barthian school I: an appreciation', 314.

[66] Ibid., 314.

[67] N. W. Porteous, 'The Barthian school II: the theology of Karl Barth', *The Expository Times* 43 (1931–32), 341–6 [342–3].

active doctrinal significance or not? It was certainly useless, in his view, as the basis for a total theological scheme. Catholic theology had built a whole theology based upon nature, as had Protestant scholasticism and Enlightenment liberalism in its train. Yet the whole presupposition, for Barth, was faulty. 'That we misunderstand and misuse what [God] says is what Barth asserts'.[68]

Porteous was keen not to overemphasize sin as a key to understand Barth's thought, for that was not where the heart of his system laid. The Swiss's gospel was wholly positive in that it held that from eternity God had chosen to be gracious to humankind in Christ and to bring men and women into fellowship with himself. Neither human sinfulness nor human creatureliness would ever thwart that gracious will. It was God's victory over human intractability which had theological priority over rebellion and unbelief. 'There is something prior to the confession that man is sinner in this stringent sense of the word which connects it with God's special revelation, and that is the glad conviction that man is a forgiven sinner'.[69] Only those who know they are under grace know that they have sinned. '[Barth] grounds everything in a Word of God which both condemns and forgives . . . That is so fundamental to the understanding of Barth's present theological position'.[70] This was a radical departure from the Lutheran and conventional evangelical scheme which would preach the law in order to convict of sin before applying the balm of the gospel. Yet it was clear from the *Christliche Dogmatik* that this counterintuitive note would be basic to Barth's whole structure. For Barth it was not a departure but an extension of his Reformed legacy concerning the absolute sovereignty of God and the election of grace. To know that one had been saved was not a matter of presumption or cheap consolation on the part of the believer. 'God alone can say the word, and all that any man can do is to bear witness to the fact that God has said it to him'.[71] The Word of God summons listeners to embrace the status of reconciliation which God has prepared for them in Christ, and this must be done in repentance and humble faith: 'We are not permitted to slip past Jesus, regarding him as a symbol for general ideas . . . We must be content to accept just this Jesus as God's Word'.[72] God in Christ, his sinless person, costly atonement and glorious resurrection has already reconciled an alienated world to himself. The church, its humanitarian service, its preaching, its scriptures and sacraments merely bear witness to that fact: 'The church is not the kingdom of God; it is merely the fellowship of those

---

[68] Ibid., 343.
[69] Ibid., 343.
[70] Ibid., 343.
[71] Ibid., 343.
[72] Ibid., 344.

who are waiting and hastening towards the kingdom, hoping and praying that it is coming'.[73]

All this was unfamiliar to those who had grown up with the benign simplicities of Scottish liberalism and disconcertingly universalistic to those who would preach salvation to sinners bound for hell. The old Calvinistic language of sovereign election and depravity through sin was being used in a way which liberals deemed old-fashioned and evangelicals thought unbalanced or unsound. The series concluded with John McConnachie's essay on Gogarten, the Methodist Vincent Taylor's insightful treatment of Bultmann and Canon J. K. Mozley's sympathetic portrayal of Brunner's thought.

McConnachie's second volume

It was with John McConnachie's *The Barthian Theology and the Man of Today* (1933), his second substantial analysis of Barth's theology in two years, that the initial period of Barth reception in Scotland reached its climax just as that work, along with the Anglican Hoskyns' translation of the *Römerbrief* and the Congregationalist Camfield's *Revelation and the Holy Spirit*, which appeared simultaneously, marked a maturing of Barth appreciation throughout the British Isles.

McConnachie's new volume, 330 pages long which rapidly went into a second edition, was more discursive, personal and confessional than the first. It also conveyed the content of Barth's most recent thought being the first English language publication to contend with the *Kirchliche Dogmatik* 1/I, Barth's opening part-volume on the prolegomena of Word of God which had appeared in German in December 1932. Barth's new beginning was more explicitly Christological than its predecessor, the *Christliche Dogmatik* of 1927, and contained in its expository and historical sections printed in smaller type throughout the text an insight into the way Barth had learned from the doctrinal and biblical tradition of the ages. Also, '[i]n his new Dogmatics [Barth] lays a deeper stress on the objectivity of the Word of God'.[74] The Scot, for his part, took the opportunity to take stock of the situation in the church and the world. Its opening chapter, a jeremiad of a minister who had been disconcerted by the dizzy changes all about, was entitled 'The Day of Crisis'. The crisis had begun in the church. 'It has lost, or largely lost, the Word of God, and proclaims instead its own bloodless word. It offers religion, beautiful services, social and cultural activities in abundance, but it is nevertheless in danger of losing its very *raison d'être* as a church' (p.19). Reflecting the rather pained situation of a stagnant if

---

[73] Ibid., 346.
[74] John McConnachie, *The Barthian Theology and the Man of Today* (London: Hodder and Stoughton, 1933), p.47. Subsequent page numbers will be included in the text.

reunited Presbyterian establishment in the 1930s, McConnachie put the blame for much of the malaise squarely at the feet of the preachers: 'Looking back on the thirty years since I became a minister, I cannot help feeling that we ministers – and I do not exonerate myself – are in no small measure to blame for the present hunger for the Word of God' (p.20). Having allowed an insipid moralism to displace the objective realities of a supernatural gospel of sin and grace, urgency had vanished from the pulpit and the congregations had grown languid and lifeless. 'Our libraries overflow with books depicting Jesus as the ideal man, the great ethical preacher, the grand exemplar of sweetness and light, while Christ the mediator, the God-man, has dropped out of sight' (p.22), he wrote. 'There has been a shallow evolutionary view of sin, a correspondingly weak view of grace . . . grace, one might almost say, has been sent into exile for a generation' (p.23).

All this could be excused as the wearied complaint of a jaded pastor, but these comments convey a feeling which characterized much of British Protestantism at the time. McConnachie was, by all accounts, a devoted parish minister and his contribution to theological scholarship had been recognized by the University of St Andrews in 1931 through the bestowal of a DD. For him, as for others, the new theology had come as a message of liberation. As a student he had eagerly affirmed all that his professors had taught him, and his Marburg sojourn in the golden days of youth had consolidated all that he had learned. 'I also think of Herrmann as "my unforgettable teacher",[75] kindest of men, to whom I owe more than I can tell . . . [but] with all his prophetic fire and brave, fearless personal faith, Hermann had not provided us with a basis for faith in the Word of God strong enough to stand a cataclysm' (pp.34, 35). Herrman had accepted the presuppositions of the Enlightenment but believed that Jesus of Nazareth as portrayed in the gospels could yet engender faith in those who allowed themselves to be captured by his personality and life. But a world war, social dislocation and decades of parish life had convinced McConnachie that the liberal Christ was not enough. 'Many of us in the ministry today have been experiencing . . . disillusionment, and have discovered that the modern theology, which once was our pride and satisfaction, has proved a broken reed to lean on in a time of crisis' (p.34).

> All the uncertainty and relativity of time and place in the gospels opened before me like a yawning gulf. I did not lose my personal faith but my theological foundations gave way, and personal faith might in course of time followed had I not been guided on to a surer

[75] See Karl Barth, 'The principles of dogmatics according to Wilhelm Herrmann' (1925), in *Theology and the Church: shorter writings, 1920–28* (London: SCM, 1962), pp.238–71 [238].

foundation . . . This conclusion I had reached before I ever heard of
Barth. (pp.35–6)

There was little wonder that he embraced the new theology as one who
had been born again.

Following a description of Barth's development since moving to Bonn in
1930, McConnachie proceeded to assess the Swiss theologian's current
stance. Whereas much of the early discussion of Barth had centred upon
epistemological matters, whether God was known through conscience and
nature or through revelation and the Word, McConnachie tried to move on
to more substantive matters about the content of his scheme. 'At the heart of
the person of a speaking God', he explained, 'who, as creator, reconciler and
redeemer seeks fellowship with his creatures. That is the central conviction
of Barth' (p.59). Gone are the mathematical analogies of the *Römerbrief*,
a line glancing a circle or God as the *totalier aliter*, and in their place the
living fellowship of a triune God. God is still the God of revelation but his
Word is no mere voice from the beyond. 'The Word of God needs no act to
complete it; it is itself an act' (p.63). Revelation for Barth is a creative act
embodying God's gracious reconciliation of created and sinful humanity to
himself. As reconciler God had already brought about humankind's salvation in Christ. 'This truly human Jesus came under the curse of the law for
us, and accepted all the consequences of our disobedience, entering, in his
love, into the sphere of the lordship of sin, that he might subdue it' (p.75).
Although a fact, this is not patent to all. In order to grasp its saving power
it needs to be affirmed as revelation in faith. The Jesus of history, so beloved
of the liberal theologians, needs to become the Christ of faith. 'There is no
historical continuity between the two, the continuity is supernatural, transcendent and spiritual; that is, it is through the Holy Spirit' (pp.81–2). The
resurrection too, though a phenomenon within history, cannot be understood according to the canons of history. Secular history deals in continuities
and as such it is of the flesh. The resurrection, which is corporeal and has
its concomitant in the empty tomb, can only be comprehended eschato-
logically, as that which has come from beyond. 'The resurrection is not to
be regarded simply as a historical event, or as belonging to the sphere
of historical events, in general. It does not belong to history but it is the
breaking in of a new world from beyond time and history' (p.82).

As for the vexed point of the extent of human depravity and the nature of
the *imago Dei*, McConnachie realizes that there were differences between
different members of the Barthian 'school'. Emil Brunner, through his apologetic method, seemed even then to be departing from the basic insights of
the new theology. 'He . . . finds the point of contact for the Word of God in
the humanity and personality of man the sinner, to whom he allows a place
for a natural knowledge of God . . . In man *qua* creature, there resides
the possibility or capacity of man for God' (p.45). Individuals' capacity for

God could never be innate. This was the key fault of both Catholic theology since Augustine and modern theology since the Enlightenment. That men and women were God's creature was not in doubt, but God was God and humanity was humanity: 'One of the fundamental convictions of Barth is that there is no direct continuity between the creator and the creature' (p.69). If there was a point of contact it would have to be created by God himself.

> [Man] is made in the image of God, but the *imago Dei* has become so buried and lost in sin that it is irrecoverable by man, and but for the grace of God is unknown to him. The divine image is not any longer a capacity which belongs to man as a thing assured . . . It is not a thing given but a thing to be given, it is not a fulfilment but a promise. (p.69)

For McConnachie the popular idea that Barth was a cultural pessimist and a theological gloom-merchant was simply wrong. The God of glory did embrace his creation and God's revelation in nature was a positive and life-affirming fact. What was equally true, and had been repudiated by the liberals, was that humankind had forfeited the ability to respond to that revelation as God required. In order to do so the divine image would have to be restored by grace. 'To the image of God lost in Adam but restored in Christ, belongs the capacity to hear the Word of God that is spoken to us, and to know it and receive it as the Word of God (p.70)'. What was truly a revelation, and not even McConnachie does full justice to this, is that restoration has already been achieved in Christ and was elucidated and confirmed in the revelation which was ever active in the world. Also, '[t]he human aspect of Christ's revelation of the Father, as we can see in both his sermons and in his new Dogmatics, is coming to occupy a larger place in the mind of Barth' (p.113).

Chapter four on the Word of God and eight entitled 'Theology of the Word' were, in the main, a recapitulation of what McConnachie had written in his earlier exposition along with an enlightening précis of the *Kirchliche Dogmatik* 1/I. This included a highly original treatment of the doctrine of the immanent trinity as constitutive of God's revelation of himself: 'He does not *become* Son, or Word of God, in the event of revelation. The event of revelation has divine truth and actuality because Jesus reveals himself as what he was before, and is in himself' (p.226). The penultimate chapter, number nine, 'The Ethics of the Word', is over dependent on Brunner's *Das Gebot und die Ordungen* (1931) ('The Command and the Orders' later to be translated as *The Divine Imperative*) for the simple reason that that was the only published volume on ethics from a member of the dialectical school available at the time. McConnachie had attended Barth's lectures on ethics in Bonn in the summer of 1930. Material from that series would be included in later volumes of the *Kirchliche Dogmatik* during the 1950s.[76] The tenor of Brunner's volume was very different from what McConnachie had heard and in designating Brunner as representing the new theology's views, he was obviously ill at ease. Brunner's concept of the ordinances was too near to being an innate characteristic of human receptivity to God. The Scotsman was now able to think Barth's thoughts for him. 'It ought to be said at this point there is a divergence between the views of Barth and Brunner' (p.266), he claimed. 'The true Reformation teaching, as well as that of the New Testament, would seem to lie with Barth rather than Brunner who, with his strong apologetic interests, makes here a concession to modern views' (p.268). McConnachie's Barthianism had now become dyed in the wool.

As well as being the most complete assessment of Barth's views currently available, McConnachie's second book offered an interesting insight into the strains and tribulations of British church life during the early 1930s. There was something wistful about his yearning for a note of authority which the church no longer possessed. He ranges freely in chapter five, mentioning Frank Buchman's Oxford Group Movement, the character of worship in the Presbyterian churches, confessional reform – he warms to John Knox's Scots Confession rather than to the Westminster creed – the effectiveness or otherwise of Sunday schools, foreign missions and the churches' failure to reach the working class. 'What we call the social problem has its origins in the industrialization of the masses during [the] last century', he wrote. 'They were uprooted and torn from their old ways of living, and from their old loyalties and obedience, and swept into the industrial maelstrom' (p.200). Even now, in 1933, '[m]any have not even a house in which they can live in decency, and bring up their children' (p.201). The church could never stand idly by while 'anonymous powers such as capital, companies, big businesses tyrannize over them, and come between them and true life' (ibid.). The fact was that 10 years earlier both the Church of Scotland and his own United Free Church had done exactly that. But what was a simple Dundee pastor to do? In the light of the Scottish establishment's triumphalism of 1929, there was something impotent and tragic in his retort: 'The social question is ultimately a question for the state, and the only remedy for this is through the state, which God has meant should be one of his greatest gifts to men' (p.202). Like others, he had little to offer an alienated people, but for those who would come to church on a Sunday morning to listen, he knew now that he had a message to preach. 'The preacher can only speak human words. That is the border and limit of his preaching. But in and through those human words he dares to believe God speaks his Word' (p.152). There was comfort enough in that.

---

[76] See John Webster, *Barth's Ethics of Reconciliation* (Cambridge: Cambridge University Press, 1995); idem., *Barth's Moral Theology: human action in Barth's thought* (Edinburgh: T & T Clark, 1998).

3

THE RECEPTION OF KARL
BARTH'S THEOLOGY IN
WALES, 1927–33

Wales and the Scottish precedence

One of the axioms of modern church history in Britain has been that whereas Anglo-Saxon thought was on the whole impervious to the appeal of Karl Barth, it was among the Scots that his theology found any real resonance. In a 1979 volume Stephen Sykes mentions the somewhat bewildered response to his publications in Britain and the United States between 1925 and the mid-1930s and goes on to say that 'from now onwards it is in Scotland that Barth is taken with the greatest seriousness in the English-speaking world'.[1] In a volume of centenary essays, R. H. Roberts traced the reception of Barth's theology 'in the Anglo-Saxon world' by quoting the evidence of such late 1920s and early 1930s figures as J. H. Morrison, John McConnachie, H. R. Mackintosh, Norman Porteous and A. J. Macdonald (who was, in fact, not a Scotsman at all but a London based Anglican clergyman) to claim that 'it is clear from an early stage that enthusiasm for Barth's work . . . was primarily a Scottish attribute'.[2] In another essay in the same volume, Colin Gunton contrasted the usual English attitude to Barth with that of theologians from other lands: 'For the most part and despite exceptions the English find it difficult to come to terms with the theology of Karl Barth',[3]

---

[1] S. W. Sykes, 'The study of Barth' in idem. (ed.), *Karl Barth: studies of his theological method* (Oxford: Clarendon Press, 1979), pp.1–16 [6].

[2] R. H. Roberts, 'The reception of the theology of Karl Barth in the Anglo-Saxon world: history, typology and prospect', in S. W. Sykes (ed.), *Karl Barth: centenary essays* (Cambridge: Cambridge University Press, 1989), pp.115–71 [124].

[3] Colin E. Gunton, 'No other foundation: an Englishman's reading of *Church Dogmatics* Chapter IV', in Sykes (ed.), *Karl Barth: centenary essays*, pp.46–68 [61].

while in a companion volume Geoffrey Bromiley noted that this was hardly the case for theologians and pastors 'in such diverse lands as Switzerland, Germany, France, Holland, Hungary, and Scotland'.[4]

Each of the volumes listed above marked the renewal of interest in Barth's work following his centenary in 1986. In her wide ranging assessment of Barth reception in Britain published in 1995, Anne-Kathrin Finke underlined the key importance of Scotland in British Barth reception, beginning with McConnachie and Mackintosh and culminating with the massive contribution of T. F. Torrance,[5] while Torrance's biographer, Alister McGrath, acceded the same point. 'Barth', he claims, 'was something of an unknown quantity in the English-language world of the 1920s',[6] and it was not until the publication of John McConnachie's assessment in *The Hibbert Journal* of 1926–27 and Hugh Ross Mackintosh's essay in *The Expository Times* of 1928 that British readers took any notice of the Swiss's ideas. McConnachie's appraisal, according to McGrath, was 'the first major indigenous assessment of Barth's thought',[7] while both men illustrated how the Scots responded more readily to his work than anyone else: 'All the evidence indicates that early interest in and enthusiasm for Barth's theology was particularly associated with Scotland'.[8] Whereas Anglicanism's emphasis on the incarnation (a doctrine which was thought to be lacking in the early Barth), its traditional hostility to German-language theology and its doctrinal insularity prevented Barth's voice from being heard in England with any degree of clarity let alone comprehension and sympathy, the dominant ecclesiastical tradition north of the border – its Reformed nature, its intellectual openness to the European continent and the importance placed upon dogmatics in the universities and the Kirk – prepared the ground for the enthusiastic reception of the Swiss Calvinist's views. It was probably no coincidence that it was another Scottish theologian, Alasdair I. C. Heron, who was chosen to close a major appraisal of Barth's contribution published in 2000. Writing of his father's experience, a ministerial student in New College, Edinburgh, in the inter-war years: 'My father was representative of many of the ablest Scottish theological students of the 1930s – the years

[4] Geoffrey W. Bromiley, 'The influence of Barth after World War II' in Nigel Biggar (ed.), *Reckoning with Barth: essays in commemoration of the centenary of Karl Barth's birth* (Oxford: Mowbray, 1989), pp.9–24 [11].

[5] Anne-Kathrin Finke, *Karl Barth in Grossbritannien: rezeption und wirkungsgeschichte* (Neukirchen-Vluyn: Neukirchener Verlag, 1995), pp.221–43.

[6] Alister E. McGrath, *T. F. Torrance: an intellectual biography* (Edinburgh: T & T Clark, 1999), p.115.

[7] Ibid., p.115.

[8] Ibid., pp.116–7

when Barth was really beginning to become well known in Britain, especially in Scotland'.[9]

This perception had developed early. It reflected the view of Adolf Keller in 1931 and John McConnachie in his authoritative German-language assessment of Barth's impact on Scottish and English religious life published in 1936.[10] As it happens, both of these commentators mention Wales in passing,[11] indeed McConnachie noted the nation's 'strong Calvinistic background and lively religious interest',[12] but names or movements were not cited. This was due undoubtedly to the fact that most of the vigour and breadth of religious life in Wales at the time took place through the medium of the Welsh language.

Theology in post-Edwardian Wales

Although Welsh theology like that in Scotland had been influenced since the 1880s by a reverent biblical criticism and a liberalized evangelicalism,[13] it was only after the First World War especially that a pronounced philosophical idealism and a more blatant liberalism came into the Nonconformist chapels, first by way of a younger generation of able preachers, some of whom had been nurtured at Mansfield College, Oxford, and then by a cohort of gifted seminary teachers who were intent on modernizing Welsh religion according to the norms of the Enlightenment.[14] The University of Wales had been established in 1893, and its theological faculty bore the imprint of Mansfield College's Scottish principal, Andrew M. Fairbairn, who had been employed by the young university to establish the curriculum in divinity. The university movement had begun decades earlier with separate colleges being established in Aberystwyth (1872), Cardiff (1883) and Bangor (1884) all of which prepared candidates for University of London degrees. The theological colleges of the Nonconformist denominations were aimed at producing preachers rather than scholars. St David's College,

---

[9] Alasdair I. C. Heron, 'Karl Barth: a personal engagement', in John Webster (ed.), *The Cambridge Companion to Karl Barth* (Cambridge: Cambridge University Press, 2000), pp.296–306 [297].

[10] John McConnachie, 'Der Einfluss Karl Barths in Schottland und England', in Ernst Wolf (ed.), *Theologische Aufsätze Karl Barth zum 50. Geburtstag* (München: Chr. Kaiser Verlag, 1936), pp.559–70.

[11] Adolf Keller, *Der Weg der dialectischen Theologie durch die kirchliche Welt* (München: Chr. Kaiser Verlag, 1931), p.112.

[12] McConnachie, 'Der Einfluss Karl Barths in Schottland und England', p.569.

[13] D. Densil Morgan, *Wales and the Word: historical perspectives on Welsh identity and religion* (Cardiff: University of Wales Press, 2008), pp.55–87.

[14] See Robert Pope, *Seeking God's Kingdom: the nonconformist social gospel in Wales, 1906–39* (Cardiff: University of Wales Press, 1999).

Lampeter, although technically a university in its own right was in fact a seminary for the Anglican Church. Such had been the contentiousness between Nonconformity and the established church that the incipient University of Wales prevented the new 'national colleges' from teaching theology as such, though there was provision for study of the biblical languages and their literature at each. Confessional divinity and ecclesiastical polity would be left to the denominational establishments though the Bible, which was thought to be doctrinally neutral, could be studied by all.

It was not long, however, before most of the seminaries migrated towards the national colleges: the two Bala Congregational colleges amalgamated and moved to Bangor in 1886 with the Llangollen Baptists following in 1892, the Pontypool College relocated to Cardiff in 1893 while the Bala college of the Calvinistic Methodists (which was by far the most academically distinguished) ceased providing a general education and became wholly a theological college in 1891 having appointed as its head Wales's foremost biblical theologian, Thomas Charles Edwards (1837–1900). In a speech entitled 'Religious thought in Wales' given to the Presbyterian Council in London in 1888, Edwards described the changes of the previous half century. Up to the 1840s religion had been deep rather than broad. For the Nonconformist fathers, 'the doctrine of the incarnation had no value or meaning . . . except as the incarnation was a necessary condition of Christ's atoning death, and the idea of any connection between Christ and the race, be it true or be it false, had not occurred to them . . . Theology, in fact, was dying of asphyxia'.[15] It was only following the broadening of horizons that occurred after 1845 not least through the influence of the Edinburgh educated Lewis Edwards, the author's father, that the piety of the Calvinistic Methodists had been combined with patristic learning and classical culture to create a more rounded faith:

> A stream of fresh air poured in when the younger generation of theological students began to read and ponder over Coleridge's *Aids to Reflection* . . . Augustine's *City of God*, Anselm's *Cur Deus Homo*, Hooker's First and Fifth Books, Locke . . . Kant . . . and Milton's *Paradise Lost*, with which students were urged to saturate their minds.[16]

Such a blend of culture, learning, doctrinal breadth and piety needed to be created anew in each generation: 'The circulating blood of theology needs constantly to be oxygenized by contact with the broad human conceptions that create and inspire and govern literature and the age . . . We are aware

---

[15] 'Religious thought in Wales', in D. D. Williams (ed.), *Thomas Charles Edwards* (Liverpool: National Eisteddfod Society, 1921), pp.103–12 [105].

[16] Edwards, 'Religious thought in Wales', p.106.

of the dangers of knowledge, but we think the dangers of ignorance to be greater'.[17]

By the post-Edwardian era, such broadmindedness had created an atmosphere in which liberal theology could flourish, and it did so, principally, among the Congregationalists.[18] Impatience with inherited doctrinal formulae had characterized key nineteenth century Independent leaders as John Roberts and Michael D. Jones, the pugnacious principal of what would become the Bala-Bangor College, but it was with David Adams (1845–1923), minister of Grove Street Welsh church in Liverpool, that Hegelianism would replace moderate Calvinism as the systematic basis of denominational thought. An early alumnus of Aberystwyth and graduate of London University, he did more than anyone to popularize Hegelian terminology and introduce the concept of evolution, a theology of immanence and the idea of the Absolute into Welsh religion. His notorious treatise *Datblygiad yn ei berthynas â'r Cwymp, yr Ymgnawdoliad a'r Atgyfodiad* ('Evolution in its relation to the Fall, the Incarnation and the Resurrection') (1893) was a wholesale reconstruction of orthodox theology according to an alien philosophical scheme. For Adams God was not a transcendent divine being but an abstract life spirit which infused all things. Sin was not so much rebellion against God as humanity's struggle against the effects of its primitive past. Far from being the incarnation of the eternal Word in the person of Jesus of Nazareth, Christ was the perfect example of humankind animated by the divine whose death had no unique atoning qualities but exemplified the clash between residual evolutionary imperfection and the Absolute's striving for synthesis and perfection. The miraculous categories of the New Testament were metaphorical rather than literal, while the supernatural modes of traditional faith needed to be reinterpreted according to the scientific laws of cause and effect. Adams' subsequent publications merely reiterated his basic assumptions while his commentary on the Epistle to the Galatians (1908) was so infused by his preconceptions that anything genuinely Pauline virtually disappeared: 'David Adams' philosophical bias was so overwhelming . . . [that] he turned the teaching of justification by faith completely on its head'.[19]

Adams was neither an able exegete, a profound theologian nor an original thinker. Even such a radical modernist as Thomas Rees admitted that '[h]is tendency was to face the problems of theology as a philosopher rather than a theologian, and reason from a few general suppositions rather than traverse slowly and carefully through the detailed history of the experience

---

[17] Ibid., p.107.

[18] See R. Tudur Jones, Robert Pope (ed.), *Congregationalism in Wales* (Cardiff: University of Wales Press, 2004), pp.235–9.

[19] R. Tudur Jones, Robert Pope (ed.), *Faith and the Crisis of a Nation: Wales, 1890–1914* (Cardiff: University of Wales Press, 2004), p.259.

and doctrines of religion'.[20] In short, 'he was no theologian at all'.[21] His significance, though, was immense. If his ideas had been considered alien in 1893, by 1913, when he ascended to the chair of the Union of Welsh Independents, his views were becoming the norm. 'Adams', according to R. Tudur Jones, the historian of Welsh Congregationalism, 'had graduated from being a heretic into one of the denomination's oracles'.[22] It was left to liberal theologians of the stature of Miall Edwards, Thomas Rees and John Morgan Jones to supply the sophistication which Adams lacked, by which time many ordinary ministers had deemed it no longer necessary to preach on sin, redemption and faith through the cross, but on Christ as the ultimate ideal and on human beings' potential for perfectability. Widespread theological change would register fully after the First World War.

The triumph of liberalism

If Adams provided the Congregationalists with a conceptual basis for their liberalism along with the conviction, all too blithely acccepted, that Hegelian idealism was a logical extention of traditional faith, it was left to three exceptionally gifted theologians to endow that liberalism with substance. Thomas Rees (1869–1926), D. Miall Edwards (1873–1941) and John Morgan Jones (1873–1946) had studied in the University of Wales before joining a glittering generation of students at Mansfield College, Oxford, destined for positions of authority within British Nonconformity.[23] The influence of Andrew M. Fairbairn, Mansfield's principal, would be seminal for Rees, though the Ritschlian theology espoused by Fairbairn's pupil, Alfred Garvie, would be important for John Morgan Jones though his personal indebtedness to Adolf von Harnack, with whom he studied in Berlin, would be even more pronounced. Rees had been appointed to the chair in Christian doctrine at the Brecon Memorial College straight from Mansfield where he had graduated with a first in Oxford's honours school of theology in 1899. After 10 years service in Brecon, he accepted the principalship of the Bala-Bangor College. His major published works, *Duw, ei Fodolaeth a'i Natur* ('God, his Existence and Nature') (1910) and his English language volume *The Holy Spirit in Thought and Experience* (1914) bear the clear

---

[20] Thomas Rees, 'Dylanwad David Adams ar ddiwinyddiaeth Cymru' ('The Influence of David Adams on Welsh theology'), in E. Keri Evans and W. Pari Huws, *Cofiant y Parchg David Adams* (Liverpool: Hughes and Sons, 1924), pp.179–98 [183].

[21] Rees, 'Dylanwad David Adams ar ddiwinyddiaeth Cymru' , p.183.

[22] R. Tudur Jones, *Yr Undeb: Hanes Undeb yr Annibynwyr Cymraeg, 1872–1972* (Abertawe: Gwasg John Penry, 1975), p.199.

[23] See Elaine Kaye, *Mansfield College, Oxford: its origin, history and significance* (Oxford: Oxford University Press, 1996), pp.111–33.

imprint of Fairbairn's Hegelianism, while his editorship of the weighty *Geiriadur Beiblaidd* ('Biblical Dictionary'), published under the auspices of the University of Wales' theological guild in 1926 and the benchmark for scholarly liberalism, crowned his career.

Rees's theology was immanentist and idealist, with the Trinity being a modalist expression of God's inner nature while the Holy Spirit brought the historical Jesus's moral influence alive. 'I used to chaff him with being a Sabellian', quipped Miall Edwards, 'and he would retort by calling me a Samosatene or even an Arian! I think we were orthodox in spirit and intention, though somewhat heterodox in form'.[24] A much more powerful thinker than David Adams and, as both professor and principal in theological colleges, the bearer of direct influence over generations of ministerial students, he reinforced the prevailing norm that the only way forward for religion in Wales was through a progressive and escalating liberalism. 'Rees's danger', according to Robert Pope, 'was to allow the philosophy of the period with its emphasis on unity and reason to destroy the doctrine [of the Holy Spirit]'s traditional purpose and meaning'.[25]

John Morgan Jones was Rees's closest Mansfield friend, his colleague as professor of church history at Bala-Bangor and his successor as principal. He combined an even more radical theological stance with a clear and attractive prose style. 'Although he taught history and was a pupil of Adolf von Harnack, the greatest church historian of his generation', wrote R. Tudur Jones, 'his heart was in the study of the New Testament, and in discussing it he revealed himself to be the most daring of the Welsh Modernists'.[26] Books such as *Paul of Tarsus: the Apostle and his Message* (1915), *Y Testament Newydd, ei Hanes a'i Amcan* ('The New Testament, its History and Aim') (1930), his commentary *Y Bedwaredd Efengyl* ('The Fourth Gospel') (1931) and his handbook *Dysgeidiaeth Iesu Grist* ('The Teaching of Jesus Christ') (1937) showed how far the liberal consensus had evolved. If Thomas Rees, who died prematurely in 1926, had departed the scene before the Barthian renewal occurred, it was left to John Morgan Jones to plead the cause of radical liberalism when J. E. Daniel, his new colleague in Bala-Bangor, emerged to challenge its asecendency in the late 1920s and 1930s.

Of these three Congregational scholars it was Miall Edwards who proved most plausible in combining the new emphases with Nonconformity's

---

[24] D. Miall Edwards, 'Dr Thomas Rees of Bangor', *The Welsh Outlook* 13 (1926), 182–5 [184].

[25] Robert Pope, *Codi Muriau Dinas Duw: Anghydffurfiaeth ac Anghydffurfwyr Cymru'r Ugeinfed Ganrif* (Bangor: Canolfan Uwchefrydiau Crefydd yng Nghymru, 2005), p.238; for an appraisal of Rees's social theology see Pope, *Seeking God's Kingdom*, pp.56–67.

[26] Jones, *Congregationalism in Wales*, p.235.

historical faith. Reared in the radical Dissent of Merionethshire and named after Edward Miall, leader of the anti-establishment Liberation Society, like both Rees and Jones he took first class honours in theology at Mansfield and, after 9 years in the pastorate, was appointed Rees's successor as professor of Christian doctrine at Brecon. According to R. Tudur Jones, '[h]e was anxious to express the faith once given to the saints in a manner that would be meaningful to his contemporaries . . . [while] his personal godliness as well as his deep reverence for the classic theologians of the church is evident on every page that he wrote'. [27] Nevertheless, '[i]t was with the thought of David Miall Edwards that popular Welsh theology lurched to the left'.[28] He was convinced that the gospel faith could only contend with the intellectual realities of the day by conceding that God was immanent within creation, that the supernatural categories of the New Testament needed to be restated in naturalist terms, and that Christ's unique deity should be understood not ontologically but in terms of the quality of his experience of God's benign fatherhood. His able treatises *The Philosophy of Religion* (1929) and *Christianity and Philosophy* (1932) forged for him a reputation as a competent philosophical theologian beyond Wales,[29] but it was as both a creative thinker and a popularizer that he affected common thought most readily. It was his systematic theology *Bannau'r Ffydd* ('The Pinnacles of Faith') (1929), however, which drew the fire of J. E. Daniel, the most striking of the young Welsh Barthians, and so created a new epoch in the nation's theological development.

By the mid-1920s pronounced liberalism had found a home for itself in all four of the major Nonconformist denominations. The Wesleyan scholars Tecwyn Evans and E. Tegla Davies, the Baptists Herbert Morgan and J. Gwili Jenkins as well as Calvinistic Methodists of the stamp of D. Francis Roberts and Griffith Arthur Edwards, now shared with the more radical Congregationalists in the new consensus: that the key to a valid theology was not an authoritative objective revelation but the fact of religious experience, that any concept of revelation needed to be in accord with enlightened rationality, that the theory of evolution had been proven to be a religious as well as a biological fact, and that there was an ontological continuity between humankind and God. 'Theology', according to Philip Josiah Jones, a minister in the Presbyterian Church of Wales, writing in 1927 was 'an attempt on the part of men to give articulation to religious experience', while '[m]odern theology can be most satisfactoraly gauged by taking as the point of our departure the movement commonly known as

---

[27] Jones, *Faith and the Crisis of a Nation*, p.240.
[28] Ibid., p.237.
[29] See Alan P. F. Sell, *The Philosophy of Religion, 1875–1980* (Bristol: Thoemmes Press, 1996), pp.30–1, 96–7.

Philosophical Idealism of the absolute type'.[30] In surveying the history of Welsh theology since the mid-nineteenth century, he delighted in the fact that traditional formulae were fast disappearing and that a radical Nonconformity was taking its place. 'Fall from innocence into sin [within the new scheme] is a fall upwards and onwards', he claimed, 'and every stage of sin contributes to the ultimate realization of perfect goodness'.[31] Christ was not so much the divine saviour but the archetype of human perfectibility. 'Atonement is, according to this teaching, a cosmic process', whereas the resurrection of the body could only be rationally interpreted in terms of the immortality of the soul: 'Whatever may be the actual implications of this challenging and attractive teaching', he continued, 'there can be but no doubt that it gives rise to questions of great importance for theology',[32] which no doubt was the case. For some young preachers it seemed that philosophical idealism had all but swallowed Christian faith whole. 'Hegelianism', he stated, with neither irony nor incongruity, 'is the most potent vindication of Christianity and Christian doctrines which has as yet been offered to human intelligence'.[33] Time was ripe for a counter movement, and in Wales it was provided not by the conservative evangelicals, who were fighting their own battles at the time,[34] but by the more substantial and innovative thought of Karl Barth.

J. D. Vernon Lewis, E. Keri Evans and J. E. Daniel

Even during its heyday not all Welsh Independents were enamoured of radical liberalism, and it was through the offices of the Congregational biblical scholar J. D. Vernon Lewis (1879–1970) that Barth's reputation was first consolidated in Wales. Like his colleagues Thomas Rees, J. Morgan Jones and Miall Edwards, he had proceeded from the University of Wales to Mansfield College, Oxford, also graduating with first class honours in the theology schools, and thence, in 1908–09, to the University of Leipzig. His first intimation of Barth had occurred in the early 1920s following discussion with a contemporary of his, a professor at Halle, who had conveyed to him the 'thrill of surprise' which the *Römerbrief* had created among continental biblical scholars. Lewis published his assessment in July 1927 in *Yr Efrydydd* ('The Student'), a monthly review published by the Student

---

[30] Philip J. Jones, 'Theology in Wales during the last eighty years', *The Treasury* 15 (1927), 8–10, 43–5 [8].

[31] Jones, 'Theology in Wales', 9.

[32] Ibid., 9.

[33] Ibid., 43.

[34] D. Densil Morgan, *The Span of the Cross: Christian religion and society in Wales, 1914–2000* (Cardiff: University of Wales Press, 1999), pp.137–44.

Christian Movement, two months after John McConnachie's article in *The Hibbert Journal*, but based on his own reading of the third German edition of the Romans commentary, the composite volume of essays *Das Wort Gottes und die Theologie* (1924) and assorted papers which had appeared on the pages of *Zwischen den Zeiten*. His approval of Barth's exegesis was hearty and his relief at the advent of a new method of reading the Bible was palpable. 'For those of us who have been raised on and satiated in the mode of exposition represented by the *International Critical Commentary* which reached its deadening, dry-boned pinnacle of dullness in the publication of W. C. Allen's barren commentary on Matthew, turning to Barth's volume is like leaving the parched stagnation of the desert for a land of abundance, vitality and delectability'.[35] Lewis's two articles described the background and content of Barth's thought to date and mentioned the response and secondary literature which it had generated in German and Dutch. What was significant for the Welshman was not only that it had signalled a new epoch in Protestant theology but that it had arisen from a pastoral context within the Swiss Reformed churches: 'Its home is Switzerland, though it has spread now to Germany, Holland and Italy'.[36] The parallels between Swiss Calvinism and Welsh Nonconformity were striking: both countries tended to be marginalized by the mainstream while their ecclesiastical traditions put a premium on the exposition of the Word. Given the overwhelmingly Calvinist nature of Welsh religion previous to the modernist phase, Barth's message was one which was likely to appeal, especially to the younger generation of servants of the Welsh pulpit.

This being so, it is not surprising that it was not an essay but a sermon which Lewis chose to translate. The text of 'Wele – yn awr!' ('Behold – now!') was 2 Cor.6: 1-2, namely the final address in *Komm, Schöpfer Geist!*, the volume of sermons authored jointly by Barth and Eduard Thurneysen, his ministerial colleague from his Safenwil days, which been published in 1924. The Welsh version appeared in the Congregationalists' weekly newspaper *Y Tyst* ('The Witness') on 3 May 1928.[37] This, it seems, was the first of Barth's work to appear in Britain, preceding the American Douglas Horton's translation of *Das Wort Gottes und die Theolgie*, namely *The Word of God and the Word of Man*, by a few months. The response it generated was remarkable. Throughout that spring and summer a stream of letters, comments and supplementary articles from Presbyterians, Methodists as well as Congregationalists, appeared in *Y Tyst* which were,

---

[35] J. D. Vernon Lewis, 'Diwinyddiaeth Karl Barth' ('The theology of Karl Barth'), *Yr Efrydydd* 3 (1926–7), 254–8, 281–7 [254].

[36] Ibid., 281.

[37] 'Pregethu'r cyfandir: trosiad J. D. Vernon Lewis o bregeth Karl Barth' ('Continental theology: a translation by J. D. Vernon Lewis of a sermon by Karl Barth'), *Y Tyst*, 3 May 1928, 6–7.

in the main, appreciative of the sermon's thrust and desirous of knowing more of its author and the new movement in continental theology. There followed two short articles by E. Keri Evans, who had been professor of philosophy at Bangor but since the religious revival of 1904–05, which had affected him profoundly, minister of Priory Street Congregational Church in Carmarthen.[38] His 'Karl Barth – the prophet', of 16 August 1928, and 'Karl Barth – the philosopher and theologian', published a week later, added nothing new to Lewis's account or to the essays already published in the theological journals by Adolf Keller, H. R. Mackintosh and John McConnachie, but they did show the interest, affirmation and excitement that Barth was generating within Wales. The fact that Evans who, incongruously for an erudite ex-Hegelian, was a trusted leader among the Welsh fundamentalists, published a further positive assessment in the conservative evangelical journal *Yr Efengylydd* ('The Evangelist') in 1930,[39] illustrated the nature of the response. Liberalism was at last being challenged not by obscurantists or blinkered pietists but by those who had partaken most deeply of scholarly modernism itself.

It was not the biblical scholar and preacher Vernon Lewis, or the former professional philosopher E. Keri Evans, who did most to facilitate the reception of Barth's thought during this initial phase in Wales, but the theologian John Edward Daniel (1902–62). Having come down from Jesus College, Oxford, in 1925 with firsts in Classical Moderations, Greats and theology, Daniel had been appointed fellow and tutor at Bala-Bangor, the Congregationalists' theological college, at the age of 23. Following Thomas Rees's death a year later, he was promoted to a full professorship. A generational change was about to occur, while Daniel's acumen as a theologian of extraordinary depth and perceptiveness was soon to be revealed. He would become, by common consent, the ablest dogmatician of his generation and a devastating critic of the prevailing Ritschlianism of the Congregational establishment.[40] His review of *The Word of God and the Word of Man* (1928) indicates puzzlement rather than commitment. Despite its strong Christocentricism, its refreshing emphasis on the strangeness of revelation and the telling nature of its critique of liberalism, for Daniel the volume was too rhetorical and strident, too one-sided in its emphasis on God's transcendence, for its underlying theology to be ultimately satifying: 'As a protest against all types of superficial evolutionary

---

[38] An autobiography, first published in Welsh in 1938, which charts his religious development appeared as *My Spiritual Pilgrimage: from philosophy to faith* (London: James Clarke, 1961).

[39] E. Keri Evans, 'Cenadwri Karl Barth' ('The Message of Karl Barth'), *Yr Efengylydd* 16 (1931), 6–7.

[40] See D. Densil Morgan, *Torri'r Seiliau Sicr: detholiad o ysgrifau J. E. Daniel* (Llandysul: Gwasg Gomer, 1993), passim.

doctrine, every sort of Pelagianism and Titanism, and especially as an expression, despite itself, of a passionate experience of God, this work will endure'.[41] But Daniel's curiosity had been aroused, his interest had been engaged and he would soon find himself jettisoning his scruples and championing Barth's theology unreservedly.

This became obvious in his assessment of what was the most elegant (though belated) apologia for theological liberalism to appear in Welsh, D. Miall Edwards's *Bannau'r Ffydd* ('The Pinnacles of Faith'). Edwards, like Daniel, was, as we have seen, a Congregational seminary professor, at the Memorial College in Brecon, and his volume took the form of a systematic theology whose integrating theme was humankind's innate capacity for God. For Edwards the touchstone of all valid theology was its ability to reflect upon and elucidate the experience of transcendence. Christianity, he claimed, begins with salvation interpreted as the believer's experience of the divine; it advances through Christology interpreted as Jesus of Nazareth's sense of sonship with the Father; and concludes with a doctrine of God as the ground of all existence. 'It is apparent', he wrote, 'that we are working on the assumption that experience is the key to doctrine'.[42] His systematic theology reflected this progression; rather than beginning with the doctrine of God and the Trinity in the fashion of the older dogmatics, he began with the doctrine of salvation and thence moves on. So subjective was this principle that few truths remained inviolate: 'If in the future "evolution" produces one whose authority in the realm of the spiritual is higher than Jesus Christ, I would be obliged to pledge my most absolute loyalty to him'.[43] It was not the Christ of apostolic testimony which was absolute any longer but an individual's 'authority in the realm of the spiritual' (even other than that of Jesus of Nazareth).

Daniel's response to his colleague's work was devastating. In an extended review in the students' journal *Yr Efrydydd*, he took Edwards to task on every single point: the axiomatic status of 'the modern mind' in religious questions, the use of experience as the sole criterion for truth, and the attempt to do theology on the basis of human perception rather than on God's objective revelation of himself as attested in scripture. In an understandable though wholly misguided attempt to be relevant, what the Brecon professor had done was to shear God of his radical otherness and make him a projection of the religious spirit of mankind. Such errors, he claimed, had already 'led to the theological and spiritual bankruptcy of Protestantism'.[44]

---

[41] J. E. Daniel, 'Gair Duw a Gair Dyn' ('The Word of God and the Word of Man'), *Yr Efrydydd* 5 (1929), 251–5 [255].

[42] D. Miall Edwards, *Bannau'r Ffydd* (Wrexham: Hughes and Son, 1929), p.xiii.

[43] Ibid., 374.

[44] J. E. Daniel, 'Diwinyddiaeth Cymru' ('Wales's theology'), *Yr Efrydydd* 5 (1929), 118–22, 173–5, 197–203 [174].

Daniel continued by challenging Edwards's adoptionist Christology and his truncated theory of atonement. If Jesus of Nazareth was a man whose particular attribute lay in his exquisite experience of the divine, anything resembling an objective salvation would be rendered impossible: 'The modernists' Christ could not perform an objective redemption even if they believed such a thing existed', he exclaimed.[45] Yet sinners needed to be redeemed. What they required was not an example – Edwards's 'expert . . . in the realm of the spiritual' – but a saviour who was actually divine: 'For me atonement is something which is wrought for us, independently, a fountain opened *before* we drink from its waters'.[46] Despite its pious talk of Jesus' fellowship with the Father and his experience of the divine, what liberal theology did was to posit an unbridgeable ontological divide between the Father and the Son which rendered true salvation impossible. On the basis of Edwards's theology the church could no longer claim that *God* in Christ had reconciled the world to himself. Despite its elegance, attractiveness and undoubted appeal, this was in fact a theology of despair. For the sake of its present doctrinal integrity and its future spiritual health, Welsh Nonconformity should, 'with the undivided tradition of the Church, reject the concept of experience and return once more to the concept of revelation'.[47] What was needed was a restatement of classic orthodoxy according to a rejuvenated theology of the Word of God.

It was clear by now that Daniel had not only made Barth's spirited polemic against Protestant liberalism his own, but that he was interacting creatively with the Swiss theologian's more systematic thought. The *Christliche Dogmatik 1: Die Lehr vom Worte Gottes*, precursor of the *Church Dogmatics* had been published in 1927. Daniel's heavily annotated copy shows that the Barthian dogmatics had arrived in north Wales by that time and was serving as a basis for the Welshman's evolving doctrinal convictions. A widely reported paper on ecclesiology and its link with the gospel which he delivered to the annual conference of the Union of Welsh Independents in 1930[48] enhanced his growing reputation as a theological *enfant terrible* while his handbook on the Pauline theology *Dysgeidiaeth yr Apostol Paul* ('The Teaching of the Apostle Paul') (1933), not only lent heavily on the *Christliche Dogmatik* and an equally heavily annotated copy of Barth's sixth edition of the *Römerbrief* (1929) but distilled all the principal themes of the orthodox Protestant reawakening of the period. By this time the

---

[45] Ibid., 197.
[46] Ibid., 198.
[47] Ibid., 121.
[48] J. E. Daniel, 'Eglwys Crist yn hanfodol i efengyl Crist' ('The Church of Christ essential to the gospel of Christ'), *Adroddiad Undeb Caernarfon* (Abertawe: Llyfrfa'r Annibynwyr, 1930), pp.107–11.

whole of Welsh Nonconformity, still the largest Christian body in the land, was being affected by the Barthian trend.[49]

Needless to say, not all were in favour of these developments. The older liberalism found the new emphases at best uncongenial and at worst reactionary and obscurantist in the extreme. D. Miall Edwards included an appendix to *Bannau'r Ffydd*, the systematic theology which was so meticulously reviewed by J. E. Daniel, entitled 'The theology of Karl Barth'. Although his response was measured, he faulted Barthianism for its one-sidedness, its lack of balance and its obvious excesses. It should be taken, he insisted, *cum grano salis!*[50] By downgrading religious experience in favour of concentrating wholly on the objective revelation of God, Barth had created an unhealthy dualism which did scant justice to the complexities of God's involvement in the history of humankind: 'By positing such an extreme antithesis as this, truth itself turns to error in his hands'.[51] It was not antithesis but a correct synthesis which was needed. 'The way to promote God's glory is not by despising all things human. In this I feel that Barth is too Calvinistic'.[52] John Gwili Jenkins, professor of New Testament at the North Wales Baptist College, made a similar point 2 years later in his exhaustive historical theology *Hanfod Duw a Pherson Crist* ('The Essence of God and the Person of Christ'):

> The tendency of the neo-Calvinism of Barth's school is to make of man nothing, and his experience worthless; to make God and his design everything, and every part of Scripture God's immediate and unconditioned Word, uncontaminated by human experience, or imprint or understanding.[53]

The most angry critique was made in the summer of 1931 on the pages of the literary monthly *The Welsh Outlook*. 'During the last two or three years', wrote Philip Josiah Jones, the Presbyterian minister who had been so insistent on the compatibility of Hegelian idealism with Christian truth, 'orthodoxy in theology has experienced something of a boom in Wales',[54] but far from being a cause for rejoicing, this trend was wholly reprehensible.

---

[49] Morgan, *The Span of the Cross*, pp.130–7; cf. Keith Robbins, *England, Ireland, Scotland, Wales: the Christian Church, 1900–2000* (Oxford: Oxford University Press, 2008), pp.249–50.

[50] Edwards, *Bannau'r Ffydd*, p.387; cf. idem, 'Yr efengyl yn ôl Karl Barth' ('The gospel according to Karl Barth'), *Y Traethodydd* 84 (1929), 150–9.

[51] Ibid., 388.

[52] Ibid., 389.

[53] J. Gwili Jenkins, *Hanfod Duw a Pherson Crist* (Liverpool: Hugh Evans, 1931), p.423.

[54] Philip J. Jones, 'The New Orthodoxy – A Criticism', *The Welsh Outlook* 18 (1931), 180–3 [180].

Its scepticism as to God's immanent presence within human enlightenment and progress belied a pessimism which was 'not merely unsatisfactory but positively pernicious'. The weaknesses of this 'panic-stricken and altogether unintelligible post-war theology' were its virtually deistic analysis of God's transcendence, its Gnostic assessment of the nature of revelation and the irrational apocalyptic which characterized its understanding of Christ: 'It would be a waste of time to expatiate on the intellectual vacuity of this theology',[55] Jones continued, but expatiate he did, and with aplomb.

> We are thus presented not with the Sovereign Central Deity of the Christian religion, but with some sort of whimsical being – the villain of the play – who delights in deluding human beings just as much as Barthianism itself . . . Judged by man's moral and religious experience, this kind of teaching deserves to be described as super-quackery.[56]

The invective of this response illustrated the rather paranoid threat which liberalism felt it was under. It was patent that there was a change in the Welsh theological climate, and that the new theology was gaining a hearing and widespread assent. The fact that it was attracting younger pastors and theologians of undoubted ability rankled considerably. 'Men of the highest scholastic attainments are to be found in the ranks of the neo-orthodox movement', admitted Philip Jones, though given the fact that 'error and superstition have never, throughout the whole course of Christian history, lacked the support of scholarship and sophisticated acumen',[57] perhaps this was inevitable. After 1933 its influence would only increase. It was clear that Barthianism was registering as perhaps the most exciting intellectual development within Welsh Protestantism for a generation or more.

[55] Ibid., 181.
[56] Ibid., 181.
[57] Ibid., 182.

4

ENGLISH NONCONFORMITY AND THE RECEPTION OF KARL BARTH, 1926–32

The Nonconformist impulse

If Barth's theology resonated most readily among the Scottish Presbyterians and the Welsh during the 1920s and early 1930s, it would also have a marked effect on the thought of the English Free Churches or Nonconformists, the post-Edwardian children of Protestant Dissent.

'Who were the Nonconformists?' was the question posed by David W. Bebbington, the historian of British evangelicalism. And his answer? 'They were those Protestants who dissociated themselves from the church recognized by the state'.[1] The Nonconformists were the chapel folk whose worship was Word-based and sermon centred, who traditionally had prized spontaneity over formality, who had eschewed ritual and elaborate liturgy in favour of puritan simplicity and for whom the church aspired to be a community of committed believers rather than a parish gathering comprising of all. With roots in seventeenth century Puritanism, their formative historical experience had been the reintroduction of Episcopal government in the national church following the restoration of the monarchy in 1660 and the compulsory enforcement in 1662 of worship according to the Book of Common Prayer. Those clergy who could not accept these strictures were forced to fulfil their ministry outside the bounds of the establishment and frequently, until 1689, outside the bounds of the law. If the more patrician of the ejected clergy namely the English Presbyterians (who were different from the Scottish Presbyterians) had tended to abandon Trinitarian orthodoxy

---

[1] David W. Bebbington, *Victorian Nonconformity* (Bangor: Headstart History, 1992), p.2; cf. James Munson, *The Nonconformists: in search of a lost culture* (London: SPCK, 1991).

during the eighteenth century, the Independents and most of the Baptists had stuck tenaciously to their inherited Calvinism. Whereas by the nineteenth century the Presbyterians' rationalistic Christianity had become Unitarianism and their movement had declined, the Independents and Baptists had been energized by the Evangelical Revival making sure that Protestant Dissent was now disseminated throughout the land. By the early Victorian era the Independents, gathered together in self-regulating covenanted churches, had taken to be called Congregationalists, though inter-congregational links had been forged nationally through the Congregational Union established in 1831.[2] The Baptists, similar in ethos to the Congregationalists, believed however that the ordinance of baptism, which was administered by immersion, should be restricted to those responsible enough to possess a personal faith. If '[m]anufacturers and shopkeepers dominated most Congregational chapels, often being elected to positions of lay leadership', the Baptists 'drew extensively on the skilled workers',[3] though both communities also attracted a significant working class clientele. The Baptists established their national union in 1812 which was strengthened and made more effective in 1832.[4] There was also a reconstituted body this time of orthodox Presbyterians, chiefly expatriate Scots and based in the English cities, who constituted the Presbyterian Church of England, formulated as a separate synod and denomination in 1844.[5]

If the Congregationalists, the Baptists, the Unitarians (and the Quakers of the radical fringe) made up the 'Old Dissent', the 'New Dissent' comprised of the Methodists. John Wesley had died in 1790, still a staunch adherent of the Anglican Church, but his vast spiritual movement had developed a momentum of its own which could hardly be contained within the establishment after he had gone. His autocratic successor Jabez Bunting, as able an organizer as Wesley but intent on centralizing power in the ministers' hands, caused dissension which created a series of secessions: the Methodist New Connexion, the Independent Methodists, the revivalistic Primitive Methodists with their intense spirituality and appeal to the poor, and the Bible Christians. Other smaller secessionist bodies had come together between 1847 and 1851 as the United Methodist Free Churches followed by the Wesleyan Reform Union, in 1859. According to the 1851 religious census there were 1,385,382 who perpetuated the piety of the Wesleyan Revival

[2] R. Tudur Jones, *Congregationalism in England, 1662–1962* (London: Independent Press, 1962), pp.242–4.

[3] Bebbington, *Victorian Nonconformity*, p.10

[4] Ernest A. Payne, *The Baptist Union: a short history* (London: Carey Kingsgate Press, 1958), pp.15–63.

[5] David Cornick, *Under God's Good Hand: a history of the traditions which have come together in the United Reformed Church* (London: United Reformed Church, 1998), pp.123–30.

in conference and class meetings, having been given their voice by Charles Wesley in his hymns.[6] By the mid-Victorian era Methodism had become a vital and energetic component within popular English Christianity.

These were not the only Methodists, however. There was also a band of Calvinistic Methodists who looked back to George Whitefield as their inspiration and to Selina, the Countess of Huntington, for an ecclesiastical home. Her connexion was liturgical, Prayer Book based but Calvinistic rather than Arminian in its creed, and by the nineteenth century had drawn close, in England at least, to the Congregationalists.[7] It was in Wales, though, that Calvinistic Methodism had triumphed having seceded from the Church of England in 1811 to become the most powerful Nonconformist denomination in the principality.[8]

By the mid-Victorian era Nonconformity had become an alternative popular establishment, untrammelled by any links with the state. Having battled against the official establishment, its disabilities had been slowly overcome. The Test and Corporation Acts had been abolished in 1828; after 1837 births and deaths were no longer required to be registered by Church of England incumbents nor marriages performed according to the Anglican rite; the Church Rate, which required all citizens to contribute towards the upkeep of parish churches, had been abolished in 1868, while the final elimination of religious tests for those wishing to graduate at Oxford and Cambridge had occurred in 1871. The Burials Act of 1880 would allow Nonconformists to be buried according to the rites of their own denominations without requiring the presence of the parish clergy. The divide between the upper classes and the burgeoning Nonconformist middle and artisan class would certainly persist and chapel people would still suffer from social prejudice and often a feeling of cultural inferiority, but as the movement expanded, the more confident it became.

Apart from within Wales, where it was universal, Nonconformity was especially prevalent in urbanized areas, the towns of the industrial north and the flourishing municipal centres of the English Midlands. Its vast new gothic edifices, which contrasted strikingly with the neat, unostentatious meeting houses of the past, tended to attract artisans and their families, clerks, shopkeepers, teachers and the like, the upwardly mobile who would fill the ranks of an emerging lower middle class. By 1870 'Nonconformity

---

[6] Rupert E. Davies, A. Raymond George, E. Gordon Rupp (eds), *A History of the Methodist Church in Great Britain*, Vol. 2 (London: Epworth Press, 1978).

[7] J. B. Figgis, *The Countess of Huntingdon and her Connexion* (London: Marshall, [1892]).

[8] William Williams, G. Davies (ed.), *Welsh Calvinistic Methodism: a historical sketch of the Presbyterian Church of Wales*, new ed. (Bridgend: Bryntirion Press, 1998); D. Densil Morgan, 'Lewis Edwards (1809–87) and Welsh Theology', *The Welsh Journal of Religious History*, 3 (2008), 15–28.

seemed the natural religion of urban England and Wales',[9] though its proletarian edges were being rubbed away. In Wales, among the Primitive Methodists and within some of the smaller sects, the working classes were still in the majority, yet the fact was that 'respectability and decorum were gradually gaining the upper hand'.[10] Along with decorum came a conviction that fresh intellectual solutions would need to be found for the novel theological problems of the Victorian age. Doctrinal change was about to occur.

It was among the Congregationalists that it registered most markedly. R. W. Dale (1829–95), minister of Carr's Lane Church, Birmingham, and, '[t]aken all in all . . . the most remarkable Congregationalist of the nineteenth century',[11] was a key figure in the transition. Although resolutely evangelical, he was acutely conscious of the moral critique of orthodoxy which had become commonplace during the Victorian age. His categories of interpretation in his classic *The Atonement* (1870) diverged radically from the Calvinism of the past. The theology of Carr's Lane during his ministry 'was a modified evangelicalism which abandoned the language of moderate Calvinism but retained a degree of consistency with the cardinal evangelical doctrines of the Revival'.[12] By then a consensus was emerging in which full-blown liberalism could flourish, which it did in the work of Andrew M. Fairbairn (1838–1912), the founding principal of Mansfield College, Oxford. His volume *The Place of Christ in Modern Theology* (1893) became 'a benchmark for the new evangelical theology'.[13] As well as being a magisterial survey of both New Testament and historical Christology, its basic axioms were clear: that the Bible contained but could not be equated with God's self revelation, that revelation was historical and progressive, that the Jesus of history could be discovered by patient, careful scholarship, that the eschatological element of the gospels was primitive and temporal, and that the church's dogmas had frequently obscured Christ's true humanity. His subsequent substantial work *The Philosophy of the Christian Religion* (1903) cast his Christology in a Hegelian mode. By the time of his death in 1912, the prevailing theology of the Congregational Union was an enlightened liberalism which majored on evolution and progress rather than redemption and sin. There was, however, one key thinker in this generation, Peter Taylor Forsyth, who paved the way for the Barthian renaissance when it came.

---

[9] Bebbington, *Victorian Nonconformity*, p.28.

[10] Ibid., p.44.

[11] Jones, *Congregationalism in England, 1662–1962*, p.266.

[12] Mark D. Johnson, *The Dissolution of Dissent, 1850–1918* (New York: Garland, 1987), p.47.

[13] Dale A. Johnson, *The Changing Shape of English Nonconformity, 1825–1925* (New York: Oxford University Press, 1999), p.149.

P. T. Forsyth, Nathaniel Micklem and 'Orthodox Dissent'

P. T. Forsyth (b. 1848), for over 20 years principal of the Congregational Hackney College, died in 1921. A brilliant Scotsman who was educated at Aberdeen and at Göttingen under Ritschl, he had trained for the ministry at New College, London, and thereafter served the Congregational churches in pastorates in Yorkshire, London, the English Midlands and Cambridge, and as a trainer of ministers himself. A keen disciple of James Baldwin Brown, the precursor of a liberalism among English Nonconformists,[14] he achieved such notoriety as an advanced liberal that the churches he served were put out of fellowship by their local Congregational union. He underwent a spiritual crisis in the 1890s which brought him back into the Christian mainstream. According to his own testimony, he was transformed from being a Christian into a believer, from being a lover of love he was made the object of grace.[15] Although he broke with dogmatic liberalism he kept faith with all its positive traits: intellectual openness, an appreciation for the historical nature of the gospel record and an understanding of Christianity as revealing God's fatherhood as well as his holy, sin-bearing love. He also kept his liberal friends.

As well as providing Congregationalism with a rationale for its high ecclesiology,[16] Forsyth's trenchant works on Christology and the atonement culminating in his classic *The Person and Place of Jesus Christ* (1909) put him in the front rank of British theologians. For the Roman Catholic Adrian Hastings writing in 1986: 'P. T. Forsyth . . . was probably the greatest British theologian of the Edwardian age, indeed almost the only one (apart from [the Jesuit George] Tyrrell) whose work can really be profitably read for its own sake seventy years later'.[17] For the Reformed scholar Alan Sell, Forsyth was the 'one twentieth century Nonconformist theologian who, more decisively than any other has driven to the heart of the gospel of God's holy love'.[18] It is hardly surprising that it was his students, Sydney Cave, John Phillips, F. W. Camfield and H. F. Lovell Cocks, whose ears were best attuned to the antitheses and discontinuities of Barth's work when it broke upon

---

[14] For Baldwin Brown see Mark Hopkins, *Nonconformity's Romantic Generation: Evangelical and Liberal Theologies in Victorian England* (Milton Keynes: Paternoster Press, 2004), pp.16–45.

[15] P. T. Forsyth, *Positive Preaching and the Modern Mind* (London: Hodder and Stoughton, 1907), pp.282–3.

[16] P. T. Forsyth, *The Church and the Sacraments* (London: Longman's, Green and Co., 1917).

[17] Adrian Hastings, *A History of English Christianity, 1920–2000* (London: SCM, 2001), p.118 (originally published as *A History of English Christianity, 1920–1985* in 1986).

[18] Alan P. F. Sell, *Nonconformist Theology in the Twentieth Century* (Milton Keynes: Paternoster, 2006), p.163.

the English scene. 'Would that so great a master of theology were still with us', wrote Canon Mozley, a friend and admirer of Forsyth's, in 1929, 'that from him we might receive such a study of Barth as he, of all British theologians, would be uniquely competent to give'.[19] Before noting the response of Forsyth's students to Barth's theology, the fact is that the tenor of Congregationalism was about to change and that liberalism would be severely challenged in its central citadel, Mansfield College, Oxford, by one who 'was clearly destined for an outstanding career in the church of his inheritance',[20] and 'whose confidence, his wit, his intellect and his charm made him a most acceptable representative of Mansfield in a wide sphere, not only theological but also in political and literary circles'.[21] His name was Nathaniel Micklem.

Nathaniel Micklem (1888–1976) was one of the most fascinating figures in twentieth-century English Christianity whose contribution has been neglected and strangely ignored.[22] The eldest son of a barrister and Liberal MP, he received a privileged upbringing. He was educated at Rugby and New College, Oxford, where he read Greats. Elected president of the Oxford Union, rather than pursuing a political career he chose the ministry, greatly admiring R. F. Horton, a family friend who had forsaken an Oxford college fellowship in 1884 to become the pastor of Lyndhurst Congregational Church in Hampstead. Micklem entered Mansfield in 1911 and was confirmed in his already liberal faith by his tutors, W. B. Selbie, the principal, who taught doctrine and philosophy, the Old Testament scholar George Buchanan Gray, and the New Testament and patristic specialist Vernon Bartlet. Ordained at Highbury Chapel, Bristol, in 1914, he took an unpopular pacifist stance during the Great War, and moved to a Manchester charge in 1916 having married his equally cultivated wife, Agatha Silcock of Bath. They left the pastorate in 1917 to run a YMCA camp in Dieppe, and in 1918 he was called by Selbie to become chaplain to the students in Mansfield. In 1921 he was appointed Old Testament lecturer at Selly Oak, Birmingham, and in 1927 crossed the Atlantic to take up the chair of New Testament at the Queen's College, Kingston, Ontario, where he became a member of the newly formed United Church of Canada.

Micklem's early publications reflect faithfully the liberalism in which he had been trained. The categories which were explicit in his books, *The Open Light: an enquiry into faith* (1919), *The Galilean: the permanent element*

[19] J. K. Mozley, 'The theology of Karl Barth', *The Review of the Churches* 9 (1929), 553–7 [557].

[20] Elaine Kaye, *Mansfield College, Oxford: its origin, history and significance* (Oxford: Oxford University Press, 1996), p.117.

[21] Ibid., p.190.

[22] But see Norman Goodall, 'Nathaniel Micklem', *Journal of the United Reformed Church History Society* 1/10 (1977), 286–95.

in religion (1920) and *God's Freemen: a tract for the times* (1922), were experience, personality, value judgement and reason. In *The Open Light* he assumed 'that which is the postulate or condition of all thinking, that reason is sovereign and that there can be no appeal beyond reason, for by reason every appeal must commend itself'.[23] The need of the time was to 'deliver Christian faith from the jargon of theology and dead metaphysics'.[24] Just as religious authority must yield to the sovereignty of autonomous rational thought, so the spiritual norm must be internal and not external in any way. 'In the course of controversy Protestantism had begun to harden', he wrote in *God's Freemen*. 'Instead of saying, "from my own inward experience of God's grace in my heart I know", men began to say "in the infallible Scriptures of the Church it stands written". The authority was not that of inward experience but of the written external Word'.[25] For the young Micklem, who would later champion the cause of 'Genevan Congregationalism' and praise the Reformers for the classic objectivity of their faith, 'Calvin and those who followed him were not free to follow the dictates of their conscience [but were] fettered by the inexpugnable authority of the Book'.[26]

Micklem, as we have seen, took part in the Eisleben consultation of Anglo-German theologians in August 1928[27] and contributed a still fairly liberal chapter to the symposium *Mysterium Christi* in 1930.[28] It was all the more surprising that in 1927, shortly before leaving Selly Oak for Canada, he published in the *Congregational Quarterly* an essay of exceptional verve and power which challenged everything which he had previously held. Entitled 'Radicalism and Fundamentalism', it portrayed the current divide in Protestantism as existing not between two different emphases within the one faith, but as having become so wide and deep as to have created two radically different religions. There was truth, he claimed, in the Roman Catholic criticism that Protestantism leads inevitably to subjectivism and unbelief. For Micklem it now transpired that the rift between a religion based on an authoritative revelation and one based on the Enlightenment suppositions of the sovereignty of human reason 'constitutes the supreme religious issue in Europe and America today'.[29] 'Modern radicals', he continued, 'have not

---

[23] Nathaniel Micklem, *The Open Light: an enquiry into faith* (London: J. Clarke, 1919), p.15.

[24] Ibid., p.166.

[25] Nathaniel Micklem, *God's Freemen: a tract for the times* (London: J. Clarke, 1922), p.74.

[26] Ibid., p.74.

[27] See Chapter 1, p.14.

[28] Nathaniel Micklem, 'A modern approach to Christology', in G. K. A. Bell and Adolf Deissmann (eds), *Mysterium Christi: christological studies by British and German theologians* (London: Longmans Green & Co, 1930), pp.143–66.

[29] Nathaniel Micklem, 'Radicalism and Fundamentalism', *The Congregational Quarterly* 5 (1927), 327–34 [328].

realized how great a chasm divides their teaching from the teaching of the New Testament and the whole church down to the period of the *Aufklärung*.[30] Historical Christianity, he insisted, was based upon revelation and dogma, not reason and philosophy. Although modern Protestantism could not go back behind the Enlightenment to a pre-critical age, the fact was that themes such as the fatherhood of God rather than the wrath of the Lamb stemmed from two diverging concepts of what the Christian gospel was all about: 'In practice is it not in very many cases a new religion that is being proclaimed?'[31] Although liberals and modernists abhorred the dogmatism of conservative Christians and fundamentalists, they too had their unshakeable dogmas, namely the benign fatherhood of God, human brotherhood and the immanent Spirit as illustrated by the life of Jesus of Nazareth: 'It is a religion, and a very high type of religion, but is it Christianity?'[32] he asked. Whereas all enlightened people would affirm all that was valuable in modernism, its sincerity and ethical fervour, the vital question was '[i]s this really the modern expression of the old faith . . . or is it in fact a new religion altogether?'[33] Revelation, he claimed, was not merely pious logic. 'To historic Christianity the Christian faith is a truth, or series of truths, which no amount of philosophizing, however pious, nor argumentation, however devotional, could attain'.[34] It was not derived from reason though it was reconcilable to it, neither was it a general truth: 'It is concerned with the interpretation of certain alleged *facts of history*, the birth, death and resurrection of Jesus Christ in the first century of our era'.[35] The church's historic conviction that Jesus of Nazareth possessed deity was not irrational or inconceivable but it could not be substantiated by reason or historical research alone. These were matters of revelation and faith.

In all, this essay was a tremendous plea, a *tour de force*, for reinstating dogma as the basis for Christianity, something that the liberals had long thought was impossible. 'It is the interpretation accepted by historic Christianity and presupposed by the New Testament. It is accepted by those who have learnt to call Jesus Christ their Saviour; apart from this it is mere words'.[36] For the historic faith the atonement was essential, but in so many of Congregationalism's modernist pulpits, the atonement was no longer being preached. 'Let it be clear', he concluded, 'that in those churches where the atoning death of Christ for our sins is not proclaimed today,

---

[30] Ibid., 328.
[31] Ibid., 329.
[32] Ibid., 329.
[33] Ibid., 330.
[34] Ibid., 330.
[35] Ibid., 330.
[36] Ibid., 333.

there has been a decisive and fundamental breach with historic Christianity'.[37] Coming from such an urbane and persuasive disciple of the liberal school, this was unexpected to say the least. It was obvious that changes were about to occur in the ideological make-up of the Congregational world.

Micklem was not alone in standing up for the historic faith. Since the mid-1920s the Cambridge historian Bernard Lord Manning (1892–1941) had been extolling with wit, erudition and a wonderful lightness of touch the qualities of what he termed 'Orthodox Dissent'.[38] Behind the superficialities of twentieth century modernism and the individualism of nineteenth century evangelicalism was the classical dignity of eighteenth-century Dissent. Not only was it true to Luther's piety of the cross and Calvin's corporate churchmanship, it was in continuity with the people's faith of Catholic medievalism. From his professional base at Jesus College and his ecclesiastical base in Emmanuel Congregational Church, he championed the cause of a churchly Dissent which rejected liberal theology outright. A sparkling 1927 essay entitled 'Some characteristics of the Older Dissent', conveyed his agenda with a reformer's zeal. The eighteenth-century Dissenters possessed both a coherent, dogmatic theology and a clear churchmanship: 'The essence of the old Dissent was an *ecclesiastical* experience'.[39] They were neither doctrinal minimalists nor pragmatic in the field of church order: 'There was a flavour of ecclesiasticism about it which would shock and offend many modern Dissenters. The old Dissenter was a great churchman'.[40] They were not cowed by the establishment nor intimidated by it, though they did stand apart. Their sacraments were objective witnesses to God's sovereign grace, they had a high concept of the ordained ministry and they would have found incomprehensible the subjectivity, triviality and individualism of later Nonconformist life. If Congregationalism were to recover from its liberal malaise it would need to recover its roots: 'We must re-explore the positive foundations of English Dissent as they were laid in Geneva and having cleared our own minds and hearts about what it is that we stand for, we must do it as openly and unblushingly as Rome and Canterbury do it and as the older Dissent did'.[41]

---

[37] Ibid., 333.

[38] See Bernard Lord Manning, *Essays in Orthodox Dissent* (London: Independent Press, 1939); for Manning see F. Brittain, *Bernard Lord Manning: a memoir* (Cambridge: Heffer's, 1942) and J. Munsay Turner, 'Bernard Lord Manning (1892–1941) as church historian', *Journal of the United Reformed Church History Society* 1/5 (1975), 126–38.

[39] Bernard Lord Manning, 'Some characteristics of the Older Dissent, with some practical reflections', *The Congregational Quarterly* 5 (1927), 286–300 [289].

[40] Ibid., 291.

[41] Ibid., 300.

Nathaniel Micklem, for all his suave sophistication, was at heart an advocate. Although his demeanor was charming, he was always stimulated by opposition. Now he had found a cause. The fissure within Congregationalism could hardly have been starker in that his student contemporary at Mansfield, C. J. Cadoux, by this time professor of New Testament at the denomination's Bradford College, had published an equally clear apologia for modernism in the *Congregational Quarterly* only three months before his own initial essay. In 'A defence of Christian modernism', Cadoux had characterized the faith of enlightened Nonconformity as depending on the sovereignty of human reason, a belief in God's immanent presence within creation, a rejection of the miraculous, and the right of individual judgement. 'In regard to the Bible', he stated, 'the modernist does not regard all its statements as true or all its teachings as divine. For him the whole is historically interesting, but he freely uses his powers of weighing evidence to reject such of its narratives as appear unreliable'.[42] Authority did not lie with the text itself but with the critic's ability to decide, according to the axioms of modernity, what was valid and what was not. 'The modernist freely picks and chooses, learning from those portions that bear the stamp of divine inspiration and putting the rest aside'.[43] Inspiration did not lead to any notion of infallibility, however loosely the concept was defined, for 'the kind of inspiration its writers enjoyed does not differ from that of Plato, Augustine, Thomas à Kempis and Wordsworth'.[44] What was exceptional about Cadoux's essay was its directness. There was no dissembling or hiding his real meaning behind a veil of evasiveness or academic ambiguity. 'As for the gospel-story, the modernist position is that the traditional church-view of Jesus unduly obscures his true humanity', he claimed, 'that the physical miracles, virgin birth, walking on water, loaves and fishes, stilling the storm, . . . corporeal resurrection and ascension are more naturally and truthfully accounted for as religious legends than historical facts'.[45] For Cadoux, 'Jesus is the embodiment of the divine in human life',[46] and as for any accusations of naturalism, 'its subjectivism is simply the recognition of a truly divine gift in man's intellect and conscience'.[47] The author seemingly rejected every maxim of traditional faith and was convinced that this was the only way that intellectual integrity could be preserved in a critical age.

---

[42] C. J. Cadoux, 'A defence of Christian modernism', *The Congregational Quarterly* 5 (1927), 164–72 [167]; for Cadoux see Elaine Kaye, *C. J. Cadoux: theologian, scholar and pacifist* (Edinburgh: Edinburgh University Press, 1988).

[43] Cadoux, 'A defence of Christian modernism', 167.

[44] Ibid., 168.

[45] Ibid., 168.

[46] Ibid., 169.

[47] Ibid., 170.

We must plant our faith 'beyond the reach of all criticism', he concluded, 'in the one part of our nature where God comes most immediately into contact with us, in the light of reason [and] the love of truth'.[48]

Congregationalists and the early Barth: Sydney Cave and John Phillips

The tensions which would arise among the Congregationalists would become most manifest in the 1930s. Although Barthian thought did not cause the divide, the way it was received helped define the doctrinal character of English Nonconformity during the inter-war years. The first Congregationalist to show an interest in Barth was Sydney Cave (1883–1953), the president of Cheshunt College, Cambridge, and, as has been noted, a student of Forsyth's. Cave was a Londoner who had served on the mission field in India before returning home to a pastorate in Bristol from which he was called to Cheshunt, the Congregational college in Cambridge, in 1920. 'Of recent Congregational theologians', wrote R. Tudur Jones in 1962, 'Cave was the most sensitive to the religious implications of the changes through which he had lived . . . Throughout he was passionately evangelical. In all his thinking he felt he was bound and liberated by an objective gospel which God had revealed to men'.[49] Evangelical as he was, he was not unaffected by the liberalism of the day, and like many liberal evangelicals, he had a consuming interest in the doctrine of the incarnation. His essay 'Recent thought on the doctrine of the Person of Christ' in *The Expository Times* of March 1926 showed his mastery of the literature in the field: he listed works by Ritschl, Herrmann, Kaftan, Häring and Harnack from abroad, Gore and Fairbairn among the home-bred kenoticists as well as the Hegelians T. H. Green and Edward Caird. He was appreciative of the moderate conservatism of James Denney's *Jesus and the Gospel* (1908), Forsyth's *Person and Place of Jesus Christ* (1909) though it was H. R. Mackintosh's *The Person of Jesus Christ* (1912) 'which seems to many of us the most suggestive and valuable on its subject in modern times'.[50] The period since the Great War, which had come to an end 8 years previously, had seen a reaction against the evolutionary liberalism of the previous two generations. 'This reaction has taken an extreme form in the "Theology of Crisis" of which

---

[48] Ibid., 172.

[49] Jones, *Congregationalism in England, 1662–1962*, p.454; cf. Ronald Bocking, 'Sydney Cave (1883–1953): Missionary, Principal, Theologian', *Journal of the United Reformed Church History Society* 7/1 (2002), 36–44.

[50] Sydney Cave, 'Recent thought on the doctrine of the Person of Christ', *The Expository Times* 27 (1925–6), 247–53 [249].

Barth's *Commentary on Romans* is perhaps the most important expression', he claimed:

> It is an amazing book – five hundred pages of violent paradox. Barth delights in emphasizing the irrationality of Paul's thought . . . Religion is for Barth no source of comfort. It is the opponent of man though disguised as his true friend . . . It is the most dangerous opponent, apart from God himself, which man has on this side of death. Religion can only serve to reveal our godlessness, for it is a human possession and work . . . It is 'flesh', even though it dresses itself out as the history of salvation . . . So our hope lies not in human piety, nor in human devotion, but in the sole act of God.[51]

This act of God was bound up with the Person of Christ, the divine saviour who had come from above, and such was the nature of the divine self-revelation that it could only be described in terms of negation and paradox. 'The book, for all its violence', continued Cave, 'is one of the most moving and impressive works in modern theology. But, if Barth be right, there can be no theology, no successful attempt to understand the mystery of God's person'.[52] All that was possible was a feeling of awed thankfulness in the face of a sublime but incomprehensible mercy.

Although he was a conventional Nonconformist scholar not given to radicalism in any way, Cave supported the campaign mounted by Nathaniel Micklem, Bernard Lord Manning and J. S. Whale during the 1930s against such advanced modernist thinkers as Frank Lenwood, Thomas Wigley and C. J. Cadoux, of which more below, and called Congregationalism back to its roots in 'Orthodox Dissent'. He was joined by John Phillips, minister of Oxford's George Street Church, whose essay on 'Barth's Theology of Crisis' of July 1926 furnished Congregationalists with a fuller resumé of Barth's work. Phillips (1886–1981) was a native of Cardiff who had graduated at the University of Wales before training for ministry in Hackney College under Forsyth. Ordained in 1913, he was inducted to the Oxford pastorate in 1926 though there is no record of him having any links with Mansfield College. His 1930 Oxford B. Litt thesis on Barth's doctrine of the Word of God[53] seems to have been the first academic dissertation on Barth's theology to have been awarded in a British university. His 1926 article was based on two of Barth's early works: the *Römerbrief*, and the volume of sermons co-authored with Eduard Thurneysen, *Komm, Schöpfer Geist!*, along with articles from *Die Christliche Welt*.

---

[51] Ibid., 252.
[52] Ibid., 252.
[53] John Phillips, 'The Doctrine of the Word in relation to Holy Scripture as presented in the Theology of Karl Barth', unpublished B Litt thesis, University of Oxford, 1930.

The operative word in Barth's theology, according to Phillips, was 'crisis'. 'The crisis comes when man in his sinful relativity stands over and against the absolutely holy God and knows that of himself he cannot bridge the gulf. That for Barth is the theme of all theology. What lies outside that is negligible and what omits it is betrayal'.[54] Phillips provided his readers with a précis of the Romans commentary: that Paul through the miracle of God becomes our contemporary, that the person who reads the epistle is drawn into its meaning and is not the spectator that modern theology had assumed: 'The establishment of the contents of the New Testament is not made by translating Greek words and their more or less plausible rearrangement, with a little historical discussion and application of psychology',[55] while the theme of the epistle was God and his revelation in Christ. 'Barth approaches *Romans* with the presupposition that Paul speaks there about Jesus Christ and nothing else, and that the epistle is a witness and a certifying of a revelation'.[56] For Barth the biblical text was self-certifying; it did not need any independent historical verification: 'Such exclusiveness is contained in Barth's idea of revelation. If the word revelation is only a term for probable human discovery, banish the full-toned word',[57] he urged. 'With all his might Barth repudiates a mere subjectivity',[58] Phillips continued, and he explained how Barth used dialectic to shed light on truth: 'One has to face inconsistencies, apparent or real, and pick one's way through a welter of paradox. But there is a certain massiveness about it that fascinates'.[59]

According to Phillips, Barth's scheme had three principal components. First, that there was a great gulf fixed between God and humankind. God was imponderable, incomprehensible while human beings were both creaturely and sinful. Education therefore, progress, mystical union and ethics were all meaningless in the context of people's approach to God, while religion would only lead them to despair: 'Religious experiences have repeatedly led men away from God'.[60] This being the case, Barth's second cardinal point was that Christ had been appointed by God in order to bridge the divide: 'If there is no way from man to God there is a way from God to man, and that is Jesus Christ, though it is only in him as risen from the dead and set as the Son of God with power'.[61] The New Testament, he claimed, was to be read in the light of the resurrection. 'Jesus Christ is a new *aeon*,

---

[54] John Phillips, 'Barth's Theology of Crisis', *The Congregational Quarterly* 4 (1926), 322–30 [323].
[55] Ibid., 324–5.
[56] Ibid., 326.
[57] Ibid., 326.
[58] Ibid., 326.
[59] Ibid., 326.
[60] Ibid., 327.
[61] Ibid., 327.

descending vertically into the plane of human probability. In him the abyss is bridged, but he touches life only as a tangent touches a circle, for he is not a fusion of man and God, either of God poured into man or of man caught up to God'.[62] According to Phillips's description this is docetism, especially as he seems to disparage the earthly life of Jesus, his parables and Sermon on the Mount: 'The historical Jesus, it would appear, is a hint or symbol of the invisible God, who is nevertheless actually present'.[63] 'About Barth's theology many questions will be asked. The only thing that emerges with clearness is his effort to maintain the transcendence of God'.[64] For Phillips, this Christ seems 'contentless',[65] yet he had plainly been intrigued by and drawn into Barth's way of thought. The third element had to do with the listener's response. The only way to respond to this revelation is by faith, not so much as psychological experience but as an existential leap: 'How God works by Christ as risen is simply incomprehensible and the only thing to do is to wonder at it'.[66] Barth's view was eschatological, not historical. God's work was beyond time and belonged to a different order of reality: 'In God's "No" God's "Yes" appears'.[67]

What the readers of *The Congregational Quarterly* made of this is difficult to say. The base of information upon which he made his assessment was narrow, and Phillips emphasised paradoxes which went beyond even Forsyth's elliptic, epigrammatic prose. There was, nevertheless, something disconcertingly immediate in Barth's work: 'Barth restores to us the trembling awe of the prophets and brings us into line with the travailing soul of Jesus to whom it was no easy thing to know the will of God'.[68] If there were aspects of his thought which seemed, on first reading, to be irrational, that was because the Swiss theologian was still *in via* and that subsequent work would surely show more clarity of vision. Barth's theology was, none the less, a mighty corrective to the currently fashionable liberalism: 'Whatever difficulties are involved in his eschatological view of the kingdom, it comes at least as a hearty reaction to the junketing utopias offered by some today'.[69]

Congregationalism's 'sharp turn to the theological right'

There was no doubt that among Congregationalists, since the late-Victorian era, liberalism had been setting the pace. Even during the late 1920s the

[62] Ibid., 327.
[63] Ibid., 327.
[64] Ibid., 327.
[65] Ibid., 327.
[66] Ibid., 327.
[67] Ibid., 327.
[68] Ibid., 329.
[69] Ibid., 329.

advanced modernist views of such representative figures as Francis Wigley, minister of Salem Chapel, Leeds, chairman of the Congregational Union in 1928–29 and T. Rhondda Williams of Brighton[70] who succeeded him a year later, illustrated how the radicals of an earlier generation had created the received orthodoxy of the next. It was on this background that R. F. Horton, minister of Lyndhurst Church, Hampstead, the family friend who had created such an impression on the young Nathaniel Micklem, appealed in 1926 for Free Churchmen to come together to meet the needs of the time for

> a presentation of Christianity equally removed from Romanism and Fundamentalism, a presentation which the intelligence and reason and knowledge of modern men can wholeheartedly accept, a presentation which, starting from the Christ who is ever the same, shows clearly what he has to say to new times and new truths.[71]

Horton (1855–1934), formerly fellow in Modern History in New College, Oxford, and before resigning his fellowship to take up the ministry in Hampstead in 1884, the first Nonconformist since the Restoration to hold a university post in Oxford, shared the liberal preconceptions of his generation though in a studied and nuanced way.[72] The pattern was the Anglican Union of Modern Churchmen whose annual conference had been held in Oxford in 1925. The first Congregational Theological Conference was held at Mansfield in the summer of 1927 with Horton in the chair. It took as its theme 'The Christian Faith in the Light of Modern Science and Criticism' and among its speakers were W. B. Selbie, principal of Mansfield College, the inveterate modernist J. Morgan Jones, a disciple of Harnack and principal of the Bala-Bangor college in Wales, the equally modernist T. Rhondda Williams, and Micklem. The tenor of the conference was liberal. Micklem was the only one to sound a jarring note. Both Congregationalism and modern Protestantism generally, he warned, were in danger of collapse 'through the presentation of a vague and sentimental religiosity without

---

[70] Wrigley (1868–1945) and Williams (1860–1945) are listed in John Taylor and Clyde Binfield (eds), *Who They Were in the Reformed Churches of England and Wales, 1901–2000* (Donington: United Reformed History Society, 2007).

[71] R. F. Horton, 'Free Churchmen and the Modern Churchmen', *The Congregational Quarterly* 4 (1926), 167–71 [171].

[72] According to R. Tudur Jones, '[W. B.] Selbie and Horton . . . were evangelical and conservative; they were always vigilant lest the essentials of traditional Christian beliefs should be surrendered', *Congregationalism in England, 1662–1962*, p.447; for Horton see A. Peel and J. A. R. Marriott, *Robert Forman Horton* (London: Geo Allen and Unwin, 1937) and E. Neale, 'A type of Congregational ministry: R. F. Horton (1855–1934) and Lyndhurst Road', *Journal of the United Reformed Church History Society* 5/4 (1997), 215–31.

justice, without judgement, without a soul-shattering mercy, without a Redeemer and without God'.[73]

During Micklem's Canadian sojourn, the Barthian theology drew sharp criticism from within senior denominational ranks. A. E. Garvie (1861–1945), principal of New College, London, had been raised within the United Free Church of Scotland but as a young man had rejected its creedalism and Calvinism *per se* and found a home within Congregationalism: 'Brought up as I have been in strict Presbyterian orthodoxy, including the belief in verbal inspiration, it can be understood how great was the shock, and how much need there as for adjustment between the new view and the old'.[74] The adoptionist Christology which he had found in Dean Farrar's humanizing *Life of Christ*, and reflected in his own *Studies in the Life of Jesus* (1907), was still the only real option for modern believers. 'The Barthian theology', he claimed, 'which is a minor evil product of the war, gives us a lower conception [of the doctrinal task]; progress lies, I am confident, in keeping to Christ in our thought and life as the true and living way to that Father'.[75] The supposition was that Barth was only interested in the transcendence of God and that his Christology was docetic and unreal.

The radical implications of Congregationalism's modernism became obvious in the career of the charismatic Frank Lenwood (1874–1934), one of the denomination's ablest servants.[76] The son of a Congregational minister, he was educated at Rugby and Corpus Christi, Oxford, where he had won first class degrees in Classical Moderations and Greats and, like Micklem, served as president of the Union. He had combined this with a radical Nonconformist witness including pacifism and teetotalism, and had been heavily involved in Student Christian Movement evangelism. Ministerial training at Fairbairn's Mansfield had introduced him to biblical criticism, but such was his effectiveness as a student missioner that he was appointed chaplain to Oxford's Nonconformist students with a tutorship in New Testament at Mansfield providing him with a base. Having married into a distinguished Nonconformist family, he set off with Gertrude Wilson, his wife, for India in 1906 to work with the London Missionary Society. Having made an ineradicable impact on the Indian work, he returned home and was appointed secretary to the LMS in December 1912.

Following the liberal impulse Lenwood had sought to find common ground between Christians, Hindus and those of other faiths on the basis of

---

[73] Nathaniel Micklem, 'What is Christian Experience?', *The Congregational Quarterly* 5 (1927), 549–55 [552].

[74] A. E. Garvie, 'Fifty Years Retrospect', *The Congregational Quarterly* 7 (1929), 18–25 [19].

[75] Ibid., 21.

[76] See Brian Stanley, 'Manliness and Mission: Frank Lenwood and the London Missionary Society', *Journal of the United Reformed History Society* 5/8 (1996), 458–77.

a shared experience of the transcendent. The critical biblical scholarship which he had imbibed at Mansfield had slowly convinced him that the orthodox formulations of Christology were mistaken and in 1922 he confided to his wife that he had doubts as to Christ's unique divinity. In fact he could no longer confess Christ as Lord.[77] An indefatigable idealism, an enduring belief in the benefit of Christian mission and the preaching of Christ as a power for good kept him in his post for a while, but he resigned his secretaryship in 1925 and a year later was inducted pastor of Greengate, Plaistow, a liberal Congregational church in east London. It was in 1930 that he made his by now well-established views known in his controversial volume *Jesus – Lord or Leader?*, 'a sustained exposition of the modernist theme that a radical revision of doctrinal orthodoxy need entail neither a repudiation of the religious experience that had undergirded orthodoxy nor any diminution of the missionary imperative'.[78] Even advanced liberals were uneasy, especially as he had renounced the explicit lordship of Christ. The Mansfield Theological Conference of 1931 discussed the book, with the author present. C. J. Cadoux accepted Lenwood's methods but disagreed with his conclusions. 'We must admit a uniqueness in Christ', he said. 'Man is akin to God. Divinity in him and in us is one and the same kind, but in him it was perfect and this constitutes uniqueness'.[79] There was, at bottom, little intellectual difference between Cadoux's modernism and Lenwood's Christ-inspired humanitarianism.

This was made clear by perhaps the most incisive, and certainly the most devastating, review of the book by the third member of Congregationalism's new orthodox triumvirate, J. S. Whale. Although Lenwood, like Origen of old, was a noble Christian soul, his theology was not only deficient but wholly erroneous. 'About Mr Lenwood's theology as set forth, there can be only one verdict. If he is right, the great central classical Christian tradition has been wrong and much of the New Testament is a grievous illusion'.[80] Whale, professor of church history at Mansfield since 1929, continued with unabated verve:

If this up-to-date Socinianism, with its unambiguously human Jesus and its denial of the incarnation and atonement, is the true answer to the question 'What think ye of Christ?', then the religion of Irenaeus and Athaniasius, of Augustine and Anselm, of Luther and Bossuet, of Wesley and Von Hügel, has been founded on a myth, and the faith

---

[77] Roger C. Wilson, *Frank Lenwood* (London: SCM, 1936), p.161.
[78] Stanley, 'Manliness and Mission', 474.
[79] R. F. Franks, 'The Theological Conference', *Mansfield College Magazine* 9 (1931–34), 88–90 [89].
[80] J. S. Whale, 'Jesus – Lord or Leader?', *The Congregational Quarterly* 9 (1931), 54–7 [54].

of Christendom is at last exposed as a glorious dream, if not shattered as a pathetic illusion.[81]

Liberal biblical criticism had taken the historical objectivity of the New Testament for granted and believed that the critic's views were value-free, but the fact was that the Bible was the document of a community with its own preconceptions about the way that God had revealed himself to humankind 'The gospels are not the source nor the explanation of our holy religion, but its product', he claimed. 'They are literary forms witnessing to the fact of Christ, and depicting the impact of his proclamation of the divine sovereignty on men. They are not biographies of Jesus'.[82] Whereas Lenwood, and Cadoux in his later *The Historic Mission of Jesus* (1941) believed that Jesus, the simple prophet of Nazareth, could be retrieved through careful, unbiased historical scholarship, the form-critical work of Weiss, Kittel, Bultmann and the innovative gospel criticism of the Anglican Edwyn Hoskyns, had shown the modernists' views to be naïve: 'The heart of traditional dogma, then, so far from being a later alien accretion, is part of the historian's data'.[83] Lenwood, though, well realised the implications of his views: 'He sees clearly that this Unitarianism implies a radical break with historic Christianity, and the setting up of something different and new'.[84] Although he took the older man to task on the basis of scholarship and criticism, for Whale the inadequacy of modernism was, at root, religious. Not only did it fail to do justice to the evidence, it was insufficient to induce worship, wonder and praise. 'There is all the difference in the world', he concluded, 'between revering the memory of a dead leader and worshipping a living and eternal Lord'.[85]

The scorching review of Lenwood's volume announced that Whale, along with Manning and Micklem, had become an instigator of a new movement within Congregationalism. Neither conservative evangelicals nor doctrinal regressionists, they were fully abreast of the latest scholarship and totally in tune with what would become the critical orthodoxy of the inter-war years.

John Seldon Whale (1896–1997), the son of a Cornwall Congregational minister, had served as a medical orderly in the Great War and proceeded to St Catherine's, Oxford, in 1919 where he graduated with first class honours in modern history. Having enrolled for ministerial training at Mansfield, there was nothing to suggest that he was anything less than a typical theological liberal. Ordained in 1925, he married the daughter of H. C. Carter,

---

[81] Ibid., 54.
[82] Ibid., 56.
[83] Ibid., 57.
[84] Ibid., 55.
[85] Ibid., 54.

B. L. Manning's minister at Emmanuel Church, Cambridge, and was called to the Mackennal chair in church history at Mansfield in 1929. By then Mansfield's 'old guard' was leaving the scene. Buchanan Gray, the Old Testament scholar, had died in 1922; Vernon Bartlet, the church historian, had retired in 1928 and Selbie would relinquish his post in 1932. A younger generation of theological teachers which included C. H. Dodd in New Testament (before his removal to the John Rylands chair in Manchester in 1930), and an older man, the erudite Baptist H. Wheeler Robinson, principal of Regent's Park College but teaching Old Testament in Mansfield from 1927, represented new emphases among the teaching staff. Rather than accepting the prevailing theological consensus uncritically, each had his qualms as to whether liberalism did full justice to the fullness of the historic faith.

Having to teach church history, Whale, was drawn to the churchmanship of Calvin's Geneva and developed an expertise in the subject which was displayed in his essay on Calvin in the 1936 Mansfield *Festschrift* entitled *Christian Worship*.[86] This culminated a quarter century later in his classic study *The Protestant Tradition* (1955). A sparkling communicator, he soon made a name for himself in both pulpit and platform. Just as C. S. Lewis would become the most acclaimed apologist for 'Mere Christianity' with his wartime broadcast talks, Whale's radio messages published as *The Christian Answer to the Problem of Evil* (1936), *What is a Living Church?* (1937), *The Christian Faith* (1938) and *Facing the Facts* (1940) were intelligent, pungent and highly effective expositions of orthodox Christianity for a popular audience. When Micklem returned to Mansfield in 1932, inheriting the mantle of principal a year later, he rejoiced to have Whale on the staff. The two men immediately became allies in calling their denomination back to the fullness of its heritage in both ecclesiology and in Calvinistic doctrine.

The stir created by 'the new Genevans' and the reaction it engendered among incensed liberals was illustrated by the heated correspondence in *The Christian World*, the weekly newspaper favoured by Congregationalists, through late 1931 and 1932. The perception that a new force was at work came at the Congregational Union's centenary meetings at Manchester in October 1931. 'The challenging brilliance' of Micklem's assembly speech was reported with astonishment, along with a realization that 'a new power had arisen in Congregationalism'.[87] 'It has never been our freedom to proclaim what we like', stated Micklem, 'or to invent a gospel . . . Apart from faith in Jesus Christ as our great High Priest, the Lamb of God,

---

[86] J. S. Whale, 'Calvin', in Nathaniel Micklem (ed.), *Christian Worship: studies in its history and meaning* (Oxford: Oxford University Press, 1936), pp.154–71.

[87] Anon, 'Congregational Union Centenary Meetings', *The Christian World*, 15 October, 1931, 5.

the saviour of the world, there is no Christianity nor ever can be'.[88] Whale, in similar vein, claimed that 'without the belief in Christ as the Son of God, without the forgiveness of sins at the foot of the cross, without the faith of the resurrection, Christianity is at an end'.[89] According to an editorial, 'The sermon of Dr J. D. Jones and the addresses of Professors Nathanial Micklem and John S. Whale arrested the interest of the assembly by a characteristic common to all: namely, a sharp turn to the theological right'.[90] A few weeks later Whale was taken to task by the modernist Thomas Wigley for apparently saying, in the Cornwall Congregational Union, that '[i]f much of our modernism is true, then St Paul was a blockhead!'[91] Although Whale refuted the words, he nevertheless stood by the sentiment.[92] By late 1931 the new orthodoxy was proving to be a potent force in contemporary Independency.

The liberals, Frank Lenwood included, could hardly take this lying down. Thomas Wigley, minister of Blackheath Congregational Church, and Lenwood held a conference on modernist themes during the 1932 meetings of the Congregational Union, and in *The Christian World* of 9 February 1933 a 'Restatement of Christian Thought' appeared. It took evolution to be axiomatic in matters of religion and held no place for the miraculous, the supernatural or much else pertaining to traditional faith. Micklem's rejoinder was withering. The restatement contained no reference to the Trinity, the atonement or to an objective salvation. 'What is there . . . in their statement that may be regarded as the equivalent of our fathers' sense of the sovereignty of God, of sin and grace . . . of God revealed as Father, Son and Holy Ghost?', he asked. In which way could the group members 'express the spiritual wealth of the gospel within their meagre-looking *schema*?'[93] Recounting the drama in the 1950s, even a mellowed Micklem remained convinced that what had been at stake was no less than the integrity of the gospel itself:

> The issue came to a head when 'the Blackheathens', as they were called, produced a new statement of faith which they proposed as a modern substitute for the old beliefs. This document did not restate, nor did its sponsors claim that it restated, the religion of the Bible; it was rather

---

[88] Ibid.

[89] 'A turn to the right', *The Christian World*, 15 October, 1931, 10.

[90] Ibid.

[91] Thomas Wigley, 'Professor Whale and the Modernists', *The Christian World*, 26 November, 1931, 5.

[92] J. S. Whale, 'Professor Whale and the Modernists: a reply', *The Christian World*, 10 December, 1931, 7.

[93] Nathaniel Micklem, 'A restatement of Christian thought', *The Christian World*, 9 March 1933, 7.

the residual faith of those who, consciously or unconsciously, were no longer holding to biblical religion.[94]

Despite his increasingly distinctive Genevan Congregationalism,[95] Micklem would never become a Barthian. He was drawn, rather, to the medieval synthesis of Thomas Aquinas which became the unlikely basis for his doctrinal teaching among the Mansfield men. There is no doubt, however, that the move towards revelation theology, classical orthodoxy and the dogmatic teaching of the undivided church did much to create a milieu in which Barth's contribution was taken seriously. It was already getting a sympathetic hearing from senior Congregationalists. By late 1931 Sydney Cave was showing himself to be an avid supporter. Reviewing Adolf Keller's assessment of the Barthian movement in Europe *Der Weg der dialectischen Theologie durch die kirchliche Welt* in the *British Weekly*, his attitude was wholly positive: 'His book is a proof, if proof be needed, of the impossibility of ignoring what has become the most significant movement in the religion and the theology of our time'.[96] Although Keller had perceived that Barth's theology had resonated more strongly in Scotland than in England, and that it was the younger theologians of Protestant Dissent who were most in tune with his teaching, there was no doubt about its universal importance: 'Barthianism has saved many on the continent from complete despair. It may help to restore to us a sober confidence which comes not from our own devout feelings nor our anxious effort, but from the certainty that God is, God rules and God has spoken'.[97]

The most zealous protagonist of Barth's views among Congregational ministers, F. W. Camfield, would publish his *Revelation and the Holy Spirit: an essay in the Barthian theology* in 1933. By the later 1930s and 1940s it was Mansfield students, Alec Whitehouse, Hubert Cunliffe-Jones, Daniel T. Jenkins and Herbert Herschwald who took the English study of Barth forward in new and fruitful directions. J. S. Whale, for his part, left Mansfield in 1933 to succeed Cave as president of Cheshunt College. It was from Cambridge, and Emmanuel Church, that he and Manning, with the support

---

[94] Nathaniel Micklem, *The Box and the Puppets* (London: Geoffrey Bles, 1957), p.78; for the Blackheath controversy, see John W. Grant, *Free Churchmanship in England , 1870–1940* (London: Independent Press, [1955]), pp.303–7 and Ian M. Randall, *Evangelical Experiences: a study in the spirituality of English Evangelicalism, 1918–39* (Carlisle: Paternoster Press, 1999), pp.179–82.

[95] Nathaniel Micklem, 'The Genevan inheritance of Protestant Dissent', *The Hibbert Journal* 25 (1936), 115–31; reprinted in idem., *The Place of Understanding* (London: Geoffrey Bles, 1963), pp.26–39.

[96] Sydney Cave, 'The teaching of Karl Barth and its influence on the churches', *The British Weekly*, 17 December, 1931, 243.

[97] Ibid.

of Micklem, Cave and Lovell Cocks, would issue their stately Genevan manifesto: 'To the Ministers of Christ's Holy Gospel in the Churches of the
Congregational Order' in 1939,[98] while his 1940 series of lectures on Christian doctrine which attracted students from all faculties, was, by all accounts,
an electrifying performance: 'One Peterhouse Methodist recalls Whale
prancing down the desk tops as if to battle, so packed were the gangways'.[99]
The book that issued from the series *Christian Doctrine*, was a classic: '[It]
became mandatory in theological colleges, and remained in print for half a
century'.[100] By calling Congregationalism back to orthodoxy with its concepts of revelation, redemption, and the objective content of God's holy
Word, these astute and remarkable (if neglected) theologians played an
important part in the broader context of Barth reception in England.

R. Birch Hoyle and the Baptist response to Barth

There was much in the Baptist culture which was in accord with that of
the Congregationalists. Both denominations were of comparable size, the
Baptists having some 250,000 members in 1930 to the Congregationalists'
300,000. (The English Presbyterians, mostly to be found in the larger cities
and the rural borderland of Northumberland, had a membership of
80,000.)[101] Both had their roots in the Older Dissent and partook of the
politicization of Nonconformity which occurred in the nineteenth century.
The Baptists, though, were less doctrinally polarized than the Congregationalists, having no discernable modernist left wing, though they were more
susceptible to fundamentalism, that belligerent attitude to biblical criticism,
hostility to ecumenism and outright opposition to the theory of evolution
which had been imported from America by the 1920s.[102] It perpetuated the
influence of the Victorian preacher C. H. Spurgeon: 'A strong body of

---

[98] See Erik Routley, *The Story of Congregationalism* (London: Independent Press, 1961),
pp.164–71.

[99] Clyde Binfield, 'A learned and gifted Protestant minister: John Seldon Whale', *Journal
of the United Reformed Church History Society* 6 (1998), 97–131 [124].

[100] Ibid.; J. S. Whale, *Christian Doctrine* (Cambridge: Cambridge University Press,
1942).

[101] R. Currie, Alan Gilbert, L. Horsley, *Churches and Churchgoers: patterns of church
growth in the British Isles since 1700* (Oxford: Oxford University Press, 1977),
pp.134, 150.

[102] See David W. Bebbington, 'Baptist Fundamentalism in inter-war Britain', in K. Robbins
(ed.), *Protestant Evangelicalism: Britain, Ireland, Germany and America, 1750–1950*
(Oxford: Blackwells, 1990), pp.297–326; cf. Ian M. Randall, '"Capturing Keswick":
Baptists and the changing spirituality of the Keswick Convention in the 1920s', *The
Baptist Quarterly* 36 (1996), 331–48.

"Spurgeonite" Baptist life continued, wary of liberal theology and stressing the evangelical hallmarks: biblical inspiration, personal conversion, the saving power of the blood of Christ shed in the sacrificial, substitutionary atonement, and the second advent'.[103] In a denomination whose grass-roots were overwhelmingly biblical, there was little sympathy for either ecumenism or a more communal or sacramental ecclesiology. 'That individualism which characterizes the Baptists perhaps more than any other denomination', noted H. Wheeler Robinson, 'supplies the chief elements of both their strength and their weakness'.[104]

Although mainstream Baptists preserved good relations with their Free Church neighbours, the tendency by the 1920s was to accentuate denominational distinctives: freedom from the state, individual responsibility and a non-creedal Biblicism. The appointment of M. E. Aubrey (1885–1957) as general secretary of the Baptist Union in 1925 had reinforced this trend. Despite having learned his theology at Mansfield College under Fairbairn and Buchanan Grey, Aubrey made sure that the denomination stuck to a centrist, non-doctrinaire, traditional evangelical faith. Baptists were not, however, without creative thinkers who desired to expand horizons rather than replicate unthinkingly older views. The most impressive among them was H. Wheeler Robinson (1872–1945), principal of Regent's Park College. Born into restricted circumstances in Northampton, his burning educational ambition had taken him to Edinburgh University in the 1890s where he had been initiated into the liberal evangelicalism which had become the Scottish Presbyterian norm. He had proceeded to Fairbairn's Mansfield to read theology and Oriental studies and had been Buchanan Grey's prize pupil, excelling in Hebrew and Semitics. Following pastorates in Perthshire and Coventry, he became tutor at Rawdon College, Manchester, and succeeded to the principalship of Regent's Park, then situated in London, in 1920. Though wedded to his denomination's ethos, he was more than a typical Baptist individualist. Holding resolutely to the need for evangelical conversion, he developed a high ecclesiology and sacramental faith in which baptism, conversion and the gift of the Holy Spirit were held tightly together.

For most Edwardian Baptists, believer's baptism was an adjunct to faith, an external extra which witnessed to an inner experience which was complete of itself. Careful exegesis and a profound knowledge of seventeenth century Baptist practice had taught Robinson that the New Testament emphasis was in a different place, that the baptismal rite was a channel of

---

[103] Keith W. Clements, *Lovers of Discord: twentieth century theological controversies in England* (London: SPCK, 1989), p.109.

[104] H. Wheeler Robinson, *The Life and Faith of the Baptists* (London: Kingsgate Press, 1927), p.v.

grace as well as witnessing to a subjective event.[105] His concept of corporate personality as a key to understanding Old Testament faith became seminal in academic circles, though it was a *The Christian Experience of the Holy Spirit* (1928) which marked him out as a major creative theologian in his own right.[106] Although he had been censured by the Baptist right following his use of higher critical methods, his deference to the authority of the text along with his affirmation of experiential evangelicalism assured his acceptance within the mainstream.[107] Robinson's espousal of human personality as a vehicle for the divine gave him affinities with Schleiermacher's liberalism, but as his faith was rooted in an objective, supernatural and historical gospel, he was wholly in accord with denominational standards. As an old Mansfield man he well knew the advantages of having a centre of Nonconformist excellence in Oxford, a seat of Anglican power, and it was he who orchestrated Regent Park's move from London to Oxford in 1927. Mansfield immediately offered him a post as Old Testament tutor in conjunction with his principalship, while the university theological faculty appointed him Reader in 1934. Centrist evangelicalism even if tinged with liberalism had now become the Baptist norm, whereas Calvinism had been superseded even at the Pastors' College, renamed Spurgeon's College following its move from Stepney to South Norwood, London, in 1923.

If Robinson was the most creative theologian, the Baptists' best known public personality was the classicist T. R. Glover (1869–1943): 'Glover and Robinson, in Cambridge and Oxford respectively, with their combination of moderate liberalism and commitment to evangelical experience, epitomized progressive inter-war Baptist opinion'.[108] The son of a scholarly, open-minded minister in Bristol, Glover won a scholarship to St John's College, Cambridge, where he excelled in the classics tripos and was elected to a fellowship. Apart from a 5-year professorship in Ontario, Canada, St John's was the scene of his labours for the rest of his life.[109] Prodigiously learned though a highly popular communicator, he produced a vast body on Greek and Latin themes and in 1920 was elected the university's Public Orator. It gave him droll satisfaction to have presented for honorary degrees six

---

[105] H. Wheeler Robinson, 'The place of baptism in Baptist churches today', *The Baptist Quarterly* 1 (1922–23), 212–18; for Robinson see E. A. Payne, *Henry Wheeler Robinson: a memoir* (London: Nisbet, 1948).

[106] See Rex Mason, 'H. Wheeler Robinson revisited', *The Baptist Quarterly* 37 (1998), 213–26.

[107] Ian M. Randall, *The English Baptists of the Twentieth Century* (Didcot: Baptist History Society, 2005), p.133.

[108] Randall, *Evangelical Experiences: a study in the spirituality of English Evangelicalism, 1918–39* , p.177.

[109] See T. R. Glover, *Cambridge Retprospect* (Cambridge: Cambridge University Press, 1943) ; cf. H. G. Wood, *Terrot Reavely Glover: a biography* (Cambridge: Cambridge University Press, 1953).

prime ministers, two kings and a god, namely the crown prince of Japan! Raucous and good natured, he was nevertheless committed to the Free Churchmanship and the simple Christianity in which he had been raised. Never a theologian in the technical sense, his commitment to Jesus cohered with an emphasis on Christ's humanity which was characteristic of Protestant liberalism. 'Judging . . . from his character and personality', the young Glover wrote to his father, 'Jesus seems more likely to be right and reliable than ordinary teachers'.[110] Although he refused to disavow Christ's deity, atonement or resurrection, it was Jesus' humanity which was well to the fore.

Glover discharged both a debt and a ministry in publishing his *Jesus of History* in 1917. It was phenomenally successful, selling some 500,000 copies within the first few years. His debt was to his religious inheritance and the tolerant faith of his father, the Revd Richard Glover. His ministry was that of a lay evangelist, especially to students. Along with William Temple and the Methodist Russell Maltby, he was the most popular speaker at SCM gatherings during the inter-war years. His expertise was in the world of classical Greece and Rome. He had belonged to that first generation of Nonconformists to benefit from an Oxbridge education. It was his responsibility and joy to share his devotion to Jesus by extolling his genius in the context of the culture of first century Greece. While Wheeler Robinson was immersing himself in the corporate nature of Hebrew thought, Glover's classicism underlined the individualism of current liberal Protestantism. He had nothing to say about the miraculous element in Christ's ministry – though he did not deny it – but much about the ethical: 'Glover's Jesus can be taken to be *the* "middle of the road" picture of Jesus as presented by non-Catholic Christians throughout the English speaking world . . . This was an Englishman's Jesus for the British Empire and the United States'.[111]

Glover's presidency of the Baptist Union in 1924–25, though frowned upon by the conservative right, was widely appreciated by the membership as a whole: 'We know quite well the elements of the gospel experience; we are scarred by the power of evil, we have known again and again the saving power of Christ'.[112] 'As I grow older', he continued, 'I want more and more to preach Christ without theory, to tell people the tremendous facts associated with him – . . . victory over sin, the changed life, and the most amazing fact of all, himself.'[113] The emphasis here was on the subjective appropriation of salvation rather than any objective doctrinal scheme. A later fracas in which Glover, having produced a series of studies for the Baptist Union entitled 'Fundamentals', explained the atonement in a minimalist and a-theological way, was defused by his claim that he could affirm all that

---

[110] Quoted in Clements, *Lovers of Discord*, p.113.
[111] Robbins, *England, Ireland, Scotland, Wales*, p.172.
[112] T. R. Glover, *The Preaching of Christ* (London: Kingsgate Press, 1924), p.29.
[113] Ibid., p.30.

was contained in the great evangelical hymns but that the church needed to connect with those for whom traditional language had become unintelligible.[114] Mainstream Baptists, therefore, were more traditionally minded than Congregationalists and less doctrinally adventurous. Few, though, knew how to respond to the theology of Karl Barth when it was unveiled in 1930, with considerable aplomb, by one of their own.

Richard Birch Hoyle (1875–1939) was a Lancastrian who studied for the ministry at Regent's Park College, London, under the Old Testament scholar George P. Gould. A Hebrew prizemen in his London University examinations, he was ordained in Gloucestershire in 1900 and ministered in Aberdeen and later in London. His contributions to *The Encyclopaedia of Religion and Ethics* were well received, as was his study *The Holy Spirit in St Paul* (1927). 'He was a man of much native ability, with few early advantages and severe physical handicaps', according to his obituary note in *The Baptist Handbook*.[115] A centrist figure within his own denomination, though never well known, he was appointed professor at the American Baptist Western Seminary in 1934, but he was forced to resign due to ill health 2 years later, and returned home. His 279-page volume *The Teaching of Karl Barth: an exposition*, which was published under the Student Christian Movement imprimatur, preceded John McConnachie's two works, and provided the first book length study of the subject in Britain. It appeared in June 1930 with a second edition in October of the same year.

Hoyle's principal sources were the Romans commentary, the *Christliche Dogmatik* (1927) and *Die Theologie und die Kirche* (1928). 'On Barth's lips the name of God carries with it an awe and an impressive force', he wrote, and, 'a challenge such as we have not listened to in this generation'.[116] The book was in three parts: chapters one to four about the man and his background; chapters five to eleven which explained Barth's key concepts such as transcendence, crisis and eschatology; and chapters twelve and thirteen which included a critique. Apart from portions of the final chapter, his tone was explanatory and appreciative rather than overtly critical. '[O]nly in so-called backward religious circles, Strict Baptists, hyper-Calvinists, "Wee Frees", is the theological terminology which Barth uses familiar' (p.40) he claimed, yet the Swiss's use of these terms, sovereignty, grace and election rather than fatherhood, feeling and experience, was quite revolutionary. 'With Barth there is always the insistence on the absolute sovereignty of God, the nullity of man and that one channel by which grace is conveyed

---

[114] See Clements, *Lovers of Discord*, pp.120–4; Randall, *The English Baptists of the Twentieth Century*, pp.171–3.

[115] *The Baptist Handbook* (London: Carey Press, 1941), p.333.

[116] R. Birch Hoyle, *The Teaching of Karl Barth: an exposition* (London: SCM Press, 1930), p.10; subsequent page references will be made in the text.

to men is the Word of God' (p.50). It was obvious that this theology had struck a chord. 'The great service rendered by Barth has been to show that the evils of the present time are to be traced to the departure from the idea of God and his relation to man as given by the Reformers' (p.73). Like McConnachie, Hoyle saw Barth as a Reformed figure whose dispute with Catholic theology underlined the theological seriousness with which he was undertaking his task. Rome, however, was not his prime target: '[Barth] is very ill at ease with present-day Protestantism' (p.53). Unlike McConnachie, however, Hoyle was more aware of the threat of Freudian psychology and the corrosive effect of Feuerbach's atheism to contemporary faith: 'Is there a God?'(p.97), he asked, and 'Is God a myth?' (p.84), reflecting his worry concerning the atheistic consensus among British intellectuals which had become the norm in the 1920s.[117]

In conveying the substance of Barth's thought, Hoyle contrasted the continental theology with 'the stress upon psychology of religion and appeal to the contents of religious experience which marks present-day British theology, *vide* H. R. Mackintosh, W. R. Matthews, H. Wheeler Robinson . . . to name a few', which were 'swept by the board' (p.113) by Barth and his friends. As humankind has no natural aptitude for the divine, it is through the Word that individuals are taken hold of by God, while 'the further British penchant for the interpretation of God in terms of the good, the beautiful and the true gets short shrift from this school' (p.117). Quoting the *Christliche Dogmatik* Hoyle made the prescient point that God's transcendence was not intended to limit human freedom but to make room for men and women to respond freely to the divine claim, but when immanentistism was all-pervasive, rhetoric like Barth's was inevitable. He also provided his readers with a fine exposition of those passages in the *Christliche Dogmatik* which underscored the mystery of incarnation, the significance of the virgin birth – which Brunner rejected outright – and the Logos-centred doctrine of incarnation which predicated Christ's humanity to the creative action of the divine:

> The human nature of Christ is a creature of the triune God, created and taken over for this to be a vessel of the Revealer . . . the 'Jesus of history', without the content of the divine essence, the 'Dearest Lord' of the mystic and pietist, the Teacher of Wisdom and Friend of Man of the *Aufklärung*, the purport of exalted humanity of Schleiermacher etc. is an empty throne without a king, the warm adoration of whom is a deifying of the creature and nothing else (*Christliche Dogmatik*, p.135).

---

[117] See Hastings, *A History of English Christianity, 1920–2000*, pp.221–39.

In his Christology Barth was flying in the face of the whole of mainstream Protestant theology for a century and a half: 'This vehement passage will explain why Barth is abhorred by these various types of mind' (p.171).

In treating Barth's concept of faith, he linked it with the person of the Spirit. 'In this mode of thinking', he explained, 'the man of faith has never any subjective assurance upon which to build' (p.184). Assurance can never be a religious possession, rather it is an ever-renewed gift of God: 'The very capacity of man is denied: to explain such a faith requires one to seek an explanation in God' (p.188). Quoting the *Dogmatik*, p.291, he states: 'Apart from the act of the Holy Ghost, apart from the event of Pentecost, all construction of the subjective possibility of revelation is once again a bridge which ends in the empty space over the abyss' (p.190). 'The Spirit of grace conveys not only grace but God to the hearts of men, and makes God accessible' (p.191). This, as Hoyle states, was characteristic of the early Reformers thought: 'With glee this school dwells on the statements of Luther that there are no perceptible signs by which the senses can discern the work of grace' (p.199). Such a view challenged Protestant scholasticism with its proofs for the existence of God, Puritanism with its workings of grace in the soul, pietistic evangelicalism with its experience of salvation, a 'heart strangely warmed', and the ethicism and felt religion of current liberal theology. God was absolute subject, possessing radical otherness as Father, Son and Spirit, and it was only through the triune revelation of himself that the transcendent God could be known.

Like Barth's earlier exegetes, Hoyle tried to do justice to Barth's concept of history as *Urgeshichte*, history not as Ritschl understood it, a secular, profane construct open to all, but eschatological history as the context for God's transcendent revelation to humankind. 'History is the sphere of the relative, the contingent, and the religious interest of Barth is centred in gaining something more stable, an absolute, on which to depend' (pp.202–3). 'Revelation preceeds history', he continued, 'determines history, is manifest in and through history, but is ever distinct from history' (p.203). Quoting the *Dogmatik*, p.239, he wrote:

> Revelation is more than eternal history: it is a point in temporal history: it is not bound to the irreversible sequence of temporal history, but around it, as a circle round a centre, it encloses all history beyond, whether divided as before and after; hence the positive relation of all history to pre-history (*Urgeschichte*) is related to it . . . as prophecy to fulfilment, as Advent to Christmas. (p.213)

However complex this language appeared, Barth's basic thought was becoming more and more plain: 'The eye which sees, however, to Barth, is the eye of faith which gazes beyond space and time into the world beyond' (p.214). Even the dialectic method, on reflection, was a surprisingly apt tool to do justice to the mysterious and apparently contradictory reality of a transcendent Lord. 'The *Dogmatic*', claimed Hoyle, '. . . is an exhaustive attempt to think through the idea of revelation and the possibility of man's receiving an authentic Word of God' (p.239). Was the whole quest beyond the wit of man? Barth and his devotees would answer with a resounding 'No!' '[T]he thinker must be a believer and obedient, realizing that his very existence depends upon his carrying through his critical enterprise. And because God, the object of his thinking, is also the pure irremovable subject, the thinking must be led by God in the thinker, God the Holy Spirit' (pp.239–40).

Further response

Hoyle's work immediately became significant as the only detailed, up-to-date and book length study of Barth's work available in English. 'Mr Birch Hoyle has attempted a difficult task and has accomplished it with great credit',[118] was the rather anodyne response of J. C. Carlisle in *The Baptist Times*, though John McConnachie, in an appendix to his own volume *The Significance of Karl Barth*, was more critical by far. The Scotsman took the Baptist to task for failing to do justice to Barth's concept of natural revelation, which although blighted by human miscomprehension through sin, was nevertheless valid and real; he questioned Hoyle's critique concerning Barth's apparently attenuated doctrine of the Holy Spirit; he rejected the suggestion that Barth's strictures against continuity between the realm of nature and the life of faith were overblown, and he faults him, quite correctly as it would transpire, for treating Barth and Brunner as though they were one. 'As a pioneer book, Mr Hoyle's volume shows wide reading and a wonderful knowledge of the literature of the subject', he concluded. 'A disciple of Barth, however, will hardly feel that Mr Hoyle has got inside his mind and purpose'.[119] The Anglo-Catholic Edwyn Hoskyns, who took the Swiss seriously enough to provide the epoch-making English translation of the *Romans* commentary in 1933, was equally trenchant. Like McConnachie, he was rather grudging about the volume's obvious virtues. 'The book is not a satisfactory book', he opined, in the *Journal of Theological Studies*, 'because it is difficult to think that the English reader will . . . understand why "ferment" has in fact arisen'.[120] Its strength was in its description of Barth's background and context; its weakness was that it substituted context for substance. More than anything else Barth was an

[118] J. C. Carlisle, 'The Teaching of Karl Barth', *The Baptist Times*, 7 August 1930, 568.
[119] John McConnachie, *The Significance of Karl Barth* (London: Hodder and Stoughton, 1931), p.288.
[120] Edwyn C. Hoskyns, 'Review', *Journal of Theological Studies* 33 (1932), 204–5 [204].

expositor of the Word: 'Barth's whole work, not only the *Römerbrief* and *Die Auferstehung der Toten* (which is a commentary on 1 Corinthians), but all his writings including the *Dogmatik*, are the product of a severe wrestling with the Scriptures'.[121] In fact Hoskyns was doing his own wrestling at the time, and was immersed not only in Barth's *Romans* but in the whole concept of theology as a biblical task: 'Barth's claim to be heard rests, and rests only, upon a decision as to whether what Barth finds in the Scriptures is really there or not'.[122] His grand and dismissive tone did him little credit. Hoyle's book was in fact very good. By October 1930 its second edition had left the press.

As for the Baptists, few took much note. Those who did tended to be critical. '[Barth's] views of history and his theory of knowledge . . . are quite unacceptable', wrote Henry Townsend, President of the Manchester Baptist College, in *The Baptist Times* in January 1932. 'He regards the human mind as passive. It would seem that only when God speaks to the human soul has He a direct contact with human nature'.[123] Yet if the Swiss helped contemporary Baptists to be biblical and preach in an awakening, experiential way – 'I am not consenting to Barth's theory of revelation in saying this' – it will have been for the good. In an assessment of the Barthian idea of revelation, David Glass, a Baptist minister, conflated Barth with Brunner and made the familiar critique that 'Barthianism' was dualistic, unbalanced and docetic: 'To insist so absolutely on the "Deus absconditus" . . . is to strengthen the position of those who take refuge in either obscurantism or in agnosticism',[124] he claimed. Basing his assertion on the English translation of Barth's volume of essays *The Word of God and the Word of Man* (1928), Barth, it seemed, had no real conception of the incarnation: 'Now this "incognito" suggestion looks dangerously like the ancient Docetic heresy which obscured and denied the truly human nature of Jesus'.[125] Although effective as a corrective to excessive liberalism, Barth's scheme had little positive to offer the contemporary church. Glass's fellow Baptist, Harold C. Rowse, was positively dismissive: 'It may be an exaggeration to assert that the Barthian movement in England is a spent force, but it is at least true to say that its public appeal has passed'.[126] Referring specifically to the office of the preacher, Barth's idea was overly dogmatic. Did not the

---

[121] Ibid., 205.

[122] Ibid., 205.

[123] Henry Townsend, 'Karl Barth and our own preaching', *The Baptist Times*, 14 January 1932, 28.

[124] David Glass, 'The Barthian idea of revelation', *The Baptist Quarterly* 6 (1932–33), 97–104 [102].

[125] Ibid., 103.

[126] Harold C. Rowse, 'The Barthian challenge to Christian thought', *The Baptist Quarterly* 7 (1934–35), 254–63 [257].

idea of incarnation imply that humanity could co-operate with God in fulfilling his saving purposes? The way forward was with a return to Phillips Brooks' ideal of truth being mediated through personality. As for Barthianism, it seemed irrational: 'The abnegation of reason is not the evidence of faith but the confession of despair'.[127]

Birch Hoyle, for his part, continued to be more positive by far. 'Barth has a message and a ring that is needed today', he asserted once more. 'Here sounds the trumpet note of a herald announcing glad tidings . . . Well may Protestantism in these isles welcome the voice from German Switzerland with its old cries, *gratia Dei sola, fidei sola, soli gloria Dei*'.[128] English Nonconformity at least was being made aware of the ferment from afar.

J. Arundel Chapman and the Methodist response to Barth

Methodism was the largest of the English Free Churches though its tendency was towards the practical rather than the theological. During the 1920s it expended much of its energy in schemes for reunion. The two main strains within Methodism were the Wesleyan, which was more churchly, clerical and organizationally minded and dominated by the Conference, and free Methodism, which was looser, more congregationally based and lay-involved. Three of the smaller Methodist bodies, the United Methodist Free Churches, the Methodist New Connexion and the Bible Christians, came together in 1907 to form the United Methodist Church, a democratic, egalitarian body of 150,000 members which preserved the missionary zeal and lay participation of nineteenth century evangelicalism at its most expansionist. Elsewhere free Methodism was represented by the Primitives, strong in County Durham and the rural north-east, with a presence down the east coast through Lincolnshire and as far as East Anglia. With 222,000 members, 1,300 ministers and an army of 13,000 lay preachers, it was significantly larger than the United Methodists though less than half the size of the Wesleyans. Its strength was that it was of the people, a proletarian movement with 'an almost Pentecostal style of worship with an authentic participation of the congregation quite different from Wesleyanism'.[129]

By the post-war years both pragmatism and a feeling for the scriptural principle of the unity of God's people, dictated that the three bodies should merge to form one strong, vibrant Methodist church which could match

---

[127] Ibid., 263.
[128] R. Birch Hoyle, 'Karl Barth and the Protestant revival', *The Churchman* 45 (1931), 113–23 [123].
[129] J. Munsey Turner, 'Methodism in England, 1900–32', in Rupert E. Davies, A. Raymond George and E. Gordon Rupp (eds), *A History of the Methodist Church in Great Britain*, Vol. 3 (London: Epworth Press, 1983), pp.309–61 [329].

the Church of England in influence and create, with the other Free Churches, a significant non-Episcopal Christian body. When, in 1928, the Wesleyan Conference overcame its qualms about lay leadership and the threat to ministerial authority, the move towards organic union had virtually been won. An enabling bill paved the way for a new structure, and in September 1932 a united conference of the three denominations signed a deed of union and the newly constituted English Methodist church was born. It included 517,500 Wesleyans, 222,000 Primitives and 180,000 United Methodists with a joint complement of 4,000 ministers and 38,000 local preachers.[130]

The movement's most ubiquitous presence was J. Scott Lidgett (1854–1953), 'arguably the boldest theologian among the Methodists in the first half of the twentieth century'.[131] Although a gifted dogmatician Lidgett was at heart a social activist: warden of the Bermondsey Settlement, he expended his prodigious energy on civic responsibilities such as the leadership of the Progressive Party on the London County Council, the vice-chancellorship of the University of London and chairmanship of the Central Council for Nursing. His works *The Atonement* (1898) and *The Fatherhood of God* (1902) were typical of their era, and although still possessing an acute doctrinal mind, by the 1920s his influence had abated. In fact the movement's theological life was repetitive and jaded, lacking in fresh ideas and drive.

From 1921 there had been a Methodist presence in Cambridge presided over by H. Maldwyn Hughes, author of *Christian Foundations: an introduction to Christian Doctrine* (1927), though it was not until 1926 that Wesley House had a college building of its own. If the Wesleyans possessed competent scholars like Hughes, C. Ryder Smith of Richmond College, Surrey, and author of *The Christian Experience: a study in the Theology of Fellowship* (1926), and the biblical expert W. F. Lofthouse at Handsworth College, Birmingham, it was only after the advent of the Barthian renewal that a more exciting scholarship, illustrated by Vincent Taylor in New Testament, R. Newton Flew in ecclesiology and Philip S. Watson and E. Gordon Rupp in Luther studies, appeared. As it happens it was Lofthouse, from the older generation, who was the first to signal an awareness of the Barthian movement within English Methodist circles. In a 1927 essay in *The Contemporary Review* he described the impact of the Romans commentary, 'which has made his reviewers, accustomed to the "scientific" work of most German professors, very angry',[132] and noted the similarity of Barth's thought with that of Rudolf Otto, the more or less unknown Soren

---

[130] See John Kent, *The Age of Disunity* (London: Epworth Press, 1966), pp.20–43; R. Currie, *Methodism Divided* (London: Faber and Faber, 1968), pp.248–92.

[131] Johnson, *The Changing Shape of English Nonconformity*, p.119; cf. Turner, 'Methodism in England, 1900–32', p.314.

[132] W. F. Lofthouse, 'A Theology of Paradox', *The Contemporary Review* 132 (1927), 211–17 [212].

Kierkegaard and the Russian novelist Dostoevsky. It was obvious that Lofthouse hardly knew what to make of Barth, whether to damn him or praise him. He gingerly affirmed the note of transcendence in his work and as a Methodist was happy to see the emphasis on the appropriation of an objective gospel through faith. But on the whole Barth was too blunt and uncompromising, beholden to the early Luther and not the maturer Reformer 'who inspired the genial piety which would gradually entice society into obedience to the Sermon on the Mount'.[133] For his generation, Barth and his friends would remain something between an enigma and an irritant.[134]

There were younger ministers, however, who were convinced that the post-war years demanded radical renewal. This was manifested in the vibrant Fellowship of the Kingdom, established in 1919, which was socially active, theologically alert and open to a fresh anointing, Wesley style, of a felt spirituality. Its exemplar was W. Russell Maltby (1866–1951), warden of the Wesley Deaconesses Movement and, along with T. R. Glover and William Temple, the best-known Christian advocate in the student world. His popular writings *The Significance of Jesus* (1929) and *Christ and His Cross* (1935) were devotional rather than scholarly, but redolent of the liberal evangelicalism which had become the received orthodoxy of the day. They were also typically Methodist. There was much talk within the Fellowship of the outpouring of the Spirit, holiness and perfectionism, though its 'spirituality . . . was based on the historical Jesus as he is described in the synoptic gospels'.[135] In other words, the liberal Christology of a humanized Jesus and an exemplarist doctrine of the atonement had become *de rigueur*.[136] Yet at least one of its leaders, J. Arundel Chapman, had become progressively more dissatisfied with this stance.

Chapman (1885–1934), who had taught at both Didsbury College, Manchester, and Leeds, had come to feel that the spiritual renewal for which he yearned needed a more definite doctrinal underpinning than the current liberalism could supply. His discovery of Barth came as a revelation. 'I owe a very deep spiritual debt to Karl Barth and Emil Brunner', he wrote in February 1931, 'and other writers who have dealt with the Theology of Crisis'.[137] For Chapman, Methodism had succumbed to a naïve belief in the immanence of God, the minimization of the difference between the

---

[133] Ibid., 213.
[134] Cf. W. F. Lofthouse, 'Karl Barth and the Gospel', *London Quarterly and Holborn Review* 158 (1933), 28–37.
[135] Gordon S. Wakefield, *Methodist Devotion: the spiritual life in the Methodist tradition, 1791–1945* (London: Epworth Press, 1966), p.90.
[136] See Randall, *Evangelical Experiences: a study in the spirituality of English Evangelicalism, 1918–39* , pp.109–41.
[137] J. Arundel Chapman, *The Theology of Karl Barth: a short introduction* (London: Epworth Press, 1931), p.vii; page numbers will be included in the text.

human and the divine, an unthinking deference to the dogma of evolution and a frankly Pelagian view of sin: 'Between Karl Barth and much that we understand by the word "modern" is a relentless war' (p.10). The Swiss's preconceptions were totally at odds with the accepted wisdom of the Protestant world. 'In his thought we are confronted by a transcendent God, the note of eternity booms out, he is a thoroughgoing dualist, his theme is righteousness, ethical distinctions are taken very seriously, humanity is fallen and broken, restoration is only possible by God's sovereign act, and it is accomplished in crisis' (p.10). Chapman's reading had been confined to Birch Hoyle's assessment, Barth's volume of essays *The Word of God and the Word of Man* (1928), Brunner's *Theology of Crisis* (1929), which meant that he only knew of the *Römerbrief* at second hand. This did not prevent him from stating that it is 'unquestionably the most remarkable commentary which has appeared in our generation. It is the work of a lonely man blazing out on a long disused trail' (p.13). What was most striking about Barth's stand, according to Chapman, was its existential rather than theoretical nature, the priority it afforded to God's transcendence, the reality of Christ and the resurrection and its concept of crisis: 'Its presence gives to his teaching the tempestuous character which it bears. It is like a river in flood, swollen and agitated. Barth even goes so far as to describe faith as agitated continuance in negation' (p.30). Although there was much in his thought that was difficult to understand, and Barth needed to take a positive rather than negative view of religious experience – an obvious point for a Methodist to make – there was something awesome about his whole scheme. 'I confess to being half a Barthian' (p.34), he wrote. Chapman's subsequent works, a Barthian critique of Schleiermacher in which he had become more sparing in his use of the category of experience,[138] a succinct work on the atonement which, in contrast to Maltby's treatise, championed the objective view,[139] and a collection of sermons and essays,[140] signifies the way in which he was travelling. Were it not for his early death, under tragic circumstances, in 1934,[141] he may well have become as influential a voice within Methodist theology as R. Newton Flew and Vincent Taylor, or as well known as his colleagues in the Fellowship of the Kingdom, the preachers Leslie Weatherhead, W. E. Sangster and Donald Soper.[142]

---

[138] J. Arundel Chapman, *An Introduction to Schleiermacher* (London: Epworth Press, 1932).

[139] J. Arundel Chapman, *Atonement and the Cross* (London: Epworth Press, 1933).

[140] J. Arundel Chapman, *The Supernatural Life* (London, Epworth Press, 1934).

[141] John Travell, *Doctor of Souls: a biography of Dr Leslie D. Weatherhead* (Cambridge: Lutterworth Press, 1999), p.46.

[142] All of whom are listed in are listed in John Vickers (ed.), *A Dictionary of Methodism* (London: Epworth Press, 2000).

As for Barth's impact on Methodism, both Flew and Taylor were not unaffected. R. Newton Flew (1886–1962), English Methodism's foremost mid-twentieth century ecclesiastical statesman, had proceeded from Merton College, Oxford, to Bonn and Marburg in 1906, attending classes by Jülicher and Herrmann, while a later travelling fellowship to Italy opened his mind to Roman Catholic thought. Following 10 years' circuit ministry, he was appointed to the New Testament chair in Wesley House in 1927, proceeding to the principalship 10 years after that. His volume *The Idea of Perfection in Christian Theology* (1934) was a meticulous piece of scholarship on a theme dear to Methodist hearts, though it was as an ecclesiologist with *Jesus and his Church* (1938), that he would exert widest influence on Protestant thought. It was through the influence of his Cambridge colleague Edwyn C. Hoskyns, the Anglo-Catholic Barth enthusiast, that Flew broke with liberalism and embraced neo-orthodoxy, and along with J. S. Whale and Bernard Lord Manning developed a higher doctrine of the church than otherwise would have been the case.[143]

Vincent Taylor (1887–1968), tutor in New Testament at Wesley College, Headingly, Leeds, wrote on Bultmann in the 1932 *Expository Times* series on Barth and his school. Already a significant biblical scholar, his *Formation of the Gospel Tradition* (1933) would signal the end of the liberal mode of gospel criticism and establish form-criticism as an essential tool in English New Testament studies.[144] 'It is undoubtedly true that in Bultmann's *Jesus*, a short volume of two hundred pages, published in 1925, we do find many ideas which remind us of the Barthians',[145] he wrote. Although the gospels do not provide readers with a historical account of Jesus, they do point to the community in which his teaching was characterized by phenomena such as crisis, eschatological urgency, the breaking in of the kingdom and discipleship as radical obedience: 'The exposition is powerful and moving, and one by one the ideas which Barth, Brunner and Gogarten have made us familiar are found in the teaching of the historical Jesus'.[146] Although the differences between Bultmann and Barth would later become much clearer, at the time both men were seen as being close colleagues: 'Bultmann's *Jesus* . . . is not only of very great interest, but is also a unique example of Barthian teaching',[147] namely the sovereignty of God, the radical nature

---

[143] Gordon S. Wakefield, *Robert Newton Flew, 1886–1962* (London: Epworth Press, 1971), pp.83–7, 91–3.

[144] See Owen E. Evans, 'Vincent Taylor', A. W. and E. Hastings, *Theologians of Our Times* (Edinburgh: T & T Clark, 1966), pp.47–56.

[145] Vincent Taylor, 'The Barthian School IV: Rudolf Bultmann', *The Expository Times* 43 (1931–32), 485–90 [486].

[146] Ibid., 486.

[147] Ibid., 489.

of sin, obedience before the Word and the miracle of forgiveness: '*Jesus*, if not a religious classic, is one of the most stimulating studies of our time'.[148]

A Presbyterian response?

In conclusion, the evidence suggests that within English Nonconformity the work of Karl Barth during its first phase impacted most strongly upon the Congregationalists. Both Sydney Cave and John Phillips became enthusiasts while the vigorous renewal of confessional orthodoxy and the Genevan tradition opened young ministers' minds and their imaginations to the 'Crisis Theology' of Safenwil and Göttingen. From 1932 both Mansfield College, Oxford, under Micklem and the Yorkshire Independent College, Bradford, where Lovell Cocks was based between 1932 and 1937, would become centres conducive to the study and assimilation of Barthian thought.[149] Among the Baptists Birch Hoyle was a-typical. Spurgeonic conservativism remained impervious to the appeal of the new theology as did the more widespread undogmatic biblicism of the T. R. Glover school. The untimely death of Arundel Chapman in 1934 put paid to a Barthian renaissance within Methodism for nearly a decade. The surprising thing is that English Presbyterianism remained unmoved. The links with Scotland were very strong while Barth was, after all, a Reformed theologian. The denomination's intellectual hub, Westminster College, Cambridge, included a distinguished faculty: John Skinner, an accomplished Old Testament scholar, C. Anderson Scott in New Testament, the urbane and ecclesiastically minded P. Carnegie Simpson teaching church history, and its celebrated principal, the philosophical theologian John Oman. Oman's thought had been long fixed. A reaction against the intransigent Orcadian Presbyterianism of his youth had made him unrepentantly liberal. He was a synthesist: faith and rationality, religion and science, revelation and experience. By 1925 he was already 65 and long confirmed in his ways. Carnegie Simpson, whose high Presbyterian ecclesiology made him potentially more open to the insights of the theologians of the Word, recollected that a student skit had included a scene in which Oman had published a book entitled *What I Owe to Karl Barth*: its pages were blank![150] Oman would retire in 1935 and Simpson in 1938.

---

[148] Ibid., 490.
[149] Elaine Kaye, *For the Work of the Ministry: a history of Northern College and its predecessors* (Edinburgh: T & T Clark, 1999), pp.193–207.
[150] P. Carnegie Simpson, *Recollections: mainly ecclesiastical but sometimes human* (London: Nisbet, 1943), p.65; for Oman see Steven Bevans, *John Oman and his Doctrine of God* (Cambridge: Cambridge University Press, 1992).

Equally paradoxical was the fact that if the professed upholders of the Reformed faith in England seemed unmoved by Barth, in 1932 a not wholly negative response came from a representative of the Society of Friends. 'To the Quaker and those of kindred thinking', wrote Carl Heath, 'what we know of the life of the Spirit comes to us from within, comes in and by the light of that indwelling reality that links us to God, and that Quakers commonly speak of as the Inner Light'.[151] Unsurprisingly Heath rejected Barth's doctrine of discontinuity between humankind and God, that God was the wholly unknown, and what he saw, on the basis of the 1926 lectures *Vom Christen Leben* ('The Christian Life') Barth's radical Calvinistic pessimism concerning the human state. Yet both Barth and Brunner were to be praised for reminding people of the fact that God existed as an objective reality, and that great Christian words such as sin, grace and redemption could mean something in the context of the post-war world. 'However one may disagree with the fundamental claims of the new teaching', he concluded, 'none the less I hold Barth to be the most challenging and prophetic spirit of the day'.[152] That Barth was more than a prophet was something which readers would begin to appreciate as the bulky volumes of the *Kirchliche Dogmatik* began to appear from 1932 onwards.

[151] Carl Heath, *The Challenge of Karl Barth: a critical comment* (London: H. R. Allenson [1932]), p.13.
[152] Heath, *The Challenge of Karl Barth*, p.34.

5

BARTH RECEPTION AND THE CHURCH OF ENGLAND, 1927–33

Barth reception and Anglican modernism

In formal terms, the theology of the Anglican church reflected its constitution in the Elizabethan settlement of 1559. Regarding itself as being in continuity with Augustine of Canterbury's earliest English church, it had preserved the three-fold ministry of bishop, priest and deacon which guaranteed its place within the apostolic succession. Its liturgy was preserved in the 1662 Book of Common Prayer and its doctrinal basis, enshrined in the 39 Articles, included the Apostles' and Nicene Creeds. Neither Romanist nor Genevan, it prided itself on being a *via media* whose authority was enshrined in the three-fold norm of reason, tradition and the Holy Scriptures. Despite marked differences of emphasis, its constituent parties, the high churchmen or Anglo-Catholics, the broad church liberals and the low church evangelicals, bore their witness within the parameters of the much vaunted 'middle way'.

Since the mid-nineteenth century, and especially since the liberalized *Lux Mundi* synthesis of 1889, the theological acumen of the Church had been with the Anglo-Catholics, nevertheless Karl Barth's theology received some of its earliest comment from those within the liberal or broad church school. According to A. M. Ramsey, '[i]t appears that the first Anglican who studied Karl Barth carefully was C. J. Shebbeare, the learned rector of Stanhope in County Durham'.[1] Shebbeare had been active in the Modern Churchman's Union, the main focus within the Anglican Church for accommodation

---

[1] A. M. Ramsey, *From Gore to Temple: the development of Anglican theology between* Lux Mundi *and the Second World War, 1889–1945* (London: Longmans and Green, 1960), p.141.

between traditional faith and contemporary scientific and naturalist thought, whose conference on 'Christ and the Creeds' held at Girton College, Cambridge, in 1921 had garnered huge publicity.[2] 'Jesus did not claim divinity for himself', asserted Hastings Rashdall, dean of Carlisle, during the conference. 'Never in any critically well-attested sayings is there anything which suggests that his conscious relation to God was other than that of a man towards God, the attitude which He wished that all men should adopt towards God'.[3] According to J. F. Betheune-Baker, Lady Margaret Professor of Divinity and fellow of Pembroke College, Cambridge: 'I can only regard this idea of the miraculous birth [of Jesus] as aetiological and honorific, in those days a natural and reasonable way of accounting for a great personality and the experience of which Jesus was the cause and centre, as it would be unnatural and irrational today'.[4] The tenor of the conference was naturalist; anything which smacked of the miraculous was to be reinterpreted according to the categories of idealist philosophy, a closed mechanistic universe, and evolutionary science while the doctrines of God, Christ, and of humanity were to be deconstructed accordingly. God was immanent within the processes of the world and the difference between creature and Creator was seriously blurred.

In his 1927 elucidation of Anglican modernism, H. D. A. Major, editor of *The Modern Churchman* and the Girton conference's leading light, listed the preconceptions which governed his movement's thinking: that the idea of evolution was axiomatic; that any concept of hell or eternal punishment was primitive and in conflict with the benign nature of God; that the idea of Christ's death as being a propitiatory sacrifice was outmoded; that eschatology generally and the idea of the parousia or second coming particularly had been made impossible by modern science; that the Bible was a fallible, human document and that Christianity was but one example among many of the genius of human spirituality. Religion, in itself, was innate and essential for human wellbeing: 'Revelation is implied in the very structure of the human mind, so that the process of thought, conscience, affection truly understood, induce the recognition of the Infinite and Eternal'.[5] For the English modernists churchgoing was beneficial but the traditional dogmas,

[2] See Roger Lloyd, *The Church of England, 1900–65* (London: SCM, 1966), pp.254–78; Alan M. G. Stephenson, *The Rise and Decline of English Modernism* (London: SPCK, 1984), pp.99–122, 123–37.

[3] Hastings Rashdall, 'Christ as Logos and as Son of God', *The Modern Churchman* 11 (1921), 278–86 [278].

[4] J. F. Betheune Baker, 'Jesus as both human and divine', *The Modern Churchman* 11 (1921), 287–301 [288–9].

[5] H. D. A. Major, *English Modernism: its origins, methods and aims* (Harvard: Harvard University Press, 1927), p.119.

being inconceivable in the light of science, needed to be reformulated radically:

> As editor of *The Modern Churchman* for thirty years I have no knowledge of Modern Churchmen who do not believe in the incarnation [and] the atonement . . . but I do know a great number . . . who do not believe in the virgin birth, in the resurrection of the physical body of Jesus Christ . . . [or] in his return to judge the quick and the dead.[6]

Although all these assertions were recited as part of the church's liturgy from Sunday to Sunday, they could no longer be believed as they stood. 'If asked why Modern Churchmen do not believe these things, the reply is that modern biblical, historical and scientific studies have made them incredible'.[7] As the established church of the realm, the Church of England was best situated to fulfil society's need for transcendence. The traditional content of the faith, however, had to be rejected outright.

Not all English modernists were as negative as the leaders of the Girton conference and though broad churchmanship generally downplayed all that was unique in the Christian faith, many liberals were careful to preserve the ontological difference between God and humankind.[8] In an essay in *The Atonement in History and Life* (1929), C. J. Shebbeare showed a working knowledge of Barth's earliest work and a surprisingly positive response to its content. The weakness of current liberalism, he claimed, was due to its idealistic bent, its overoptimistic assessment of human rationality and its inability to allow for the realities of tragedy, evil and sin. There were entirely salutary reasons that '[j]ust now the doctrines of sin, grace, redemption, atonement, election, the fall, which had fallen somewhat into the background for at least a generation, are receiving renewed attention'[9] as they reflected a permanent religious reality which optimistic liberalism had blithely ignored. Far from being primitive and unsophisticated, the great doctrines of classic orthodoxy reflected a spiritual reality which no true religion could afford to disregard: 'It would have been a defect in Christianity if it had wholly failed to meet the cravings and requirements which seem native to the religion of mankind'.[10]

---

[6] Letter in *The Times*, 4 September, 1945; quoted by Lloyd, *The Church of England, 1900–65*, p.261.

[7] Lloyd, *The Church of England, 1900–65*, p.261.

[8] See Ramsey, *From Gore to Temple*, pp.60–76.

[9] C. J. Shebbeare, 'The Atonement and some tendencies of modern thought', in L. W. Grensted, *The Atonement in History and Modern Life* (London: SPCK, 1929), pp.299–321 [300].

[10] Shebbeare, 'The Atonement and some tendencies of modern thought', p.300.

Much of Shebbeare's essay is taken up with recounting the major themes in 'that remarkable book, Karl Barth's Commentary on the Epistle to the Romans . . . even a cursory reading [of which] is enough to show that the book is a great book, and of vastly higher religious and intellectual value that [Rudolf] Otto's *Idea of the Holy*, from which . . . the recent changes in theological outlook may also be illustrated'.[11] With evident relish, the author quoted key passages to illustrate Barth's treatment of concepts of sin, righteousness, judgement and redemption, noting both how rhetorically effective they were and how essential they remained in order to assuage humankind's basic religious needs.

> To those of us . . . who are accustomed to evangelical theology, and especially to evangelical religion, many of these epigrams will present no difficulty when once we have been accustomed to their unfamiliar setting – they agree so remarkably well with the customary language of old-fashioned evangelicalism.[12]

Although Shebbeare had moved away from the evangelicalism of his youth, he obviously retained an affection for it and an appreciation of its abiding spiritual value. 'In older evangelicals, then, it awakens memories of familiar language when Barth speaks of what does, and what does not, justify a man in the sight of God'.[13] For the evangelical, all human righteousness was as filthy rags; justification was an alien righteousness, wrought through Christ's costly sacrifice and affirmed by faith alone. 'For Barth faith is never identical with piety . . . but rather the inward restlessness, convulsion and awe, the sense of amazement and astonishment, of respect for that which is above us . . . a humility, an awed submission before God'.[14]

Shebbeare's standpoint was that of the psychology of religion. Barth's weakness, he felt, was in a latent antinomianism which he detected in his work and in an element of irrationalism in his scheme. 'There exists in the modern world a really strong reaction against some aspects of theological liberalism; first against its predominantly ethical conception of religion, and secondly, against its impatience of paradox'.[15] Yet Barth was obviously a powerful thinker and one from whom he wished to learn and not to disparage or reject. 'Can Barth's passionate sense of the sharp opposition between nature and grace, flesh and spirit, be recognized with that belief in the unity of the world which is vital to a rational theology?',[16] he asked.

---

[11] Ibid., p.301.
[12] Ibid., p.303.
[13] Ibid., p.304.
[14] Ibid., p.306.
[15] Ibid., p.309.
[16] Ibid., p.310.

If so, as a corrective to the current weaknesses of liberal Anglicanism, it would be salutary indeed. There were other Anglican modernists, alas, who would need more convincing than the learned rector of Stanhope.

In a second altogether more hostile essay by G. L. H. Harvey in 1931, Barth's theology was described as being 'desperado theology', the result of the collapse of civilization and a cynical flight to the irrational: 'Barth's theology . . . is not Christian, or at the very most is only semi-Christian. It is derived from 4 *Esdras* and is characteristic of a period of collapse and inflation'.[17] Unlike Shebbeare, Harvey referred more to Barth's *Christliche Dogmatik* of 1927 than to the Romans commentary, though hardly to its gain. If the commentary was a passionate affair though irrational and dual-istic, the later volume showed that '[t]he glowing mass is becoming solidified. Here and there something of the old fire breaks forth anew, but in the process of petrefaction the original glow has in a large measure disappeared'.[18] The four characteristics of Barth's scheme, all of which the critic found lamentable, were first its dependency on the concept of an unverified, external revelation: 'he warns the historian, the psychologist, the logician off his ground as trespassers. They must not lay their cuckoo's eggs within the sphere of Barthian theology';[19] second the radical subjectivism of his concept of God: '[Barth] hypostasizes the elements of a grammatical analysis. God is revealer, He is revelation, He is the thing revealed, hence the Trinity. Barth is driven to such arid abstractions because he empties reality as we know it of all content;'[20] third his unhistorical concept of the Word of God through which 'Barth is compelled by his presuppositions to ignore what the modernist values as partial or relative truth;'[21] and fourth his docetic Christology. What Hervey found especially obscurantist was Barth's championing of the concept of the virgin birth:

> Barth's treatment of the virgin-birth well illustrates three outstanding characteristics of his system and his method – his pseudo-orthodoxy, his dexterity in transferring ideas appropriate to one plane . . . to another . . ., a dexterity which can only be fitly described as sleight-of-hand, and a dry intellectualism which alternates with *sacrificium intellectus*.[22]

---

[17] G. L. H. Harvey, 'Barthianism and Modernism', *The Modern Churchman* 20 (1930–31), 586–95 [586].
[18] Ibid., 587.
[19] Ibid., 588.
[20] Ibid., 589.
[21] Ibid., 590.
[22] Ibid., 594.

This would not be the last savaging that Barth's theology would receive from the Anglican modernists. The influential Cambridge theologian Charles Raven would say much in the same vein during the 1940s. But for this early critic, '[w]hether or not there exists an unbridgeable gap between time and eternity, there is certainly an unbridgeable gulf between Barthianism and Modernism, at any rate as we know Modernism in England'.[23] With invective like this, it may have been all for the best.

Barthianism and evangelicalism

As C. J. Shebbeare had suggested, there was ostensibly much in common between Barth's theology and the convictions of the evangelical party within the established church, but of the three schools of Anglican churchmanship during the inter-war years, the evangelical was least receptive to any fresh thinking. 'The Evangelicals', remarked Hensley Henson, bishop of Durham, 'were exhibiting all the marks of a moribund party. They were out of touch with the prevailing tendencies, social and intellectual, of the time'.[24] They possessed no leaders of weight – Christopher Chevasse, vicar of St Aldate's, Oxford, would become bishop of Rochester in the 1930s but would never achieve eminence on the Episcopal bench – and almost no scholars of note. Backward looking and uninspired, clinging to inherited positions such as the concept of penal substitution which were everywhere being undermined, and progressively unsure how to tackle the challenges of biblical criticism and modern scientific thought, they had become introverted and dispirited. Their unreflective support, on the basis of a staunch Protestant erastianism, of the parliamentary majority who had rejected the revised Prayer Book of 1928, had made them pariahs among many of their fellow churchmen. They seemed unable to provide a credible apologia for the evangelical faith in the face of both liberalism and a resurgent high churchmanship.

Although not a single evangelical held a divinity chair at either Oxford, Cambridge, Durham or King's College, London, at the time, the party was not wholly bereft of capable men. Allan John Macdonald (1887–1959), author of the accomplished *The Evangelical Doctrine of Holy Communion* (1930) and Hulsean lecturer at Cambridge in 1931–32, was rector of St Dunstan-in-the-west, Fleet Street, and prominent in the Church of England Council on Foreign Relations. A centrist evangelical, he was keen to promote Barth's thought among his fellow churchmen. His paper on

[23] Ibid., 588.
[24] H. Hensley Henson, *Retrospect of an Unimportant Life*, Vol. 1 (Oxford: Oxford University Press, 1942), p.157.

Barth's theology at the Oxford Conference of Evangelical Churchmen in April 1932 accompanied by a series of essays in the mainly Anglo-Catholic monthly *Theology*, showed him to be keenly appreciative of the continental movement. His *Theology* essays were based mainly on the assessments of John McConnachie and Birch Hoyle, but he also quoted directly from the *Römerbrief* and the *Christliche Dogmatik*. 'As we proceed we shall see that [Barth's] teaching is almost entirely orthodox, and if some details sound a little strange to English ears, that may be because they are inherited by him from his Swiss Reformed theology and from the ancient Logos theology of the Greek thinkers'.[25] Whereas the modernists were all too ready to dismiss Barth's thought as being the product of the disenchantment of post-war Germany, Macdonald was adamant that this was not the case: 'Karl Barth's theology springs not from the war crisis – with which it certainly grapples – but from the prophet's discontent with contemporary religious teaching, and from the preacher's need for a message'.[26] He commended Barth's doctrine of revelation as a healthy corrective to the fashionable liberal psychologizing of religion and the immanentism of the modernists, and saw it for what it was: an example of healthy dogmatic deliberation: 'This is the angle of approach of prophetic men, of Isaiah and Jeremiah, of Paul and Luther and Calvin'.[27] The objective reality of God, and God's qualitative difference from humankind, is something which he found both refreshing and essential: 'The necessary prerequisite for reconciliation with God is to realize that God is completely and distinctly *other* than oneself, and is not to be grasped by any subjective movement of human thought, but is only to be apprehended after a movement from the other side, by revelation from Himself'.[28] Whereas the modernist Harvey believed Barth's Trinitarian doctrine to be abstract and content-less, Macdonald was insistent that it was innovative and profound. Far from being docetist, it did full justice to Christ's humanity though that humanity was the predicate of his divinity and not the God-consciousness of a uniquely pious man. 'The miracle of the virgin birth gives him no trouble',[29] he asserted, in fact it was wholly apposite on directly theological grounds: 'Other events of this kind are myths. This event is prevented from being a myth by our theological knowledge'.[30]

Macdonald's second essay was not on Barth but on Brunner and the ethical content of the neo-orthodox movement generally taking Brunner's *Mittler* ('The Mediator') as its base, but his third essay was on Barth's

---

[25] A. J. Macdonald, 'The message and theology of Barth and Brunner', *Theology* 24 (1932), 197–207, 252–8, 324–32 [199].

[26] Ibid., 200.

[27] Ibid., 201.

[28] Ibid., 201.

[29] Ibid., 207.

[30] Ibid., 206.

understanding of the Bible, revelation and history: 'In the Bible we find a new world the world of God, striking in its freshness because it is to be found nowhere else'.[31] Preaching is derivative of the Word of God and as such is a vital, engaging and dynamic task: 'The self-revelation of the Word of God, the Word of God in its first form, speaks to us through its second form in Holy Scripture, and so no other will it be in its third form, the ground and norm of Christian preaching'.[32] The church, therefore, is not a creative but a mediatorial reality that listens to the testimony of the prophets and apostles and places itself wholly under their rule. Although revelation occurs concretely within history, its unique nature makes it difficult to perceive using the criteria of ordinary history. It is only thus that the mystery of Christ's corporeal resurrection can be understood: 'This is surely a strikingly fruitful idea in Barth's exegesis'.[33] Moreover, there is an inner necessity within God's open creation which can only be fulfilled by a bodily resurrection such as that demonstrated by Christ himself having been raised from the dead: 'Human corporeality must be redeemed and resurrected because it has been created, and cannot escape the natural *dénoument* of its existence', he wrote. 'We shall rise from the dead because we have been created – the question of judgement comes later. This exhilarating notion certainly reinforces whatever is optimistic in Barth's theory of election'.[34]

In his address to the Oxford evangelical conference, Macdonald was equally positive. The theme of the conference was revival, and Macdonald's lecture portrayed the Barthian movement as being a genuine revival of piety as well as creative theology among continental Protestants. He began by conveying the now familiar description of Barth's background as a son of the manse, his training in liberal Protestantism and disenchantment with the thought of Ritschl, Harnack and Herrmann as a young parish minister in Safenwil. It was then that Barth discovered through patient and passionate study of the Bible that the essence of Christianity was not the human quest for God but God's quest for humankind: 'Man is incapable of finding God by his own efforts. God seeks man and finds him. I think Barth is right'.[35] God's quest is not disembodied, and revelation is not merely verbal or conceptual. In the process of incarnation, both revealer and revelation are one: 'In the person of Jesus, the Word of God was revealed. It crashed into human thought in the midst of its blind, stumbling course. The same process takes place in individuals today'.[36] For Barth it was the

---

[31] Ibid., 325.
[32] Ibid., 327.
[33] Ibid., 331.
[34] Ibid., 332.
[35] A. J. Macdonald, 'Professor Karl Barth and the Theology of Crisis', *The Churchman* 46 (1932), 192–201 [195].
[36] Ibid., 195.

Holy Spirit rather than the immanence of the human spirit which was the link between the human and the divine, while the Bible, which was open to be interpreted by ordinary critical methods, was nevertheless the means whereby God was revealed through the Holy Word. As he had said in his *Theology* articles, Jesus of Nazareth was fully human though his humanity was not that of a God-inspired individual but that which bore his unique nature as God's divine Son. Christology, therefore, was not a species of religious psychology with the rabbi of Nazareth as its subject but an affirmation of God's unique act for human salvation in Christ. The function of the church was to bear witness to this fact through the faithful preaching of the biblical Word. 'So far as the church fails to fulfil this function', he claimed, 'she comes under the lash of Barth's invective . . . The church has authority in imparting to us the context of scripture, but it is a mediate authority, the original authority is in scripture itself'.[37] As an evangelical Macdonald was keen to find common ground between his own tradition and Barth, and he found it in the Swiss theologian's dynamic concept of the Word. There was no doubt, in his mind, that Barth held to the plenary inspiration of canonical scripture, but his method of interpretation was existential rather than static: 'I have to make a decision on the truth which approaches me'.[38] Both election and resurrection were activated within human history and not on some ethereal, non-realist plane, but due to their very nature as divine events that could not be naturally perceived.

For the rector of St Dunstan-in-the-west, this theology was not a new theology but a revival of the spiritual content of Reformation theology with many of the crudities removed: 'Barthianism does not go back merely to the Reformation. It is a revival of ancient church history . . . It is more, it is the most striking manifestation today of the Spirit's activity within the churches'.[39] It was a blessing to all and 'supplies the tired preacher with a burning evangelical message'[40] which, if applied, could transform even the languid and over-conformist Anglican church and make it vital once more.

A. J. Macdonald seems to have been the sole evangelical who, during this first phase, interacted with the theology of Karl Barth. His paper aroused mild interest in the Oxford Conference, but there is no evidence on the pages of *The Churchman* or elsewhere of a widespread evangelical response to Barthianism within the established church. Although 'individual Evangelicals welcomed [Barth's] teaching', reported Kenneth Hylson-Smith, 'and the Oxford conference gave a warm, if muted assent to it',[41] little else

---

[37] Ibid., 199.
[38] Ibid., 199.
[39] Ibid., 201.
[40] Ibid., 201.
[41] Kenneth Hylson-Smith, *Evangelicals in the Church of England, 1734–1984* (Edinburgh: T & T Clark, 1984), p.270.

happened. On the whole, somnolence prevailed. 'The influence of Barth was part of a remarkable Christian intellectual revival in the period 1930 to 1945, of which the Evangelicals of the time did not seem to be aware'.[42] With striking irony, it was among the Anglo-Catholic high churchmen that Barthian thought was to make its deepest Anglican mark.

Anglo-Catholicism: John Kenneth Mozley and Edwyn Clement Hoskyns

The two figures from within Anglo-Catholic high churchmanship who were most enamoured of Karl Barth's contribution were J. K. Mozley (1883–1946), one time fellow of Pembroke College, Cambridge, warden of St Augustine House, Reading, and thereafter canon of St Paul's Cathedral, and Sir E. C. Hoskyns, clergyman and hereditary baronet, fellow of Corpus Christi College and between 1919 and his untimely death at the age of 52 in 1937, Cambridge faculty lecturer in New Testament. Mozley's works included *The Doctrine of the Atonement* (1915), *The Heart of the Gospel* (1925) and a learned study on the divine attributes entitled *The Impassibility of God* (1926). Both men were established scholars within the *Lux Mundi* tradition of liberal catholicism though it was said of the former: 'He left no one in doubt of his own resolute and undeviating churchmanship, and perhaps for that very reason he had many friends who were not Anglicans; indeed it would be difficult to say whether Bishop Gore or Principal [P. T.] Forsyth . . . exercised the greater influence on his thought'.[43] Although holding to the orthodoxy of the creeds, they belonged to a younger generation of Anglo-Catholic liberals who had been affected by the French Roman Catholic biblical scholar Alfred Loisy's *L'Évangile et l'Église* (1902) which held that religious authority was to be found not so much in the letter of scripture or the pronouncements of popes and councils but in the ongoing *experience* of the risen Christ mediated through the sacraments of the evolving catholic church. Like the theologians of Protestant liberalism – indeed Hoskyns had studied under Adolf von Harnack in Berlin – for them the category of experience was an important element in discerning theological truth. The result of Barth's thought would be to raise questions in their minds as to that category's propriety, and to revert to the concept of revelation and the sovereign authority of God's Word.

Mozley's first published response to Barth was a somewhat inquisitive 1929 review of Douglas Horton's translation, *The Word of God and the*

---

[42] Ibid., p.270.
[43] E. G. Selwyn 'Preface', to J. K. Mozley, *Some Tendencies in British Theology: from the publication of* Lux Mundi *to the present day* (London: SPCK, 1952), p.8.

Word of Man. Barth, he admitted, was an unknown quantity, 'a stormy petrel of theology . . . to some he stands for the illumination of the theological sky, to others he suggests its darkening'.[44] The reviewer was intrigued by his biblicism, and chose to focus on the two chapters, 'The Strange New World of the Bible', and 'Biblical Questions, Insights and Vistas': 'It must clearly be understood that Barth is not what is called a Fundamentalist. He has no quarrel with the methods of higher criticism; he does not object to its findings, that they are irreconcilable with a doctrine of verbal inerrancy'.[45] The important thing for Barth was the theology that was done *after* the critics had completed their task, a theology which centred on the divine. The principal theme of these chapters was the strangeness of the biblical revelation, its alien quality and how it contravened the usual canons of religious thought. 'Nothing is more baffling than Barth's attitude to . . . the truth of biblical history', he claimed. 'What he means is that where the action of God is concerned it is no use our supposing that those historical canons are applicable which have become normative for us through our attention to the history of man . . . This seems to be the key to his extremely difficult statement on the resurrection of Christ'.[46] The only way to begin to do justice to the disparity between human relativity and the divine absolute was through the dialectic method:

> As Barth himself expresses it, every Yes and No is no more than a *witness* to God's truth, and misunderstanding can be avoided only when the Yes is adequately limited by the No and the No by the Yes. And though the dialectical method is truer than any other, the dialectician must remember that he also cannot really speak of God. Only God can do that.[47]

Along with his treatment of dialectic and the Bible, Mozley was highly intrigued by Barth's critique of the category of experience as a means of apprehending the divine. 'The unprepared reader may well feel surprised at Barth's polemics against religion', he claimed. 'For Barth, religion always lies on this side of the gulf which separates God from man'.[48] All that religion did was to reveal the depth of human relativity though it remained an ambiguous essential in the response to, if not the quest for God: 'Here we meet with the supremely Calvinistic character of Barth's thought,

[44] J. K. Mozley, 'The theology of Karl Barth', *The Review of the Churches* 6 (1929), 553–7 [553].
[45] Ibid., 553.
[46] Ibid., 554.
[47] Ibid., 555.
[48] Ibid., 555.

though it is not the Calvinism of contrasted individualistic election or reprobation'.[49] For this Swiss Calvinist, election, grace and faith do not belong to the realm of individualistic piety, but according to the exegesis of Romans 6, they have to do with the nature and essence of God.

Whereas other critics had feared that Barth's Calvinistic God-sovereignty would lead to a depreciation of the ethical task, Mozely did not believe this to be the case. The striking chapter 'The Problem of Ethics Today' showed that Barth was exceedingly concerned with Christian conduct, though any true system of morals had to be securely grounded in a valid doctrine of God. The bane of late-nineteenth century Protestant theology had been its moralism, that it had collapsed the ethical into the religious and God's radical otherness had been compromised as a result. 'Barth argues that man is bound to recognize his inability to reach that moral objective which, nevertheless he feels constrained to seek'.[50] It is there, in his power-lessness, that he meets God. It was no wonder, therefore, that he made so much of the ideas of revelation, forgiveness and grace: 'The supreme experience of what he calls "the new world", the world of an utterly different order of reality from anything anywhere discoverable except in the Bible, is in the forgiveness of sins'.[51] Mozley was convinced that all Barth's metaphysics and epistemology lead ultimately to the reality of ethics: 'The discussion of "The Problem of Ethics Today" works up towards these conclusions',[52] namely the justification of the unrighteous. It is the covering of sins by grace which makes an authentic Christian ethics possible.

The reader of *The Word of God and the Word of Man* 'may feel like an explorer in an unknown country',[53] yet traversing the ground was an exciting and rewarding task: 'The extraordinary unlikeness of Barth's theology to anything with which we usually meet in Anglican or Free Church circles makes it all the more worthy of study'.[54] This Swiss Calvinist – 'It is not difficult to think of Barth as a Protestant of the Protestants, one who wears Calvin's own Geneva gown'[55] – was, nonetheless, difficult to categorize; he did not conform either to orthodox or the liberal norms: 'Anyone who came straight to Barth from a work steeped in the atmosphere of rational orthodoxy which is the finest type of the Anglican tradition might well feel like a stranger who had wandered into a Christian service at

---

[49] Ibid., 555.
[50] Ibid., 556.
[51] Ibid., 556.
[52] Ibid., 556.
[53] Ibid., 556.
[54] Ibid., 557.
[55] Ibid., 556.

Corinth in the first century and heard believers speaking in tongues'.[56] This vital new voice demanded a hearing: 'If we neglect him we will miss a great deal'.[57]

Mozley, however worthy, was never destined to be a major figure in English theological history. Hoskyns, however, has been credited with creating an epoch. For Alan Wilkinson he became 'the leading exponent of neo-orthodoxy in England'.[58] 'His article on "The Christ of the Synoptic Gospels" is . . . epoch-making',[59] according to Adrian Hastings, turning the tide in New Testament studies and virtually creating a new era in biblical theology. For Roger Lloyd, he was the scholar who more or less single-handedly engineered 'the eclipse of liberalism'.[60] 'Hoskyns', he claimed, 'had destroyed an idol'.[61] 'To many Anglicans, as indeed to many who were not', related A. M. Ramsey, who attended his lectures at Cambridge in 1926, 'it was Edwyn Clement Hoskyns who became the symbol of what seemed a startlingly new approach to the Bible'.[62] 'His lectures on the theology and ethics of the New Testament were exceptionally vivid, forceful, trenchant, and unexpected', stated his friend and colleague, Charles Smyth, 'and were delivered with a sustained enthusiasm and excitement which it is impossible . . . ever to forget . . . It was through these lectures, and through his college teaching and supervisions, that he left his abiding mark on the Church of England'.[63]

The son of a Tractarian and titled bishop of Stepney, the family baronetcy having first been bestowed by Charles II in 1676, Sir Edwyn C. Hoskyns (1884–1937) had read for the history tripos in Jesus College Cambridge where he had been an indifferent rather than brilliant scholar. The college dean, the advanced modernist F. J. Foakes-Jackson, realized his latent academic potential and sent him to Berlin for further studies with the great liberal Protestant church historian, Adolf von Harnack. It was in Germany in 1906 that Hoskyns became familiar with the work of Albert Schweitzer whose *Reimarus zu Wrede*, published in that year, would be translated as *The Quest for the Historical Jesus* (1910). The young Englishman became fascinated by Schweitzer's revolutionary eschatological interpretation of Jesus and the gospel narrative. His Jesus was no gentle religious sage but

---

[56] Ibid., 557.

[57] Ibid., 557.

[58] Alan Wilkinson, *Dissent or Conform? War, Peace and the English Churches, 1900–45* (London: SCM, 1986), p.205.

[59] Hastings, *A History of English Christianity, 1920–2000*, p.235.

[60] Lloyd, *The Church of England, 1900–65*, p.271.

[61] Ibid., p.278.

[62] Ramsey, *From Gore to Temple*, p.131.

[63] Charles Smyth, introduction to Edwyn Clement Hoskyns, *Cambridge Sermons* (London: SPCK, 1938), p.xix.

a thwarted apocalyptic seer whose Kingdom of God would not be achieved through progressive human goodness but as a divine catastrophe. Ethics, which were so central to conventional religiosity, had merely interim status in this scheme, its paramount feature being the breaking-in of a calamitous, other-worldly, divine reality. Following ministerial training at Wells Theological College, Hoskyns was ordained to the deaconate in 1908 and worked as curate in a Sunderland parish before taking up an appointment as warden to the Anglican hostel of Sheffield University in 1912. He volunteered for chaplaincy duty at the outbreak of war and served with distinction both on the Western Front and in the Middle East and was decorated with the Military Cross in 1918.

It was his appointment to a fellowship at Corpus Christi College, Cambridge, in 1919 at the age of 35, along with a faculty lectureship in New Testament, which would mark the beginning of his influence on Anglican thought. Virtually the sole Anglo-Catholic on the Cambridge Faculty of Divinity, he found himself having to counter the overwhelming influence of modernism, not least as personified by the immensely powerful J. F. Betheune-Baker, Lady Margaret Professor of Divinity. 'To be of Anglo-Catholic opinions in this group was to be a man apart', recounted Owen Chadwick. 'Betheune-Baker regarded Anglo-Catholicism as part of the nonsense it was his mission to destroy. Hoskyns, sitting at meetings of the faculty, felt alone. His sense of isolation was the chief suffering of his life in Cambridge'.[64] He was not wholly bereft, however, of congenial fellowship. His academic, indeed his spiritual home was his college and the company of a cabal of like-minded churchmen including the scientist Will Spens, the historian Charles Smyth, E. G. Selwyn, editor of the journal *Theology* and of the volume which did for the inter-war generation what *Lux Mundi* had done for the late Victorians, namely *Essays Catholic and Critical* (1926), and a few others: 'The most important features of inter-war Corpus', reminisced Maurice Cowling, 'were that it was a small college and that it was a Conservative-Anglican plot'.[65] Unlike the left-leaning social democrat Barth, Hoskyns's increasingly radical critique of theological liberalism corresponded with a fairly reactionary political stance.[66]

As noted in Chapter 1, Hoskyns had already been drawn into the remarkable fellowship of English and German biblical scholars instituted

[64] Owen Chadwick, *Michael Ramsey: a life* (Oxford: Clarendon Press, 1990), p.28.
[65] Maurice Cowling, *Religion and Public Doctrine in Modern England* (Cambridge: Cambridge University Press, 1980), p.73.
[66] For Hoskyns's patrician Toryism and right-wing political views see Cowling, *Religion and Public Doctrine in Modern England*, pp.90–6 and Gordon S. Wakefield, 'Biographical Introduction', E. C. Hoskyns and Noel Davey, *Crucifixion–Resurrection: the pattern of the theology and ethics of the New Testament* (London: SPCK, 1981), pp.27–81 [60–6 esp.].

by George Bell and Adolf Deissmann which met at Canterbury and Eisenach in 1927 and 1928, and whose work culminated in the volume *Mysterium Christi* (1930). There, in the company of Karl Ludwig Schmidt, Gerhart Kittel, Paul Althaus and others, he had seen how Schweitzer's apocalyptic understanding of Jesus had created a by now long established consensus in continental New Testament scholarship. This confirmed his own radical interpretation of the synoptic data, that the minute, scholarly and painstaking examination of the text revealed not a liberal Christ, the simple carpenter of Nazareth who had been deified by his followers, St Paul most of all, but the strange, alien, mysterious figure of Jesus whose divinity, replete with miracles, belonged to even the earliest strata of the material. Consequently, rather than being an extraneous and illegitimate declension from the simplicities of the beginning, the historic faith of the church was in genuine continuity with the mission of Jesus himself. His two conference essays, 'The other-worldly Kingdom of God in the New Testament' (1927) and 'Jesus Christ, Son of God, Saviour' (1928) along with his chapter 'Jesus the messiah' in *Mysterium Christi*,[67] made the case for an apocalyptic, messianic Christ, as had his succinct and highly memorable chapter 'The Christ of the Synoptic Gospels' in Selwyn's *Essays Catholic and Critical*: 'There seems no reason to doubt that the characteristic features of catholic piety have their origin in our Lord's interpretation of his own person and of the significance of his disciples for the world'.[68] In the words of A. M. Ramsey: 'The ground was being cut from beneath the feet of modernism'.[69]

Just as his lectures were electrifying undergraduates, Hoskyns' sermons in the chapel of Corpus Christi College were providing a thundering apologia for a renewed and exciting biblical orthodoxy. His 1926–27 series on eschatology, and 1927–28 series on the concept of sin were especially arresting. Gone was the idea that Christianity could be reconciled with philosophy in order to provide a rational apologetic for sound religion. The faith of the cross was at odds with all that was natural and demure. Men, and women, were under God's wrath. Salvation could only come from beyond. 'Eschatology [is] the expectation of a new order of things entering catastrophically at any moment, and felt to be at hand'.[70] 'The intensity of St Paul's missionary activity largely depended on this belief; men and women were going to destruction, and conversion to Christianity was the only means of salvation from the wrath of God. The time was short'.[71] With a wealth of biblical illustration, Hoskyns took his listeners into a biblical world which was

---

[67] See Chapter 1, pp.10–15.
[68] Edwyn C. Hoskyns, 'The Christ of the Synoptic Gospels', in E. G. Selwyn (ed.), *Essays Catholic and Critical* (London: SPCK, 1926), pp.151–78 [178].
[69] Ramsey, *From Gore to Temple*, p.107.
[70] Hoskyns, *Cambridge Sermons*, p.3.
[71] Ibid., p.8.

strange, alien and disconcerting, radically different from the blithe conformity of the Anglican way:

> The *ecclesia* of God, the church of Christ, stands in the world as the home of salvation, because within it God is actively at work: it is the sphere of his authority, the realm of his Spirit, the body of his Son. Salvation from sin, from pessimism, from the sense that all things pass to inevitable destruction, from materialism, is not for us Christians to be attained by dreaming of a world beyond this world . . . but by plunging head first into Christian faith and fellowship, believing that the *ecclesia* of God is the visible expression of his love and his mercy.[72]

This was a vision of the church which was imbued with an earthy sacramental realism which neither the broad churchmen nor the evangelicals could comprehend. 'Far more important than this', he continued, 'is the belief that God acts catastrophically in human life, that He works miracles, that men are transformed from sin to righteousness, that prayer calls forth an act of God, that it does not merely effect an adaptation of the laws of nature'.[73] True and vital churchmanship was a matter of affirming gospel realities and a supernaturalism which modernity could never overturn: 'To deprive the saint of the conviction that God has acted and does act miraculously in turning the hearts of the unrighteous to the wisdom of the just . . . is to deprive Christian piety of its very life blood'.[74]

Hoskyns and Barth

The language of the Cambridge sermons was influenced by the idiom of Karl Barth. 'It is not what we think about God and Christ and the church and the scriptures which in the end matters very much, but rather what God thinks about us, how we are judged by the Christ and by the living Word of God, made manifest in the scriptures and in the church'.[75] The post-*Lux Mundi* Anglo-Catholic synthesis of orthodox faith, cultural openness and critical thought was yielding to something less compromising. 'It is a hard truth for us to learn, we in the pride of our achievements, we with our doctrines of evolution, we with our petty impertinence convinced that God can only speak to men through men, through human personalities'.[76]

---

[72] Ibid., p.28.
[73] Ibid., p.35.
[74] Ibid., pp.35–6.
[75] Ibid., p.45.
[76] Ibid., p.62.

It was patent that Hoskyns was already immersing himself in Barth's writings, a process which would culminate in his immensely significant translation of the *Römerbrief* which would afford English readers access to that key text in 1933: 'Can you . . . maintain a paradox? Can you explain No from Yes, and a Yes from No? and see the truth in a contrast because it is a contrast without any attempt at a synthesis? . . . There is the paradox, and there is no synthesis in this world'.[77] A review of a continental volume on Barth in the *Journal of Theological Studies* in 1928 conveyed the trend of his thought. 'Since the revival which is associated with the name of Karl Barth is perhaps the most important religious movement in Swiss, German and Dutch Protestantism at the present time', he wrote, 'it is important that a serious attempt should be made in England to understand its significance'.[78] 'The assumption which underlies everything that Barth writes is that God is God, and men are men, and that the line which separates the two can be crossed neither by human thought nor by human experience'.[79] God is not object but subject and humankind is under the searing indictment of the divine judgement. God's elective action alone brings men and women into his sphere: 'God's action descends vertically, miraculously upon those who believe and are under *krisis*'.[80] 'The problem', he stated in words the sense of which he would repeat in the chapel of Corpus Christi College, 'is not what Barth thinks about God but what God thinks about Barth'.[81] All the believer can do is bear witness to a revelation which is received, not automatically but miraculously: 'He can only bear witness to revelation and await a miracle'.[82]

For Barth, he claimed, human perception of theological truth was by its very nature dialectical. Synthesis was not a possibility: 'The method is valuable simply because it is a means not of speaking about God, but of making room for him to speak and act'.[83] Revelation is mediated through the Holy Scriptures, not that the Bible itself is objective truth but that it functions as the means whereby God is made known: 'For this reason Barth is supported by Rudolf Bultmann and by an increasing number of younger radical German theologians'.[84] God, for Barth, 'is the Completely Other, the New World, the Resurrection of the Dead, unknown, He speaks in his

---

[77] Ibid., pp.80–1.

[78] Edwyn C. Hoskyns, review of Th. L. Haitjema, *Karl Barths 'Kritische Theologie'*, German translation by Peter Schumacher (Wageninen: H. Veenman & Zonen, 1926), *Journal of Theological Studies* 29 (1928), 201–4 [201].

[79] Hoskyns, *Karl Barths 'Kritische Theologie'*, 202.

[80] Ibid., 202.

[81] Ibid., 202.

[82] Ibid., 202.

[83] Ibid., 202.

[84] Ibid., 202.

silence, merciful in his unapproachable holiness. He who says "God" says miracle, revelation'.[85] Barth's Christology was an aspect of his concept of revelation. Jesus Christ is God's revelation in history when two worlds intersect: 'The point at which these two worlds cross and intersect is Jesus, the historical Jesus of Nazareth. But again, it is impossible to speak of him *in abstractio*'.[86] This Jesus is not the Jesus of history as revered by popular piety or understood by historical criticism, but a much more mysterious entity, God's appointed witness to miracle. 'Barth can never think of [the death and resurrection of Jesus Christ] as direct, impersonal, independent, historical events'.[87] Revelation is oblique for the simple reason that God is God, transcendent and other, whereas history is human, mundane and ordinary. God can only be affirmed and perceived by faith; the risen Christ is pure eschatology, beyond history and psychology: 'Here Barth ends'.[88]

It has been stated incessantly that Hoskyns was never a Barthian. J. O. Cobham, principal of the Queen's College, Birmingham, was the first to assert this soon after Hoskyns' death in 1937. 'Hoskyns was never a Barthian. That, I am sure, wants saying', he claimed. 'But at the same time when his own work on the New Testament was forcing him away from Catholic Modernism, he discovered Barth as someone who supplied him with a language through which to express what he himself was discovering in the New Testament'.[89] 'It would be an injustice both to Barth and to Hoskyns to say that Hoskyns was a "Barthian"', stated Alec Vidler. 'He did however more than anyone else in England – or at least in the Church of England – regard Barth as the prophet for that time'.[90] 'Hoskyns was no Barthian', echoed Roger Lloyd, 'though he understood Barth and greatly admired him. None the less, he became to Anglican theology the same kind of moving and disturbing force that Karl Barth was to European Protestantism'.[91] The typical Anglican disdain for the uncompromising character of continental theology is all too obvious in these comments. What a Barthian actually was, was never defined, though J. K. Mozley who knew him as well as anyone certainly linked him inextricably with Barth: 'The exposition of Christianity which we associate with Karl Barth and his school and the late Sir Edwyn Hoskyns in England, is characterized by a deep suspicion of the tendency to present Christianity as a philosophy of religion'.[92] It was Hoskyns, after all, who undertook the onerous task of

[85] Ibid., 203.
[86] Ibid., 203.
[87] Ibid., 204.
[88] Ibid., 204.
[89] Quoted in introduction to Hoskyns, *Cambridge Sermons*, p.xvii.
[90] Alec R. Vidler, *Twentieth Century Defenders of the Faith* (London: SCM, 1965), p.91.
[91] Lloyd, *The Church of England, 1900–65*, p.278.
[92] Mozley, *Some Tendencies in British Theology*, p.56.

translating the *Romërbrief*, and what is more, it was he who wrote the striking 'Letter from England' in *Theologische Aufsätze: Karl Barth zum 50. Geburtstag*, the volume charting the reception of Barth's work in Europe up to 1936. To the extent that inter-war Anglican theology responded to Barth at all, it did so through the medium of Hoskyns. 'It became customary to describe Hoskyns as a Barthian', reminisced A. M. Ramsey. 'What I think Hoskyns chiefly got from Barth . . . was *eloquence, language*. He caught something of Barth's tone of speech and mode of expression . . . Perhaps also . . . a deepening of his own perception that the biblical theologian exists not to be commending a system, but to be constantly subjecting every attempt at system to be judged by the cross'.[93]

Nevertheless Anglicanism, unlike sections of Scottish Presbyterianism and Welsh Nonconformity, would never be at home in Barth's world of revelation, election and the Word of God. That is not to say that individual Anglicans would not learn from Barth and some, like the young evangelicals Geoffrey Bromiley and T. H. L. Parker, students during the 1930s who would make a huge contribution to English Barth reception in later years. As Ramsey, whose remarkable *The Gospel and the Catholic Church* (1936) represented perhaps the finest flowering of early Anglo-Catholic biblicism, stated: '[Barth] was in a sense a sort of experience through which many Anglicans passed'.[94]

[93] Ramsey, *From Gore to Temple*, p.137.
[94] Ibid., p.141.

6

BARTH, BRITAIN AND
THE MID-1930S

Hoskyns's translation of Romans

The second phase of Barth reception in Britain began in 1933 with the publication of two of Barth's expositional works, the 1924 exegesis of 1 Corinthians which appeared as *The Resurrection of the Dead*, along with Edwyn C. Hoskyns's translation of the second 1922 edition of the *Römerbrief*, as *The Epistle to the Romans*. The former, which arguably provides a clearer insight into Barth's understanding of the eschatological nature of revelation and its connection with temporal history, was wholly overshadowed by the latter. Just as the original *Römerbrief* of 1919, the so-called bomb exploding on the playground of the theologians, made such an extraordinary impact on continental Protestant thought, so it was Hoskyns's translation which attracted almost exclusive attention at the time. The Corinthians volume seems to have made no impression at all.[1]

Hoskyns's translation had been completed by mid 1932 and the author had provided an appreciative preface dated October of that year. Barth's knowledge of English was imperfect despite the coaching he had received by the Scottish theologian John A. Mackay, later president of the Princeton Seminary, in preparation for his British visit in 1930.[2] He was confident, however, having compared it with the original, that 'Sir Edwyn . . . has performed his task with great skill'.[3] The author was keen to make the point that the commentary which would now be available for the direct perusal of the English-reading public had been written over a decade

---

[1] Karl Barth, *The Resurrection of the Dead* (London: SCM, 1933); the translator was H. J. Stenning.

[2] Eberhart Busch, *Karl Barth: his life from letters and autobiographical texts* (London: SCM, 1976), p.204.

[3] Karl Barth, *The Epistle to the Romans* (Oxford: Oxford University Press, 1933), p v.

previously, indeed the original version had been composed even earlier: 'The man who sat writing his commentary was then just a young country pastor . . . [who had] tumbled himself into a conflict, the inward and outward significance of which he could not foresee'.[4] By 1932 the world had moved on, and so had Barth: 'When . . . I look back at the book, it seems to have been written by another man to meet a situation belonging to a past epoch'.[5] He implored his readers not to judge his present theological position in the light of this early work.

He was also keen, even at this stage, to distance himself from Emil Brunner. Brunner was by far the best known exponent of the new theology in the English-speaking world. His triumphant visit to America in 1929 where he popularized the new emphases, his lectures being published as *The Theology of Crisis* (1929), showed him to be an immensely engaging figure. When serving as visiting professor at Princeton Seminary in 1938, his impact on students would be remarkable. 'Of all the lecturers I have ever sat under', stated the New Testament textual critic Bruce M. Metzger who was there at the time, 'I found Brunner to be by far the most dynamic . . . His ability to use simple English to express profound thoughts could be electrifying'.[6] Yet Barth felt that Brunner's smooth biblicism and rational apologetic method compromised everything that he, Barth, was attempting to do.[7] The titles such as 'Crisis Theology', 'Dialectical Theology' or 'the Theology of the Word' with which the Zürich professor was wholly comfortable, gave the impression of a unified school whereas, in fact, the differences between Barth, Brunner, Gogarten and Bultmann were already glaring and becoming more acute by the day. 'May I ask my English readers . . . not to look at me simply through the spectacles of Emil Brunner, not to conform me to his pattern, and, above all, not to think of me as the representative of a particular "theological school"'.[8]

He insisted also that he was engaged not in forging a new theological trend but quite simply in the exegesis of a text. 'In writing this book, I set out neither to compose a free fantasia upon the theme of religion, nor to evolve a philosophy of it. My sole aim was to interpret scripture', he claimed. 'In writing this book, I felt myself bound to the actual words of the text, and did not in any way propose to engage myself in free theologizing'.[9] As always, Barth desired nothing more than to understand clearly and

---

[4] Ibid., p.v.
[5] Ibid., p.vi.
[6] Bruce M. Metzger, *Reminisces of an Octogenarian* (Peabody, Ma: Hendrickson, 1997), p.22.
[7] See John W. Hart, *Karl Barth versus Emil Brunner: the formation and dissolution of a theological alliance, 1916–36* (New York: Peter Lang, 2001).
[8] Barth, *The Epistle to the Romans*, p.vii.
[9] Barth, *The Epistle to the Romans*, p.ix.

explicate faithfully the content of scripture as God's holy Word. His review-ers, alas, were loath to believe him. For the Congregationalist Sydney Cave, the commentary's significance was not 'as a contribution to the study of St Paul, but as the fountainhead of the Barthian movement which . . . has become of decisive importance in continental Protestant theology'.[10] For the Anglican J. K. Mozley, its content was 'at least as illuminative of the purposes of Barth as of the purposes of St Paul',[11] while Charles S. Nye in the *Church Quarterly Review* commented that 'many will approach this translation as a text book of the Barthian position from which they may decide for themselves as to its nature and value'.[12]

Cave was already conversant with the first volume of the *Kirchliche Dogmatik* which had appeared in December 1932 and included sections on the human appropriation of revelation, 'The Word of God and Experience' and 'The Word of God and Faith', which had not been apparent in Barth's earlier published work. He was happy, therefore, to affirm the contention that the commentary should not be made the measuring stick for Barth's current position. Yet he found the Swiss's exegesis paradoxical, often obscure and in parts, overly severe. Whereas the apostle had gloried in the recogni-tion of God's glory in Christ, '[i]n Barth's commentary there is scarcely a trace of the joy of that discovery'.[13] Yet there was no doubt about the volume's potency and its outstanding intensity.

> Whatever be the defects of Barth's interpretation . . . at least this commentary does seek to do what most of our conventional com-mentaries fail to do: it seeks to interpret this epistle as to show that it has something to say to our age as well as the age in which it was written.[14]

Mozley was similarly impressed. If the Anglican had qualms as to Barth's concept of the human capacity for recognizing God, 'his errors lie in what he has to say about man and in a theory of knowledge . . . which . . . leaves man face to face with the bare Word of revelation, to which he can apply no tests whatever',[15] he wholly agreed with the emphasis on both the grace and the sheer Godness of God. 'To look on Barth as simply the great "Misleader"

---

[10] Sydney Cave, review of Karl Barth, *The Epistle to the Romans, Journal of Theological Study* 34 (1933), 412–6 [413].

[11] J. K. Mozley, review of Karl Barth, *The Epistle to the Romans, Theology* 29 (1934), 368–72 [368].

[12] Charles S. Nye, review of Karl Barth, *The Epistle to the Romans, Church Quarterly Review* 117 (1933–4), 359–61 [360].

[13] Cave, review of Barth, *The Epistle to the Romans*, 415.

[14] Ibid., 416.

[15] Mozley, review of Barth, *The Epistle to the Romans*, 372.

is a profound mistake', he claimed, 'while any attempt to explain him as a post-war phenomenon of reaction and obscurantism is mere trifling'.[16] His theology was, in fact, salutary and sound, and his faithfulness to scripture was sorely needed by the church of the day. 'The strength of Barth – and it is strength of immense value – lies in what he has to say about God . . . about his transcendence, his holiness and his love'.[17] As for the translator, Mozley's close friend and fellow Anglo-Catholic, Edwyn Hoskyns: 'A translator can hardly ever have deserved to a fuller extent the gratitude and admiration of his readers . . . for his labour, even though that has been a labour of love'.[18] Norman Porteous, writing in T. S. Eliot's literary magazine *The Criterion*, stated that Hoskyns had 'done the English speaking world an inestimable service' in translating Barth's commentary and was 'to be congratulated on the remarkable skill and insight which he has exhibited in performing this difficult task'.[19] It was, in all 'a brilliant performance'.[20] Hoskyns's reputation as England's foremost exponent of the theology of Karl Barth was rapidly being sealed.

In a most unexpected turn, the Romans commentary and the whole Barthian venture to date received a remarkably positive response from, of all places, Ripon Hall Oxford, the nerve centre of English modernism. In an extended assessment in *The Hibbert Journal*, Melville Chaning-Pearce both expounded the main themes of the author's Paulinism, and elucidated his scheme as a whole. If he began by suggesting that the theology was an aspect of the crisis of the times, namely the tragedy of a post-war Europe on the brink of being plunged into tyranny once more, – by now Hitler had come to power – he concluded by maintaining that its principal truths were not new at all but faithful to classic Christianity as it had been perceived by the Protestant Reformers. The crisis of which Barth wrote was not so much the crisis of the times, but that of being judged by the eternal Word of God; it was that searing occurrence that made both the resurrection and eschatology such central categories in the exposition: 'This note of crisis is the essential feature of real religion; it reaches its climax in the Christian revelation in the fact and witness of the resurrection'.[21] God, being God, could only be hidden from humankind; revelation could be the only way in which God allowed himself to be known; the resurrection, although occurring within history, could never be perceived in terms of history; although dialectic

---

[16] Ibid., 372.
[17] Ibid., 372.
[18] Ibid., 372.
[19] Norman Porteous, review of Karl Barth, *The Epistle to the Romans*, *The Criterion* 13 (1933–4), 342–4 [342].
[20] Ibid., 344.
[21] M. Chaning-Pearce, 'The Theology of Crisis', *The Hibbert Journal* 32 (1933–4), 161–74; 437–50 [166].

issued in paradox, all Christian theology worth the name had an element of paradox at its root: '"What manner of God is he who can be proved?", asks Barth. "Revelation means . . . truth recognized as being true only by him who permits it to be told to him. It is truth carrying its own trustworthiness within itself . . . It is, as Calvin expresses it, autopistic"'.[22]

'Again', stated Chaning-Pearce, 'it is no new doctrine',[23] rather a new exposition, in particularly uncompromising form, of what the Reformers had always believed and which Roman theology with its *analogia entis*, 'upon which foundation doctrine the Roman Catholic Church erects all her majestic system of the perfectibility of the soul and the attainment, with the aids of grace, of the beatific vision',[24] had rejected out of hand. What Barth was doing was taking Protestant thought back to first principles and clearing the way for a true engagement between the only two viable alternatives for Christian truth, Catholicism or the revelation of the Word. The usual criticisms that Barth was irrational and world-denying were wholly wide of the mark. Resurrection led to life and the crisis of the Word re-created rather than nullified human activity and culture. For Chaning-Pearce, this was 'a theology which seeks to give to an age of crisis a faith of and for crisis . . . [whose] strange and significant stirring among the "dry bones" of Reformation doctrine is a force to be reckoned with'.[25]

F. W. *Camfield's* Revelation and the Holy Spirit

Melville Chaning-Pearce, an Anglican layman, would become an important spiritual author during the Second World War whose bleak assessment of the human condition contributed to the revival of Christian realism of a Niebuhrian type which characterized those years. Writing under the pseudonym 'Nicodemus', his London notebook *The Midnight Hour* (1942), which was redolent with the spirit of the Blitz, became significant reading for many.[26] It was Kierkegaard, however, who was his guiding light,[27] though he remained a thoughtful reader of Barth's works during the coming decade. But there would be others whose names would become linked with Karl Barth during 1933 and after. Although John McConnachie's insightful

---

[22] Ibid., 171.
[23] Ibid., 173.
[24] Ibid., 172.
[25] Ibid., 437.
[26] See Alan Wilkinson, *Dissent or Conform?: war, peace and the English churches, 1900–45* (London, SCM, 1986), pp.221–2.
[27] M. Chaning-Pearce, *The Terrible Crystal: studies in Kierkegaard and modern Christianity* (London: Keegan Paul, 1940); idem., *Soren Kierkegaard: a study* (London: James Clark, 1945).

analysis *The Barthian Theology and the Man of Today* had appeared early in the year, 'a masterpiece', according to Adolf Keller, 'of up-to-date interpretation of Barthianism',[28] the first book-length application of Barthian categories to an explicit theological theme was published almost immediately afterwards, namely Frederick William Camfield's *Revelation and the Holy Spirit: an essay in Barthian theology*, the substance of a London DD which had been examined by McConnachie. Camfield (1882–1950) was a Congregational minister who had trained at Hackney College under P. T. Forsyth before serving charges at West Hackney and then Worthing in Sussex. He began by challenging the popular concept of revelation as a human undertaking, the seeker's ability to perceive truth through the process of discovery, and put it back squarely within the province of the divine. The Christian contention, for Camfield, was that revelation is an objective reality, vouchsafed by God and witnessed to exclusively in the scriptural narrative which culminates in Christ, the Word. Temporal history cannot guarantee its validity, in fact the events of revelation 'are historical in the sense that they witness to the fact that something has happened, but they are not historical in the usual sense, but only by a new faculty . . . which is called faith'.[29] Faith was neither an innate human capacity nor a theological virtue but, like revelation, a gift: 'It is not our act but God's act in us. Faith is the gift of God. It is miracle'.[30] For Camfield there was no continuity between human spirituality, human consciousness, human religiosity or ethical endeavour and God. Instead there existed an unbridgeable divide between them. It was this discontinuity which gave both Christ and the New Testament their strangeness and elusive, mysterious quality. 'Christ [and] the secret of his person is not capable of historical or psychological explanation', he claimed.

> It is cognizable [*sic*] not by reason as such, but by that entirely new kind of reason called faith, a reason conditioned by a new and transcendental relation set up, not from our side at all, but from the other side of that boundary where our human thought stumbles upon not a rational continuity but a fundamental discontinuity. In other words Jesus is to be understood as revelation only in and through the Holy Spirit.[31]

---

[28] Adolf Keller, *Karl Barth and Christian Unity: the influence of the Barthian Movement upon the churches of the world* (London: Macmillan, 1933), p.177.

[29] F. W. Camfield, *Revelation and the Holy Spirit: an essay in Barthian theology* (London: Elliott Stock, 1933), p.32.

[30] Ibid., p.152.

[31] Ibid., p.60.

Nothing which pertained to the witness could be directly posited as divine, not even people's discernment of Christ's human character as the historic figure of Jesus of Nazareth, and certainly not his wholly miraculous resurrection from the dead. 'Rational proof is out of the question where the subject matter of revelation is not amenable to rational treatment'.[32] This had radical implications for biblical scholarship, apologetics as well as the everyday relation between theology, religion and other human activities, both intellectual and ethical. Divine truth could only be validated by means of the divine, which meant that the Holy Spirit was essential to understand and affirm religious reality. 'No rational explanation of the atonement is possible. Rationally it must ever remain a mystery. But to faith its secret is disclosed, because faith is the work of the Holy Spirit, the transcendent, supra-temporal, supra-rational understanding, which links man's consciousness on to the deed of revelation'.[33]

In his zeal to safeguard the unique character of revelation, Camfield was in danger of slipping into Nestorianism in Christology and docetism in his perception of the divine. Even his doctrine of the Holy Spirit, apart from the exposition in his penultimate chapter, was attenuated, relating not so much to creation and providence as to epistemology and the knowledge of God. 'Christ means the entrance into history of something that is new', he claimed. 'In that which makes him Christ, the revelation of God, he is not continuous with history but discontinuous. He is in history but not of history'.[34] Whereas Edwyn Hoskyns and Nathaniel Micklem, as New Testament scholars, could demonstrate through painstaking critical analysis that the strange, mysterious and miraculous elements in the gospel narrative were not extraneous but embedded in the earliest strands of the text,[35] Camfield appeared to be ambivalent about the value of their work: 'It is useless . . . to expect that criticism will have any positive contribution to make to revelation', he wrote. 'The data of criticism are not the data of revelation. The sphere in which criticism does its work is cut off from that in which revelation functions'.[36] Yet the volume as a whole was a powerful indication that its author had mastered Barth's early work, the Romans commentary and the *Christliche Dogmatik* especially, and was not averse to using such outmoded concepts as the immanent Trinity and the hypostatic union in the context of the contemporary doctrinal discourse. Camfield's closing chapter, 'The Holy Spirit and the Incarnation' was perhaps the most creative, with its

---

[32] Ibid., p.79.
[33] Ibid., p.73.
[34] Ibid., p.96
[35] Nathaniel Micklem, 'The historical problem of the gospels', *Mansfield College Magazine* 9 (1931–4), 102–16.
[36] Camfield, *Revelation and the Holy Spirit*, p.65.

highly atypical – by the standards of English Nonconformity – championing of the patristic concept of *anhypostasia* or the impersonal nature of Christ's humanity: 'The person of Christ, the innermost secret and reality of his being, was divine and not human'.[37] Conscious of the dangers of his standpoint, that it was an abstraction which tended to undercut the full humanity of Christ, he stuck by it nevertheless and posited that it was essential for a true understanding of the atoning sacrifice of Calvary.

Camfield's volume created something of a stir. For the Anglican K. D. Mackenzie writing in *Theology*, it was a 'remarkable book' and 'a brilliant piece of work, of extraordinary clarity and interest'.[38] Although Anglo-Catholics would not normally be drawn to the Barthian disparagement of profane history as a vehicle for perceiving divine revelation, to the downgrading of the innate capacity of the soul to comprehend religious truths or the relativizing of human ethical endeavour, nevertheless the reviewer had nothing but praise for the book. It was, he said 'a noble and refreshing work of pure theology'.[39] Although very positive, Camfield's fellow Congregationalist, E. J. Price, principal of the Yorkshire Independent College, Bradford, wondered whether such a radical discontinuity between the human and the divine in the appropriation of the knowledge of God did not defeat the end, admirable in itself, of preserving the sovereignty of revelation: 'We have not escaped from subjectivity if the theologian can be submitted to no tests, and if the New Testament witness is declared to include an *Urgeschichte* which is beyond the reach of the historians'.[40] There was no doubt, however, of the high quality of the assessment and of its extraordinary fervour. 'This "Essay in Barthian Theology" is a sufficient statement that the Congregational ministry is ceasing to produce theologians',[41] he stated. 'This book will certainly take its place as the leading exposition in England of the theology of crisis'.[42]

To complement the two key English texts of 1933, Hoskyns's translation of Romans and Camfield's *Revelation and the Holy Spirit*, a panoramic journalistic portrayal entitled *Karl Barth and Christian Unity: the influence of the Barthian Movement upon the churches of the world* was issued from the prolific pen of the Swiss ecumenist Adolf Keller. More an advocate and Christian activist than creative theologian in his own right, Keller was being drawn more and more towards Barth's work as providing the necessary

---

[37] Ibid., p.272.
[38] K. D. Mackenzie, review of Camfield, *Revelation and the Holy Spirit*, *Theology* 29 (1934), 55–6 [56].
[39] Ibid., p.56.
[40] E. J. Price, review of Camfield, *Revelation and the Holy Spirit*, *The Congregational Quarterly* 12 (1934), 107–8 [107].
[41] Price, review of Camfield, *Revelation and the Holy Spirit*, p.107.
[42] Ibid., p.108.

radical edge which continental Protestantism needed were it to play its part in an ecumenical rapprochement of any kind. The Protestant churches needed to know what they believed and Barth's theology, he thought, could help them clarify their vision: 'With this new theology dominant central viewpoints are now emerging which might well be employed in a new general orientation within the present form of Christianity'.[43]

In some 350 pages the ever-expansive Keller provided an absorbing account of Barth reception mostly in Europe, with insightful comments on England, Scotland and the United States. 'In no other country do tradition, national and psychological idiosyncracy, "common sense" and then again a certain Platonic factor in the national ecclesiastical thought', he stated, 'offer such unique preliminary conditions for a discussion as in England'.[44] The English distaste for abstract thought, its abhorrence of extremism, its practical bent and genius for compromise, 'the spirit of Erasmus is still active in Anglicanism',[45] would seemingly make it impervious not only to the appeal of Barth but to an understanding of what the younger Swiss's theology actually entailed. Although Nonconformity was vigorous and Anglicanism was a revered if increasingly neglected aspect of national life, neither of these two traditions had been shaken by the crisis which had characterized continental theology for a decade and more. Instancing the words of the Congregationalist Alfred E. Garvie, the liberal principal of Hackney and New College, in 1932: 'The revival of Calvinism by Barth is to be regarded as disastrous, as a tragic theological reaction',[46] Keller showed how far common perceptions diverged from the essence of the new emphases. 'How far Dr Garvie is from understanding the deep spiritual concern of this theology may be seen from his judgment that Barthianism is one of the minor evils of the consequences of the war'.[47]

The same was true, in his view, of the Anglicans who could only think in terms of synthesis, especially between religion and science but also between faith and criticism and reason and revelation. The tenor of the 1930 Lambeth conference had been wholly immanentist: 'The spiritual life in man enables him to enter into relationship with God. God and man are united. The human and the divine do not exclude each other. In the highest ideals which human consciousness recognizes there is found a revelation of the ideals which are present with the divine Spirit'.[48] These ideas were not only passé in continental Protestantism, but pereceived as being spiritually

---

[43] Keller, *Karl Barth and Christian Unity*, pp.xv–xvi.
[44] Ibid., p.158.
[45] Ibid., p.159.
[46] A. E. Garvie, *The Christian Belief in God* (London: Hodder and Stoughton, 1932), p.449.
[47] Keller, *Karl Barth and Christian Unity*, p.165.
[48] Ibid., p.163.

bankrupt: 'In this aspiration [for synthesis] there still lives a theological optimism which continental theology no longer possesses . . . Lambeth theology as yet knows no theology of despair'.[49] Despite the muted interest of some younger ministers and Anglican priests, England was not yet ready for Karl Barth: 'Wherever in the foreground of theological interest there stands such a synthesis of science and gospel, of faith and criticism, wherever the impossibility of the human situation is not realized to the point of crying out, there can be no appreciation of the final tensions which have called forth the Barthian theology'.[50] The assiduous Swiss commentator knew little about the doctrinal renewal that was already underway among the 'new Genevans' of the Congregational order, neither had he been informed of the work which was being done by Hoskyns among the Anglo-Catholics or Camfield among the Nonconformists. He was, though, full of foreboding as to the political situation in Germany which would be decisive, through the German Church Struggle and the Barmen Declaration of 1934, for the current phase of the reception of Barth's work. His informative volume, however, helped make 1933 a significant year for dissemination of Barth's contribution in the United Kingdom and the United States.

The 'first blast' of the German Church Struggle

Up to January 1933 Karl Barth's reputation in Great Britain was solely as a radical and not fully understood theologian, but by the end of that year he was being recognized as an uncompromising opponent of the policies of the Nazi Party, especially as they affected the Christian churches. Hitler had been elected chancellor and leader of a coalition government comprising of Nazis and other right wing factions on 30 January and within less than a month, on 27 February, Berlin's Reichstag building had been burned down. The carefully prepared Decree of the Reich President for the Safety of the Nation and the State had been issued within hours of the blaze in which Hitler virtually abolished civic democracy and took executive powers as Germany's sole governor. The state now possessed the right to imprison persons for indefinite periods without trial, to impose censorship on the public media and to prohibit what it deemed were subversive activities. The Enabling Laws which transferred the legislative powers from the German parliament to the Nazi Party were enacted on 24 March while all opposition parties, including the Social Democrats which Barth had joined 2 years earlier, were progressively banned. Trades unions were abolished on 1 May. The police had already been put under the jurisdiction of the SS, Hitler's

---

[49] Ibid., p.163.
[50] Ibid., p.164.

blackshirted personal guard, while the Gestapo, or secret police, would be granted autonomous powers. The army stood apart from these measures, but its conservative and instinctively loyal officer corps knew that it would be a beneficiary of the new regime, the new chancellor having promised to restore the forces to their former strength and prestige. By mid-summer the first phase of the establishment of the Third Reich was complete.

Few people realized how momentous or indeed how sinister these actions were. For many of the German people Hitler was merely restoring necessary authority following the economic chaos and moral corruption of the Weimar Republic and countering the threat of communism and anarchy. The perceived injustices of the Versailles Treaty still rankled while the bulk of the clergy and many within their congregations who had supported the conservative DNVP, the German National People's Party, felt that the forced abdication of the Kaiser in 1919 had been a humiliation and the imposition of a republic alien to the hierarchic nature of German society. Lutheran piety was infused with a deep reverence for ordained authority and its 'two kingdoms' doctrine which separated absolutely the spiritual from the secular, provided no means of critiquing the status quo. German Protestantism possessed no tradition of radical dissent. More regrettable was the dark shadow of anti-Semitism. Although understated and hardly ideological, distaste for the Jews had been gathering momentum since the nineteenth century. It remains one of the tragedies of the legacy of Martin Luther that an intemperate hostility to the Jews can be traced back to the writings of the Reformer himself.[51] Even though this animus was religious and not racial, Luther's antagonism to the Jews, common as it was during the middle ages, could all too easily become a justification for later generations' indulgent bigotry. According to Richard V. Pierard: 'Because the clergy were so tightly linked with the DNVP, anti-Semitism permeated the Evangelical churches like a virulent cancer'.[52] Nazi zealots could and did tap into this aversion towards the decadent, materialistic, cosmopolitan Jew, and, if possible, fan the embers into a flame. With Adolf Hitler posing readily as a man of faith, paragraph 24 of the Nazi manifesto expressing that 'positive Christianity' would be the moral basis for the new Germany and a credulous religiosity instilling some transcendent purpose into the revolutionary changes of early 1933, conventional Christianity readily embraced the new regime.

Just as the political revolution was underway, a religious movement was paralleling the expansion of Nazi ideology. The Faith Movement of German Christians (*Deutsche Christien*), established in 1930 and enjoying

[51] See 'On the Jews and their Lies' (1543), *Luther's Works*, Vol. 47 (Philadelphia: Fortress Press, 1971), pp.121–306; Gerhart Falk, *The Jew in Christian Theology: Martin Luther's anti-Jewish 'Von Schem Hamporas'* (1544) (Jefferson NC: McFarland, 1992).

[52] Richard V. Pierard, 'Why did Protestants welcome Hitler?', *Fides et Historia* 10 (1978), 8–29 [19].

the patronage of such luminaries as the church historian Emmanuel Hirsch, Barth's erstwhile colleague at Göttingen and the dogmatician Paul Althaus of Erlangen, one of the mainstays of the Anglo-German theological conferences of the late 1920s, demanded the creation of a specifically German Christianity in keeping with the values of the new dispensation and shorn of all the vestiges of Judaism. Just as the Nazi leader had unified the country, its first call was for the creation from the 28 disparate *Landeskirchen* or territorial churches, one single Protestant church serving the people, the *Volk*, as a whole. In April 1933 Hermann Kapler, a United Church pastor and president of the German Church Federation, August Marahens, Lutheran bishop of Hanover, and Hermann Hesse of Elberfeld, representing the Reformed Church, met, at Kepler's behest, to establish a new church constitution which would create a single unified established church. This ostensibly was a reasonable development, while the heady atmosphere of national revival made such a move propitious. On 20 May this 'Committee of Three' issued a manifesto calling for a unified church under a single *Reichsbishof* who would have ultimate spiritual responsibility for the new structure. Conscious of the revolutionary nature of the proposal and the need to find a conciliating national bishop who would be respected by all, they took it upon themselves to invite Friedrich von Bodelshwingh, director of the Bethel institute near Bielfield which comprised of an orphanage and care home for the handicapped, to take on the task.[53] The German Christians were appalled by this move. They disapproved of von Bodelshwingh, contested his appointment vigorously and canvassed for one of their own, the undistinguished military chaplain Ludwig Müller, to be given the post.

In the midst of this upheaval the government itself intervened by appointing in June 1933 the lawyer August Jäger as commissar for church affairs in Prussia. Although nominally a churchman, he was, in fact, a party apparatchik imposed to ensure that the wishes of the regime were enforced. Finding his authority undermined, von Bodelshwingh, whose integrity was total, resigned before he could properly commence his responsibilities. With that Ludwig Müller, accompanied by a party of brown shirted henchmen, seized control of the headquarters of the Church Federation and announced that, under emergency measures, he was assuming the role of president himself. Jäger immediately declared Müller head of the Old Prussian Union, by far the largest and most influential of the *Landeskirchen*. The constitution of the putative *Reichskirche* was confirmed by state law on 14 July and a campaign of propaganda, bullying tactics and pressurization led to a

---

[53] For these developments see Arthur C. Cochraine, *The Church's Confession under Hitler* (Philadelphia: Westminster Press, 1962), pp.98–128; John S. Conway, *The Nazi Persecution of the Churches, 1933–45* (London: Weidenfield and Nicolson, 1968), pp.45–139; Klaus Scholder, *The Churches and the Third Reich*, Vol.1: *The Time of Illusions, 1918–34* (London: SCM, 1988), pp.219–356.

sweeping victory for the German Christians in the church elections of 26 July. The convocation of the Prussian General Synod confirmed Ludwig Müller's appointment as synod leader on 4 August, and at the first general synod of the new German Evangelical Church at Wittenburg on 27 September 1933 he was elected *Reichbishof*. Thus the first phase of the ecclesiastical revolution was also complete.

As these events were unfolding, Barth could not help but to be drawn into opposition to the new regime. He was 47 when Hitler came to power and in the middle of delivering four lectures a week on nineteenth-century Protestant theology along with leading a twice-weekly seminar on Book Three of Calvin's *Institutio*. His first theological response was to compose a lecture on 'The First Commandment as a Theological Axiom' which he delivered in Copenhagen and then in Aarhaus on a short visit to Denmark in early March.[54] He reminded his listeners of the absolute sovereignty of the Word of God and warned that they should give no quarter whatever to natural theology. In late May, as the academic year neared its end, he was involved with his fellow Reformed ministers, Wilhelm Niesel and Hermann Hesse, in drafting the '14 Dusseldorf Theses' which began by quoting the opening thesis of the Berne Disputation of 1528: 'The Holy Christian Church, whose sole head is Christ, is born of the Word of God, abides in him and hears not the voice of a stranger'. Hesse, who had so recently been one of the 'Committee of Three' had now been convinced by Barth that there could be no compromise with ecclesiastical relativism and that the basis for all opposition to the current measures must be a theology of revelation. The theses were 'a striking testimony to the belief that the times of the Reformation had returned in which the great confessions had appeared to combat the heresies then threatening the unity and faith of the church'.[55] Yet this was only a prelude to Barth's contribution to the defence of Protestant integrity. His ferocious pamphlet *Theologische existens heute!*, 'the first trumpet blast of the Confessing Church',[56] would set out the rationale for opposition to the German Christians and their sympathizers, and provoke incensed reaction. It had sold out within days with a second edition being rushed off the presses by early July. It was banned by the authorities on 28 July, by which time 37,000 copies had been circulated. Karl Barth had become notorious.

---

[54] Karl Barth, 'Das erste Gebot als theologische Axiom', *Zwischen den Zeiten* 13 (1933), 127–43; 'The first commandment as an axiom of theology', in H. Martin Rumsheidt (ed.), *The Way of Theology in Karl Barth: essays and comments* (Allison Park, PA: Pickwick Press, 1986), pp.63–78.

[55] Cochraine, *The Church's Confession under Hitler*, p.97; the text of the Dusseldorf Theses is quoted in full as appendix IV, p.229.

[56] Busch, *Karl Barth: his life from letters*, p.226.

The history of the *Kirchenkampf*, the German Church Struggle, has been told many times and in great detail.[57] There was the imposition by September 1933 of an 'Aryan paragraph' which both introduced so-called racial purity rather than baptism and Christian faith as a criterion for church membership and potentially excluded pastors of Jewish background from the ministry of the Evangelical Church. Then there was the infamous speech by Reinhold Krause, head of the Berlin branch of the German Christians before an enthusiastic crowd of 20,000 in the city's vast sports arena on 13 November crudely lambasting such biblical fundamentals as the Old Testament, the messiahship of Christ in the New, 'the theology of the Rabbi Paul with its scapegoats and inferiority complex',[58] lampooning the symbol of the cross and calling for a new revelation of specifically Aryan 'Christianity'. Krause over-reached himself and, not surprisingly, produced a virulent backlash against the German Christians causing many of the staunchly conservative Evangelical clergy to realize, for the first time, the malign nature of the movement. Müller was obliged to dismiss Krause and censure the German Christians for their excesses. Martin Niemöller, himself the most deep-dyed of patriots and minister of the Berlin-Dahlem parish, had already called together concerned clergy in the Pastors' Emergency League which, following the sports palace fiasco, attracted thousands thus strengthening a body which was determined to resist the new church government on theological grounds. By the spring of 1934 it had evolved into the German Confessing Church, its first national synod being convened in Barmen between 29 and 31 of May. Along with the formation of a 'Council of Brethren' in order to lead the new body, the synod's most significant act was the approval of a 'Theological Declaration concerning the Present Situation of the German Evangelical Church' – the Barmen Declaration – with its memorable first thesis: 'Jesus Christ as he is attested for us in Holy Scripture is the one Word of God which we have to hear, trust and obey in life and in death'.[59] Its main and virtually sole author was Karl Barth.[60]

British Christians were intensely interested in the German Church Struggle from the beginning.[61] The World Alliance for the Promoting of Friendship

---

[57] See Victoria Barnett, *For the Soul of the People: Protestant protest against Hitler* (New York: Oxford University Press, 1992) as well as n. 53 above.

[58] Quoted by Doris L. Bergen, *Twisted Cross: the German Christian Movement and the Third Reich* (Chapel Hill: University of North Carolina Press, 1996), p.158.

[59] Cochrane, *The Church's Confession under Hitler*, appendix II, pp.238–42 [239].

[60] For the detail of Barth's part in writing of the declaration, see Busch, *Karl Barth: his life from letters*, pp.245–8.

[61] See M. Daphne Hampson, 'The British Response to the German Church Struggle, 1933–9', unpublished Oxford University D Phil dissertation, 1973; Keith Robbins, 'Martin Niemöller, the German Church Struggle, and English opinion', 'Church and Politics: Dorothy Buxton and the German Church Struggle' in *History, Religion and Identity in Modern Britain* (London: Hambledon Press, 1993), pp.161–94; Andrew

through the Churches was only one of the numerous manifestations of international solidarity which had burgeoned during the 1920s echoing a new Europeanism which the League of Nations represented in the political realm. The nascent ecumenical movement which William Temple would later call 'the great new fact of our era', the conferences of Life and Work in Stockholm 1925 and Faith and Order in Lausanne 1927 as well as the important Anglo-German theological consultations of the late 1920s, cemented the conviction that the Christian church as the Body of Christ was the one single entity which could overcome factionalism and national self-interest and bind the wounds of a broken humanity which had been scarred first by the war and then by a calamitous economic depression. The advent of Hitler, though in many ways expected following the injustices of Versailles, was a cause of apprehension and dismay. What was unexpected and increasingly unintelligible was the deepening animosity towards ortho-dox Christian faith: 'It was a matter of incredulity that in the heart of historical Christendom, in a society which had been comparable to our own, Christians should find themselves persecuted for their faith'.[62] It was this persecution which would afford the Church Struggle its drama, poignancy and perplexity as well.

If Barth's pamphlet of June 1933 had been the first blast of the Confessing Church, it was also the opening salvo of the campaign to enlighten British church people as to the Confessionalists' cause. The work was issued in translation by R. Birch Hoyle, the Baptist author of *The Teaching of Karl Barth: an exposition* (1930), and appeared as early as October 1933.[63] The verve, seriousness and pugnacity of the work expressed both the extra-ordinary nature of the crisis in Germany but also the compelling quality of Barth's theology in its own right. In one way the church crisis was inconse-quential. The task of theology remained the same whatever the political situation in which the witnessing community found itself: 'It is the unani-mous opinion within the church that God is never for us . . . except in his Word, that this Word for us has no other name and content but Jesus Christ, and that Jesus Christ is never to be found on our behalf save every day afresh in the Holy Scripture of the Old and New Testaments'.[64] The constant

Chandler, *Brethren in Adversity: Bishop George Bell, the Church of England and the crisis of German Protestantism, 1933-9* (Woodbridge: Boydell Press, 1997); Keith W. Clements, *Bonhoeffer in Britain* (London: Churches Together in Britain and Ireland, 2006).

[62] Hampson, 'The British Response to the German Church Struggle', p.5.

[63] For the correspondence between Birch Hoyle and Barth concerning the translation, see Eberhardt Busch et al. (ed.), *Karl Barth: Brief des Jehres 1933* (Zürich: Theologischer Verlag, 2004), pp.417–8, 427.

[64] Karl Barth, *Theological Existence Today!* (London: Hodder and Stoughton, 1933), pp.12–13.

temptation of humankind was to seek God everywhere but where God himself had ordained to be found. This was especially true of the professing church: 'Under the stormy assault of principalities, powers and rulers of this world's darkness, we seek for God elsewhere than in his Word, and seek his Word somewhere else than in Jesus Christ, and seek Jesus Christ elsewhere than in the Holy Scriptures of the Old and New Testaments'.[65] In applying these truths to the present malaise, the great fault of an over-excited and unexpectedly popular German Protestantism was to believe that the national renewal of January 1933 and the unthinking enthusiasm that it has inspired, had its source in God rather than in historical exigencies as such. The clamour for church reform in the shape of a unified church body controlled by its *Reichsbishof* had not arisen from a fresh appraisal of scripture or a renewed conviction concerning the gospel but had simply arisen as a matter of circumstance.

Barth spared neither the German Christians nor the more theologically responsible New Reformation Movement, a doctrinally sound grouping which sought to use the new situation in order to ensure that the *Reichskirche* would be faithful to the classic doctrines of Luther: 'In order to have particular importance, the demand for an independent church must contain a positive, confessional, theological content. This, at any rate, was lacking in . . . the New Reformation men'.[66] As for Ludwig Müller, the Nazi court theologians and the German Christians, his contempt was withering: 'The veriest tyro in theology knows that with their thinking we are already with a small collection of odds and ends from the great theological dustbins of the despised eighteenth and nineteenth centuries'.[67] The problem again was a theology of nature, not of grace, of human religiosity and not the divine Word, of the spirituality of a diffuse, this-worldly immanence and not the unique revelation of God in Jesus Christ. Were they to be implemented, both the ideas of the New Reformation and certainly the practices of the odious German Christians 'would only result in perpetual adjustments and compromise, creation *and* redemption, nature *and* grace, nationalism *and* the gospel, which . . . has ever been more congenial to the "natural" man than the characteristic solution which Christianity gives'.[68]

Gerhart Kittel, Cambridge and Edwyn G. Hoskyns

By the time Barth's pamphlet had circulated among English readers, the name of Martin Niemöller was being heard abroad as leader of the

[65] Ibid., p.15.
[66] Ibid., p.68.
[67] Ibid., p.53.
[68] Ibid., p.70.

German resistance. Back in Bonn the tensions between Barth and his erstwhile collaborator Freidrich Gogarten who had recently taken up a chair in Barth's former faculty at Göttingen, had reached breaking point. Although not officially aligned with the German Christians, Gogarten was wholly in accord with the nationalist renewal and sympathetic to plans to reformulate the church according to the present scheme. What was more, he had recently written that God's law had been made manifest for Germans within the national renewal movement and that Nazism could act as a schoolmaster or custodian leading them to Christ. Barth was furious, and in a biting rejoinder of 18 October 1933 he terminated his link with the now ailing *Zwischen den Zeiten*, the platform of the dialectical theologians, which immediately ceased publication. Barth refused consistently to compromise with what he regarded as heresy. He had already resigned from the Bonn church synod to which he had been elected on 23 July and although fully involved in his academic activities lecturing through the autumn on what would become the *Kirchliche Dogmatik* 1/II, the doctrine of Holy Scripture, he was active within both the German Reformed churches' opposition to the ongoing ecclesiastical measures and within the Confessing Church itself.

The ambiguity of British response both to elements of the Confessing Church's witness and to the essence of Barth's concerns was shown in an essay by R. J. C. Gutteridge, a former pupil of Edwyn C. Hoskyns, published in *Theology* in November 1933. Although both the Dean of Chichester, A. S. Duncan-Jones and A. J. Macdonald, the evangelical vicar of St Dunstans-in-the-west, who had written so glowingly on Karl Barth's theology in 1932,[69] had visited Germany on behalf of the Church of England Council on Foreign Relations in July and September 1933 respectively,[70] it was the essay by the much younger Gutteridge which informed many ministers and clergy of what was happening on the ground. Its author was an Anglican ordinand who had been studying with the New Testament scholar Gerhard Kittel at Tübingen throughout the religious and political upheaval. Despite striving to be objective, there is no doubt that he was deeply impressed by many aspects of the new regime, not least its seemingly positive attitude towards Christianity. Accepting the (at the time not improbable) view that Hitler was a sincerely religious man, 'there is no real evidence to show that the government has in any way directly meddled in what is usually character-ized as the inner, as opposed to the official or outer, life of the church',[71] he claimed. The *Reichskirche* had been promised full autonomy with the bounds of the state and complete freedom to uphold an unambiguous

---

[69] See above, Chapter 5, pp.105–8.
[70] See Chandler, *Brethren in Adversity: Bishop Bell and the crisis of German Protestant-ism*, pp.52–60.
[71] R. J. C. Gutteridge, 'German Protestantism and the Hitler regime', *Theology* 27 (1933–34), 241–64 [248].

Christian creed. He did, however, concede that the state intervention in the form of the support of August Jäger, the Prussian commissar for church affairs, for Ludwig Müller's seizure of the presidency of the Church Federation as well as the tactics used in the church elections of the preceding July, had given the German Christians a power and presence which they did not deserve. Yet he was adamant in his claim: 'In summary, there is no real evidence to show that the state at any time interfered directly in questions of religious faith and dogma'.[72]

As for those matters of religious faith and dogma, Gutteridge was not convinced that even the German Christians were wholly beyond the pale. Apart from a common commitment to German nationalism, which he did not see as being particularly sinister, there was little theological unanimity among them. If some were mystical pantheists, others were conventional if rather liberal Christian believers. He was not blind to their deficiencies, especially their downplaying of the doctrines of sin, repentance and salvation in favour of talk of blood, nation and people: 'No Englishman can be brought into contact with the German Christian Movement without sensing the dangers inherent in it'.[73] He was, however, more than willing to give them the benefit of the doubt. The importance of Barth's *Theologische existens heute!*, he thought, was to sound a warning in this matter. Yet even Gutteridge, the young idealist, was not wholly comfortable with what he had seen: 'It requires no prophet to suggest that a stern struggle may some day take place within the ranks of the German Christians, or, indeed, of the whole German Protestant Church, between those who seek salvation from outside themselves, and those who seek it from within'.[74] 'Will the German people be brought under the cross', he concluded, 'or will they try to find a satisfaction for the craving for religion in acceptance of a narrow creed of German idealism? The position is nothing more or less than a choice between the Christian gospel or national idealism'.[75]

Neither Gutteridge[76] nor his Cambridge mentor Edwyn Hoskyns nor, as it would transpire, the evangelical Macdonald fully realized the malign intentions of Hitler and the Nazis, whether the enormity of their aversion towards the Jews or to the opportunistic nature of their apparent religiosity. In 1933 Gerhart Kittel had published a lecture entitled *Die Judenfrage* ('The Jewish Question') echoing the popular anti-Semitic sentiments which blamed current problems on the decadent, secular and materialistic Jews and

---

[72] Ibid., 252.
[73] Ibid., 258.
[74] Ibid., 258.
[75] Ibid., 263.
[76] Much later in his career, he wrote a searing indictment of Christian anti-Semitism in his volume *Open Thy Mouth for the Dumb: the German Evangelical Church and the Jews, 1879–1950* (Oxford: Blackwell, 1976).

advocated, within the context of the national awakening, the formation of specifically designated churches where the Jews could be assimilated into mainstream German Christianity. Although this caused distress among his admirers and the sharp censure of Karl Barth, in Cambridge it won the approval of the patrician high-Tory Hoskyns who arranged for it to be translated, by their mutual student Gutteridge, and published through T. S. Eliot's company Faber and Faber. In the light of potential criticisms, however, Kittel vetoed its publication in England. The German theologian did consent, though, to visit Cambridge in October 1937 to deliver a short series of lectures in the Divinity Faculty on the compilation of his famous *Wortbuch*. Hoskyns, who had issued the invitation, had died, aged only 52, three months before. Although the theme of the lectures was wholly academic, the audience was scandalized by the fact that Kittel was wearing his Nazi lapel badge.[77] Despite having translated the *Römerbrief* and championed a Barth-inspired renewal of biblical theology within Anglican circles, Hoskyns could little sympathize with Barth's political stance or comprehend how it linked in with his theology. As to the situation in Germany at the time, 'there is no evidence', wrote Gordon S. Wakefield, 'that [Hoskyns] was ever awakened to the enormities of National Socialism'.[78] His untimely death, of course, precluded him from knowing the terrible way in which the story would progress, but it remains troubling that one who was instrumental in the renewal of biblical thought within the Church of England and, apparently, was on the same wavelength as Karl Barth, was so impervious to the moral, spiritual and political realities of the time.

Between Gutteridge's article of November 1933 and Kittel's visit to Cambridge in October 1937, the political situation to say nothing of the *Kirchenkampf* had changed utterly. Late June 1934 had witnessed the Röhm purge when Adolf Hitler brutally eliminated any potential threat to his authority by ordering the death of his erstwhile colleague, Ernst Röhm, leader of the SA brown shirt movement. On 2 August the elderly President Hindenberg, who had provided an increasingly tenuous link between the post-1919 Weimar democracy and the new regime, died. On the previous day, the government, at Hitler's request, had combined the offices of president and chancellor and issued an edict requiring that all officials swear a loyalty oath to the chancellor. On 19 August Hitler proclaimed himself *Führer*, both president and chancellor of the Third Reich. Throughout 1935 individual rights were steadily eroded while a more open and virulent anti-Semitism, encouraged by the official media, spread. A new wave of

---

[77] See Robert P. Eriksen, 'Theology in the Third Reich: the case of Gerhart Kittel', *Journal of Contemporary History* 12 (1977), 596–662.

[78] Gordon S. Wakefield, 'Biographical Introduction', Edwyn C. Hoskyns and Noel Davey, *Crucifixion-Resurrection: the pattern of the theology and ethics of the New Testament* (London: SPCK, 1980), pp.1–81 [65].

'Aryan' laws was passed in September 1935, severely restricting the liberties and privileges of German citizens of Jewish extraction, while the activities of the secret police were intensified. On 10 February 1936 the Gestapo was given absolute powers beyond the rule of law. It was becoming increasingly obvious that Germany had become a dictatorial tyranny, though a continued fear of communism and a blend of naïve patriotism and ingrained deference to authority prevented widespread disaffection. The state's pretence of support for 'positive Christianity' had slowly melted away, and instead a note of blatant paganism had come to the fore. By May 1936 state officials were prohibited from holding church office. Christianity, whether in its Protestant or Catholic guise, while still tolerated, was recognized as being potentially a subversive force. The official state ideology would now be a mystically tinged nationalistic secularism. Within the Confessing Church a spirit of opposition persisted, and while by mid-1935 the increasingly ineffectual Ludwig Müller and the 'German Christians' forfeited Hitler's support, being 'left by the authorities to rot away in full regalia as the contemporary phrase had it',[79] an even more obdurate administration led by Hans Kerrl, the new minister for church affairs, enforced Nazi rule with hardly a veneer of regard for Christian sensibilities.

A. J. Macdonald and opposition to the Confessing Church

A. J. Macdonald, for his part, saw this panorama unfolding before his eyes but was totally blind to its significance. Between 1934 and as late as 1939 a division of opinion had occurred within British Christianity as to the nature of the German church regime. The majority view was that the situation was intolerable and that the Confessing Church represented the only valid Christian response. Commenting on the German situation in March 1934, the General Assembly of the Church of Scotland declared that it 'deplored the grievous violation of that freedom of testimony, self-government and action in obedience to the Word of God which is essential to the Church of God',[80] a view which was echoed by the Presbyterian Church of England at its general assembly during the same year [81] as well as by the British delegates at the Baptist World Alliance conference in Berlin in August. 'A church that is not free to go as God directs cannot carry out its task of

---

[79] Richard M. Griffiths, *Fellow Travellers of the Right: British enthusiasts for Nazi Germany, 1933–9* (London: Constable, 1980), p.249.

[80] *Acts, Proceedings and Debates of the General Assembly of the Church of Scotland* (Edinburgh: William Blackwood and Sons, 1934), pp.67–70 [67].

[81] *Minutes of the General Assembly of the Presbyterian Church of England* (London: Presbyterian Church of England, 1934), pp.317–8.

saving humanity', stated M. E. Aubrey, Secretary of the Baptist Union of Great Britain. 'To bind the church is to tie the hands of God. We stand by the noble declaration of the Synod of Barmen which ended on June 1'.[82] There were those, however, who were uneasy with both the Confessing Church's theology and its ecclesiastical stance. The modernist Ernest Barnes of Birmingham speaking to his fellow bishops at the convocation of the Church of England in early June, noted that 'the theological armour of the opposition was largely derived from the teaching of Karl Barth', while the Barmen Declaration, which had just been read out for the first time in England by George Bell, by then bishop of Chichester, 'was practically an assertion that the Word of God was to be heard only in the gospel record, and that we do not find the witness of the Holy Spirit in modern scholarship, science and culture generally'.[83] In Barnes's view it would be appalling for their lordships' to associate themselves with such an absolutist and restrictive theology as this.

This opinion was shared emphatically by Arthur Cayley Headlam, formerly Regius Professor of Divinity at Oxford and since 1923 bishop of Gloucester. A distinguished scholar, ecumenist and chair of the Church of England Council on Foreign Relations, he was 'proud of being a solid, orthodox, middle-of-the-road Church of England man'.[84] He had been suspicious of Barth's doctrine from the beginning, especially its cavalier dismissal of natural theology, rejection of common sense ethicism and downplaying of reason in favour of the revealed Word. His knowledge of the German situation would be supplied by A. J. Macdonald who visited the country on behalf of the Church of England Council on Foreign Relations. Like most Anglican evangelicals, Macdonald was an Erastian. For him the established Church of England was a force for good, it underpinned the existing social order and provided stability in the face of potential anarchy or unrest. He admired the fact that Hitler had restored authority, had effectively challenged communism, and had given the people pride in themselves once more. It was reasonable to expect the church to uphold the rule of law and, as long as biblical faith was not proscribed, to be loyal to the government of the day.

Macdonald's views on the current situation became apparent in the memorandum he prepared for Headlam and Cosmo Gordon Lang, the archbishop of Canterbury, following his visit to Germany in December 1936.

---

[82] M. E. Aubrey, 'Young Baptists and their tradition', in J. H. Rushbrooke (ed.), *Fifth Baptist World Congress, Berlin August 4–10* (London: Baptist World Alliance, 1934), pp.182–3 [182].

[83] *Chronicles of Convocation of the Church of England*, session 18 (1934), pp.283–96, 321–5 [291]; quoted in Hampson, 'The British Response to the German Church Struggle', p.61.

[84] Ronald Jasper, *Arthur Cayley Headlam* (London: Faith Press, 1960), p.340.

Although his tone was amicable and his respect for Niemöller was sincere: 'He has the martyr spirit, and honestly believes that he is engaged in a cause as vital as that upheld by Martin Luther',[85] he had plainly misjudged the malign nature of the administration. 'Occasionally I saw members of the National Socialist Party, in the uniform of the party and wearing its badges, present at public worship . . . obviously taking part as devout Christian people'.[86] For Macdonald it was the Confessional Church which was at fault in provoking the Reich's church government and for not fulfilling a parish-based gospel ministry within the limits proscribed by the regime. It may have been orthodox in creed but it was using the gospel for political ends while there were many among the German Christians 'whose views on the Old Testament were no more pronounced than that of liberal evangelicals or Modern Churchmen in this country, yet holding orthodox views on the person and ministry of Christ, and loyal to the scriptural doctrine of atonement and resurrection'.[87] The need, according to the rector of St Dunstan's-in-the-west, was for the Confessionalists to eschew controversy, to lay down their theological weapons and work loyally within the structures of the established German Protestant Church.

This tone of sweet reasonableness extended even to the most callous enforcers of the status quo. Reichsminister Kerrl, claimed Macdonald, 'strives honourably on behalf of the Church'.[88] Converted at the age of 13, he read his New Testament daily. This did not prevent him from being a passionate Nazi and zealous upholder of the Party's line against both the Jews and ultimately against the church itself. For Macdonald, however, 'Herr Kerrl impressed me as belonging to a type of Christian layman with whom many of us are familiar in this country. A robust and kindly personality, a man who is doing his best in a difficult situation and ready to meet sympathy with sympathy'.[89] The naiveté of the clergyman's views became even more apparent in his description of the officials of Goebbel's Ministry of Propaganda: 'The personnel in every case impressed me as a fine body of bright, honest young men, trying to do their duty',[90] whereas the staff of Berlin's Hitler Youth headquarters 'resembled the best type of boy scout master and assistant scout commissioner in this country'.[91] Under both Müller and Kerrl the Protestant youth movement had been absorbed

---

[85] 'Memorandum by A. J. Macdonald, 23 March 1937', in Chandler, *Brethren in Adversity: Bishop Bell and the crisis of German Protestantism*, pp.107–18 [111].

[86] Ibid., p.110.

[87] Ibid., p.112.

[88] Ibid., p.113.

[89] 'Memorandum by A. J. Macdonald', p.115.

[90] Ibid., p.116.

[91] Ibid., p.116.

into the Hitler Youth despite the protestations of the church authorities. The London rector, for his part, had 'received the impression that any intelligent and tactful pastor should be able to co-operate with these bright open hearted young men'.[92] Macdonald's watchwords were tact, reasonableness and co-operation. He was oblivious to the fact that the days for diplomacy were over and that evil had to be recognized as such and denounced. He knew that his opinions were unpopular but he stuck to them nevertheless: 'My visit last December supplied fresh evidence for the conviction already held that in the German Church dispute . . . there are and have been . . . two sides to the question'.[93] If Bishop Bell and Dean Duncan-Jones were tenacious in their witness to one side, both he and Bishop Headlam were equally insistent on the validity of the other. Karl Barth's name was not mentioned.

The dismal saga of Dr Macdonald was concluded with an article entitled 'Church and State in Germany' published in the periodical *The Nineteenth Century and After* in March 1938 which paralleled Headlam's notorious apologia for the Nazi church-state pact in the Anglican paper *The Guardian* in September of that year. Like Macdonald, Headlam had recently visited Germany to explore the situation for himself. Rejecting the idea that Christianity was being persecuted or that a process of paganization had occurred, it was the Confessing Church that was at fault for refusing to support a legally instituted regime. The German Christians, he claimed,

> supported Herr Hitler because he had restored to the German people their belief in God and their belief in themselves . . . What they were opposed to was the theology of Karl Barth . . . The theology of most of those that I met is much more in harmony with the teaching of the Church of England than that of the Confessional Church, which has been influenced by Calvinism and the teaching of Karl Barth . . . It is quite untrue to say that National-Socialism is incompatible with Christianity . . . it is a foolish and dangerous thing to say so.[94]

This was too much even for his friends; the acerbic but shrewd Hensley Henson, bishop of Durham, wrote of him as 'the pertinacious apologist of the Nazi government in its treatment of the German churches, and the

---

[92] Ibid., p.116.
[93] Ibid., p.110.
[94] Bishop of Gloucester, 'The German Church', *The Guardian*, 2 September 1938; for Headlam in his context see Wilkinson, *Dissent or Conform?: war, peace and the English Churches*, pp.145–50; Robbins, 'Dorothy Buxton and the German Church Struggle', pp.185–94; Adrian Hastings, *A History of English Christianity, 1920–2000* (London: SCM, 2001), pp.321–2.

singularly ungenerous critic of its victims'.[95] If Headlam had some grounds to advocate caution in the Anglican church's dealings with German Protestants in 1933, there was no shred of an excuse to do so in 1938. The same was true of Macdonald, his advisor. His piece in *The Nineteenth Century and After* was taken word for word from his memorandum to Cosmo Lang of a year earlier.[96] Despite the fact that all the evidence was to the contrary, he still gave the Nazis the benefit of the doubt and claimed that were the Confessionalists to be more compromising, that the church crisis could be resolved. No-one was taken in. 'It looks as though he was completely bamboozled by the Nazis',[97] was the comment of a senior Foreign Office official, while Theodore Heckel, director of the overseas office of the German Evangelical Church knew that the London cleric was one of the regime's staunchest allies: 'Macdonald held the most positive view of the Third Reich, and thought any opposition on the part of the Church to the state laws inadmissible'.[98] In 1936 he had been invited by the London-based Nazi apologist, Baron Friedrich von der Ropp, to join the Anglo-German Brotherhood, a forum to foster good relations between Germany and the English clergy. 'What is significant', according to the historian of British collaboration with Nazism, 'is that such a society could flourish at the very time of the major persecution of the Confessional Church'.[99] Macdonald's short chapter entitled 'Why I believe in Hitler' in the volume *Germany in the Third Reich*, written at von der Ropp's request, shows how badly he had been duped.[100] If neither Arthur C. Headlam nor Allan John Macdonald were Nazis themselves, their gullibility and, in Headlam's case, obstinacy were culpable. Their conflicting views on the virtues of the theology of Karl Barth had little bearing on their painful naïveté in the face of incontestable evil.

Barth by mid-decade

As English attitudes towards the German Church Struggle were developing in their different ways, in Bonn Barth's theological stance was hardening and his personal circumstances were becoming ever more difficult. Following the implementation of the Barmen declaration by the Confessing Church

---

[95] H. Hensley Henson, *Retrospect of an Unimportant Life*, Vol. 2 (Oxford: Oxford University Press), p.413.
[96] A. J. Macdonald, 'Church and State in Germany' *The Nineteenth Century and After*, 123 (1938), 338–50.
[97] Hampson, 'The British Response to the German Church Struggle', p.209.
[98] Quoted in Hampson, 'The British Response to the German Church Struggle', p.238.
[99] Griffiths, *Fellow Travellers of the Right: British enthusiasts for Nazi Germany*, p.252.
[100] A. J. Macdonald, 'Why I believe in Hitler', in Gustav Schad (ed.), *Germany in the Third Reich* (Frankfurt, 1936), pp.15–23.

in late May 1934, his relationship with Emil Brunner deteriorated seriously. His frankly polemical tract *Nein! Antwort an Emil Brunner* ('No! An Answer to Emil Brunner') of October was an explosive response to his Zürich's colleague attempt to convince Barth in his *Natur und Gnade: zum Gespräche mit Karl Barth* ('Nature and Grace: a Discussion with Karl Barth') (1934) that they should be working towards a modest but valid natural theology. Brunner had always been much more apologetically inclined than Barth and through his idea of eristics, an existential awakening of individuals as a 'point of contact' between them and the Word of God, had sought to develop a method through which revelation could be grounded in the human quest for meaning.[101] Barth's response was testy but inevitable. He rejected outright Brunner's thesis that the contradiction of human self-existence, being innate in all, was a means towards God, he challenged in withering fashion Brunner's exegesis of Romans 1 and the nature Psalms, and he was contemptuous of his historical analysis of Calvin's doctrine of the *semen religionis*, 'the seed of religion' with was implanted in all. It was because the two men had, ostensibly, so much in common that Barth's attack was so fierce. Although it was clearly provoked – Brunner had been upbraiding Barth publicly on this point since 1929 – it put paid to their collaboration permanently and virtually destroyed their friendship. It was not until 1966, when Brunner was nearing death, that the two men were reconciled: 'The time when I thought that I had to say "No" to him is now long past', he wrote, 'since we all live by virtue of the great God's merciful "Yes."'[102] The fracture did serve, however, to clarify Barth's own position in the public mind and to free him from the encumbrance, against which he had long chafed, of belonging to a particular theological 'school'.

Although Barth was still immersed in classroom work and continuing his lecture course on revelation, scripture and the doctrine of the Word, the authorities were closing in upon him. The second synod of the Confessing Church had been held at Berlin-Dahlem on 19–20 October 1934, but he did not take a leading part in its affairs. He had already been placed on civil probation in May for non-compliance with the church laws and refusing to give the Hitler salute at the beginning of his lectures, while relations with his fellow Confessionalists were becoming more strained. He despaired of the senior Lutherans, the bishops especially, who seemed constantly to be seeking a way to reconcile the Confessing Church with Ludwig Müller's Nazi-friendly Protestant establishment. Along with the equally disillusioned Martin Niemöller, he resigned from the Council of Brethren in November

---

[101] See Emil Brunner, 'Die andere Aufgabe der Theologie', *Zwischen den Zeiten* 9 (1929), 255–76; cf. Bruce L. McCormack, *Karl Barth's Critically Realistic Dialectical Theology: its genesis and development, 1909–36* (Oxford: Clarendon Press, 1995), pp.403–6.

[102] Busch, *Karl Barth: his life from letters*, pp.476–7.

pouring his ecclesiastical energies thereafter into the Reformed grouping which was more resolute in its loyalty to the Barmen decrees and saw in a much clearer light what was at stake. The loyalty oath to Hitler had been operative for all civil servants, including both Protestant clergy and university professors, since August and Barth's only concession was that he could accept it 'within my responsibilities as an Evangelical Christian'.[103] This was hardly enough to assuage the powers that be, and on 26 November he was suspended from his post. It fell to the vice-chancellor of the university, on 21 December 1934, to issue him with notice to quit. The drama of the occasion was described vividly by a student, the Welshman Ivor Oswy Davies, who was present when the university was informed of Barth's dismissal:

> A great crowd gathered together and nervous anticipation filled the air. I saw from the back of the hall, unusually, the small band of grey shirted theological students who were zealous for Hitler . . . They glared at the rest of us, who supported Professor Barth, like birds of prey. It was clear that their only role was to provide backing for the vice-chancellor in the execution of his shameful deed . . . He entered through a small door at the side of the stage and walked excitedly towards the podium glancing anxiously at the assembly. He read the reasons for Barth's dismissal awkwardly from a script . . . He became progressively more flustered as he listed the professor's supposed misdemeanours to the sound of our catcalls and the stamping of feet. The blackshirts' vocal support was feeble in comparison . . . We thought that a riot might ensue, while the vice-chancellor was sweating profusely as he concluded his dirge. It only lasted ten minutes but it will be etched on my memory forever. For there, in that ritual of darkness, I witnessed the University of Bonn losing its very soul.[104]

Barth, who even at this stage had no desire to leave Germany and the fray, lodged an appeal that lasted throughout the spring of 1935. Although no longer in receipt of a salary and barred from entering the university, he continued to hold a graduate seminar in the form of a Bible study group at his home taking the first chapter of the Gospel of Luke as its theme. The respite did, at least, give him an opportunity to travel, and a series of lectures entitled *Credo* based upon the Apostles Creed and dedicated to Hans Asmussen, Hermann Hesse, Martin Niemöller and other pastors of the Confessing Church, were delivered at the university of Utrecht in Holland in February and early March. The appeal, alas, was in vain, and Barth was told on 22 June 1935 by the minister of cultural affairs that he

---

[103] Busch, *Karl Barth: his life from letters*, p.255.
[104] Ivor Oswy Davies, 'Karl Barth', *Y Drysorfa* 112 (1942), 10–13, 44–9 [13].

was no longer welcome on German soil. Deliverance was at hand, happily, from his native city. He was appointed professor of Systematic Theology at the University of Basel on 25 June and left, with his family, immediately. He would watch the tragedy of war unfolding from neighbouring Switzerland and would return to Germany only in 1946.

The excitement emanating from Barth's progress and thought carried on unabatedly in Great Britain during this time. Adolf Keller and John McConnachie were his staunchest advocates. In a stirring address to the National Free Church Council meeting at Birkenhead in March 1934, Keller was incisive. 'Adolf Hitler cannot understand his fighting pastors if he does not study some theology',[105] he said. The struggle was neither academic nor inconsequential; it had to do with the very essence of the Christian faith: 'It is the controversy whether Christendom shall, in the future, be based on a theology of creation or on a theology of redemption, whether the primary data of creation, our human existence, the blood, the race, the state, shall be the fundamental element of the Christian faith or the revealed gospel of sin and grace'.[106] Whatever contribution others had made to the struggle, its premier champion had been Karl Barth:

> He has forged the theological weapons for that valiant army of intrepid pastors, protesting synods, disobeying presbyteries and faithful parishes . . . which, like Elijah, sees the heavenly cavalry protecting the city of God besieged by a hostile power. Just as the prophet prayed to God to show him that invisible presence, Karl Barth is opening the eyes of thousands of believers to the true spiritual nature of the church of Jesus Christ.[107]

Rhetoric apart, Keller informed his Free Church audience plainly what was at issue and underlined the significance of the Confessing Church's stand: 'This battle, fought so heroically and with such great sacrifices, means a rebirth of the spirit of the Reformation, such as we have perhaps not seen for three centuries', he claimed. 'Again, as in Luther's time, Christian men are taking their stand with Christ, trusting in God alone and defending the Bible, the whole Bible of the New and Old Testaments'.[108] 'Today, a new church-consciousness is awakening, a new *ecclesia militans*, struggling for its place in the modern world'.[109]

---

[105] Adolf Keller, *The Three Struggles of the Protestant Churches of Europe* (London: Free Church Council, 1934), p.11.

[106] Ibid., p.11.

[107] Ibid., p.11.

[108] Ibid., p.10.

[109] Ibid., p.12.

John McConnachie was also keen to explain the significance of Barth's latest actions. In an article in the *Expository Times* in July 1934, he supported Barth's contention against Brunner that there could be no compromising with natural theology. Whatever the validity of St Augustine's speculations concerning the *vestigia trinitatis* within the structures of human life or even Luther's contention that reason postulates vaguely the existence of God, the historical fact was that theology had never been content to leave these as signs or suggestions but had always used them to build a natural theology which either compromised or utterly nullified the specific revelation in Christ: 'In the whole idea of a *revelatio generalis* we are to beware of an old Trojan horse in whose body the ancient enemy – the false continuity doctrine of St Thomas – is allowed to enter all too unquestioningly into the theological Illium'.[110] Whether it was the Catholic *analogia entis* or the Protestant framing of theology in terms of the philosophy of the day, the result was that specific revelation had been conceded and the gospel had been eclipsed. 'We have had since the eighteenth century revelation *and* reason (Kant)', he claimed, 'revelation *and* the religious consciousness (Schleiermacher), revelation *and* culture (Ritschl), revelation *and* the history of religions (Troeltsch) and now, last of all, in our own day, revelation *and* the ordinances of creation (Gogarten and the "German Christians")'.[111] As Adolf Keller had contended, the current malaise had brought the theological issue to the surface in an unprecedented form. 'The whole question of revelation in its relation to natural theology [has been brought] into the foreground with a clarity and urgency such as has not been known since the Reformation. Indeed, the question was not raised in such acuteness even by Luther and Calvin'.[112] 'Against this whole modern theory of the "and" . . . Barth, as the theological and spiritual teacher of the opposition in Germany, strongly protests'.[113] Fearing the criticism that such a radical emphasis on revelation would lead to scepticism and, for most people, ignorance of God altogether, McConnachie insisted that special revelation was accessible by all and created its own point of contact with the human consciousness, that the *imago Dei* remained a fact though it too required wholesale, radical and not merely partial renewal, and that God's gracious election of humankind in Christ was the only true and effective basis of continuity between men, women and God.

In Wales it was the Presbyterian Ivor Oswy Davies who enlightened his countryman on what was at stake. As part of his ministerial training he had spent the winter semester of 1933 in Zürich attending the classes of

---

[110] John McConnachie, 'Natural religion or revelation?', *Expository Times* 45 (1933–34), 441–7 [443].

[111] Ibid., 442.

[112] Ibid., 441.

[113] Ibid., 443.

Emil Brunner. In his first article on continental church life in *Y Goleuad* ('The Lantern'), the Presbyterian Church of Wales's weekly, he shared his impressions of meeting with and learning directly from his Swiss teacher: 'He faces each problem from the standpoint of Christianity, that is from the standpoint of his doctrinal convictions, those of "the Dialectical Theology"'.[114] Yet it was not Brunner but Barth who was destined to have the most lasting effect on the young Welshman, and in April 1934, a few weeks before the Synod of Barmen, he crossed the Swiss border and made for Bonn. 'Professor Barth plays a dual role in the life of German Protestantism today', he stated, first as the leader of the theological movement which challenged the preconceptions of the older liberalism, and secondly as a leader of the Confessing Church.

> This church has claimed during the last few weeks that it is the one *true* Protestant church in wholesale opposition to Müller's church. The latter is, to a great extent, *a paper church*, only supported by a few ministers and laymen from among the 'German Christians' . . . The great majority of the people stand with the opposition as members of the Confessing Church.[115]

Davies's reports became vitally important in informing the Welsh religious public of the gravity of political and religious developments in Germany at the time.[116] When the situation became critical it was he, more than anyone else, who kept his church informed of the fate of the German Confessing Church and its members.

> The 'German Christians' hold to the view that the 'historic moment' of the national revolution (which began nearly two years ago) *is an independent source of revelation to them as a German people*, side by side with God's Word in the Bible. Contrary to this Barth and the Confessing Church state absolutely and unconditionally that *God has given his revelation to his church once and for all in the incarnation of our Lord Jesus Christ*. It is very difficult for us to realize how hard it is for a German who is also a committed Christian to think clearly about the meaning of Christianity when so much propaganda in the press, on the wireless, from the platform, in the schools and universities as

---

[114] Ivor Oswy Davies, 'Adlais o'r Swistir' ('An echo from Switzerland'), *Y Goleuad*, 17 January 1934, 8–9 [8].

[115] Ivor Oswy Davies, 'Karl Barth: y dyn' ('Karl Barth: the man'), *Y Goleuad*, 24 November 1934, 2–3 [2].

[116] See D. Densil Morgan, *Cedyrn Canrif: Crefydd a Chymdeithas yng Nghymru'r Ugeinfed Ganrif* (Caerdydd: Gwasg Prifysgol Cymru, 2001), pp.132–57.

well as through movements especially formed for that purpose, deify nationalism and loyalty to the state.[117]

In the rest of the article he described Barth's background and theological development, his personal characteristics and relationship to his students, his method of teaching in the 7 a. m. lecture four times a week which always began with a scripture reading and the singing of a hymn, and in the more informal 'open evening' at home each Wednesday, and his unembellished though powerful preaching in the university's Castle Church: 'What is its secret? Perhaps the absence of any apologetic note. The gospel which he has to proclaim is a miracle; this is his underlying conviction; he proclaims it thus quite unassumingly allowing it to speak for itself.'[118] Yet it was his teacher's closing words at the last 'open house' of the summer semester which had impressed themselves on the young Welshman before returning home: 'I would urge you to do one thing', he had said, 'that is – take your theology seriously'. In the uncertain future which lay ahead, faith in God's free and gracious sovereignty was the only anchor. God alone would usher in his Kingdom, it was their responsibility to stay faithful to him.[119]

[117] Davies, 'Karl Barth: y dyn', 2.
[118] Ibid., 2.
[119] Ibid., 3.

7

TOWARDS THE SECOND
WORLD WAR

Edwyn C. Hoskyns's 'Letter from England'

By the mid-1930s Barth was beginning to be known through his own writings and not just via his interpreters. In 1934 the Americans George W. Richards and Elmer Homrighausen issued *Come, Holy Spirit*, a translation of *Komm, Schopfer Geist!*, Barth's and Thurneysen's joint 1924 volume of sermons, and followed this a year later with *God's Search for Man*, their rendition of *Suchet Gott, so werdet ihr Leben!* ('Seek God so that you may Live!'), the Swiss pair's sermon compendium of 1928. 1936 was even more propitious for those who wanted first-hand information about Barth with J. Strathearn McNab's rendition of the Utrecht lectures of the previous year issued as *Credo: a presentation of the chief problems of dogmatics with reference to the Apostles' creed*, along with an accessible translation by Homrighausen's of some of Barth's more recent brief essays entitled *God in Action: theological addresses*. '[This] little book', commented Austin Farrar, 'shows with what earnestness, simplicity and practical import the great theologian can impress the truths of the gospel . . . on ordinary people'.[1] Of more lasting significance was G. T. Thomson's translation of the *Kirchliche Dogmatik* 1/1 as *The Doctrine of the Word of God*. Thomson, who was professor of systematic theology at Aberdeen, was wholly convinced of the original's significance. It was, he claimed, 'the greatest treatise of the Trinity since the Reformation . . . I have read nothing like it except Martin Luther and John Calvin'.[2] The volume would remain the only part of the *Church Dogmatics* available in English for the next 20 years which meant

---

[1] Austin Farrar, review of Karl Barth, *God in Action: theological addresses* (Edinburgh: T & T Clark, 1936), in *Theology* 33 (1936), 373.

[2] G. T. Thomson, 'Introduction', Karl Barth, *The Doctrine of the Word of God* (Edinburgh: T & T Clark, 1936), p.v.

that while Barth was moving on rapidly in the *Kirchliche Dogmatik* II and III to deal with the more substantive issues of God, election and the doctrine of creation, English readers remained in a sort of epistemological groove believing that most of what Barth had to say related to the concept of revelation alone and that his Trinitarian doctrine had more to do with how God was known than with who God was in essence.

By now enjoying the safety of Basel, Karl Barth celebrated his fiftieth birthday in 1936. The Munich publisher Christian Kaiser Verlag issued a *Festschrift* entitled *Theologische Auftsätze* ('Theological Essays'), edited by Ernst Wolf, noting the occasion. The volume included, in English, Edwyn C. Hoskyns's 'A Letter from England' and John McConnachie's overview 'Der Einfluss Karl Barths in Schottland und England' ('The Influence of Karl Barth in Scotland and England'). McConnachie had already published a short article entitled 'The Barthian theology in Great Britain' in an American assessment of his work in the *Union Seminary Review*, a conservative journal emanating from Richmond, Virginia, along with a German version of the same piece in *Reformierte Kirchenzeitung*, the magazine of the German Reformed churches:[3] 'Within the last few years a great change has undoubtedly taken place and Barth's name has become a name to conjure with among theologians'.[4] Appreciation was, on the whole, generational, with those whose experience had been formed by the mores and religion of the Victorian age looking askance and the younger generation being drawn towards the Swiss. 'Among the young men . . . it is being recognized that Barth is the only really challenging theologian in the field, the one chief religious thinker to be reckoned with today'.[5] Apart from in Wales, 'particularly among the Welsh Calvinistic Methodists where he has many followers', it was in Scotland that the greatest appreciation had been shown: 'When we turn to Scotland, with its Calvinistic training, we find the soil more congenial to Barthian teaching, for wherever Calvin has gone before, Barth finds easier entrance'.[6] McConnachie listed H. R. Mackintosh, who belonged, a-typically, to the older generation, Norman Porteous and G. T. Thomson as devotees, though not yet George S. Hendry, the young Church of Scotland minister at Bridge of Allan who would soon make his mark as Barth's most decided disciple in the north. Even for those who had not become followers, it was a mark of Barth's stature that he had changed the vocabulary if not quite the ground rules of the theological enterprise.

---

[3] John McConnachie, 'Karl Barth in Grossbritannien', *Reformierte Kirchenzeitung* 38 (1935), 259–61.
[4] John McConnachie, 'Karl Barth in Great Britain', *Union Seminary Review* 46 (1935), 302–7 [302].
[5] Ibid., 302.
[6] Ibid., 303.

No longer did preachers talk of religion, God within, values and ideals but of revelation, faith and the sovereignty of grace. 'This, in brief, is Great Britain's present debt to Karl Barth. He is helping to bring theology, and with it Christian preaching, back to its proper theme'.[7]

McConnachie's contribution to the *Festschrift* was, in essence, an expansion of his *Union Seminary Review* article. He began by listing his sources including the essays of the 1920s by Mackintosh, Keller and others, and described the earliest responses. 'It was said that Barth was less a dogmatician than a prophet',[8] but that soon an indirect influence, mitigated partly by the practical, anti-metaphysical bent of most British theology and the fact that few could read him in the original, nevertheless began to be felt. This was certainly true in Scotland though the Calvinistic heritage, although preparing the ground, was in fact ambiguous, its rigorous sabbatarianism and other forbidding features having created a prejudice in many minds: 'Barth's link with Calvin has rather harmed him than helped him in "Young Scotland"'.[9] Neither was McConnachie's own Church of Scotland a monochrome entity. It included old-fashioned scholastic confessionalists, modernists, social-gospellers and some Scotto-Catholics who looked for inspiration towards Iona and a misty Celtic past rather than towards Geneva and Basel. 'The most common theological position in Scotland could be described as a compromise between orthodoxy and modernism',[10] a mediating theology which tended to downplay sin in favour of the concept of a benign divine fatherhood. This, however, was being seen as increasingly inadequate to carry a realistic and vital spirituality and the way was open to embrace Barth and his thought. McConnachie was equally confident that the Basel theologian was being heard in the pews: 'His influence is tangible among the educated laypeople of the Kirk who read his books (presumably the sermons *Come, Holy Spirit* and *God's Search for Man*) avidly and have followed his fight for the faith'.[11] Neither was this influence confined to the Church of Scotland; it was noticeable among the Congegationalists and the Baptists – R. Birch Hoyle had, of course, ministered in Aberdeen. He repeated his contention that religious people no longer spoke quite as they did in the past of religion, God within, values and ideals but rather of revelation, crisis, faith and the sovereignty of grace.

---

[7] Ibid., 307.
[8] John McConnachie, 'Der Einfluss Karl Barths in Schottland und England', in Ernst Wolf (ed.), *Theologische Auftsätze Karl Barth zum 50. Geburstag* (München: Chr. Kaiser Verlag, 1936), pp.559–70 [559].
[9] Ibid., p.561.
[10] Ibid., pp.561–2.
[11] Ibid., p.564.

In turning to England McConnachie mentioned the mediation of Barth's views by A. J. Macdonald representing the 'Low Church Evangelicals'[12] and his popularity among some of the 'more liberal members of the Anglo-Catholic party'[13] of whom Sir Edwyn Hoskyns was the best known. Anglicanism, alas, was incurably Pelagian, and the church's modernists were only taking their ingrained Pelagianism to its logical conclusion. Charles Raven in Cambridge and A. G. Matthews, dean of St Paul's, were implacably opposed to Barth's views, as were some within the Nonconformist churches, especially the fundamentalists whose minds were closed. The situation was much brighter among the younger Congregationalists, while their colleges, Cheshunt in Cambridge under John Whale, Nathaniel Micklem's Mansfield, Oxford, as well as Bradford where Lovell Cocks was teaching and New College, London, under Sydney Cave, were not only receptive to Barthian teaching but were being transformed by 'a positive theology'[14] linked with his name. Finally, McConnachie was glowing in his reference to Wales. 'In the Welsh churches, especially the Presbyterian Church which is called in Wales the Calvinistic Methodist Church, with its strong Calvinistic background and lively religious interest, Barth's direct influence is more noticeable than anywhere in England',[15] he claimed. Barth's books were widely disseminated and avidly discussed – he mentions an animated conversation about Barth that he had recently enjoyed in a Welsh village with the local postmaster! – and there was no reason to believe that this trend was on the wane. 'Today', he concluded, 'both Scotland and England (and presumably Wales) are indebted to Karl Barth. Church, theology and Christian preaching have been given by him a new authenticity and brought back to their true object'.[16]

If McConnachie's essays were destined hardly to be known in Britain, the same was not true of Hoskyns's striking 'Letter from England', the sole contribution in the *Festschrift* which appeared in English. Dated 'Tuesday in Holy Week, 1936', and written from Corpus Christi College, Cambridge, Hoskyns addressed Barth as 'My Dear Colleague', and confessed that they had never met. The English baronet stated immediately the differences between himself and the Swiss Calvinist professor: 'We are separated by the very real barrier of a different language, a different political tradition, a different quality of piety or impiety, a different structure even of theological and un-theological heritage',[17] yet the essentials of faith were identical, and

---

[12] Ibid., p.566.
[13] Ibid., p.567.
[14] Ibid., p.568.
[15] Ibid., p.569.
[16] Ibid., p.570.
[17] Edwyn C. Hoskyns, 'A Letter from England', in Wolf (ed.) *Theologische Aufsätze*, pp.525–7 [525].

for those who had discovered the same answers to the theological question, they could stand side by side.

> You will therefore perhaps understand and forgive me if, for one moment, I break through the reserve that has been imposed upon us, in order to assure you that your work has not been altogether misunderstood in England, and to assure you that your purpose in permitting your book to appear in English has not been altogether overlooked.[18]

It was very obvious that Hoskyns revered Barth for having rediscovered the Bible, its excitement and profundity; he said nothing of Barth's doctrinal scheme nor did he mention the *Kirchliche Dogmatik*. What he found compelling was Barth's revitalization of stark biblical categories vis-à-vis 'for want of a better word be described as "humanism"'.[19] 'For us, as for you in Central Europe, the subject matter of the Bible is difficult, strange and foreign', but Barth's genius had been to make his readers see this with an unsurpassed clarity and respond as the gospel would have them do. Whereas 'the characteristic English substitution of piety for theology'[20] had eclipsed the biblical world, Barth had rediscovered it and led people back to its shores: 'We too know that we are standing where those men once stood to whom apostles and evangelists and prophets once spoke, and that we have to take seriously what they said'.[21] He was effusive in his gratitude for Barth's religious stand, though he mentions nothing of his political views or of the alarming situation which was developing in Germany at the time. Of Barth having been so recently dismissed by the Nazi regime he was silent. The tone, though, was reverential and his appreciation for him having '[borne] witness to the glory of God and to his love of men through Jesus Christ our Lord'[22] was patently sincere.

Hoskyns, as we have seen, was a man with a following, and his 'Letter from England', which was reprinted in his *Cambridge Sermons* (1938), was often quoted whenever Barth's influence was mentioned. Hoskyns' untimely death in 1937 and the evangelical A. J. Macdonald's drawing away from the Swiss's work at around the same time following his uncongenial (for him) contacts with the Confessing Church, marked the virtual end of a possible Barthian movement within England's established church. Yet Barth's impact would not abate. 'In spite of ever-recurring rumours that his influence is waning', wrote H. R. Mackintosh in 1936, 'there is every likelihood that it

---

[18] Ibid., p.525.
[19] Ibid., p.526.
[20] Ibid., p.526.
[21] Ibid., p.526.
[22] Ibid., p.527.

will increase, and that the problems he has compelled the church to face will more and more engage attention'.[23] It would be principally in Scotland, Wales and among the younger English Congregationalists of the Church Order Group and through the lively journal *The Presbyter* that this would be the case.

Developments in Wales

John McConnachie had stated that in Wales it had been among the Calvinistic Methodists, the Presbyterian Church of Wales, that Barth's views had found a most ready response. As we have seen, it was one of their number, Ivor Oswy Davies (1906–64), who had been to the continent to learn about Barth for himself. Following undergraduate courses at the University of Wales and Oxford, Davies had been drawn to 'modern theological movement in Germany'[24] during his training for the ministry at the church's theological college at Aberystwyth in 1930–32. A graduate thesis written during his pastoral year at the Bala seminary in 1933 indicated his mastery of the current trends within continental theology at the time. 'Today we find a new post-war theological movement in Germany', he noted, which was intent on retreating from the direction which Protestantism had been taken by Kant and Schleiermacher and returning to the classic doctrines of Luther and Calvin.[25] Whereas Kant's philosophy had posited an unbridgeable gap between reality and knowledge, and Schleiermacher's romanticism had made experience the criterion of all valid piety, by affirming the concept of a divinely authenticated revelation the new theologians had vaulted the Kantian divide and restored an element of objectivity to Protestant theology once more. 'The value of revelation is not that the human spirit stumbles across some new vision', he wrote, 'but that God actively impinges upon human consciousness, and coercively reveals himself to his creatures, – it is God discovering man, rather than man discovering God'.[26]

Whereas by 1933, when this dissertation was composed, Anglophone theology was becoming slowly more conscious of the work of the younger German language theologians, Davies's sources were in the original, Barth's *Christliche Dogmatik* (1927), Rudolf Bultmann's *Jesus* (1929) and, more especially, Emil Brunner's second edition of *Der Mittler* ('The Mediator') (1932). His treatment of Schleiermacher was already influenced by the

---

[23] Hugh Ross Mackintosh, *Types of Modern Theology: Schleiermacher to Barth* (London: Nisbet, 1937), p.264.

[24] Ivor Oswy Davies, 'Schleiermacher in relation to the modern theological movement in Germany', Ivor Oswy Davies MSS, Bangor University Archive, pp.1–78.

[25] Ibid., p.3.

[26] Ibid., p.41.

thought of 'the dialectical school', whose work 'might be characterized as a throwing down of the gauntlet of a Neo-Calvinistic theology, as constituting the essential nature and truth of Christian Faith'.[27] Following his critique of the still prevalent Protestant liberalism, he described the new theology as being biblical, dialectical, revolutionary and existentialist. Although he was not yet wholly convinced of its validity – its still all too blatant Kantianism, its supra-rational character and 'the incognito of the historical Jesus'[28] caused Davies consternation – its attraction was in its radical nature and uncompromising stance. Its practitioners were not ashamed of the gospel: 'In this lies the immense value and importance of their work for our own time', he claimed: 'They have certainly indicated, at least roughly for us, the way we must traverse if the distinctiveness and solitary supremacy of the faith as absolute and final, is to be effectively maintained'.[29]

Davies's sojourn on the continent first at Zürich with Brunner and latterly at Bonn where he had been taught by Barth, took him to the heart of the Confessing controversy. Not only had he witnessed the tense drama of Barth's dismissal from the university in December 1934,[30] but he had experienced the camaraderie of his professor's Wednesday evening Bible class on the Gospel of Luke at his home during the spring of 1935. He was also present at Bremen on 24 November 1934 when Barth preached what was, for the Welshman, a tremendously moving sermon on Mathew 14:22-33, Jesus stilling the waters while the disciples were in fear as the storm raged. The boat, of course, was God's church in the land of Martin Luther, the storm was Nazi oppression and they, the faithful, were the disciples. Barth then led his congregation in prayer: 'God is our refuge and strength, a very present help in trouble. Therefore we will not fear, though the earth be removed and though the mountains be carried into the midst of the sea . . .'. Davies felt that he was witnessing one of the latter day acts of the apostles and martyrs. 'So long as I live I will remember that hour'.[31] It is hardly surprising that Ivor Oswy Davies's championing of the Barthian theology in Wales would thereafter be infinitely more than an academic preference.

If Ivor Oswy Davies functioned as an observer and interpreter of current events, it was the Congregationalist J. E. Daniel who did most to infuse Barthianism into the bloodstream of Welsh Nonconformist theology. His 1933 handbook on the Pauline theology *Dysgeidiaeth yr Apostol Paul* ('The Teaching of the Apostle Paul') which was heavily indebted to the

---

[27] Ibid., p.56.

[28] Ibid., p.73.

[29] Ibid., p.77.

[30] See above, Chapter 6, p.144.

[31] Ivor Oswy Davies, 'Karl Barth', *Y Drysorfa* 112 (1942), 10–13, 44–9 [48–9]; for the text of the sermon see Kurt I. Johanson (ed.), *The Word in this World: two sermons by Karl Barth* (Vancouver: Regent College, 2007).

Römerbrief, had been written explicitly from the standpoint of 'the new traditionalism',[32] and it was radically different from what Welsh readers had been used to when considering the life and mission of the great apostle from Tarsus: 'Always remember that it was not through studying the moral and religious experience of Jesus of Nazareth in the manner of T. R. Glover's *Jesus of History* that made Paul a Christian but an overwhelming conviction that he was the messiah'.[33] Daniel had spent a semester in Marburg with Bultmann in 1929 and the experience had clearly left its mark. He had little to say either about the psychology of St Paul or about the personality of Jesus. Christ's significance was that he was the divine redeemer who had been sent by the Father to be the saviour of the world: 'It is true that Paul nowhere calls Jesus God; his Jewish heritage would never allow him to do so, but he says unequivocally that it is on the godward side of the line separating God from man that Jesus's essence is to be found'.[34] It was in his divine sovereignty and vicarious sacrifice that Christ's uniqueness lay: 'Despite the fashion of many teachers to dispense with the wrath of God, it is obvious enough in Paul'.[35] The essence of Pauline religion and the Christian gospel as construed by Paul was not that men and women were naturally open to God, but that God, unbidden, had come to them. 'Let the mind of the philosopher or the scientist search the mysteries of their own psyche or the secrets of the universe', he wrote, 'yet they will never come across God. There is no human net whose mesh is small enough to catch him'. Revelation was the only way in which the transcendent God could ever be known by man:

> Imagine a castle, stronger even than Harlech castle, a castle which resisted every siege, a castle which no raider or marauder ever succeeded in conquering. You seek entrance to that castle. It is surrounded by a deep moat, its base is washed by the sea waves and it is situated on a rocky cliff. How can you ever gain your wish? You must first have the permission of the castle's inhabitants, that they lower the drawbridge so that you can cross the moat and enter in.[36]

By the mid-1930s, Daniel's popularity among his students and significance for Welsh Nonconformity generally was being recognized. He had become the leading Barthian of his time.

---

[32] J. E. Daniel, *Dysgeidiaeth yr Apostol Paul* (Abertawe: Llyfrfa'r Annibynwyr, 1933), p.iii.

[33] Ibid., p.101.

[34] Ibid., p.101.

[35] Ibid., p.86.

[36] Ibid. , p.74.

Neither was he alone. More and more Welsh preachers were being attracted by Barth and his message. The New Testament scholar T. Ellis Jones, later principal of the Bangor Baptist College, enlightened his fellow ministers concerning the theology of Barth and his companions in 1934.[37] In a thoughtful series of essays in the Methodist monthly *Yr Eurgrawn* ('The Periodical') in 1935 drawn from the available sources in English and Welsh, George Breeze, a Wesleyan preacher of the older generation, described the essence of Barth's thought. Mentioning his concept of revelation, God as the transcendent 'other', history as *Urgeschishte* and the rest, he was especially taken by his Christology. 'There is little doubt that Barth and Brunner would consider our current interest in the Jesus of history as an attempt to know Christ after the flesh',[38] he claimed. Yet the Christ of the New Testament was, above all, the resurrected Lord: 'Biblical criticism as an historical science can only reveal Christ "after the flesh". It is the gracious privilege of faith alone to perceive Christ as the revelation of God'.[39] For a jaded minister in need of both spiritual refreshment and a vital message to preach, Barth had been a Godsend: 'Although I cannot follow him in all he says, I must admit that no other religious thinker has ever had such an influence upon me. He has forced me to reconsider God for myself, reconsider him not in terms of Calvinism but of the divine revelation in scripture'.[40] Similar sentiments were voiced by T. Ivon Jones, a Calvinistic Methodist minister in the heart of the North Wales slate quarry district a year later. It was Barth who had reminded evangelical Protestants what the gospel was all about and that the preaching of the Word was not only a privilege but a tremendous force for the salvation of the world.[41]

Barth's expulsion from Germany and return to his home city of Basel in the summer of 1935 had coincided with Oswy Davies's ordination to the ministry of the Presbyterian Church of Wales. Davies contributed a succinct précis of Barth's theology to date in *Y Goleuad* in September 1937, as well as an assessment of its author's significance: 'The *emphasis* within Christian theology in each Protestant church throughout the world has changed during the last ten years', he claimed, and it was due to Barth and his colleagues that this had come about.[42] The renewal of the German church

---

[37] T. Ellis Jones, 'Y Barthiaid' ('The Barthians'), *Seren Gomer* 26 (1934), 100–10.

[38] George E. Breeze, 'Karl Barth: y dyn a'i genadwri' ('Karl Barth: the man and his message'), *Yr Eurgrawn* 127 (1935), 13–16, 63–6, 85–9, 144–8, 187–92, 247–51 [189].

[39] Ibid., 191.

[40] Ibid., 14.

[41] T. Ivon Jones, 'Pregethu'r Gair yn ôl Karl Barth' ('Preaching the Word according to Karl Barth'), *Y Traethodydd* N. S. 5 (1936), 18–27.

[42] Ivor Oswy Davies, 'Mudiad Karl Barth' ('Karl Barth's movement'), *Y Goleuad*, 22 September 1937, 9–10 [9].

under the Word of God had already begun before Hitler had come to power, he stated, but

> [T]oday a host of young theologians in Germany are in leadership positions within the Confessing Church in direct response to the work of Karl Barth. The debt which German Protestantism owes him is immeasurable; Barth's strong personality and his definite and undeviating leadership, from the beginning of 1933 to his forced expulsion in mid-1935, not only made 'opposition' a possibility but kept it alive as well.[43]

Yet it was not Barth's political role which Davies emphasized, but his doctrinal stance. The key conviction concerning God's revelation of himself in Christ, witnessed to in scripture and coming ever alive in the preaching of the gospel, had become a startling imperative, even for preachers!

> There is no doubt that Barth's standpoint has met a need which many had perceived for a long time. We felt that we had to accept the new and scientific way of treating the Bible and its literature, – but the theology of Modernism, even when at its best, had failed to satisfy. Then came Barth to show us where we had gone astray. The *theological content* of the Bible as revelation, as the *Word of God*, was something which the net of the scientific method of treating the text could never catch, – it was essential to look at Scripture from God's side as both Speaker and Executor, and listen to his message. The testimony of the prophets and the apostles to the Word must *become* God's living and powerful Word *to us, anew*, constantly, every day.[44]

The one objective criterion of theology was the Word, God's specific and unique revelation of himself: 'There is no standard outside of revelation with which to judge God's truth'. Unlike philosophy, theology was not a free science but one which functioned within its own sphere, that of the church, and under a discipline, that of the Christian life: 'Love of Christ, obedience to his will, and consecration to his service, – such are the conditions of interpreting the Word'.[45] Yet this revelation was not impersonal and bare, rather it was clothed in the gospel and in the form of Christ. 'We must put God, the Creator, the Lord, and the Redeemer, once more in the centre', he claimed, 'That is the message of Barth'.[46]

[43] Ibid., 10.
[44] Ibid., 10.
[45] Ibid., 10.
[46] Ibid., 10.

By the late 1930s the new theology had not only gained a hearing but had found a niche within Welsh Nonconformity. Its practitioners were gaining influence within their denominations and their profile was being raised ever higher. J. D. Vernon Lewis's appointment as professor of Christian doctrine at the Brecon Memorial College in 1934 in succession to D. Miall Edwards illustrated the nature of the development. In lecture rooms and, more importantly (given the still considerable popular influence of chapel religion), in pulpits, the older liberalism was yielding to the new orthodoxy. Ivor Oswy Davies's reputation as a leading representative of the Barthian position was registered as having a salutary influence on his denomination. In an address to its assembly in June 1938, only a few months before Neville Chamberlain's last attempt at appeasing Hitler at Munich, the note he struck was uncompromisingly positive. His subject was 'God in History'. Whereas by any secular standard, humankind could glean little of comfort from the present situation, yet the church would reign triumphant whatever was about to occur. 'We interpret this well-nigh uninterpretable phenomenon called "history" by faith, not by sight', he claimed:

> Although there is much in the past, present and future, we do *not* know, yet, we speak authoritatively and dogmatically, about the deepest, ultimate and eternal *meaning* of what men call 'world-history', in virtue of the revealed Word of God, the Lord Jesus Christ, as the Lord of History, and of Eternity. That God, the Father of Jesus, is *in* history, cannot be logically proven, – it can only be believed. The more we obey His Lordship in our own lives, the stronger shall our conviction of His Lordship in the world, and its history, become. The Kingdom or Lordship of God as at hand, *today*; 'repent ye, and believe this divine proclamation'.[47]

According to the Presbyterian historian R. Buick Knox: 'In a conference where the tone of many speeches was gloomy, Davies spoke of Christ's Kingdom as present in the world as judgement and redemption; he said that God could use the encircling darkness, as He had done on the Cross, to bring His light to view'.[48] The effect this had on his congregation was considerable, and it suggested that the new emphases had something supremely pertinent to say to the Welsh churches at the time. On the eve of war, this was a message to which Welsh Christians could assuredly respond.

---

[47] Ivor Oswy Davies, 'God in History', pp.1–8 [3], Ivor Oswy Davies MSS, Bangor University Archive.

[48] R. Buick Knox, *Voices from the Past: a history of the English conference of the Presbyterian Church of Wales, 1889–1938* (Llandysul: Gomer Press, 1969), p.54.

The Scottish connection in the later 1930s

Between mid-decade and the outbreak of the Second World War, Barth's influence would stabilize within Great Britain and his theology would win new and important adherents. In Scotland the fact that G. T. Thomson (1887–1958) 'whose vigorous defence of orthodoxy had something of a military flavour',[49] would be joined in the Barthian cause by an even more senior figure, Edinburgh's H. R. Mackintosh. Thomson's translation of the *Kirchliche Dogmatik* 1/I as *The Doctrine of the Word of God* would be read throughout the English-speaking world while Mackintosh, though rooted in his own land and church, was revered as one of the foremost English language theologians of his generation.

Mackintosh, who had already commented on Barth during the mid-1920s,[50] made his commitment to Barth's scheme explicit in his 1933 Croall Lectures, published posthumously in 1937 as *Types of Modern Theology*. Although some observers have questioned whether Mackintosh really ever embraced Barth's theology fully at all,[51] the weight of the evidence shows conclusively that he came to espouse a revelation-based theology of the Word of God in which the Barthian categories were elemental. The 65-page final chapter of his book comprises an insightful assessment and deep appreciation of Barth's work. That it has more to say about revelation and the way in which God could be known than of who God actually is, reflects the progress of Barth's thought to date. He defends Barth vigorously against accusations of irrationality and a lack of historical concreteness. The eschatological references in the *Römerbrief* were to be understood as Barth intended and not in any docetic mode: 'The suggestion that Barth in the last resort is indifferent to the historical existence of Jesus Christ must be unconditionally repelled'.[52] He has no doubt about Barth's significance: 'In him we have incontestably the greatest figure in Christian theology that has appeared for decades'.[53] His concluding paragraph stated his views decisively:

He is compelling us to face again the problems of life and death. He thrusts upon us those terrible questions that are rampant in our

---

[49] Art. by D. F. Wright in Nigel M deCameron (ed.), *Dictionary of Scottish Church History and Theology* (Edinburgh: T & T Clark, 1993), p.821.

[50] See above, Chapter 2, pp.25–9.

[51] See John Lewis McPake, 'H. R. Mackintosh, T. F. Torrance and the reception of the theology of Karl Barth in Scotland', unpublished Edinburgh University PhD, 1994, pp.104–77; for the contrary view see T. F. Torrance, 'H. R. Mackintosh: Theologian of the Cross', *Scottish Journal of Evangelical Theology* 5 (1987), pp.160–73; Robert R. Redman Jr., *Reformulating Reformed Theology: Jesus Christ in the theology of Hugh Ross Mackintosh* (Lanham PA: University Press of America, 1997), pp.23–5.

[52] Mackintosh, *Types of Modern Theology*, p.305.

[53] Ibid., p.263.

world . . . Nothing more enriching for the whole church could be thought of than the time for completion should be given him, if God will, and that more and more of his living influence should pass from land to land.[54]

If Mackintosh belonged to the generation that was passing away, George S. Hendry (1904–93) displayed youthful zeal and glorious impetuosity. A native of Aberdeenshire who had been educated in classics at Aberdeen before proceeding to study divinity at New College, Edinburgh, he had been inducted into the parish ministry at Bridge of Allan near Stirling in 1930. Invited to give Hastie Lectures at Glasgow in 1935, he showed himself not only to have mastered Barth's thought but to be a persuasive and highly erudite exponent of its claims. 'Hendry's book *God the Creator* (1937)', wrote Alec Cheyne, 'announced to the world that Barthianism had at last established a firm bridgehead north of the Tweed'.[55] In his opening chapter he set out his presuppositions unflinchingly: 'Revelation disqualifies every attempt to reach the knowledge of God by philosophical thought as incompetent and futile'.[56] Although ostensibly centred upon the doctrine of God, the work was in fact about epistemology. For Hendry the one true God was not the god of the philosophers, still less the god of religion, spirituality or striving after the divine, rather God is the God of Holy Scripture revealed uniquely and incontrovertibly in Jesus Christ the Lord:

It is a fundamental axiom of Christian theology that God is to be known only by the fact that He makes himself to be known . . . God makes himself known by revelation. He is not made known by some faculty of man which is capable of apprehending him. He himself gives the faith by which his revelation is received.[57]

Repeating in rather dogmatic fashion what many of Barth's earliest proponents had already claimed, the minister from Bridge of Allan emphasized the fact that revelation was not a matter of general spiritual enlightenment, a heightened human apprehension of the divine, but the unique and otherwise unattainable gift of God: 'The Christian notion of revelation is opposed to every conception of it which postulates a continuity between God and man . . . It has no point of contact in our existence'.[58] Revelation can only

---

[54] Ibid., p.319.
[55] A. C. Cheyne, *The Transforming of the Kirk: Victorian Scotland's religious revolution* (Edinburgh: St Andrew's Press, 1983), pp.215–6.
[56] George S. Hendry, *God the Creator* (London: Hodder and Stoughton, 1937), pp.7–8.
[57] Ibid., pp.8, 16.
[58] Ibid., p.20.

be conceived, understood and affirmed by faith: 'Faith is unique, *sui generis*'.[59] 'The theology of revelation is in real contradiction with the conclusions of all natural theology', he continued, 'for the nature of God, as it is revealed to faith, is incomprehensible to reason, and, indeed, it is an offence to it'.[60] Echoing Barth's controversy with Emil Brunner, and with a pronounced polemic verve of his own, Hendry was adamant that true religion was a matter of revelation engendering faith, crisis and decision leading to a justification which was, in true Reformation fashion, *sola gratia*. 'The Christian faith is based on revelation, and revelation is not a category of thought or an extension of it', he claimed, 'but something absolutely unique, which moves in a direction contrary to that of thought and which in its impact upon thought creates a crisis'.[61]

Had he confined himself to making these affirmations alone, Hendry's volume would hardly have advanced Barthian studies at all. What made it both significant was not its rhetorical power, which it possessed in abundance, nor its uncompromising tone but its mastery of classical, patristic and medieval sources, and his copious and apposite quotations from Luther, virtually an unknown quantity among English-language scholars at the time.[62] Beginning with Platonic, Aristotelian and Stoic thought, advancing through the Apostolic Fathers, Apologists such as Clement of Alexandria, before reaching Augustine and Aquinas, he defended his contention that the ultimate metaphysical principle which philosophers and religious thinkers had sought as the integrative rational ideal underpinning the universe was not a reflection of the true God but a fallible human speculation. In direct and constant opposition to this ideal was the God of the Bible: 'The basic element in the testimony of the Old Testament is the contingent or historical character of God's revelation of himself'.[63] What validated human activity and the world itself was the fact that they existed within God's good creation which differed from, though were not independent of, their sovereign Lord. It was the particular genius of Luther that, after a millennium of speculation, he had brought this fact to light: 'Luther was brought face to face with a living, personal God, the Creator, who stands in such a relation to man that it cannot be conceived in intellectual terms at all. God is to be encountered by faith alone in his revelation of himself in his Word'.[64] Luther's *theologia crucis* was the result of his own searing experience of the real God.

---

[59] Ibid., p.21.
[60] Ibid., p.27.
[61] Ibid., p.152.
[62] For a discussion of the state of Luther studies in English, see E. Gordon Rupp, *The Righteousness of God: Luther Studies* (London: Hodder and Stoughton, 1953), pp.49–55.
[63] Hendry, *God the Creator*, p.39.
[64] Ibid., p.83.

Henceforth it would become axiomatic that God is unique and cannot be known through a process of human analogy; that God can only be known in Christ, God's gift to humankind; and that this knowledge can only be accessed through the crisis of faith leading to the justification of the ungodly. Consequently '[t]he natural idea of God is a *phantasma*, a *figmentum*, or in more modern language, a projection of the human mind'.[65]

For George Hendry it was essential that Luther's discovery be made anew in each generation. The excitement and energy which was being engendered by 'the theological awakening of the present day'[66] was proof that the process was well under way: 'The theological movement which is associated with the name of Karl Barth marks the end of the age-old acquiescence of theology in its Babylonian captivity to modern thought and beginning of a new apprehension of the godhead of God'.[67] Although entitled *God the Creator*, Hendry's book was, in fact, about revelation and epistemology rather than about God's work in creation as such. He has the briefest suggestion in the final chapter of how a treatise on God as Creator would look with the concepts of *creatio ex nihilo*, *creatio per verbum* and *creatio continua* well to the fore.[68] The book's significance, however, was not in being about creation. Precocious and supremely confident, it showed how Barth was capturing the imagination of the ablest of the younger theologians and creating fresh and innovative thought.

By the latter part of the 1930s Scotland was leading the way with New College, Edinburgh, becoming a focus for Barth's influence within the British Isles. It was to Edinburgh that the ordinands of the Yorkshire College of the Congregational Union would come for graduate study while a small stream of North American researchers chose to work with G. T. Thomson, H. R. Macintosh's successor in the chair of Christian Dogmatics, on Barthian themes.[69] Not all Scottish reaction to Barth, however, was positive. R. W. Stewart, minister at Ferryhill South Church in Aberdeen, had written scathingly in *The Hibbert Journal* that 'Barth's commentary on Romans is one of the longest books in existence and almost impossibly difficult in style'.[70] His substantive criticism was that Barth's concept of revelation

---

[65] Ibid., p.102.
[66] Ibid., p.3.
[67] Ibid., pp.154–5.
[68] Ibid., pp.178–82.
[69] The Canadian Arthur C. Cochrain, later professor at Dubuque Theological School, Iowa, and a leading proponent of Barth's thought in America, completed his PhD dissertation 'The Relation of Karl Barth to the Historic Creeds and Standards of the Church' at New College in 1937 as did the Southern Baptist Harold W. Tribble with his 'The Doctrine of Sanctification in the Theology of Karl Barth' in the same year.
[70] R. W. Stewart, 'The Theology of Crisis: a criticism', *The Hibbert Journal* 32 (1933–4), 451–4 [454].

contained no element of continuity but, like quantum theory, was a matter of 'spurts, or jerks, or blobs'.[71] Not only was this disruptive of the concept of growth or progress but it was fatal for ethics. 'The good life', claimed Stewart, 'is not character, or disposition, or purpose or anything suggesting a flow or a current: it is a series of jerks, of decisions to obey these flashes of revelation'.[72] 'May not one be amused at the incessant italics and jingling repetitions of catchwords that Barthians confuse with penetrating thought and arresting statement?'[73] he concluded. In fact, Stewart had no patience with either Barth or his Scottish disciples at all. John Baillie (1886–1960), professor of theology at Union Seminary in New York between 1930 and 1934 and thereafter holder of the Edinburgh chair of divinity (and as such H. R. Macintosh's and G. T. Thomson's colleague), was an altogether more perceptive critic, though a critic he would remain. 'In debate with my theological friends in this country', he wrote during his American sojourn, 'I have, more often than otherwise, found myself defending the Barthian positions against the very opposite principles which are professed by perhaps a majority of them'.[74] His appreciation for Barth, however, was for those elements in his work which would not, in the longer run, be most theologically significant.

> Its protests against our overweening humanism, our cheap evolutionism, our smug immanentism . . . have been most challenging, and in what it has to say about our human insignificance as over against God and our utter dependence on him for our salvation it is difficult to do anything but rejoice.[75]

Yet all this could be found, as he stated readily, in Baron von Hügel and others, thinkers which the liberal Baillie found much more congenial. As for Barth's explicit Biblicism, his refusal to countenance natural religion as a valid source of God's self-revelation as well as his highly innovative doctrine of election in which Christ, from eternity, became a covenant partner with humankind, these things rather passed him by.[76]

---

[71] Ibid., 451.

[72] Ibid., 453.

[73] Ibid., 454.

[74] John Baillie, 'Confessions of a Transplanted Scot', in Veriglius Ferm (ed.), *Contemporary American Theology* (New York: Round Table Press, 1933), pp.33–59 [53].

[75] Ibid., p.53.

[76] See David Fergusson, 'John Baillie: orthodox liberal', in idem., *Christ, Church and Society: essays on John and Donald Baillie* (Edinburgh: T& T Clark, 1993), pp.123–53.

Nathaniel Micklem and 'Natural Theology'

The links between Scotland and English Nonconformity were not insubstantial while it was among the Congregationalists, as we have seen, that Barth's thought was finding its most fruitful soil. Nathaniel Micklem was continuing his urbane crusade to call Congregationalists back to their historical legacy. 'There have arisen some amongst us who frankly reject the testimony of the prophets and apostles as the standard and rule of our churches', he told the Congregational Theological Conference in July 1934. 'This is an issue on which there can be no compromise. It is a fundamental principle of our common Protestantism that it is the preaching of the Word of God that constitutes the church'.[77] His polished blueprint for doctrinal orthodoxy *What is the Faith?* appeared in 1936 followed a year later by a trenchant apologia for a Congregational high churchmanship entitled *Congregationalism Today.* Both expanded upon what had become a passionate conviction: 'Congregationalism had stood, stands today and will stand inside, not outside, the common catholic and evangelical tradition of Latin Christendom'.[78] Neither was this a matter of religious convenience but it had implications for the very nature of salvation and the church: 'If anyone should deny that we are redeemed by the precious blood of Christ, he would be cutting himself off from the church catholic'.[79]

Yet Micklem's premier contribution in the late 1930s was as a lifeline to the Confessing Church. His visits to Germany, first over Easter 1937 when he took part in the illegal ordination of a pastor into the Church's ministry, and then a year later, in the company of his student Alec Whitehouse, when he covertly supported the Catholic Church during its troubles with the Nazis, were key events in the Christian opposition to the regime: 'Few, if any, other English visitors were privileged to share so fully in the daily life of the Confessing Church'.[80] In two remarkable articles, one on the theological issues in the German Church Conflict and a second in which he linked Barth's Barmen theology with the campaign against the dominance of liberal theology within his own communion, he elucidated the current situation with startling clarity. 'Herr Hitler does not add to his other striking

---

[77] Nathaniel Micklem, 'The Holy Spirit and a new creed', *The Congregational Quarterly* 12 (1934), 545–57 [552].

[78] Ibid., 552.

[79] Ibid., 556.

[80] Elaine Kaye, *Mansfield College: its origin, history and significance* (Oxford: Oxford University Press, 1996), p.207; cf. M. Daphne Hampson, 'The British response to the German Church Struggle, 1933–9', unpublished Oxford University DPhil dissertation, 1973, p.198; for Micklem's own recollections of this period see his autobiography *The Box and the Puppets* (London: Geoffrey Bles, 1957), pp.105–13.

gifts the competence of a theologian',[81] he informed the readers of the Chicago-based journal *Christendom*, yet the character of his movement possessed a malign spirituality which had been championed by Alfred Rosenberg, the Nazi's court philosopher with his myth of blood and soil. The church, by definition, could only be concerned with its inner life and the hope of a world to come, while the *Weltanschauung* or world order was one in which the state reigned supreme:

> The church must confine its attention to the esoteric experiences of its members . . . abandoning without qualification its prophetic ministry and its claim to speak to the nation in the name of God . . . Hence in Herr Hitler's view, there are no martyrs of the faith in Germany, but only politically minded parsons who forget their place and calling.[82]

Rosenberg's theories had demonized the Jews, reinterpreted Christianity bizarrely as an Aryan faith, and created a 'pure' spirituality in which the virtues of humility and lowliness had given way to an ethic of racial superiority. There were Christians in Germany, both Catholic and Protestant, who realized the implications of this policy, but the churches as such had been emasculated and those who did speak out were treated as political rather than religious dissidents. 'Protestantism is deeply under the influence of Professor Karl Barth',[83] he reported, while even Catholics with their own Christian *Weltanschauung* based upon the philosophy of St Thomas Aquinas realized the power of Barth's doctrine in the day of trial: 'A world that is half mad must be confronted solely with the Word of God'.[84] Yet both communions were presently under the cross: 'Never have the two been so near together, never has there been such a good understanding between them as now . . . The Protestants would have us understand that the integrity of the Christian gospel is at stake: the Romans that Christian civilization in Europe is now jeopardized. I think that they both are right'.[85] Benign English tolerance and the enlightened (and Enlightenment) American division of church and state were of little help in trying to comprehend the enormity of the situation in Germany or its impending evil, but the bonds of a common confession of Christ's lordship compelled Christians to involve themselves in the current struggle. These issues 'come before us with

---

[81] Nathanial Micklem, 'Theological issues in the German Church Conflict', *Christendom* 3 (1938), 250–9 [250].

[82] Ibid., 251.

[83] Ibid., 255.

[84] Ibid., 255.

[85] Ibid., 256.

particular pathos because our German brethren are facing them, not in the calm of academic thought, but in the flames of persecution'.[86]

His second essay had to do specifically with a valid theology of the church. Of the three variants of contemporary faith there was the Catholic, the Protestant and the liberal: 'Here the concept is that faith is a more or less confident assent to a *Weltanschauung* or philosophy of life . . . it is distinguishable from knowledge but scarcely from opinion'.[87] It was this view which had infected bourgeois Nonconformity for two generations and was proving lethal in contemporary Germany: 'This is the view of faith which . . . has virtually driven out from a large part of the Protestant world the notion of faith held by the Reformers. It is rationalism, not Protestant-ism. It takes the name of faith but it generally corresponds to what our fathers deemed to be unbelief'.[88] It was against this that Barth's theology and the Barman Declaration had waged total war. According to this view it may well have been that God had not left himself without witness within nature, culture, history and philosophy as well as that which was good and wholesome in ordinary human life. It was apposite for the philosophers to philosophize and for creative people to reflect on the source of life: 'But all this has nothing to do with the distinctive Christian revelation, which is revelation in a different mode'.[89] In the gospel a radical disjunction had occurred: 'In Jesus Christ discussion ended, for God came himself, "and we beheld his glory"'.[90] It was this conviction, commonplace among the Protestant fathers and witnessed to even by the two-tier theology of St Thomas Aquinas and the Catholic Church, that had been fatally dissi-pated by Protestant liberalism: 'The German controversy . . . is only a striking and crucial instance of a hidden conflict throughout Protestantism in all other lands'.[91]

For the Nazi-supporting 'German Christians' whose theology was so plausible and whose ethos was in accord with the folk religion of their land – a point which had been emphasized so positively by Bishop Headlam and Dr A. J. Macdonald – their only aim had been to make Christianity relevant once more. 'This is simply the contemporary German form of that which in an English or American idiom scores of our ministers have been saying for a generation', he wrote. 'Christianity must be accommodated to the "modern mind"; it must not be tied to outworn formulations; it must

---

[86] Ibid., 259.
[87] Nathaniel Micklem, 'The faith by which the church lives', *International Review of Missions* 38 (1938), 321–32 [322].
[88] Ibid., 322.
[89] Ibid., 324.
[90] Ibid., 324.
[91] Ibid. 325.

be restated in the light of modern ideals and the thought-forms of the age'.[92] The one defect in this otherwise admirable scheme was that it cut itself off from the normative authority of the Bible: 'It has, in effect, repudiated that first principle upon which all our churches rest – that the Holy Scriptures of the Old and New Testaments are the standard and rule of faith'.[93] Taking an example from an American source of a recent attempt to modernize the faith very much like that of the Blackheath Group among English Congregationalists that he had fulminated against a few years before, he repeated his contention: 'I do not doubt that we have here a more or less Christianized *Weltanschuung* or philosophy of life; I do not doubt that we have a basis for a civilizing mission. But we are not within sight of the Christian gospel . . . We are apt to smile at such extravagances as heretical. This is not heresy, it is unbelief'.[94] For Micklem, Karl Barth's great contribution had been to clarify the issue once and for all, while the task of the Confessing Church had been to witness unflinchingly to it in practice:

> There is no doubt what is the heart and kernel of the Christian gospel, and there is no doubt what is missing from these syncretistic modernisms, whether in Germany or America or England. We greatly deceive ourselves if we think that the German Church Conflict, as we call it, is a local matter for the Germans. It represents in the clearest form the issue which confronts us all.[95]

Barth himself, visiting Britain in the spring of 1937 to deliver the Gifford Lectures at Aberdeen, had already clarified from the perspective of the Confessing Church what the theological issues really were. For most British observers, the struggle was more about freedom of opinion than doctrinal purity as such. What appalled most church people was that Christians were being imprisoned for speaking their minds. For Barth, Dietrich Bonhoeffer and Martin Niemöller (who would be detained and placed in solitary confinement on 3 July), the matter had everything to do with costly obedience to the demands of the gospel. In a reception at the Russell Hotel in London sponsored by the Evangelical Alliance, a body which was wholly supportive of Barth's theology during these years,[96] Barth said:

> The fact that 'freedom of conscience' and 'freedom of the Church' are approved in Britain and that all atrocities are detested and that these

---

[92] Ibid. 326.
[93] Ibid., 327.
[94] Ibid., 330.
[95] Ibid., 332.
[96] See Ian M. Randall and David Hilborn, *One Body in Christ: the history and significance of the Evangelical Alliance* (Carlisle: Paternoster Press, 2001), pp.202–5.

views find ready expression is well known in Germany, but it makes not the slightest impression on the National Socialists . . . And the Confessional Church is not thereby helped because the fight is not about freedom but about the necessary bondage of the conscience, and not about the *freedom* but about the *substance* of the Church. It is about the preservation, rediscovery and authentication of the true Christian faith. It is not waiting to hear the voice of the British citizen saying once again what every stout Briton has been saying for many centuries, but . . . the voice of the Church in Britain saying now what can only be said in the Holy Spirit, only in recollection of what the Holy Scriptures say.[97]

Rather than admiring the Confessing Church for its stand, the best thing that British Christians could do was to make the theology of the Barmen Declaration its own:

The only real help, apart from your prayers, which you can render the German Church would consist in this: in declaring with as much publicity and solemnity as was done in Barmen itself that in your conviction also, a conviction arising from Holy Scripture, [that] this statement . . . is the right and necessary expression of the Christian faith for our day and therefore also *your* confession of faith.[98]

The Congregational Theological Conference took place in Oxford on 12–15 July 1937, a week following Niemöller's arrest. The conference theme was 'Revelation and Faith' in which the liberal minister Thomas Wigley speaking on the subject 'Faith, Fact and Knowledge' was countered directly by F. W. Camfield in a paper entitled 'The Barthian Challenge'. The fact that the more mediating figures of R. S. Franks, John Short, H. Cunliffe-Jones and John Marsh could agree that true religion needed to be rooted in revelation, that revelation, though rational, shone in its own light, that the key to its interpretation was Israel and Christ, knowledge of both being accessed through faith which in turn was God's unique gift, showed the extent of Barth's impact.[99] It was patent that Micklem's campaign was succeeding and that a new theological consensus among the younger ministers of the Congregational order, was being achieved.

It was no coincidence that it was Mansfield College that hosted a reception for Barth when he was in Oxford a year later to receive an

---

[97] 'Karl Barth answers a question: how can churches abroad help the German Evangelical Church?', *The British Weekly*, 22 April 1937, 71.

[98] 'Karl Barth answers a question', 71.

[99] John Marsh and Geoffrey F. Nuttall, 'The Congregational Theological Conference, 1937', *The Congregational Quarterly* 15 (1937), 498–505.

honorary DD before making his way to Aberdeen for the second series of his Gifford Lectures.[100] This was the occasion of a remarkable lecture, 'Trouble and Promise in the Struggle of the Church in Germany', which he gave in Lady Margaret Hall on 4 March 1938. By then, and despite Bishop Headlam's support for the German regime which was manipulated deftly by the Nazi propaganda machine,[101] all pretences had vanished and people had come to recognize Hitler for what he was. Niemöller's detention in a concentration camp as the Führer's 'personal prisoner' in February 1938 had inflamed popular opinion in Britain even more, and Barth's fierce lecture served to solidify opposition. Although, as a Swiss, he was no longer directly involved in the activities of the Confessing Church and remaining highly critical of its Lutheran bishops who refused to engage in a political critique of the Nazi ideology, he extolled the Church's virtues and its heroism: 'The courage, the patience, the faithfulness, and, not least, the nerves of even the best people in the Confessing Church have by this time been subjected to a hard trial after nearly five years of unbroken struggle.'[102] Despite its narrow remit and concern for its own ecclesiastical discipline rather than wider issues including the defence of the Jews, it was the Confessing Church which had provided a foil to the Nazis when political parties, the judiciary, the universities and trades unions had either capitulated or been silenced. The Roman Catholics had been muzzled while the Free Churches (though Barth did not mention this), the Baptists and the Methodists, had made their peace with the regime. It was only the Confessing pastors and their flocks who continued to stand fast: 'In the midst of these men, who have failed often and in many respects, there lived and lives a power that has not failed, and that power was the Word of God'.[103] The troubles were still manifest, and Barth implored his audience to do all they could to support the Confessional Church in as many ways as possible. Yet he was far from being cast down. God's promises remained valid while the miracle of the divine presence had manifested itself again and again in this Church under the cross: 'In the course of this trouble the church in Germany has been allowed to make a discovery; the discovery, in fact, of the majesty of the foundation

---

[100] Kaye, *Mansfield College*, p.208; Eberhart Busch, *Karl Barth: his life from letters and autobiographical texts* (London: SCM, 1976), p.287.

[101] *Der Bishof von Gloucester über Volkstum, Christentum und Kirche in England und Deutschland* (Berlin, 1939) which was a translation of his article in the Anglican newspaper *The Guardian* of 2 September 1938 extolling the virtues of the official Protestant church and its link with the German state; see Hampson, 'The British Response to the German Church Struggle, 1933–9', p.290.

[102] Karl Barth, *Trouble and Promise in the Struggle of the Church in Germany* (Oxford: Clarendon Press, 1938), p.16.

[103] Ibid., p.22.

on which the church stands, of the *majesty of the Word of God*.[104] It was this Word and not the might of armies or the whims of dictators which would last forever.

The Gifford Lectures and their implications

By the late 1930s there was little reason for the theology of Karl Barth to be unknown or misunderstood in Britain. His most faithful interpreters, John McConnachie, R. Birch Hoyle, H. R. Mackintosh and now George S. Hendry, had prepared the ground thoroughly while the essence of his mature theology was coming more and more into the public domain. Although his contribution to the thought of the incipient ecumenical movement, an essay in John Baillie's preparatory symposium for the important gatherings of the Council for Life and Work in Oxford, July 1937, and Faith and Order in Edinburgh a month later, traversed the perhaps over-familiar ground of 'revelation',[105] other works such as *Credo*, the essays in *God in Action* to say nothing of the bold trinitarianism of *The Doctrine of the Word of God* illustrated something of the breadth of Barth's vision. R. Birch Hoyle's further translation of a 1929 lecture as *The Holy Ghost and the Christian Life* (1938) gave a further insight into the content of Barth's evolving theology.[106] It was the Gifford Lectures, however, which made quite explicit where Barth stood on a whole range of doctrinal issues. The quite remarkable though little commented on series of lectures delivered in Aberdeen in two phases, the first in March 1937 and the second a year later, show how Barth's mature theology, already present in embryo in the Göttingen cycle of 1924–25,[107] was brought to bear on John Knox's little-known (even in Scotland) Scottish Confession of 1560. Barth had, in fact, immersed himself in the confessional theology of the Protestant Reformers as early as 1923,[108] and was now keen to convince the theologians of Aberdeen that their heritage was not to be despised: 'The confession of John Knox is a good confession and moreover, in many respects a very original

---

[104] Ibid., p.20.
[105] Karl Barth, 'Chapter 2' in John Baillie and Hugh Martin, *Revelation* (London: Faber and Faber, 1937), pp.41–81.
[106] Karl Barth, *The Holy Ghost and the Christian Life* (London: Fredrick Muller, 1938).
[107] See Bruce L. McCormack, *Karl Barth's Critically Realistic Dialectical Theology: its genesis and development, 1909–36* (Oxford: Clarendon Press, 1995), pp.327–74.
[108] See Karl Barth, *The Theology of the Reformed Confessions* (Louisville: Westminster Press, 2002); cf. John Webster, *Karl Barth's Early Theology* (Edinburgh: T & T Clark,), pp.41–66.

and interesting confession'.[109] It was on the basis of this that he explained to a British audience what his own theological scheme was all about.

The Gifford Lectures, of course, were explicitly intended to elucidate the meaning of natural theology. The dilemma of Barth was acute: 'I certainly see – with astonishment – that such a science as Lord Gifford had in mind does exist, but I do not see how it is possible for it to exist. I am convinced that so far as it has existed and still exists, it owes its existence to a radical error'.[110] In order to show how erroneous, in his own eyes, the concept was, he used the confession – with the ready approval of his Scottish hosts – to highlight its perceived errors: 'The background and antithesis to "natural theology" . . . is the knowledge of God according to the teaching of the Reformation',[111] and he proceeded, as a Reformed theologian, to set out his thesis. In his ten lectures, corresponding to Articles 1–10 of Knox's Confession, he explained what had become his own highly original version of the Reformed faith. God was not just the sovereign Lord, rather He had acted in his very essence in order to be for and with humankind: 'The Reformed church and Reformed theology have never spoken about God and man as if God were everything and man were nothing. That is a carica-ture of Reformed teaching'.[112] God as creator presupposes a creation in which He has chosen to be bounteous and merciful. Moreover, He has done this from eternity in Christ: 'Let us proceed from the simple fact that in the revelation of God in Jesus Christ, God and man meet, and therefore are really together'.[113] In Christ humankind becomes not God's antithesis or his servant still less his slave but his covenant partner and consort. Humankind too possesses glory.

Man, of course, as the gospel had always claimed, is still a sinner. There is no room for any Enlightenment optimism as to human perfectibility or guiltlessness; humans are fallen and under judgement and the object of the divine wrath. But there is something more central to human disobedience and God's righteous condemnation, namely that God has chosen for human-kind: 'That man is *against* God is true and important and has to be taken seriously. But what is ever truer, *more* important and to be taken *more* seri-ously is the other fact that God in Jesus Christ is *for* man'.[114] It is here that Barth's celebrated universal Christocentricism shows itself in clear relief: 'In this Lord and head, Jesus Christ, God and man, God and sinful man, are one. For this reason God maintains fellowship with all the men that belong

---

[109] Karl Barth, *The Knowledge of God and the Service of God* (London: Hodder and Stoughton, 1938), p.11.

[110] Ibid., p.5.

[111] Ibid., p.8.

[112] Ibid., p.35.

[113] Ibid., p.36.

[114] Ibid., p.46.

to that people (namely humankind), whose Lord and head is Jesus Christ'.[115] This is not fortuitous; it has nothing to do with man as man; man is sinner and as such is damned, his will is in bondage and the *imago Dei* has been hopelessly marred. In no way can sin be downplayed. Yet God is for humankind because he has chosen, or elected, to do so. Election is no abstraction, neither does it have to do with two distinct groups, the reprobate and the saved. It has, rather, to do with Adam, the whole human race, and even more basically with the Second Adam, Jesus Christ: 'God's eternal decree and man's election and thus the whole of what is called the doctrine of predestination cannot but be misunderstood unless it is understood in its connection with the truth of the divine-human nature of Jesus Christ'.[116]

Barth had been contemplating this radical recasting of the doctrine of election for a long time. His friend the French Reformed pastor Pierre Maury had also been led along the same path, in his case for explicitly pastoral reasons – how could those in anguish of soul know that they were among the elect? – and in the international Calvinist conference in Geneva in 1936 Maury gave a paper on election from a Christological standpoint which sharpened Barth's views considerably.[117] Going beyond the view of the *Göttingen Dogmatics* that election was to be understood existentially and dynamically and not according to a rationalistic scheme which posited the existence of a fixed decree in which God had chosen pre-temporally who would be saved and who would be damned, Maury, and thereafter Barth, had grounded the decree in the eternal choice of Jesus Christ as God's elect. It was a revolutionary reworking of the system. It would be treated in detail by Barth in the *Kirchliche Dogmatik* II/2 (1942) though it found its way, in a much paired down form, into the seventh Aberdeen lecture, 'God's Decision and Man's Election'. What is remarkable is that no-one, even in Calvinistic Scotland, seems to have remarked upon its novelty at the time. When Barth's lectures, translated by two young theologians, the Scot Ian Henderson and the Belfast Presbyterian J. L. M. Haire, was published as a substantial 240-page volume at the end of 1938, they scarcely created a ripple. The book was hardly reviewed, and when it was, as by A. L. Lilley in the *Journal of Theological Studies*, its significance was not apparent.[118] As the outbreak of war loomed ever nearer, Barth's theology, if not his courageous stand against Hitler, was either misconstrued or else ignored by bulk of Britain's religious establishment.

---

[115] Ibid., p.59.

[116] Ibid., p.77.

[117] See Pierre Maury, *Predestination and Other Papers* (London: SCM, 1960); cf. McCormack, *Karl Barth's Critically Realistic Dialectical Theology*, pp.453–8.

[118] A. L. Lilley, review of Barth, *The Knowledge of God and the Service of God*, in *The Journal of Theological Studies* 41 (1940), 212–4.

8

BARTH RECEPTION IN
WARTIME AND BEYOND

Daniel T. Jenkins and the catholicity of the Word

'The small group of faithful followers of Karl Barth in this country have begun almost to despair of his ever being understood by the mass of English theological writers'.[1] The young Congregationalist Daniel T. Jenkins's sigh of frustration, shared with the world in December 1939, was not without justification. Of those who had been arrested by Barth, they still tended to see him only as the prophet of divine transcendence and the one key theologian who had reminded the church that a unique revelation was essential for a true knowledge of God. For those who had been immune to Barth's allure or repelled by his certainties, they reacted either with incredulity or with scorn.

C. J. Cadoux, Jenkins's teacher of church history at Mansfield College, Oxford, found himself completely out of sympathy with the new doctrinal consensus which was being forged. Commenting on C. H. Dodd's *History and the Gospel* (1938), he deplored the refusal to go behind the kerygma in order to discover the historical figure of 'the real Jesus', and resented the Barthian shibboleth of 'judgement' and the idea of an extreme moral incapacity due to sin: 'It is quite foreign to the mind of Jesus as he is described in the gospels'.[2] Dodd, Norris-Hulse Professor of Divinity at Cambridge, had vacated the Yates chair in New Testament in Mansfield College in 1930 and had become probably the premier New Testament scholar of his generation.[3] His descent into obscurantism was, for the more enlightened Cadoux,

---

[1] Daniel Jenkins, 'Mr Demant and Karl Barth', *Theology* 39 (1939), 412–20 [412].
[2] C. J. Cadoux, review of C. H. Dodd, *History and the Gospel* (London: Nisbet, 1938) in *Mansfield College Magazine* 10 (1934–41), 588–92 [591].
[3] See F. W. Dillistone, *C. H. Dodd, Interpreter of the New Testament* (London: Hodder and Stoughton, 1977).

wholly regrettable: 'The frequent occurrence of technical terms and phrases characteristic of the Barthian theology makes it clear (for the first time so far as my knowledge goes) that Dodd has definite leanings in the direction of Barthianism'.[4] Cadoux's even then superseded method of ignoring the miraculous elements in the gospel in order to discover the 'ethical and spiritual grandeur' of Christ's person in his simple obedience to the Father's will, was at odds with Dodd's insistence that his person could not be divorced from the apostolic interpretation of his significance: 'Barthians, at least, will cordially approve of the methods adopted. Those, however, who regard the Barthian theology as obscurantist and reactionary, will necessarily feel some hesitation on the matter'.[5] It was not only Congregationalists who were appalled by the Barthian tenets, Anglicans were similarly aggrieved. 'I must confess to finding Barth's teaching almost impossible to understand', wrote the Anglo-Catholic E. G. Selwyn, formerly editor of *Theology* and brother-in-law of the late Sir Edwyn C. Hoskyns. 'It suffers, I believe, from precisely the same irrationality as the [Roman] doctrine of infallibility. The truth it asserts is left *in vacuo*, unrelated to any of the ordinary operations of human thought, incapable of being criticized and therefore incapable of being understood'.[6] Epithets such as obscurantist and reactionary, irrational and incomprehensible were the common currency of the time.

Just as John McConnachie and F. W. Camfield had been compelled to enlighten English-speaking people as to Barth's contribution during the inter-war years, Daniel T. Jenkins took the lead in spreading the Barthian message, especially as it applied to church order, during the 1940s and 1950s. Responding to the Anglican social theologian Vigo Demant's criticism of 'neo-Calvinist transcendental supernaturalism'[7] in his volume *The Religious Prospect* (1939), he quailed at what appeared to be a wilful caricature: 'No theologian can ever have been subject to more irrelevant criticism and few can have been so frequently damned with a faint praise which has been given for the wrong reasons'.[8] For Demant, the only answer to the problem of existence at such a critical period in European history was a catholic social teaching of the Anglican variety. The renewal of natural law would be essential for society's wellbeing with a second world war already in sight. For him, 'the neo-Lutheranism and neo-Calvinism which have appeared in the forceful teaching of Karl Barth and his followers are, in fact, an evasion of the problem'.[9] By positing such a radical bifurcation between nature and grace, Barth's neo-Calvinism had become

[4] Cadoux, review of C. H. Dodd, *History and the Gospel*, 590.
[5] Ibid., *History and the Gospel*, 590.
[6] E. G. Selwyn, 'The outlook for English theology', *Theology* 40 (1940), 6–14 [10].
[7] V. A. Demant, *The Religious Prospect* (London: Frederick Muller, 1939), p.182.
[8] Jenkins, 'Mr Demant and Karl Barth', 412.
[9] Demant, *The Religious Prospect*, p.179.

virtually heretical: 'The identity of God as creator and preserver, and God as redeemer and saviour, is no more than a verbal affirmation', he claimed. What is more, 'God's hand cannot be discerned in history. The incarnation becomes not a central point which infuses meaning into history, but a historical event unrelated to all other historical happenings'.[10] 'The abstract transcendentalism of theological Protestantism'[11] condemned everything to the wrath of God and the divine 'No', he was sure, making ethical discernment impossible and all moral effort redundant.

There was little wonder that Jenkins viewed such prejudice with a weary disdain. By that time not only some of Barth's earliest essays had been long available, but the Romans commentary, the *Credo* volume, the essays in *God in Action* and *Revelation*, the treatise on the Holy Spirit and, more pointedly, *Church Dogmatics* I/1 and the Gifford lectures, provided a body of material which allowed a much more informed assessment of Barth's constructive thought to be made: 'Practically every point that [Mr Demant] makes can be confuted out of Barth's own words'.[12] Jenkins proceeded to show that Barth's concept of faith was highly objective, that the ethical note had been there from the beginning, that the extended treatment of the Trinity in *Church Dogmatics* I/1 posited the nature of the difference between God as creator and God as redeemer in an unambiguous way, and that Demant's own concept of natural law needed to be challenged by something exterior to itself: 'Mr Demant cannot evaluate the theology expounded by Barth from the view-point of a Catholic philosophy of being without at least recognizing the fact that Barth, with full self-consciousness, has delivered a terrific onslaught on the very foundations of that philosophy'.[13] It was too glib to say that both Barth's own thought and that of his followers was the result of a cultural pessimism engendered by the malaise of the age:

> For our part, it was not any 'wave of apocalyptic pessimism' which drove us to Barth's teaching, but a discovery that here at last was a theologian who did justice to biblical revelation and, because he did that, did justice to the conditions of life on this earth as well, who, in fact, provided a sound ethical criterion, without the externality of Catholic ethics on the one hand and without the irrelevance of liberal pacifist ethics on the other.[14]

What was remarkable about Jenkins's article was that its author was still only a theological student at the time. Its sure grasp of Barth's thought,

---

[10] Ibid., pp.179–80.
[11] Ibid., pp.181.
[12] Jenkins, 'Mr Demant and Karl Barth', 412.
[13] Ibid., 418.
[14] Ibid., 416.

illustrated by a mastery of the available material, is complemented by an enviable maturity of thought and strength of expression. 'Barth claims that he has rediscovered the true theological method, that of attempting to let the Word of God speak for itself',[15] he continued.

> The church . . . does not possess the Word of God once for all as an assured possession; she is always in process of becoming the body of Christ, and therefore she must constantly be making the movement of re-formation, of bringing herself ever anew into subjection to the Word of God, if she is to continue to be the church.[16]

This, too, was the basis of a true scheme of biblical ethics. God's command was not a static entity, accessible through a process of logical deduction and innate within human consciousness, but a dynamic reality in which God's sovereignty was preserved: 'Mr Demant's preoccupation with natural law refuses to take this seriously . . . Ultimately, it is a debate concerning the nature of the operation of the Holy Spirit, and therefore concerning the nature of God himself'.[17] 'The scripture', he concluded, 'must ever be *becoming* the Word of God to us and the constraints of existence must ever be *acquiring* the character of God's commands through God's Word to us'.[18]

Daniel Thomas Jenkins (1914–2002) was a Welsh Congregationalist, the son of a brick-mason, from Dowlais, Glamorgan, in the industrial heartland. He had entered the Yorkshire United Independent College at Bradford in 1932 where E. J. Price was principal and H. F. Lovell Cocks, a pupil of P. T. Forsyth, taught doctrine. Following a long-standing arrangement, arts students were enrolled at Edinburgh University to read for a preparatory degree before returning to Bradford to study for the post-graduate BD. Consequently, between 1932 and 1935 Jenkins was in Edinburgh being exposed to Reformed churchmanship and taking in something of the Barthian renewal that was being felt north of the border at the time. At Bradford both Price and Cocks were in full sympathy with the Genevan renaissance which was being so effectively championed by Bernard Lord Manning, Nathaniel Micklem and John Whale. Cocks, whose own theology approximated that of his mentor, Forsyth,[19] confirmed Jenkins in his churchmanship and emboldened his appropriation of Barth's thought. In 1937 Jenkins was in Mansfield College, Oxford, which was (despite the presence

---

[15] Ibid., 417.

[16] Ibid., 417.

[17] Ibid., 419.

[18] Ibid., 419.

[19] See Alan P. F. Sell, 'Theology for All: the contribution of H. F. Lovell Cocks', in *Commemorations: studies in Christian thought and history* (Cardiff: University of Wales Press, 1993), 303–40.

of C. J. Cadoux as professor of church history) the intellectual centre of the Genevan movement.[20] There he made the acquaintance of W. A. (Alec) Whitehouse and John Huxtable, ministerial candidates and future leaders of the churchly and orthodox renewal among Congregationalists during the 1940s and 1950s. Jenkins's ordination, aged 26, at the Vineyard Congregational Church, Richmond, Surrey, in 1940, signalled the beginning of an extraordinarily fruitful period of literary and ecumenical activity which would include the publication of a series of volumes including *The Nature of Catholicity* (1942), *Prayer and the Service of God* (1944) and *The Gift of Ministry* (1947), membership of J. H. Oldham's high-powered discussion group 'the Moot',[21] the secretaryship of the Christian Frontier Council, the editorship of *The Christian News-Letter* (1945–47) and, in 1948, a Commonwealth Fund Fellowship to study in Union Seminary, New York. Not the least of his activities during these frenetic years was to found and co-edit the journal *The Presbyter: a journal of confessional and Catholic churchmanship* (1943–48), which would prove the principal forum for Barth reception in Britain at the time.

Jenkins's first book, *Britain and the Future*, was based on a series of sermons delivered during the spring of 1941 when the Luftwaffe's bombs were raining down from the London skies. Despite the grim nature of the situation, it exudes the steely confidence which was characteristic of the Christian realism of the time. The volume's underlying theology is of Christ as revealer of true humanity which Jenkins would develop more fully over the subsequent years: 'The faith of our forefathers in the living God who made and rules all things and in the light of whose revelation of himself in Jesus Christ they saw their own true nature and the way to attain the fullness of manhood'.[22] Sin was as much a refusal to attain the status of human maturity as wilful disobedience to the divine command. The only alternative to Hitler on the one hand and indolence and apathy on the other was 'Jesus Christ as proper man'.[23] The genius of Congregationalism was that it presupposed full equality within the Body of Christ whereby each individual could rediscover the full measure of their true humanity: 'The true life of humanity is that of the Body of Christ, and it is only as members of that body that we are able to act like *men*.'[24] For Jenkins, Barth's theology

---

[20] See Elaine Kaye, *Mansfield College, Oxford: its Origin, history and significance* (Oxford: Oxford University Press, 1996), pp.189–210.

[21] See Keith W. Clements, *Faith on the Frontier: a life of J. H. Oldham* (Edinburgh: T & T Clark, 1999), pp.363–88; William Taylor and Marjorie Reeves, 'Intellectuals in debate: the Moot' in Marjorie Reeves (ed.), *Christian Thinking and Social Order: conviction politics from the 1930s to the present day* (London: Cassell, 1999), pp.24–48.

[22] Daniel T. Jenkins, *Britain and the Future* (London: SCM, 1941), p.20.

[23] Ibid., p.22.

[24] Ibid., p.64.

was essential for a churchly renewal which would energize the body for the onerous tasks which would lie ahead. 'The best way in which we can serve mankind', he claimed, 'is not by listening in the first place to what men are saying about God, but by listening to what God is saying to man in Jesus Christ'.[25] The renewal of the church was key to the wider renewal of civic society along Christian lines: 'It is only in the light of the revelation of God, the creator of all things, in Jesus Christ, that we are able to understand what man is and what the divine laws governing society are'.[26] For Jenkins Christendom was a given while Congregationalism's role was prophetically to critique the status quo but not to diverge fundamentally from it. In allying himself with a rather bourgeois if theologically informed churchliness, the brick-mason's son from Dowlais would shed not only much of his Welshness but lose something of the outsider's angularity as well. Nevertheless, it was Daniel Jenkins who would provide much of the energy for the Barthian renewal which contributed so signally to the vitality of English Christianity at the time.

The wartime years were strangely stimulating and conducive to a reappraisal of Christianity as an apposite basis for civil regeneration.[27] Even such an inveterate agnostic as Winston Churchill could use the rhetoric of 'the survival of Christian civilization' to inspire the people to vanquish Nazism as being both a pernicious and an anti-religious evil.[28] The flow of English culture during the 1930s had been from irreligion to religion, from agnosticism to faith and, within the churches, from modernism to orthodoxy. The rediscovery of vital Christianity by such key cultural figures as T. S. Eliot, Rosalind Murray, C. S. Lewis and Dorothy Sayers would register forcefully a decade later. In fact, this 'collective return of Christianity' by 'some of the most influential figures in contemporary culture . . . represents one of the most significant characteristics of the 1935–45 years'.[29] It was paralleled by the flowering of Christian creativity in France through such towering literary figures as Paul Claudel, François Mauriac and Georges Bernanos and Jacques Maritain, Etienne Gilson and Yves Congar in the fields of philosophy and theology. Daniel Jenkins, for his part, was inspired by 'the tremendous Christian renewal of this generation,'[30] and was among those who were girding themselves to create a more just and equitable social

---

[25] Ibid., p.36.

[26] Ibid., p.75.

[27] Keith Robbins, *England, Ireland, Scotland, Wales: the Christian Church, 1900–2000* (Oxford: Oxford University Press, 2008), pp.279–93.

[28] See Keith Robbins, 'Britain, 1940 and "Christian Civilization"' in *History, Religion and Identity in Modern Britain* (London: Hambledon Press, 1993), pp.195–214.

[29] Adrian Hastings, *A History of English Christianity, 1920–2000* (London: SCM, 2001), p.290.

[30] Jenkins, *Britain and the Future*, p.38.

order after the war had been won. The missionary statesman J. H. Oldham's *Christian News-Letter*, established in October 1939, encapsulated this ideal perfectly. Its aim would be 'the growth of a body of people dedicated to the task of creating a new order of society' beyond fascism and communism, 'a community of free persons united under the rule of law, directing its activities increasingly to Christian ends and leavened by Christian insights, values and standards'.[31] For Jenkins it was inconceivable that the new Europe to emerge after the war could be anything less than Christian. As Karl Barth and the German Church Struggle had shown, a Christianity of the Word was the only way to check tyranny and create a truly humane order according to the divine plan. Despite the parlous situation of the country in the spring of 1941, there was no hint of defeatism. In the current Christian renewal, faith and fortitude had come together. 'We have rediscovered the apostolic faith which made Europe great', he claimed. 'This is the most significant fact about the world today'.[32]

Just as the work of Hoskyns and Dodd in New Testament studies had restored confidence in the basic historical reliability of the gospels and the congruence of its creed with the facts of apostolic Christianity, the inter-war years had seen a renewed interest in ecclesiology and the concept of churchmanship. If Anglo-Catholicism with its already developed ecclesiality had become more biblical, Protestant Nonconformity had become more churchly. Nathaniel Micklem, the Methodist R. Newton Flew and others had reacted violently against the unchecked individualism which they believed had vitiated the witness of the Edwardian piety in which they had been raised, while the biblical scholarship of Wheeler Robinson and William Manson had emphasized the corporate implications of evangelical faith. Neither was Barth's switch from *Christian* Dogmatics in 1927 to *Church* Dogmatics in 1932 inconsequential. C. H. Dodd's reconstruction of the earliest Christian preaching illustrated how the gospel message contained an announcement of Christ's messianic status in which the community of a new Israel was constituted. Forgiveness of sin, the promise of salvation and the gift of the Holy Spirit included a shared appropriation of God's redemptive Word in Christ. Faith, therefore, was not a matter of individual conviction but a deeply corporate reality.[33] For Flew the liberal idea that Jesus had not intended to found a church was deeply flawed. The thesis of his influential *Jesus and his Church* (1938) was that the preaching of the Kingdom presupposed the calling of an *ecclesia*, a 'little flock' or covenanted community

---

[31] *The Christian News-Letter*, 22 November 1939, 3; for *The Christian News-Letter* see Clements, *Faith on the Frontier*, pp.389–406; Marjorie Reeves and Elaine Kaye, 'Tracts for Wartime: *The Christian News-Letter*' in Reeves (ed.), *Christian Thinking and Social Order*, pp.49–79.

[32] Jenkins, *Britain and the Future*, p.37.

[33] C. H. Dodd, *The Apostolic Preaching and Its Developments* (London: Nisbet, 1937).

which would mediate Christ's saving and sacramental presence until his coming again in glory.[34] The kingdom, therefore, would not yield to the church during the present dispensation and churchmanship was essential to the gospel. It was on this background that Daniel Jenkins issued his *The Nature of Catholicity* in 1942. It was a highly accomplished work which would 'mark an epoch', as Lovell Cocks was soon to write, in the development of Dissenting ecclesiology.[35] It was also the ablest treatise to date to blend Barth's dogmatic concerns with the renewal of British Reformed churchmanship which was already under way.

The 28-year-old Congregationalist laid out his presuppositions clearly: 'To take the church seriously is more than to be concerned over questions of order and organization. It is to conceive of the concrete, given church as the normal channel of God's grace'.[36] Jenkins's ecclesiology was both Dissenting and Reformed. 'In 1662 it was the Ejected Ministers (namely the clergy who had forfeited their livings in the national church by their refusal to accept the Book of Common Prayer) who were the true witnesses on behalf of the Body of Christ'.[37] Whereas the post-restoration Church of England had reverted to being an engine of the state, 'the fundamental position of Reformed churchmen is that the nature of catholicity can be determined only in the light of God's Word, Jesus Christ, and that church order has significance only in relation to the gospel'.[38] If catholic ecclesiology celebrated the apostolic succession, Reformed churchmanship spoke of the catholicity of the Word: 'It is by making scripture the rule of faith that the Reformed church stands in the apostolic succession'.[39] A critical distance between the bearers of succession and the ever-renewing presence of the risen Christ was essential to preserve his Lordship over the church and it was through the concept of witness that this distance was maintained: 'It is their *testimony* which constitutes the apostles as apostles'.[40] Whatever the legitimacy of the ancient rite of the laying on of hands, its corresponding theology had served to limit God's grace which was, of necessity, a free and sovereign gift. 'The apostles', he continued, 'have authority only in so far as they forget themselves in being faithful witnesses to Jesus Christ, like John the Baptist in the Isenheim altar-piece so beloved of Barth'.[41] Drawing on

---

[34] R. Newton Flew, *Jesus and his Church: a study of the idea of the Ecclesia in the New Testament* (London: Epworth Press, 1938).

[35] H. F. Lovell Cocks, 'The Gospel and the Church', in John Marsh (ed.), *Congregationalism Today* (London: Independent Press, 1942), pp.30–45 [39].

[36] Daniel T. Jenkins, *The Nature of Catholicity* (London: Faber and Faber, 1942), p.10.

[37] Ibid., p.9.

[38] Ibid., p.13.

[39] Ibid., p.37.

[40] Ibid., p.24.

[41] Ibid., p.24.

Barth's *Church Dogmatics* I/1 and even more heavily on the Gifford Lectures, *The Knowledge of God and the Service of God* (1938), Jenkins was insistent that the only norm to judge apostolicity was the Bible, interpreted dynamically through Christ: 'It is only when the discipline of κρίσις is undergone that we are in a position to understand the scriptures and produce properly theological exegesis and stand in the succession of the apostles'.[42] Christ, therefore, manifests his Lordship not in any static sense as a given possession of the church but repeatedly and dynamically through the ever-renewing miracle of the Holy Spirit: 'The apparent argument in a circle is inevitable just because it is Jesus Christ, who cannot be trapped in any human categories, who is the subject of our inquiry'.[43]

For Daniel Jenkins, it was the quality of the false church to be static, whether the Church of Rome with its concept of papal infallibility, Anglo-Catholicism with its undialectical notion of Episcopal succession or those twins of modernity, liberal modernism and biblical fundamentalism which posited ethical experience or human rationality as theological norms. 'According to Reformed theology', on the other hand, 'the church possesses Christ never as an assured possession which she is able to take for granted ... but always in faith, that is, in such a way that Christ retains his sovereignty over her'.[44] In other words, the true church was always being 'brought under the κρίσις of the Word of God, Jesus Christ'.[45]

> Just as, in this world, faith, existing in a constant tension with unbelief, is a series of constantly repeated acts of repentance – of turning back from the self to God and acknowledging his Lordship in judgement, forgiveness and newness of life – so also is the life of the church on earth a series of constantly repeated acts of public repentance, of examining herself critically under the Word of God and of re-forming herself ever and anew in the light of that Word.[46]

In developing his thesis, Jenkins drew out the implications of Barth's thought for the ecclesiology of contemporary English Dissent. 'The Reformed theologian – and Barth is the Reformed theologian *par excellence* – fixes his eye on Jesus Christ and tries never to waver from him'.[47] Natural theology, whether Romanist, Anglican or liberal, of necessity threatened the absolute Lordship of Christ: 'Natural theology involves a turning away from Jesus Christ who is the life of the church' towards something innate in human

---

[42] Ibid., p.34.
[43] Ibid., p.48.
[44] Ibid., p.72.
[45] Ibid., p.48.
[46] Ibid., p.49.
[47] Ibid., p.68.

consciousness, experience or reason.[48] This is something that Reformed theology had always held: 'Practically all the criticism of Barth which is heard in England . . . is, from the point of view of Reformed theology, entirely irrelevant because the critics show no sign of understanding the terms of reference which he uses'.[49] In all the volume was something of a *tour de force* which not only established Jenkins's reputation as the leading younger Congregational theologian of his generation, but ensured that Barth would be afforded an intelligent hearing in the midst of the churchly renewal which was gathering strength as the Second World War progressed.

The mission of The Presbyter

The most vigorous forum for Barth reception in Britain during the 1940s was the monthly journal edited by Daniel T. Jenkins and Alexander Miller entitled *The Presbyter: a journal of confessional and Catholic churchmanship*. Originally a cyclostyled news-sheet produced by a group of younger ministers, it was re-launched in January 1943 under an editorial team including H. F. Lovell Cocks, W. A. Whitehouse, Hubert Cunliffe-Jones and T. Ralph Morton, the Presbyterian minister of St Columba's, Cambridge, with a wider denominational remit. Among its editorial supporters were Nathaniel Micklem, John Marsh, chaplain and philosophy tutor at Mansfield College, Thomas F. Torrance, Church of Scotland parish minister in Alyth, Perthshire, Alec Vidler, the Anglo-Catholic editor of *Theology* who was, at that time, heavily influenced by the theology of crisis, the Welsh Barthian theologian J. E. Daniel, and another Congregationalist, John Whale, president of Cheshunt College, Cambridge. Whale's stately proclamation in his popular *Christian Doctrine* (1941) encapsulated the feel of *The Presbyter* perfectly: 'I happen to be a minister of the Churches of the Congregational Order, one who stands gratefully and proudly in the Reformed tradition of Genevan High Churchmanship'.[50] Genevan churchmanship and Barthian theology were set to complement each other once more.

The Presbyter's manifesto, 'The transformation of theology in the twentieth century', was laid out by Daniel Jenkins clearly in its opening issue. 'The modern Reformed revival is best understood . . . as an attempted revival of the theology of the apostles and Reformers'. The task of the church was 'to listen attentively, humbly and as self-critically as possible to the testimony

---

[48] Ibid., p.69.
[49] Ibid., pp.67–8.
[50] John S. Whale, *Christian Doctrine: eight lectures delivered in the University of Cambridge to undergraduates of all faculties* (Cambridge: Cambridge University Press, 1941), p.131.

of the apostles as witnesses to Jesus Christ'.[51] It was no longer valid to attempt to go behind the apostolic testimony to a supposed Jesus of history who was little other than the sum of the liberal theologians' most cherished ideals:

> It is this which has lit up for us with a new vividness, of course through the pressure of God's Spirit upon us in the events of the world in which we live, the biblical understanding of the doctrines of God, sin, faith, the church and the divinity of Jesus Christ about which we differ most clearly from many in the generation which has gone before us.[52]

Whereas the older generation had interpreted the Reformers as harbingers of modernity and champions of the individual conscience, they had been blind to their churchly convictions and dogmatic concerns: 'Luther and Calvin have come alive for us again and we are able to read them with ready understanding and the warmest gratitude'.[53] But not even the Reformers were perfect. They had sometimes failed to maintain the inner consistency of their views, in the fields of natural theology and ecclesiology for instance. The challenge to the present generation of younger Barthian theologians and 'new Genevans' was to apply the Reformers' insights to the vastly different intellectual world of the twentieth-century Protestant church.

The verve and energy of *The Presbyter* would be maintained throughout the war years and beyond. It provided a platform for such promising talents as T. F. Torrance, E. Gordon Rupp, C. K. Barrett as well as those on its editorial team. Torrance's essays 'Kierkegaard on the knowledge of God' (March 1943) and 'In Hoc Signo Vinces' (November 1945) would be the first fruits of an extraordinarily productive career which would be crucial for the reception of Barth's work in the English-speaking world. Rupp's '. . . and the English Reformers' (November 1943) and the Presbyterian Basil Hall's 'The Contemporary relevance of the [Westminster] Confession' (December 1943) displayed the youthful talents of two church historians who would make signal contribution to English Luther studies and Calvin scholarship respectively. Although overwhelmingly Nonconformist in tone, the journal also engaged the interest of the occasional Reformed Anglican. T. H. L. Parker, who would become the Church of England's premier Calvin scholar,[54] wrote from Cambridge in August 1943: 'I must say how glad

---

[51] Daniel T. Jenkins, 'The transformation of theology in the twentieth century', *The Presbyter: journal of confessional and Catholic churchmanship* 1/1 (January 1943), 4–7 [7].

[52] Ibid., 4–5.

[53] Ibid., 5.

[54] For the earliest example of his work see T. H. L. Parker, 'The approach to Calvin', *The Evangelical Quarterly* 16 (1944), 165–72.

I was to make the acquaintance of *The Presbyter*. Perhaps one of its most useful functions . . . is to provide a meeting place for those who are romantically surprised that there are seven thousand others!' The regular essays and reviews by Lovell Cocks, John Marsh, Cunliffe-Jones, Alec Whitehouse and Jenkins were suffused with Barthian themes and informed by his writings.

Perhaps the most unusual among this group was Alexander ('Lex') Miller (1908–60). As a student in his native New Zealand, he had been heavily involved in both the SCM and radical social causes, and following the depression of the early 1930s he had been drawn towards Marxism. As a ministerial student he had also partaken of the theological renewal emanating from Europe. 'The impact of Karl Barth's teaching, and the continental theology generally', he wrote in an autobiographical piece in 1944, 'transformed the thinking of the live elements in the colleges and of the younger men in the ministry, and remodelled the theological outlook of a significant minority'.[55] Whereas Marx had provided a key to understand the dynamics of social upheaval, Barth had inspired him with a vision of radical churchmanship and a virile gospel: 'What Barth did for us was to confirm the conviction, forced upon us by Marxism and the facts of the case, that our analysis of the social problem must be driven deep enough to take account of the dynamics of power and class, and that there is both biblical warrant and biblical guidance for so doing'.[56] Having left for Britain in 1939, he took a Presbyterian charge in Stepney, London, where he applied his heady blend of social radicalism and Barthian Biblicism: 'The horrors of the blitz', reminisced one contemporary, 'strengthened his pacifism and as a stranger not quite at home in England, made him extreme in his Calvinism and in his revolutionary politics'.[57] By September 1942 he had been appointed deputy leader of the Iona Community, the ecumenical experiment established by George MacLeod, the powerful and privileged minister of Glasgow's Old Govan parish, which attempted to bridge the divide between established Scottish Christianity and the disaffiliated urban populace of Glasgow and other inner-city areas. Miller soon became a disturbing presence there. The autocratic MacLeod, whose misty Celtic Christianity was closer to Catholicism than Calvinism, had found his foil; his complaints about 'Karl Marx through the week and Karl Barth on Sundays'[58] illustrated the tensions between two strong personalities with differing visions about how radical Christianity should be practised. In fact, MacLeod was relieved

---

[55] Alexander Miller, 'Theology and lay responsibility', *The Christian News-Letter*, supplement 206, 19 April 1944, 5–12 [6].

[56] Ibid., 6–7.

[57] T. Ralph Morton, *The Iona Community: personal impressions of the early years* (Edinburgh: St Andrew's Press, 1977), p.41.

[58] Ronald Ferguson, *George MacLead: founder of the Iona community* (Glasgow: Collins, 1990), p.210.

when Miller resigned in 1945 and returned to New Zealand. He would later move to Canada, and eventually took up a professorship at Stanford University in California before dying at the early age of 52.

With Lex Miller *The Presbyter* gained not only a social conscience but developed a liberation theology with its own preferential option for the poor. His volumes *Biblical Politics: studies in Christian Social Doctrine* (1943) and *The Christian Significance of Karl Marx* (1946) reflected the social commitment which the journal espoused. 'It is unquestionably true that a good deal of theologizing which claims the name "catholic" or "confessional" or "Reformed" tends towards a pretty barren ecclesiasticism, divorced from any radical concern with Christian obedience in terms of contemporary political or economic facts'.[59] The challenge was to combine biblical orthodoxy with costly social commitment which was earthed in the complex realities of a fallen world: 'There is a suspicion on the part of some who are concerned with the social problem', opined an editorial in September 1943, 'that sections of the church are reacting to the contemporary crisis by retiring into a shell of ecclesiastical order and of theological "rightness" which has little relation to the vexing questions that effect the life of men'.[60] Yet none of this involved a toning down of Miller's uncompromising doctrinal stance. This would become patent in his polemical treatment of the liberalism of Charles Raven and Nathaniel Micklem's nemesis at Mansfield College, C. J. Cadoux.

Raven and Cadoux were perhaps the foremost and most vociferous opponents of the new theology and viewed the mission of *The Presbyter* with irritation if not outright disdain. Although Charles E. Raven (1885–1964), since 1932 Regius Professor of Divinity at Cambridge, had been trained as a classicist, he was a naturalist at heart who had already distinguished himself in the field of biology. A magnetic presence and popular speaker in SCM circles, he had personified the theology of synthesis which had characterized much Anglicanism into the 1920s. His volume *Apollinarianism* (1923) had sought to delineate the dangers of a less than fully human Christology. During the 1920s he was at the forefront of all that was popular, progressive and enlightened in the Christian world. Christianity, for him, was a matter of God's evolutionary presence within creation drawing out human goodness towards the pinnacle of the cosmic Christ. Although he had experienced the horrors of combat during the Great War and knew something about the tragic sense of life, he was wholly unprepared for the change of theological atmosphere which occurred with Barth's

---

[59] Alexander Miller, 'Questions about the Reformed Faith: has it a social message?', *The Presbyter* 1/8 (August 1943), 9–11 [9].

[60] Alexander Miller, 'Editorial', *The Presbyter* 1/9 (September 1943), 3.

Romans commentary and the ensuing eclipse of liberalism: 'By the late 1930s Raven for all his brilliance and pursuit of relevance, found himself regarded as irrelevant',[61] and the experience stung. His feeling of aggrievement was compounded by the fact that he felt himself being frozen out by both the ecumenical establishment and the Anglican Church: 'I had been dropped out of almost all ecumenical work in spite of my share in COPEC and the Jerusalem conference',[62] he would inform J. H. Oldham in 1948:

> I had also no position at all in my own church except a nominal connection with Ely . . . I think you will realise how hard it was then to find myself entirely alone and unwanted by the movements in the church in which I was particularly interested . . . It left a deep mark and has made me feel scarred ever since.[63]

Whereas a man of his ability and influence would ordinarily have been chosen for a senior episcopal position, his disapproval of Anglo-Catholicism and even more pronounced liberalism put him at odds with the trend of the time. In all he found himself 'half-bitterly, half-defiantly'[64] on the outside.

Knowing of his theological stance, Daniel Jenkins invited Raven to respond to *The Presbyter's* spirited manifesto of January 1943. The older man did so with alacrity: 'This theology as expounded in Mr Jenkins' article . . . seems to me to be in fact reactionary, ill-founded and if not itself transformed, disastrous.'[65] He was appalled, as he had been by the work of his Cambridge colleague Edwyn C. Hoskyns, by the replacement of the Jesus of history by the kerygmatic Christ, with the downgrading of mundane history as the sphere of divine activity and saw in this 'theology of a "divine intruder", a "God incognito" . . . the reducing of the incarnation to the level of a stage-play'.[66] The younger theologians had made a fetish both of the Reformers and the concept of the Word and had nothing consequential to say about the doctrine of the Holy Spirit: 'It is a reformation not in terms of Chalcedon, Luther and Dr Barth [that we need] but in those of the twentieth century, of Christ as the consummation of the creative process, of the scientific

---

[61] Hastings, *A History of English Christianity, 1920–2000*, p.294.

[62] COPEC, the Conference on Politics, Economics and Citizenship held under the chairmanship of William Temple in Birmingham in 1924; the Jerusalem conference of the International Missionary Council, 1928.

[63] F. W. Dillistone, *Charles Raven: naturalist, historian, theologian* (London: Hodder and Stoughton, 1975), p.275.

[64] Ibid., p.277.

[65] Charles E. Raven, 'Questions about the Reformed Faith: is the new expression of it valid?', *The Presbyter* 1/3 (March 1943), 8–9 [8].

[66] Raven, 'Is the new expression valid?', 8.

method and outlook'.[67] Whereas Raven's generation had put forward a new hope for humankind based on synthesis and evolution, 'it is to the reaction, the obscurantism and escapism of the "new theology" that the destruction of that hope is due'.[68] Raven's pique was intensified by the strident confidence with which the new theologians held their views: 'Is all this insistence upon their own novelty and revolutionism by what is after all a small and not (as yet) very distinguished group of students really justified? We cannot feel that wisdom is the necessary perquisite of the neophyte'.[69]

Jenkins's reply was courteous but uncompromising nevertheless. 'May it not be that we sound arrogant in the ears of liberals because we have a different conception of the nature of theological truth than theirs? They are more at home in approaching truth through probabilities and relativities, which approach they may think is the more humble and reverent one. We do not, and give reasons for our position'.[70] He distanced himself from all those who would drive a wedge between historical criticism and the New Testament Christ: 'Possibly Dr Raven has been moved to make this criticism by certain phrases of Bultmann, by which no responsible Reformed theologian would wish his position to be judged'.[71] The New Testament, however, could only really be understood by an evangelical appropriation of its message and not by merely dispassionate academic research. He wholly refuted the fact that the new theology had abjured the doctrine of the Holy Spirit: Barth had written extensively on it in both his *Dogmatics* and in *The Holy Ghost and the Christian Life*: 'Dr Raven may not like the modern Reformed doctrine of the Holy Spirit, but we are at a loss to understand why he says it does not exist'.[72] The fact was that Raven's understanding of the Spirit and the new theology's account of it did not amount to the same thing. The Holy Spirit in classic Christian theology was not another name for the innate power energizing the universe but the Third Person of the eternal God: 'Dr Raven's diffused world-spirit manifesting itself everywhere with large-hearted comprehensiveness is like a signpost pointing in all directions', he claimed. 'Because it is not closely enough linked to God's word to man, Jesus Christ, speaking to us in judgment and promise, it can frequently do no more than echo without discrimination the voice of the spirit of the age'.[73]

---

[67] Ibid., 9.
[68] Ibid., 9.
[69] Ibid., 8.
[70] Daniel T. Jenkins, 'Questions about the Reformed Faith: do liberals understand it?', *The Presbyter* 1/4(April 1943), 9–10, 13 [9].
[71] Jenkins, 'Do liberals understand it?', 9.
[72] Ibid., 10.
[73] Ibid., 10, 13.

This is the Message *and* Good News of God

If Jenkins's riposte was courteous, Lex Miller's review of Raven's *Science, Religion and the Future* (1943) and even more pointedly his *Good News of God* (1943) amounted to a blistering attack. If the former volume, a course of eight lectures delivered at Cambridge, purported to be for the academic market, 'Good News of God is a far more slap-dash book, part written at a furious pace, part dictated during a critical illness'.[74] Both, however, were contemptuous of the new theology and its practitioners. 'Barth's school . . . in Britain and America was neither impressive in quality nor (at first) strong in numbers',[75] Raven claimed, and while 'the abler minds of Christendom' were working towards the synthesis of science and religion, 'these "revolutionaries" reverted to the legends and superstitions of the old order or to an irrationalism which contentedly writes meaningless rhetoric and justifies it as the proper language to apply to the ineffable'.[76] Evidence of this was that 'an exaggerated enthusiasm exalts the strange and diseased genius of Kierkegaard into the place of the most profound Christian theologians'.[77] There was no doubt in Raven's mind that 'since the outbreak of war such theology . . . has been plainly pathological'.[78] In his second book, his mocking condescension became positively toxic:

> The message of the lions of *Theology* and the *Student Movement* [the magazine of the SCM] . . . is affected, priggish, arrogant, contemptuous of what it does not understand, and apparently incapable of seeing much beyond its own glibly enunciated formulae; its claims when tested amount to little but ill-digested borrowings from Kierkegaard and Barth, and its assets boil down to a few clichés, 'vertical and horizontal', 'irruptions into history', 'not victory in this world but vindication at the last day' which sound nice but mean nothing, and an extensive vocabulary of abuse applied to all who have laboured for critical scholarship, for historical research, for philosophical theology and for a reasonable faith.[79]

---

[74] Alexander Miller, 'Theological counter-revolution', *The Presbyter* 2/1 (January 1944), 12–14.

[75] Charles E. Raven, *Science, Religion and the Future* (Cambridge: Cambridge University Press), p.76.

[76] Ibid., p.77.

[77] Ibid., p.79.

[78] Ibid., p.78.

[79] Charles E. Raven, *Good News of God: being eight letters . . . based upon Romans I–VIII* (London: Hodder and Stoughton), pp.19–20.

If Raven revelled in the tradition of the 'reasonable religion' of Cambridge Platonism, he patently reviled 'our theological reactionaries, these loud-voiced champions of a new and biblical theology'.[80] Again there was no doubt that 'the characteristic theology [of *The Student Movement* and *The Presbyter*] is plainly pathological'.[81]

Given this level of invective, it was hardly surprising that Miller responded in kind. 'Dr Raven's counter-revolutionary fretfulness makes him . . . hysterical', stated the review. 'To give this as a summary of what serious Reformation theology says about science and rational investigation is to convict oneself of illiteracy in this field'.[82] Having countered 'Dr Raven's phobias . . . one would search for a long time in the literature of "neo-orthodoxy" for such an instance of such regulated and undocumented abuse'.[83] The younger man was at a loss to understand why a regius professor was reacting in such a bizarrely volatile way. It was clear that something elemental was at stake and that the liberals' combativeness was masking a potentially deep crisis of faith: 'Manifestly Dr Raven would not dig his own grave as a serious theological controversialist unless he were sorely provoked'.[84] The response seemed to be out of proportion to the provocation itself. It served to confirm the fact that liberalism was not only outmoded but perhaps delusional as well.

Lex Miller's article, not unexpectedly, 'stirred Charles to indignation and anger', wrote his biographer. 'This was perhaps the severest treatment that Charles ever received and he resented it deeply'.[85] It was not, alas, the end of his woes. An even more trenchant though cooler response came in the Lutheran and former Confessing Church pastor Franz Hildebrandt's *This is the Message: a continental reply to Charles Raven* (1944). Hildebrandt (1909–85) had been one of Dietrich Bonhoeffer's closest friends who had been forced to flee Germany due to his Jewish ancestry. He had acted as Martin Niemöller's curate at Dahlem and after arriving in Britain in 1937, had been active in the work of the Confessing Church abroad. By the outbreak of war he was pastor of the Cambridge Lutheran congregation and had enrolled for a PhD in Christ's College which was subsequently published as *Melanchthon: alien or ally?* (1946). A man of immense charm but steely will, he and Raven were personally close. Their theologies, however, were poles apart, and such was the onslaught in *Good News of God* that the German felt that he had no choice but to reply.

---

[80] Ibid., p.31.
[81] Ibid., p.6.
[82] Miller, 'Theological counter-revolution', 12.
[83] Ibid., 13.
[84] Ibid., 13.
[85] Dillistone, *Charles Raven*, pp.288–9.

Whereas Raven's book was curt and bitter, Hildebrandt's reply was elegant and urbane. He took his stand on the unique nature of the revelation in Christ, and apart from the Bible, his only authorities were Luther and John Wesley: 'It is not by either continental or confessional standards as such that we will be judged, but by our faithfulness to Holy Scripture'.[86] After the war Hildebrandt became a Methodist minister serving circuits in Cambridge and Edinburgh and at Drew Seminary in New Jersey, USA. His Berlin thesis *Est: Das Lutherische Prinzip* (1931) had been critical of Barth especially on the subject of the inversion of the law-gospel postulate,[87] but the tenor of his thought was generally Barthian: 'He is intensely Lutheran and biblical in his approach, with a keen appreciation of Wesley's special emphasis. If not a Barthian, his sympathies lie in that direction'.[88] *This is the Message* was penned as a series of letters, loosely based upon 1 John, addressed politely: 'My dear Charles'. Although friendly, and often witty, no punches were pulled. In Germany, he said, those who had been keenest to forge a synthesis between Christianity, science and the modern mind were the first to welcome Hitler as having been sent by God: 'What corresponded to the Modern Churchman's Union turned out to be, ninety-nine times out of a hundred cases, the champions of the "German (Nazi) Christian" movement'.[89] For the Lutheran, revelation was not a general phenomenon of nature but a matter of '[Christ's] own Word coming down to us from heaven, carried by his messengers, the prophets and apostles, and embodied in the scriptures of the Old and New Testaments'.[90] The categories which Raven used: religion, unity, experience, were open to severe misunderstanding: 'Even the word "religion" is no longer safe to express the divine promise of the gospel', he wrote. 'To us it has come to denote man's offer to God rather than God's offer to man'.[91] He criticized Raven for positing an immediacy between God and humankind which dispensed with the appointed means of grace. Whereas nature, for the professor, was a straightforward emanation of God's glory, for Hildebrandt it had been blighted by sin: 'I believe that our position is fundamentally different from Adam in the garden; living after the fall, we have lost the immediacy between creation

---

[86] Franz Hildebrandt, *This is the Message: a continental reply to Charles Raven* (London: Lutterworth Press, 1944), p.6.

[87] Franz Hildebrandt, *Est: Das Lutherische Prinzip* (Göttingen: Vandenhoeck und Ruprecht, 1931), pp.21–4, 30–1; cf. Holger Roggelin, *Franz Hildebrant: Ein lutherischer Dissenter im Kirchenkampf und Exil* (Göttingen: Vandenhoeck und Ruprecht, 1999), pp.34–7.

[88] Amos Cresswell and Max Tow, *Dr Franz Hildebrandt: Mr Valiant-for truth* (Leominster: Gracewing, 2000), p.148.

[89] Hildebrandt, *This is the Message*, p.11.

[90] Ibid., p.12.

[91] Ibid., p.21.

and creator and the direct understanding of the language of plant and animal'.[92] The gospel was not a commonplace dependent on individuals' 'capacity' for God; it was, rather, a message of redemption for otherwise lost sinners and a gift of free grace: 'Christ is the only source of our proclamation, the only Word of promise. Nothing short of the Barmen safeguard can end the confusion of voices in our pulpits and prevent the doctrinal chaos which is the common plague of your church and mine'.[93]

The scripturalism of Hildebrandt, the 'new Genevans' and the devotees of the Barthian renaissance was foreign to Charles Raven and for him, much too narrowly based. 'What worries us "continentals" beyond measure', wrote the younger man, 'whenever we enter the theological discussion with our English friends is the almost complete absence of biblical arguments from the debate'.[94] It was on the basis of scripture that the younger theologians had been drawn to the unique nature of Christ and to a renewed sensitivity to the church as the community of the Word. If Raven was disillusioned with the ecclesiastical establishment and found solace in the idealism of a wider humanity, Hildebrandt had no choice but to remain a man of the church: 'There is an unmistakable demarcation line between the church and the world which we have neither right nor power to change nor ignore'.[95] Although the good God was undoubtedly at work in his world, there was no biblical warrant for equating the fruit of Holy Spirit with the natural virtues of humankind: 'I wonder whether this is not to mistake enthusiasm for the spiritual life?'[96] Similarly, when Raven was appalled by a primitive literalism which took evil, the devil and the apocalyptic language of the New Testament seriously, the Lutheran could only point to the iniquity of Hitler's regime: 'You have your scientists, I have my Nazis to consider'.[97] Niemöller was still in Gestapo hands and soon Bonhoeffer, Hildebrandt's closest friend, would be hanged at Flossenberg prison in Berlin. Suddenly Raven's concerns seemed inconsequential and trite. Theology was a serious matter which demanded a gospel which was commensurate with the needs of the time: 'The "deity" which to my horror I find mentioned on p.53 of your book may be within the reach of scientific "evidence" for its "existence and nature"; the God and father of our Lord Jesus Christ is accessible only by faith'.[98] There was no neutral ground on which these matters could be decided: 'We can only proclaim the good news'.[99]

---

[92] Ibid., p.110.
[93] Ibid., p.26.
[94] Ibid., p.13.
[95] Ibid., p.41.
[96] Ibid., p.83.
[97] Ibid., p.96.
[98] Ibid., p.112.
[99] Ibid., p.113.

Anything farther from pathological could hardly be imagined. The tone of *This is the Message* was mild and its content was balanced and clear. Raven, however, was mortified and their association came to a bitter end: 'Charles felt that he had been wounded by a friend'.[100] Although the missionary statesman Max Warren, former vicar of Holy Trinity, Cambridge, tried to engineer a reconciliation between the two men, nothing came of it: 'The use of my Christian name on the dust cover', Raven claimed haughtily, being 'a failure to appreciate the nuances of English manners',[101] was what he had resented most. It was a sad end to what had been a sincere friendship. Hildebrandt's wistful final letter to Raven, on 27 December 1948, expressed the distance and exclusivity between both men's views:

> When I felt the pain that I had caused you, I knew that I had made my first mistake, and that 'confessions' of this kind, however laudable in the German situation, were not really wanted here . . . That one could ever act as a bridge-builder, that another point of view but that of the Cambridge tradition could ever find a hearing in the university, was a hope, which I have once had, but have buried long since.[102]

As in the case of other advocates of the new theology and their opponents, there would never be a meeting of minds.

The clash between Raven and Hildebrandt, however, neither stemmed the influence of the new theology among its followers nor boosted its reputation among its detractors. *The Presbyter* continued to provide the principal forum for Barth reception in England while one of its sponsors, J. E. Daniel, proceeded to apply Barth's insights to the ongoing chapel life of Wales. Daniel Jenkins, Alec Whitehouse, Lovell Cocks and T. F. Torrance, joined with John McConnachie and George S. Hendry, to contribute to what would become a milestone of British Barth reception, F. W. Camfield's symposium *Reformation Old and New* (1947). Just as Raven had used the pages of *The Presbyter* to express his disapproval of Barthianism, C. H. Cadoux did the same. Responding, though good-naturedly, to Lex Miller's pugnacious review 'Militant Liberalism' (July 1943) of his *Pilgrim's Further Progress* (1943), Cadoux made a significant confession: 'Miller makes much of the fact that I have not read much of Barth or Brunner. But surely one can know (and say) how one stands towards Barthianism without having personally

---

[100] Dillistone, *Charles Raven*, p.311; the controversy is described and analysed by Alan Wilkinson, *Dissent or Conform? war, peace and the English churches 1900–45* (London: SCM, 1986), pp.224–7 and Roggelin, *Franz Hildebrant: Ein lutherischer Dissenter*, pp.234–8.

[101] Dillistone, *Charles Raven*, p.437.

[102] Quoted in Roggelin, *Franz Hildebrant: Ein lutherischer Dissenter*, p.237.

waded through Barth's enormous tomes'.[103] Whether this referred to the *Kirchliche Dogmatik* 1 and 2 which were now available in German or to the English works, G. T. Thompson's *Doctrine of the Word of God* (1936) and the Aberdeen Giffords (1938), was not clear. It was evidence, though, that Barth was better known by reputation, whether good or ill, than by a careful perusal of his written texts. 'During the last fifteen years or so, I have listened to and read countless discussions and quotations of his views: and one cannot do that without gleaning an approximately correct view of what he stands for. It is the same story every time: and life is too short to enable me to do more'.[104]

J. E. Daniel, R. Ifor Parry and developments in Wales

As these controversies were being enacted in Cambridge and on the pages of *The Presbyter*, Barth's influence in Wales was gaining ground steadily. This was clear in the welcome given to the popular volume *Sylfeini'r Ffydd Ddoe a Heddiw* ('Foundations of the Faith Yesterday and Today') published in 1942 by what had been the staunchly liberal Student Christian Movement. Each of its nine essays bore the imprint of the renewed biblicism of the neo-orthodox movement. Its tenor was struck by the words of the editor: 'As believers in Wales we must recognize once more the authority of the Bible as the Word of God and listen in humility to what God has to tell us.'[105] There was no question any longer that religious authority was vested in human piety, speculation or reason, but solely in God's gracious self-revelation in Christ. The keynote essay was J. E. Daniel's 'Pwyslais Diwinyddiaeth Heddiw' ('The Emphasis in Theology Today'), which was a succinct, trenchant and vigorous résumé of the Barthian theology:

> We stand in the line which leads from the New Testament, through Marcion (with a slight deviation), and Tertullian, and Augustine and St. Bernard and Luther and Calvin and Kierkegaard and Barth. We do not stand on the line which leads through Origen and Erigena and Lessing and Schleiermacher and Ritschl. Among Welsh theologians we stand with Thomas Jones of Denbigh rather than with David Adams and Miall Edwards.[106]

Daniel was defining a position in which he placed the Welsh experience in the mainstream of classical western orthodoxy. Patently it was Barth more

---

[103] C. J. Cadoux, 'What is theology?', *The Presbyter* 2/10 (October 1944), 15.
[104] Ibid., 15.
[105] John Wyn Roberts (ed.), *Sylfeini'r Ffydd Ddoe a Heddiw* (London: SCM, 1942), p.3.
[106] J. E. Daniel, 'Pwyslais Diwinyddiaeth Heddiw', pp.89–92 [89].

than anyone else who had provided the stimulus for Welsh Nonconformity's more recent doctrinal renewal. Daniel's subsequent wartime essays, 'Y syniad seciwlar am ddyn' ('The secular estimate of man') and 'Gwaed y teulu' ('The blood of the family'), constituted a small but striking body of revelation theology which synthesized the old and the new with verve and extraordinary intellectual distinction.[107] In a 1944 radio broadcast he repeated how the new theology had rejuvenated the old. 'Now there is nothing new in any of this', he claimed:

> This is the essence of the gospel as it is to be found in the New Testament, as it was rediscovered by the Protestant Reformers, and as it is still believed by an innumerable amount of simple Christians in many lands. Karl Barth's service is to have restored the ancient scandal of the gospel to our self-sufficient world, without concern for the views of the philosophers or scientists, but mindful only of the claims of the gospel. The anvil of truth has nothing to fear from the blows which assail it; this is an anvil, as Beza said of the church, which has worn out many hammers, and which will surely do so again.[108]

Few outside Wales realized either how the nation's theology was developing or how different its religious situation was from that on the eastern side of Offa's Dyke. 'Wales is still something of a terra incognita to most Englishmen', wrote Daniel Jenkins in 1946. 'The actual facts of life in modern Wales such as the eisteddfod and the chapels are regarded as quaint and unreal, suitable for philistine Anglo-Saxon humour'.[109] Although Jenkins had been immersed in English church life for over a decade, he resented such ignorance and neglect: 'The tacit assumption that it is either mildly amusing or tiresome for Welshmen to regard their country as one not very important part of England does not make for harmonious relations between the two peoples'.[110] The dynamic of Welsh Christianity needed to be pondered and sympathetically understood. 'Wales is a religious nation in a sense that England is not',[111] and as such deserved especial respect. Drawing upon his own background in Dowlais, Jenkins took pride in the fact that Wales was still a chapel-going, working-class nation in which education

---

[107] For the essays see D. Densil Morgan, *Torri'r Seiliau Sicr: Detholiad o Ysgrifau J. E. Daniel* (Llandysul: Gwasg Gomer, 1992), pp.158–69; cf. idem. *The Span of the Cross: Christian religion and society in Wales, 1914–2000* (Cardiff: University of Wales Press, 1999), pp.144–7.

[108] J. E. Daniel, 'Karl Barth', *Y Dysgedydd* 128 (1945), 7–10 [10].

[109] Daniel T. Jenkins, 'Report on Wales', *The Christian News-Letter*, supplement 259, 1 May 1946, 5–12 [5].

[110] Ibid., 5.

[111] Ibid., 5.

was highly prized: 'The characteristic form of Welsh life is that of a chapel-centred democracy whose leader is the minister'.[112] Even in post-war, industrialized Wales this was still the norm, and as such was highly unusual: 'This working-class culture of Wales has the limitations of its nature, but of its kind it must be unique. Nearly every mining village boasts its poets and musicians, its choir, its philosophy class and its flourishing chapel life'.[113] This was not just romanticism, in fact Wales had been deeply scarred by the depression of the 1930s and the process of Anglicization and secularization was proceeding apace. Yet there were signs of vigour and rejuvenation: 'The Welsh tradition is giving plenty of evidence that it is by no means dead',[114] and along with the Labour movement, the Nationalist Party and the Welsh League of Youth, it was through the chapels that the potential for renewal could be best fulfilled. This was not to say that Nonconformity was not in need of reformation. To perpetuate conventional chapel life was not an option: 'Although the Welsh churches have had an intense congregational life there has been little strong churchmanship or consciousness of the church as a universal divine society . . . [or] a passionate desire to heal the broken body of Christ'.[115] Ecumenism and churchly renewal would henceforth be essential, as would be an application of the gospel to the complexities of contemporary life, but the Barthian movement which J. E. Daniel and others had spearheaded was having a salutary effect on students and the younger generation of preachers especially: 'Its influence is likely to grow'.[116]

Not all were as sanguine in their hopes or assessment as Daniel Jenkins. There were both liberals and evangelicals who could find little good in either Barthianism or in ecumenism and the churchly renewal as such. The philosopher Hywel D. Lewis, a colleague of J. E. Daniel's at Bangor would later occupy the chair of philosophy of religion in King's College, London. His *Morals and the New Theology* (1947) was a swingeing indictment of neo-orthodoxy in its entirety. According to its precepts as evidenced by the work of Reinhold Niebuhr's *The Nature and Destiny of Man* (1941–42) and Emil Brunner's *The Divine Imperative* (1942), there was no common ground between moral evil as understood by the philosophers and the biblical reality of sin. The moral autonomy which rendered individuals responsible for their actions was hopelessly compromised by such orthodox concepts as collectivism and solidarity 'in Adam' which had become the staple fare of the new theologians: 'It is just not possible to retain the idea of genuine sinfulness and guilt with the presuppositions of traditionalist

---

[112] Ibid., 6.
[113] Ibid., 6.
[114] Ibid., 9.
[115] Ibid., 10.
[116] Ibid., 11.

theology'.[117] A self-confessed liberal, he was appalled by the pessimistic and authoritarian tone of 'Barthianism' which, for him, encompassed the work of Niebuhr and Brunner as well as that of Karl Barth. He found 'the pessimism of Barth in regard to all human endeavour'[118] reprehensible, and his system blighted by 'a wholly reactionary dogmatism'.[119] In a spectacularly wrongheaded chapter he took Barth to task for providing a justification for the Lutheran two kingdoms dualism which had characterized the witness of the Confessing Church: 'In the subsequent humiliation and sufferings of the Confessional Churches themselves the nemesis of their own teaching is visible to all'.[120] In the light of the integrity and suffering of those who had challenged Nazi tyranny on the basis of the theology of the Word, his criticism was staggeringly inept. Barth, for Lewis, was the villain of the piece. Rather than providing a means of undermining authoritarianism, his theology merely served to reinforce its very structures: 'Witness the fulsome, almost blasphemous reverence of the state in the celebrated pamphlet on *Church and State* by Barth'.[121] The fact that the Confessing Church provided the only effective, if muted, opposition to Hitlerism during the 1930s was apparently immaterial, as was Barth's rejection of Lutheran quietism on the basis of a Reformed conception of God's authority over the political realm. Despite berating 'Barthianism', the Welsh philosopher did not interact at all with Barth's explicitly doctrinal works. It was enough to demonize 'that theology' for its reactionary character, and rebuke it for 'the murkiness of its ethical thinking'.[122]

At the other end of the spectrum, there were conservative evangelicals who were as suspicious of neo-orthodoxy as the most combative liberal. Martyn Lloyd-Jones, who was still nominally a Welsh Calvinistic Methodist though ministering at the time in the Congregational Westminster Chapel in London, could never find it in him to believe that Barth, his colleagues or their followers, were really converted at all. Writing of D. R. Davies, whose *On to Orthodoxy* (1939) was perhaps the most effective popular treatment of the new orthodoxy to have appeared by that time, he said: 'He, like Brunner and Barth falls short of the real thing. I feel he has had some kind of "intellectual conversion" and nothing more.'[123] His advice to enquirers was uncompromising: 'Don't waste time reading Barth and Brunner.

---

[117] H. D. Lewis, *Morals and the New Theology* (London: Victor Gollancz, 1947), p.145.

[118] Ibid., p.110.

[119] Ibid., p.9.

[120] Ibid., p.107.

[121] Ibid., p.101; the reference is to Karl Barth, *Church and State* (London: SCM, 1939).

[122] Ibid., p.101; idem., *Gwybod am Dduw* (Caerdydd: Gwasg Prifysgol Cymru, 1952), pp.55–77.

[123] Iain H. Murray (ed.), *D. Martyn Lloyd-Jones: letters 1919–81* (Edinburgh: Banner of Truth Trust, 1994), p.46.

You will get nothing from them to aid you with preaching. Read Pink.'[124] Arthur Pink was an eccentric hyper-Calvinist biblical expositor whose obscurity was only equalled by his extreme sectarianism; he spent the last decade of his life in seclusion in Stornoway on the Isle of Lewis refusing to join any form of Christian fellowship as neither the Free Church of Scotland congregation nor that of the Free Presbyterians was sufficiently pure and Reformed for his liking.[125] Any virtues which his biblical expositions contained were undermined by such excessive individualism. Yet, for Lloyd-Jones, he was infinitely preferable to Brunner, Barth or such errant evangelicals as T. F. Torrance. In a letter to the young evangelical theologian Philip E. Hughes in 1942, he stated: 'Apart from T. F. Torrance, who is far too Barthian for my liking, you are the only man who has aroused my interest deeply.'[126] Lloyd-Jones's opinions reflected the Calvinistic scholasticism of Cornelius Van Til of Westminster Seminary, Philadelphia, whose *The New Modernism* (1946) was an intemperate and gratuitous censure of the Barthian theology as a whole.[127] In an interesting Welsh-language radio broadcast in 1947 surveying the state of religion at the time, Lloyd-Jones (though in more conciliatory mood) still bemoaned the erroneous nature of the increasingly influential neo-orthodoxy in Wales and beyond:

> Has not the time come for us to consider the real value of the new theological movement? Although it challenges the importance of human intellect and reason, does it touch anything apart from the human mind? And although it scorns philosophy, is it anything apart from a new emphasis in philosophy? Isn't this why its literature is so difficult to comprehend? If we can be thankful for all prominence which is given to the Word and to theology, we must remember that there is a difference between preaching the Word and preaching about the Word. Preaching the Word alone can save mankind, and that is the aim of the gospel – not to provide individuals with an intellectual conversion or persuade them to change their philosophy, but to regenerate them and renew them totally.[128]

---

[124] Iain H. Murray, *D. Martyn Lloyd-Jones: the Fight of Faith, 1939–81* (Edinburgh: Banner of Truth Trust, 1990), p.137.

[125] Iain H. Murray, *The Life of Arthur W. Pink* (Edinburgh: Banner of Truth Trust, 1981).

[126] Murray (ed.), *D. Martyn Lloyd-Jones: letters 1919–81*, p.61.

[127] Its 'grotesque' nature was challenged forcefully by the Catholic Hans Urs Von Balthassar in *The Theology of Karl Barth* (San Francisco: Ignatius Press, [1951] 1991), pp.61–2, and the Reformed G. C. Berkouwer in *The Triumph of Grace in the Theology of Karl Barth* (Grand Rapids: Eerdmans, 1956), pp.385–93.

[128] Martyn Lloyd-Jones, *Crefydd Heddiw ac Yfory* (Llandybïe: Llyfrau'r Dryw, 1947), pp.11–12.

This, apparently, was what the new theology was failing to do.

The fullest assessment of Barth's contribution to appear in Welsh though not, alas, the most discerning, was R. Ifor Parry's *Diwinyddiaeth Karl Barth: Traethawd Beirniadol* (1949) ('The Theology of Karl Barth: A Critical Essay'). Parry, a Congregational minister and former student of J. E. Daniel, tried valiantly to show sympathy with his subject but his penchant for a doctrine of human analogy and the autonomous status of reason conditioned his response: 'Our need is for a new synthesis between faith and biblical criticism, between theology and the scientific spirit of our times'.[129] Although Barth was for him 'the most important theologian of our age'[130] who had 'inaugurated the most significant theological movement of our period,'[131] his assessment was negative due, in part, to his familiarity with only Barth's early works: 'Personally, we believe that his "prophetic" influence between 1919 and 1926 is more satisfactory than his "theological" influence after that'.[132] Parry's chapter on God and his Word was seriously misleading in that it interpreted the divine sovereignty independently from the reality of Christ, something which Barth had precluded in even the earliest of his works. 'Creation', maintained Parry, 'was an act of naked omnipotence',[133] and again, 'The tendency of neo-Calvinism is to interpret God as naked will'.[134] As to God's being-in-becoming, his essentially Trinitarian nature and humankind's vocation to be God's covenant partner in Christ, Parry seemed to be wholly unaware. His succeeding chapters on humanity and its state and history and its meaning repeated the pre-war, liberal critique that Barth's thought negated human personhood and deprived history of its meaning, while 'the invincible Word destroys both religion and morality'.[135] In a gracious review, Barth's student Ivor Oswy Davies was nevertheless pointedly critical: 'It is a very difficult task to interpret Barth's mind clearly even when the interpreter agrees with him in essence. It is much more difficult to interpret him plainly and fairly when the reviewer's opinion is radically divergent. I was surprised that Mr Parry has succeeded to the extent that he has'.[136] The lack of interaction with the *Kirchliche Dogmatik*, or even the Gifford Lectures at Aberdeen was, however, glaring, as was his failure to assess Barth's Trinitarian doctrine of God or his teaching

---

[129] R. Ifor Parry, *Diwinyddiaeth Karl Barth: Traethawd Beirniadol* (Llandybïe: Llyfrau'r Dryw, 1949), p.96.

[130] Ibid., p.7.

[131] Ibid., p.22.

[132] Ibid., p.93.

[133] Ibid., p.39.

[134] Ibid., p.38.

[135] Ibid., p.39.

[136] Ivor Oswy Davies, review of *Diwinyddiaeth Karl Barth*, *Y Traethodydd*, 3rd series 18 (1950), 92–4 [92].

on the Holy Spirit. The author, however, who was remarkably free from any animus towards his subject, admitted that Barth's influence was gaining ground: 'In Wales, the majority of Barth's disciples are among the younger ministers'.[137] It would be their task to confirm the Barthian principles during the post-war years.

Towards Reformation Old and New

As these events were occurring in the land of his birth, Daniel Jenkins had become the most prolific of the English-based Barthians. Between 1944 and 1947 three volumes, a pamphlet and a series of substantial articles would flow from his pen. In *The Church Meeting and Democracy* (1944), one of the 'Forward Books' published by the Independent Press, he applied the principles of Congregationalism to the democratic needs of a reconstructed post-war world: 'The concern for the right of all men to responsible personal existence before God has received its most distinctive expression and justification in classic Independency',[138] he claimed. Independency, the term used in the eighteenth century (as it still was in Wales) for Congregationalism, was never identical with individualism or with the isolated self-sufficiency of each separate congregation. It was, rather, the mechanism by which each person within the covenanted community was made responsible for their existence before God. Within the priesthood of believers the function of the church meeting was to facilitate this very fact: '[The church meeting] is a finely-wrought instrument, fashioned by God's own hand, for helping us discern his will and to live together in harmony as his children'.[139] This was not a matter of pragmatism but of deep doctrinal principle: 'We must recapture the important truth that there is such a thing as church order, which springs from the gospel and witnesses to the gospel and gives to the church its distinctive shape in the world'.[140] The high Genevan churchmanship which had become *de rigueur* among young Congregationalists was fed by the Barthian renaissance: 'If we believe in the visible church at all, as we most emphatically do, we cannot treat the form which Christ's body has in the world as a mere matter of administrative convenience'.[141] The church was a given reality born of the unique revelation in Christ while the ministry existed to facilitate the constant refashioning of the believing congregation according to the norms of Christ: 'It is one of the chief

---

[137] Parry, *Diwinyddiaeth Karl Barth*, p.93.
[138] Daniel T. Jenkins, *The Church Meeting and Democracy* (London: Independent Press, 1944), p.9.
[139] Ibid., p.30.
[140] Ibid., p.21.
[141] Ibid., pp.21–2.

functions of the ministry of the Word in the church to be the public conscience, checking itself by the one infallible guide, Jesus Christ as the scriptures declare him'.[142]

One of the themes which would become prominent in Jenkins's thinking was that a Christian humanism based on the gospel of redemption was essential for the renewal of European society. 'The whole trend of characteristic modern society has been towards creating not a community of free men, but a mass, people who have so lost their humanity as to become a herd'.[143] The antidote to this was the creation of an organic and corporate life in Christ: 'We find our fulfilment, our integration and our personal freedom, the fullness of the stature of our manhood, only in the fellowship of the Body of Christ and the discipline of common life'.[144] This theme was developed in *Prayer and the Service of God* (1944), an expansion of the essay 'Concerning Prayer' which had appeared in *The Christian News-Letter* of November 1942. What characterized secular modernity was atomization and a negation of personhood. Echoing T. S. Eliot's 'the hollow men', he wrote of '"the masses", the semi-depersonalized multitudes of humanity who drag out their existence aimlessly . . . the seething anonymous throngs . . . people without a history . . . because their lives have had no direction and no creative power'.[145] The gospel was not just a religious truth but had to do with human personhood. It was here that the evangelistic and humanitarian message of the church coalesced.

As well as being a thoughtful treatise on the concept of prayer, Jenkins's volume reflected many of the themes which Barth would express in the *Dogmatics*: the absolute authority of revelation, religion as a highly ambiguous project, and prayer, consequently, as a potential flight *from* God: 'Prayer as such is not necessarily a good thing. Unless it is directed to the right Person in the way He has laid down it can become a demonic thing and do untold damage to men and nations.'[146] Sin was not as a promethean endeavour, a wilful rebellion against God, but indolence and slothfulness born of a refusal to rise to the stature of full humanity in Christ: 'The one thing which "mass man" flees from is genuine personal relationship because that involves responsibility and decision, assuming the burden of attaining unto the fullness of the stature of manhood and taking actions in freedom'.[147] It was only through costly repentance and vital faith that this dire situation, so typical of bourgeois life, could be remedied.

---

[142] Ibid., p.49.

[143] Ibid., p.7.

[144] Ibid., p.23.

[145] Daniel T. Jenkins, *Prayer and the Service of God* (London: Faber and Faber, 1944), p.16.

[146] Ibid., p.20.

[147] Ibid., pp.30–1.

Jenkins's essays in *The Presbyter* and the *Christian News-Letter* were written 'in the light of the theological clarification granted to the church in these last days'.[148] In January 1944 he elaborated on the place of the church within a theology of reconstruction which would include not only the stabilizing of Barth's doctrinal renewal but also the flourishing of a Christian politics under the Word.[149] In October 1944 he answered the question 'Is an ecumenical theology emerging?' with a tentative 'yes'. The concept of a biblical theology which took the unity and authority of the Scriptures seriously and centred in the objective revelation of the divine Christ along with the surprising receptivity of Anglo-Catholics like Lionel Thornton, A. M. Ramsay and A. G. Herbert to the concerns of the Reformed, augured well for a general theological renewal. But 'first there is the appearance of a great ecumenical dogmatic system – that of Karl Barth . . . Here in fact is a great system which sets old controversies in a new perspective and provides a point of reference for future discussions'.[150] He repeated his contention in *The Christian News-Letter* in April 1945:

> The Protestant revival, largely . . . under the influence of Karl Barth, is still a comparatively new movement in this country and has only begun to show fruits in the life of ordinary churches. But it has undoubtedly transformed the theological situation within Protestantism and . . . created a new frame of reference for all theological discussion. It has suffered more than any other theological movement in recent history from misunderstanding and misrepresentation . . . It is still widely believed, even apparently by some eminent scholars, that Barth asserts that the Word of God is entirely irrational, that there is no contact between God and man even in faith, and that the natural order is irredeemable, and in consequence what he really says is given scant attention. Nevertheless, his indirect influence is immense and growing.[151]

In *The Place of a Faculty of Theology in the University of Today* (1946), he carefully delineated the role of Christian theology within a secular university according to the standard he had learned from Karl Barth: 'To insist that theology can be taught in a university only if . . . it is treated as an aspect of human experience on a level with others is a form of sheer

---

[148] Ibid., p.7.

[149] Daniel T. Jenkins, 'A theology of reconstruction: the place of the church', *The Presbyter* 2/1 (January 1944), 4–8.

[150] Daniel T. Jenkins, 'Is an ecumenical theology emerging?', *The Presbyter* 2/10 (October 1944), 4–6 [4].

[151] Daniel T. Jenkins, 'A map of theology today', *The Christian News-Letter*, supplement 232, April 1945, 7–12 [7].

persecution in the interests of a liberal agnostic ideology', he claimed. 'Theology ... has its own criteria, its own procedure and its own method of presentation, conditioned by its own subject matter, the self-revelation of the living God'.[152] By now the war was over, the horrors of Buchenwald and Belsen had been revealed, the atom bomb had been exploded over Hiroshima and Nagasaki, but still Jenkins was ebullient about future change: 'There are numerous signs from all over the world that we are at the beginning of what may turn out to be a great Christian renaissance'.[153]

The ignorance or misunderstanding of Barth's thought only began to be redressed at the end of this period. Modest scholarly work on Barth, based on a knowledge of the original texts, had been undergone, principally at Edinburgh where some PhD dissertations supervised by John Baillie and G. T. Thomson had appeared at the beginning of the decade[154] while F. W. Camfield had provided the readers of *Theology* with a short précis of Barth's idea of election in 1943.[155] It was not until 1945, however, with a Mansfield College based Oxford DPhil, that a level of sophistication was achieved which lifted Barth's thought from beyond the level of cliché. Barth himself had been working assiduously in Basle throughout the war and had completed *Kirchliche Dogmatik* II/1, on God's being-in-becoming and the divine perfections, in 1940, *Kirchliche Dogmatik* II/2 on the ambiguities of 'religion' and the doctrine of election in 1942, while *Kirchliche Dogmatik* III/1, his first part-volume on creation, was issued in 1945. Very few people in Britain were in a position to keep up with this welter of publication, but one of them was the Confessing Church refugee Herbert Hirschwald.

Hirschwald (1894–1989) had served in the German army during the Great War where he had been awarded the Iron Cross for bravery. Following legal training at Erlangen he had been appointed to the Prussian Supreme Court at the age of 32 to become the youngest high court judge in his land. A committed Lutheran layman, he had joined the Confessing Church in 1934 and become immediately involved in the legal defence of Jews. Deprived of his professional status under the Nuremberg laws, he had come into contact with George Bell, bishop of Chichester, and the office for non-Aryan

---

[152] Daniel T. Jenkins, *The Place of a Faculty of Theology in the University of Today* (London: SCM, 1946), p.14.

[153] Ibid., p.21.

[154] John Henderson, 'The Controversy between Karl Barth and Emil Brunner concerning Natural Theology', unpublished PhD, New College Edinburgh, 1940; Ivor Francis Morris, 'The Relation of the Word of God to the Doctrine of the Imago Dei in the Theology of Professor Karl Barth', unpublished PhD, New College Edinburgh, 1941; cf. A. M. Fairweather, *The Word as Truth: a critical examination of the Christian doctrine of revelation in Thomas Aquinas and Karl Barth* (London: Lutterworth Press, 1944) which was based on an Edinburgh PhD supervised by the philosopher Norman Kemp Smith.

[155] F. W. Camfield, 'Barth's doctrine of God', *Theology* 46 (1943), 3–8.

Christians, and later with Nathaniel Micklem and John Marsh. Having escaped from Germany in 1939, he was invited to Mansfield College where he began training for the Congregational ministry. Like Franz Hildebrandt in Cambridge, he enrolled for the Oxford DPhil which was awarded in 1945. 'Karl Barth's Conception of Grace and its Place in his Theology' was the most detailed and insightful study of Barth's work yet to appear in English, which predated the Dutch scholar G. C. Berkouwer by a decade in positing 'the triumph of grace' to be the keystone of Barth's whole system: 'Grace is the central pivot or core of Barth's theology and the key to the true understanding of it',[156] the dissertation claimed. 'This message proclaims the absolute sovereignty of the grace of God and its sufficiency for every man, which latter has an almost totalitarian character, and the present war and total destruction has every reason to listen to that message very attentively'.[157]

What was novel in the British context was Hirschwald's exposition of *Kirchliche Dogmatik* II/1, God's loving in freedom, God's existence as the event of reaching out to humankind and creating communion in Christ. Also, his elucidation (which was present in the Aberdeen Gifford Lectures but hardly noticed at the time) of the radical shape of election from *Kirchliche Dogmatik* II/2. The tendency among his British disciples was to see Barth if no longer as a prophet then as a system builder whose dogmatics, when mastered, were there to be applied. Even in Daniel Jenkins, the impression gleaned was that Barth was a somewhat conventional, if brilliant, Reformed theologian. Hirschwald was sure that this was not the case and that Barth belonged to a category of his own. Grace, though wholly gratuitous, is irresistible because God is God. It is never coercive and there is no synergy between God and the human will: 'We are not invited to understand his idea of ruling grace in terms of sheer power and tyranny forcing its acts and decisions upon man by the mere weight of God's omnipotence'.[158] Man's total freedom was a postulate, through the *analogia fidei*, of the absolute freedom of God. It was the sheer graciousness of God's elective action, which arose from his inner Trinitarian being, which was most striking in Barth's scheme, a theme which only came to the fore as the *Kirchliche Dogmatik* unfolded: 'In Barth's theology a place of the first magnitude has been assigned to the idea of grace as never before in the history of the doctrine of grace'.[159] This made all previous writing on his work redundant.

The Swiss's fatal flaw, for Hirschwald, was in his idea that the *imago Dei* had been totally obscured: 'It is in Barth's doctrine of the total loss of

---

[156] Herbert Hirschwald, 'Karl Barth's Conception of Grace and its Place in his Theology', unpublished DPhil, St Catherine's Society, Oxford, 1945, p.ii.
[157] Ibid., p.10.
[158] Ibid., p.123.
[159] Ibid., p.5.

the image of God in man which makes it virtually impossible for him to acknowledge the moral independence of man'.[160] Like many critics, Hirschwald wondered whether this allowed a sufficient basis for ethics: 'If man's life as seen from God's side is a continuous falling and therefore is in constant need of new acts of divine grace, is it not conceivable how there can be moral development and moral progress on the part of man?'[161] Neither was he convinced that the extreme emphasis on grace was wholly scriptural: 'Holy scriptures say nowhere nor do they allow to say by way of interpretation or by way of direct conclusions that God's nature is wholly grace'.[162] Nevertheless, the treatment was learned, balanced and provided the most knowledgeable assessment to date of the totality of Barth's thought: 'A right understanding of Barth's theology, which because of the personality of its author, and because of its great influence on the life of the churches, especially on the continent of Europe, rightly claims our attention'.[163]

Hirschwald's dissertation, though erudite and astute, remained unpublished while, following ordination, his pastoral work among German refugees prevented him from accomplishing the sustained contribution to theological studies which he surely could have made. It was not until 1964 that he would issue his study *The Theology of Karl Barth: an introduction* under the anglicized name of Herbert Hartwell. By 1946, however, other scholars were mediating Barth's work to an English language readership: J. H. Oldham provided a précis of *Kirchliche Dogmatik* III/1, Barth's treatment of creation and covenant, his Christological interpretation of the Genesis saga and God's 'Yes' to his creation, in *The Christian News-Letter*[164] with Alec White-house fulfilling the same task on the pages of *The Presbyter*.[165] F. W. Camfield, who had left the Congregational ministry in 1942 to seek orders in the Anglican Church, provided a more extensive description of *Kirchliche Dogmatik* II/1 on God's being-in-becoming and the divine perfections, and *Kirchliche Dogmatik* II/2 centring on the doctrine of election, in the opening chapters of his edited volume *Reformation Old and New* (1947). The volume was presented to Barth as a tribute on his sixtieth birthday and its editor had no qualms about the significance of the Swiss theologian's accomplishment: 'For the first time in the history of the Christian church, a theology of vast range and of striking coherence and clarity, has been built

---

[160] Ibid., p.523.

[161] Ibid., p.474.

[162] Ibid., p.451.

[163] Ibid., p.8.

[164] J. H. Oldham, 'Karl Barth on the doctrine of creation', *The Christian News-Letter*, supplement 271, 16 October 1946, 6–16.

[165] A. W. Whitehouse, 'Karl Barth and the doctrine of creation', *The Presbyter* 4/4 (Winter 1946), 1–7; reprinted in idem., *The Authority of Grace: essays in response to Karl Barth* (Edinburgh: T & T Clark, 1981), pp.9–16.

wholly on the foundation of the Word of God as attested in the biblical witness to revelation'.[166] Herbert Hirschwald returned to the field in the same year with a detailed assessment of the *imago Dei*, contrasting Barth's earlier view in *Romans* (1922), *The Holy Ghost and the Christian Life* (1929) and *The Doctrine of the Word of God* (1936), of which he disapproved, with the communal understanding put forward in *Kirchliche Dogmatik* III/1, a work which had not appeared when he had been working on his doctoral dissertation: 'Man (male and female) who has been created not only by God . . . but for God . . . as God's partner in His covenant with man, is called to reflect in his own form of life the dynamic relationship that exists within the Godhead'.[167] For Hirschwald this was a much more fruitful avenue of thought but one which was not devoid of difficulties. What was more, it 'not only differs from the Reformers but in a most striking way appears to be at variance with Barth's own teaching on the same subject in the fist volume, part one, of his *Church Dogmatics*'.[168]

The growing critique

In all it was a boon to allow English readers access to Barth's more recent and innovative thought, but each of these contributions, though worthy, suffered from what Hans Frei was to describe decades later as Barth's vigorous prose 'dying on one's hands': 'There is nothing as wooden to read as one's own or others' restatements of Barth's terms, his technical themes and their development . . . For that reason reading "Barthians", unlike Barth himself, can often be painfully boring'.[169] In fact, the exhilaration and stimulus of Barth's contribution was beginning to pall. Alexander Miller had warned as early as 1944 that, for all their zeal and enthusiasm, all was not well among the new theology's British protégées:

> It would be impossible to claim that we in Britain have seriously reckoned with Barth. We easily assume that we have come to terms with his emphases or over-emphases as we care to regard it upon this or that question of doctrine, but in point of fact we are a thousand

---

[166] F. W. Camfield, 'Development and present stage of the theology of Karl Barth', in idem. (ed.), *Reformation Old and New: a tribute to Karl Barth* (London: Lutterworth Press, 1947), pp.12–100 [27].

[167] Herbert Hirschwald, 'The teaching of Karl Barth on the doctrine of the *Imago Dei*', *The Presbyter* 5/4 (Winter 1947), 1–17 [11].

[168] Ibid., 2.

[169] Hans Frei's review of Eberhart Busch, *Karl Barth: his life from letters and autobiographical texts* (London: SCM, 1976) in H. Martin Rumscheit (ed.), *Karl Barth in Re-View* (Pittsburg: Pickwick Press, 1981), pp.95–116 [112].

miles from having grappled in an existential way with the issues that he raises.[170]

It was not just that the disciples were failing to grapple with the work of the master; some were beginning to lose patience with the master himself. Responding to the volume *Natural Theology* (1946), the English translation of Emil Brunner's *Natur und Gnade* along with Barth's volcanic response, *Nein!* of 1934, even Daniel Jenkins withheld his wholesale support. He certainly approved of Barth's cardinal criticisms: that Brunner's distinction between the formal and the material *imago Dei* was abstract and forced, that his idea of a *theologia naturalis* was inept, and that the Holy Spirit provides its own point of contact with the recipient of the Word which was independent of any inherent capacity that human beings possessed. He was, though, exasperated with Barth for 'his attitude of truculent indifference' to Brunner's valid apologetic concerns. '[Barth] does not sufficiently recognize that Brunner is trying to meet a real need',[171] that of sympathetically understanding the cultural context of those who are addressed by the Word: 'The question of the relation of the gospel to secular modern culture is not the decisive one for the theologian but it has its own importance on its own level'.[172] Barth, for all his genius, was seriously at fault for his lack of engagement with the contextual aspect of the theological task. For Jenkins, there was room for *both* Swiss doctors in the pantheon:

> We shall always sit at the feet of Karl Barth, the mighty doctor of Holy Scripture whom God has raised up for our illumination and strengthening in this dark time, but we shall not allow him to intimidate us into heeding what Emil Brunner, the wise and balanced teacher who with infinite learning and clarity helps us to see our way through the tangled maze of this life, says to us either.[173]

Camfield's volume *Reformation Old and New* contained valuable work. In a chapter entitled 'Reformation issues today', the stalwart John McConnachie, now in his seventies, returned to a theme which he had raised in a 1944 essay on the Westminster Confession,[174] contending that Barth

---

[170] Alexander Miller, 'From a height in the Cairngorms: a theological survey of war-time Britain', *The Presbyter* 2/10 (October 1944), 4–7 [4].

[171] Daniel T. Jenkins, review of *Natural Theology: comprising 'Nature and Grace' by Professor Dr Emil Brunner and the reply 'No!' by Dr Karl Barth* (London: Geoffrey Bles, 1946), in *The Presbyter* 5/2 (April 1947), 34–36 [35].

[172] Ibid., 35.

[173] Ibid., 35.

[174] John McConnachie, 'The Westminster Confession of faith', *The Evangelical Quarterly* 16 (1944), 268–81.

had carried through a truer reformation wholly on the basis of God's Word than the heirs of the Reformation ever succeeded in doing. In his chapter 'The rediscovery of the Bible'[175] George S. Hendry, still in parish ministry in the Bridge of Allan, showed that his zeal for Barth's thought had not abated. His blunt criticism of the 'notorious doctrine of verbal infallibility'[176] would prove contentious, especially in the 1950s, when British evangelicalism, under the influence of Cornelius Van Til's *The New Modernism* (1946), Martyn Lloyd-Jones and the Inter Varsity Fellowship, would become increasingly vociferous in its opposition to Barth. T. F. Torrance's 'The Word of God and the nature of man' which treated the vexed question of 'natural religion' in Calvin and Barth, as well as other essays by Lovell Cocks on saving faith, Daniel Jenkins on Barth and the congregation and Alec Whitehouse on natural law, confirmed the fact Barth was still exercising the imagination of British theologians. The excitement of fresh discovery, however, was beginning to subside.

Hubert Cunliffe-Jones, who had formerly been within the Barthian orbit and was now principal of the Yorkshire Independent College, was prepared to make his criticisms explicit. For all its rhetoric about God's sovereignty over creation through the Word, there was a serious disconnect between Barth's scheme and the ordinary lives of every day Christians, he claimed. As a pastoral and practical theology it was proving ineffective. Also, if the Word did embed itself in the stuff of human life and experience, those realities needed to be incorporated more deeply into the theological venture than Barth's dogmas allowed. The extreme antipathy between revelation and experience which may have been polemically necessary in the revolt against liberalism, was no longer valid in the post-war world. History, too, was problematic. *Urgeschichte* was one thing, but both the biblical world and modern life existed in the realm of the temporal and the mundane. There were implications to this in the field of biblical criticism and the miraculous that Barthianism was still unwilling to face. Although Barth remained 'in my judgement . . . a magnificent witness to Christian truth, and a persistent stimulus to more discerning and penetrating theology',[177]

---

[175] This complemented an earlier essay 'The Old Testament in the Christian Church' in the American Reformed journal *Crisis Christology* 3 (1945), 3–13; *Crisis Christology*, published between 1943 and 1949 at the theological school of the University of Dubuque, Iowa, performed a similar function to *The Presbyter* in providing a platform for Barth reception in the American context.

[176] George S. Hendry, 'The Rediscovery of the Bible', in Camfield (ed.), *Reformation Old and New*, pp.142–56 [145].

[177] H. Cunliffe-Jones, review of *Reformation Old and New* in *The Presbyter* 5/4 (October 1947), 24–7 [27].

his scheme as a whole had proved unworkable. It could no longer provide 'the basis for all future theology'.[178]

The increasing feeling of despondency and fatigue was well expressed by Basil Hall, one of *The Presbyter's* faithful: 'A clutch of ex-SCM secretaries, a covey of theological intellectuals and an odd lot of individualists who have a little Barth do not constitute a Reformed church',[179] he wrote in 1947. There was, in his own denomination, a worrying lack of spiritual vigour and a truncated sense of history: 'The only dogmatic offered seems to be a variant of Barthianism, but this is well on the road to becoming a scholasticism as recondite as that of seventeenth century Basle'.[180] The verve of discovery which had been so conspicuous less than a decade earlier was slowly dissipating. There was soon to be a divergence among those who would remain faithful to Barth as they developed their own insights into matters which Barth had been, at best, ambivalent about: Alec Whitehouse on the concept of natural law and T. F. Torrance on revelation and the physical sciences being cases in point. Daniel Jenkins however, his appreciation for Brunner notwithstanding, would remain staunch: 'The work of reformation has still largely to be done', he claimed. 'When Karl Barth finally completes his stupendous *Dogmatik* it will not be the beginning of the end. It will indeed be the end of the beginning'.[181]

---

[178] Ibid., 25.
[179] Basil Hall, 'The Presbyterian Church and its future', *The Presbyter* 5/1 (January 1947), 25–33 [32].
[180] Ibid., 32–3.
[181] Daniel T. Jenkins, *The Gift of Ministry* (London: Faber and Faber, 1947), p.174.

9

BARTH RECEPTION DURING
THE POST-WAR YEARS,
1948–56 (I)

The World Council of Churches and the clash with Reinhold Niebuhr

Karl Barth was spending his second summer semester teaching in the bomb-damaged University of Bonn when *Reformation Old and New* appeared. Now aged 60, he had been temporarily relieved of his duties by his home university at Basel in order to assist in the reconstruction of German academic life following the war. He had first spent time there between May and August 1946 lecturing at 7 a.m. every weekday on the Apostles' Creed among the ruins. It was there that he made the acquaintance of the young Scottish theologian Ronald Gregor Smith, a contemporary of T. F. Torrance and co-founder of the Scottish Church Theology Society. Smith, like his colleague Ian Henderson who was appointed to the Glasgow chair of Systematic Theology in 1948, would diverge fundamentally from Barth (and Torrance) on the substance of the Christian message and become during the late 1950s and 1960s a leading proponent of demythologizing and the thought of Rudolf Bultmann.[1] Barth and his followers in Britain would soon find themselves being challenged from both the evangelical right and from a resurgent liberal left. The stirring lectures on the Apostles' Creed appeared in 1948 as *Dogmatik im grundriss*, immediately translated by G. T. Thomson as *Dogmatics in Outline* (1949). Presented to a variegated audience of students from all faculties, the lectures were intended as a

---

[1] See Keith W. Clements, *The Theology of Ronald Gregor Smith* (Leiden: Brill, 1986).

new catechesis of basic biblical Christianity for the youth of a war-damaged Europe.

Along with this catechetical teaching,[2] Barth was drawn at the same time into the preparatory work for the establishment of the World Council of Churches. Unlike his erstwhile colleague from his curate days in Geneva, Adolf Keller, he had never been fired by the ecumenical vision, but he now felt that the need to strive for the visible unity of the church was both a theological imperative and worthwhile for its own sake. The movement for the unity of the churches had been gathering pace throughout the century though the Edinburgh Missionary Conference of 1910 was regarded as its official beginning. This would culminate in the formation of the World Council of Churches and its first assembly, in Amsterdam, in August 1948.[3] Along with the Swedish Lutheran Gustav Aulén, the Orthodox George Florovsky and others, Barth had been invited to contribute to the assembly's understanding of the doctrine of the church. For a Reformed churchman his ecclesiology was surprisingly Congregationalist. 'The principle of Congregationalism – the free congregation of the free Word of God – is sound enough',[4] he claimed. It was the local congregation, in fraternal unity with other congregations in which the Word was preached and the sacraments duly administered, which was the indispensable unit of church life. The danger for any congregation was to lapse into lifelessness or apostasy through disobedience to the direct call of Christ in his Word. When this happens 'the life of the congregation ceases to be *event*, the congregation ceases to be a *living* congregation'[5] so creating 'the phenomenon of the nominal church, the church which is merely an ecclesiastical shell'.[6] Yet the miracle of the Word through the Holy Spirit meant that even apparently lifeless congregations could be quickened: 'The renewal of the living congregation, which also constitutes her unity, is the work of the living Lord'.[7] For Barth the true church could never be an institution and the perpetuation of the churches' historical existence through institutional means whether episcopacy or a formal inherited ecclesiastical order was deeply ambiguous. Rather the church was an eschatological reality witnessing to the risen

---

[2] During the 1947 semester Barth lectured on the Heidelberg Catechism, see Karl Barth, *The Heidelberg Catechism for Today* (Richmond: John Knox Press, 1964).

[3] See G. K. A. Bell, *The Kingship of Christ: the story of the World Council of Churches* (London: Penguin, 1954); W. A. Visser't Hooft, *The Genesis and Formation of the World Council of Churches* (Geneva: WCC, 1982).

[4] Karl Barth, 'The living congregation of the living Lord Jesus Christ', in *The Universal Church in God's Design*, Vol. 1 (London: SCM, 1948), pp.67–76 [75].

[5] Ibid., p.71.

[6] Ibid., p.71.

[7] Ibid., p.72.

Christ's already achieved conquest over sin and death, and awaiting his coming again in glory:

> In this final period the congregation is the *event* which consists in gathering together those men and women whom the living Lord Jesus Christ chooses and calls to be witnesses to the victory he has already won, and heralds of its future universal manifestation.[8]

This was not pietism or otherworldliness. Barth was keen to emphasize the church's witness and service to the world, the sphere wherein Christ had risen from the dead and exercises his continuing Lordship under the guise of secular realities and political facts.

It was not only Barth's stark and unexpected ecclesiology which created a stir, but his contribution to the general debate. 'No one who was present on the first Monday afternoon, 23 August, will forget the prophetic warnings and grave eloquence of Professor Karl Barth of Basel, and the way in which he pointed out the danger of all our counsels coming to nought',[9] recounted George Bell, the bishop of Chichester. Suspicious of the activism of the American churches especially and their 'Christian Marshall Plans' – the Marshall Plan was the generous American operation to rebuild Europe following the Second World War – he reminded the delegates that the kingdom of God was God's and not a human construct, and that it already existed as an eschatological reality. God's design, which was the assembly's watchword, 'is already present, victorious, already founded kingdom in all its majesty, our Lord Jesus Christ, who has already robbed sin and death, the devil and hell of their power, and already vindicated divine and human justice in his own person'.[10] Lesslie Newbigin, a young bishop in the Church of South India, was duly impressed. 'Karl Barth gave us a tremendous oration on the fundamental theme of the conference. It was real prophecy and compelled everyone, I think, to look beyond all our plans and self-importance to the living God. Some people were very annoyed by it, but I more and more feel that it was needed'.[11]

Among those who were sorely annoyed was the American ethicist Reinhold Niebuhr (1892–1971). Niebuhr had gained a reputation as being an ally of Barth and an insightful proponent of neo-orthodoxy. Both a political and religious liberal, his early volume *Moral Man and Immoral Society* (1932) had broken with doctrinaire liberalism and dealt a body blow to glib American optimism and the doctrine of inevitable progress,

---

[8] Ibid., p.68.
[9] Bell, *The Kingship of Christ*, p.53.
[10] Ibid., p.54.
[11] Lesslie Newbigin, *Unfinished Agenda: an autobiography* (London: SPCK, 1985), pp.116–7.

while his Gifford Lectures *The Nature and Destiny of Man* (1941–43) delivered in Edinburgh in 1939, a year after Barth had concluded his own Gifford series, had analysed the enigma of human sinfulness and provided an underpinning for his scheme of Christian realism. Niebuhr's affinity with Barth, however, was apparent and not real. In fact the two men were light years apart. Although invariably referred to as a theologian, Niebuhr was in truth a social ethicist with minimal theological interests. His break with liberalism had been politically and never doctrinally motivated. By espousing a theoretically Augustinian view of human sinfulness, he found a more effective key to understand the bleak ambiguities of the human condition than the trite optimism which had been *de rigueur* among his fellow intellectuals. For him Protestant religiosity was an aspect of the culture of the bourgeois elite to which he belonged. As a professor in New York's fashionable Union Seminary he had become America's 'official establishment theologian',[12] championed by Henry Luce, publisher of the magazines *Time* and *Life* and feted by politicians and socialites alike. It was because the biblical doctrine of redemption and sin offered a more potent description of human experience that he took it as his key, not because it possessed any intrinsic theological value as such. In fact Niebuhr remained doctrinally a minimalist, rejecting the concept of miracle, the supernatural and the factual basis of Christian orthodoxy as being incompatible with the demands of Enlightenment rationality. For him incarnation, atonement and resurrection were symbolic rather than actual truths.[13] Few realized this at the time – though it was expressed unambiguously in the second volume of his Gifford Lectures, 'The Destiny of Man', – and many took it for granted that he and Barth were upholders of virtually identical truths. In reality Niebuhr regarded Barth's theology as being 'no better than "magic"'. Niebuhr was not interested, then or later, in making a careful study of Barth's work'.[14]

Although this fact was not in the public domain, the animus against Karl Barth was clear in his response to the Amsterdam appeal. In an article in *The Christian News-Letter* in October 1948, the American ethicist took the Swiss theologian to task for his oration. For Niebuhr, Barth's address was a characteristic expression of 'continental theology' at its most perverse: rhetorical, unrealistic and uninvolved. Rather than busying itself with the demands of social reconstruction, Barth took solace in eschatological abstractions which were in danger of blunting the witness of the newly established World Council. Pious rhetoric about Christ's already won victory may be stirring, but 'did not these conclusions tend to rob the Christian

---

[12] Richard Fox, *Reinhold Niebuhr: a biography* (New York: Pantheon Books, 1985), p.234.

[13] Cf. Stanley Hauerwas, *With the Grain of the Universe: the Church's witness and natural theology* (London: SCM, 2001), pp.87–140.

[14] Fox, *Reinhold Niebuhr: a biography*, p.117.

life of its sense of responsibility? Did they not deal in an irresponsible manner with all the trials and perplexities, the judgements and discriminations which Christians face in the daily round of their individual and collective life?'[15] For Niebuhr the weakness of Barth's emphasis 'is that it tempts the Christian to share the victory and the glory of the risen Lord (which he regarded in metaphoric rather than realistic terms) without participating in the crucifixion of the self, which is the scriptural presupposition of a new life'.[16] Even he, though, was obliged to admit that the theology of the Word had provided a mighty challenge to the tyranny of the Hitler regime. The problem, of course, was that now the war was over and the church was faced with new problems which called for nuance, balance and compromise rather than out-and-out opposition. Faith in God's absolute Lordship 'resulted in a very powerful witness to Christ in the hour of crisis. But perhaps this theology is constructed too much for the crises of history. It seems to have no guidance for a Christian statesman in his day-to-day responsibilities'.[17] Barth, in his view, was indulging in reckless theological triumphalism: 'We seem always to be God rather than men in this theology, viewing the world not from the standpoint of the special perplexities and problems of given periods, but *sub specie aeternitatis*'.[18] A dogmatic faith in the finality of Christ's victory undermined the need for responsible activity within the secular realm which, symbolism apart, was the only domain which really mattered. Biblical literalism like Barth's undercut reality: 'Christian faith . . . may . . . degenerate into a too simple determination and irresponsibility when the divine grace is regarded as a way of escape from, rather than a source of engagement with, the anxieties, perplexities, sins and pretensions of human existence'.[19] For Niebuhr this was all too clear in Barth's Amsterdam address. 'The wheel has turned full circle. It is now in danger of offering a crown without a cross, a triumph without a battle . . . a faith which has annulled rather than transmuted perplexity'.[20] In all Barth's Christian supranaturalism was irrelevant to the post-war world.

Karl Barth was flabbergasted by this response. What made matters worse was that Niebuhr, who was a German-speaking American with roots deep in continental piety, had called on Barth in Basel in the spring of 1947 to discuss the political and religious situation and both had concurred,

---

[15] Reinhold Niebuhr, 'We are men and not God', *The Christian News-Letter*, supplement 323, 27 October 1948, 11–16 [11–12].
[16] Ibid., 12.
[17] Ibid., 14.
[18] Ibid., 15.
[19] Ibid., 15–16.
[20] Ibid., 16.

apparently, in their analysis of the malaise.[21] 'In the light of what I have read of his writings', Barth replied, 'of a good talk which I had with him here in Basel and of his speech in Amsterdam, I had in all good faith looked on him as belonging to the dissenting element among the "Anglo-Saxons", and now I find him to my utter surprise – *et tu Brute!* – entering the lists against me as spokesman of the "Anglo-Saxon" world'.[22] Whereas in his essay Niebuhr had attributed the disparity in their approach to the difference between 'continental' and 'Anglo-Saxon' theology, Barth was not convinced: 'I know some American theologians, and in Great Britain entire groups of theologians and certain magazines (a reference to *The Presbyter* and its constituency) which, with greater or less definiteness, must be regarded as belonging decidedly to the "continental" type'.[23] The difference was not due to any competing cultural or national ethos but to conflicting understandings of the essence of the faith. Whereas Niebuhr and the liberals used Christian symbolism to shed light on basically non-theological realities, the Christian faith judged the world according to its own unique norms. The Bible was not a repository of convenient symbols to enlighten mundane or secular experiences but the point of entry into a completely different world.

This, apparently, was something that Niebuhr did not comprehend: 'What dumbfounds me is that so distinguished, accomplished and certainly well-meaning a spokesman of "Anglo-Saxon" theology should be unable to give any other picture of us than a caricature'.[24] Despite the apparent biblicism of Niebuhr's analysis of the human condition, his actual theology was flat and one-dimensional and typical of so much of the thinking which had become apparent at Amsterdam:

> It seemed to be a quite unfamiliar demand that in the church one must not simply speak in general terms of 'the mind of Jesus', but must always fundamentally think and argue also from definite biblical texts and contexts, and when one put forward this demand, one had to be prepared to be written off as a 'Biblicist' or 'legalist' or 'literalist' – a charge which Niebuhr has repeated once again.[25]

What was lacking in the new liberalism was a definite theological *a priori*: 'I am chilled by this framework . . . Those who think in these terms cannot

---

[21] Eberhart Busch, *Karl Barth: his life from letters and autobiographical texts* (London: SCM, 1976), p.342; Fox, *Reinhold Niebuhr: a biography*, p.231.
[22] Karl Barth, 'A preliminary reply to Dr Reinhold Niebuhr', *The Christian News-Letter*, supplement 326, 8 December 1948, 9–16 [10].
[23] Ibid., 9–10.
[24] Ibid., 13.
[25] Ibid., 15.

understand me'.[26] The Christian theologian like the Christian lay man in the secular world, cannot think in conventional dualisms of good and evil, justice and oppression, progress and regression and the like, but knows the reality of a third dimension which controls the other two: 'I am encouraged by the fact that it is precisely the Bible that knows not only these two dimensions but also a third that is decisive – the Word of God, the Holy Spirit, God's free choice, God's grace and judgement, creation, reconciliation, the kingdom, sanctification, the congregation'.[27] It was this dimension 'of mystery' to which both Niebuhr and too many of the religious activists of the World Council of Churches seemed totally blind. The so-called 'Anglo-Saxon' theology lacked mystery and as such was ineffective and, frankly, boring and trite: 'My own explanation of this lack of mystery is that it has not yet seen the third dimension in the Bible'.[28] Niebuhr's 'Answer to Karl Barth' of March 1949 failed to take the discussion forward in any meaningful way. The American could hardly differentiate Barth's thought from a form of sophisticated, or perhaps not so sophisticated, fundamentalism. After protesting against 'the hazards of biblical literalism',[29] for the time being at least he let the matter rest.

This would not be the last time that the two men would clash. Preparations for the second assembly of the World Council of Churches, scheduled to take place in the Chicago suburb of Evanston, Illinois, in 1954, began 4 years earlier when the central committee decided on the concept of hope as the conference theme. A commission of 25 leading theologians was selected to prepare a document which would serve as a basis for discussion, deliberation and action. Ostensibly the theme was perfectly apposite. It had been 5 years since the ending of the war, western Europe was being slowly rebuilt, American confidence was booming as was its economy, while the anti-religious bias of the communist regimes beyond the iron curtain provided a threat which encouraged the need to exercise hope. Western Protestantism was in a fairly healthy state; in America it was thriving. In all the 1950s was a quietly optimistic time for the churches. In choosing the topic of hope no one, it seems, realized how contentious it would become. 'I am far from sure', noted Willem Visser't Hooft, general secretary of the World Council of Churches, 'that the Central Council would have taken this decision if it had realized what a theological tempest it would have to face'.[30]

---

[26] Ibid., 15.
[27] Ibid., 15.
[28] Ibid., 16.
[29] Reinhold Niebuhr, 'Answer to Karl Barth', *The Christian News-Letter*, supplement 332, 2 March 1949, 74–80 [78].
[30] W. A. Visser't Hooft, *Memoirs* (London: SCM, 1970), p.246.

The source of the tempest would be the conflicting understandings of the meaning of Christian hope and how it should be interpreted in the modern world. Was it a this-worldly or other-worldly entity? Was hope a transcendent divine reality or a product of human striving? To what extent was it exclusively kingdom-based or did it include the evangelical and humanitarian mission of the church? How did the resurrection and ascension of Christ fit into the idea of hope, and how were these realities to be interpreted anyway? Was resurrection a historical or an a-historical concept? Then there was the New Testament conviction concerning the parousia, Christ's coming again in glory. Was this a symbolic way of expressing idealism and human progress or was the creation of a new heaven and a new earth an authentic apocalyptic reality? How should religious symbolism and venerable theological convictions be understood in the midst of a modern, increasingly technological world? With eschatology already a burning question among the theologians, the fact that Barth and Niebuhr had been invited to serve on the preparatory commission meant that there would be no unanimity on these questions. 'Was it not fantastic to expect that Karl Barth and Reinhold Niebuhr, Emil Brunner and George Florovsky, Hendrik Kraemer and Henry Van Dusen would find a common word on such an extraordinarily difficult theme?'[31] reflected Visser't Hooft wistfully. The decision, however, had been made, and the invitations had been accepted.

The first of the three preparatory meetings was held at the village of Rolle on Lake Geneva on 20–30 July 1951. 'Barth', according to Lesslie Newbigin, 'was at his most polemical'.[32] He was rather contemptuous of the Americans, 'Niebuhr at their head, with bright, healthy teeth, great determination and few problems',[33] and it was not long before the conflict manifested itself. The American contingent conceptualized hope in terms of social betterment and incremental development inspired by the example of Christ whereas the European theologians were intent on taking the theological category of hope seriously. For Niebuhr God was beyond history. All theological formulations were culture bound and provisional. It was religious experience including the consciousness of sin and release of redemption, which were absolute while the mission of the church was to partake in ethical renewal. Barth had little patience with religiously tinged optimism, and when Niebuhr suggested that eschatology should be put to one side and even that the word 'hope' be dropped from the assembly's title, the Swiss exploded. It was only the diplomacy of Newbigin and Edmund Schlink from Heidelberg that prevented Niebuhr from packing his bags and leaving forthwith. Newbigin, who would be chosen chairman for the

---

[31] Visser't Hooft, *Memoirs*, p.246.
[32] Newbigin, *Unfinished Agenda*, p.131.
[33] Busch, *Karl Barth: his life from letters*, p.395.

succeeding meetings at Château Bossey, Geneva, in 1952 and 1953, was intent that the biblical concept of hope should inform the deliberations: 'Eschatology was at that time an issue which the western liberal establishment was unwilling to face'.[34] Consequently his sympathies were with Barth. Following the first difficult meeting relations did improve, a consensus of sorts was achieved and Barth was given the task of preparing the final draft of the report. 'I found him sitting surrounded by papers in the middle of the Bossey lawn, looking much dishevelled', recounted Newbigin. '"You look as if you are in trouble", I said. "I am", he replied. "This is a task for some great ecumenical theologian"'.[35] For Barth consensus did not come easily, and the final report was more theologically informed than otherwise would have been the case.[36] Niebuhr's only retort was: 'We did nothing more than capitulate more than was wise to Karl Barth'.[37]

The establishment of The Scottish Journal of Theology

As well as being the year which inaugurated the World Council of Churches, 1948 witnessed the establishment of *The Scottish Journal of Theology* which would become the major platform for the dissemination of Barthian influence in Britain and, indeed, the English speaking world. It also saw Daniel T. Jenkins's removal to the United States as a Commonwealth Fund Fellow at Union Seminary New York and thereafter, between 1949 and 1961, as a part-time professor at the Chicago Divinity School which he combined with a British pastorate, first at the Oxted Congregational Church in Surrey and from 1956, at the King's Weigh House in London's west end. During the next decade Jenkins, like T. F. Torrance, would write extensively on church based issues, with volumes such as *Tradition and the Spirit* (1951), *Congregationalism: a restatement* (1954), *The Strangeness of the Church* (1955) and *The Protestant Ministry* (1958) expanding on the thesis which he had initiated so masterfully in his early *The Nature of Catholicity* (1942). 'I consider Karl Barth a theologian without a peer in the world today',[38] he wrote from Chicago in 1951, a theological school not noted for its appreciation of theological orthodoxy. His work, like Torrance's, would be to combine a commitment to ecumenism with a basic faithfulness to Barth in order to

---

[34] Newbigin, *Unfinished Agenda*, p.133.

[35] Ibid., p.140.

[36] See *Report of the Advisory Commission on the Main Theme of the Second Assembly: Christ, the Hope of the World* (New York: Harper and Brothers, 1954).

[37] Fox, *Reinhold Niebuhr: a biography*, p.244.

[38] Daniel T. Jenkins, *Europe and America: their contribution to the World Church* (Philadelphia: Westminster Press, 1951), p.16.

provide Protestants with a richer ecclesiology than they would otherwise have had.

Others from among the British Barthians were moving on. Alec White-house had left the pastoral ministry at Elland, Yorkshire, for an academic post in the University of Durham in 1948, while a year later George S. Hendry, after nearly two decades ministering to a Church of Scotland parish in the Bridge of Allen, Stirling, was appointed to the Charles Hodge Chair of Theology at the Princeton Theological Seminary. Princeton, along with the small divinity school of Iowa's University of Dubuque, was one of the few institutions in the United States where Barth's work was appreciated and actually read. At Princeton Hendry would find as colleagues Elmer G. Homrighausen, translator of some of Barth's earliest works, the German New Testament scholar Otto Piper, Hugh T. Kerr Jr., and the president, his fellow Scot John A. Mackay, all of whom were in accord with Barth's basic orientation and sympathetic to his work.[39] With Geoffrey Bromiley's departure from Edinburgh for Fuller Seminary in Pasedena, California, in 1958,[40] the reception of Barth's theology through the medium of English would take an even more pronounced transatlantic turn.

A not unrelated factor contributing to the increasing welcome which was being afforded to the Barthian theology in England during the 1950s, was the highly erudite and arresting volume entitled *The Catholicity of Protestantism* (1951) edited by the Methodist scholars R. Newton Flew and Rupert Davies, presented to the Archbishop of Canterbury in response to his 1946 appeal to the Free Churches 'to take episcopacy into their system'. The ecumenical rapprochement had been gathering momentum since the end of the war, and although there would be no ultimate union between the Church of England and Nonconformity, it did engender fresh theological thinking and historical research. Building on the Luther scholarship of E. Gordon Rupp and his fellow Methodist Philip S. Watson and enshrining the Geneva Catholicism of Nathaniel Micklem, the report presented a magisterial account of the Word-centred revelation theology and ecclesiological seriousness of the new Nonconformity. Along with Rupp, Watson and Micklem, its authors included H. F. Lovell Cocks and John Marsh, the Baptist Ernest Payne and others. As well as being a rediscovery of evangelical grace and justification by faith alone, the Reformation had entailed a renewal of the church as a divine ordinance replete with an ordered gospel ministry and effective sacraments. It was by now apparent that Micklem's generation-long struggle to call his fellow Congregationalists, and Protestant Nonconformists generally, to the fullness of their doctrinal heritage

[39] See William K. Selden, *Princeton Theological Seminary: a narrative history, 1812–1992* (Princeton: PTS, 1992), pp.115–40.

[40] See George Marsden, *Reforming Fundamentalism: Fuller Seminary and the New Evangelicalism* (Grand Rapids: Eerdmans, 1987), p.188.

was paying off. 'There are signs of reviving life and witness', Micklem had told a University of Chicago audience in 1946. 'Over against the old guard of the rationalists stands the new theological movement inspired by the Swiss theologian Karl Barth, though many are coming to see that P. T. Forsyth a generation ago was representing the same witness in a more intelligible or digestible form'.[41] The long term outcome of this movement, among the Congregationalists and the English Presbyterians at least, would be the formation, in 1972, of the United Reformed Church, though the acids of 1960s secular modernism would vitiate the doctrinal seriousness of that denomination from the outset. In the late 1940s and 1950s, however, signs of renewal were particularly high:

> Among the Congregationalists there is a revival of Genevan high-churchmanship which by its opponents is called sometimes 'Barthianism', sometimes 'Thomism', sometimes merely 'obscurantism', for the gulf between those who take the incarnation seriously and those who regard it as a metaphor goes very deep.[42]

It was Scotland, however, which would provide the prime momentum for Barth reception in the United Kingdom from the 1950s onwards. *The Scottish Journal of Theology* had arisen from the extraordinary vitality which had been evident in New College, Edinburgh, especially in the mid-1930s and early 1940s. 'The action of a few raw ministers of the Church of Scotland, ordained for barely one or two years, in throwing themselves into an association for the study of theology, might pardonably be judged to bear the appearance of . . . juvenility',[43] remarked one of them, J. K. S. Reid, in 1945. Just as those who had congregated around Daniel Jenkins and made *The Presbyter* their forum, north of the border many of Reid's New College contemporaries such as T. F. Torrance, Ronald Gregor Smith, Ian Henderson and others had established the Scottish Church Theology Society in August 1940 in order to study theology seriously as an aspect of the church's ongoing mission to the world. In 1945–46 the *Institutio* was taken as the members' set text, with especial note being given to the vexed question of natural revelation in Book 1. 'It is with no desire to absolutize the theology of the Reformation that our society has taken up the study of Calvin's *Institutes*', wrote John McConnachie, 'still less that we should seek to return to that Calvinism which later lost the insight of the Reformers and laid its heavy hand on the Church of Scotland, with its bleak prohibitions

---

[41] Nathaniel Micklem, 'The religious situation in Great Britain', *Journal of Religion* 26 (1946), 44–8 [47].
[42] Ibid., 47.
[43] J. K. S. Reid, 'Ne taceretur', *Crisis Christology* 3/2 (Winter 1945–46), 32–4 [32].

and dogmatic presentation of Christianity'.[44] There was, though, no doubt that the renewal reflected all the characteristics of the Barthian scheme: deep doctrinal seriousness, a pastoral orientation within the Reformed tradition, the conviction that religion began with revelation not reason, that revelation was a matter of God's saving self-disclosure in Christ which issued in the renewal of preaching within the church.

T. F. Torrance, recently returned from war service as a chaplain in Italy, conveyed these convictions with stark intensity. 'Christianity means Christ himself and nothing else but Christ; and that means that the Person of Christ displaces and banishes all vague natural religion with only "God" in it',[45] he claimed. Notional religion was worse than useless as was that which did not begin with the crucified Christ: 'Many a time one knew that, had it not been for the cross, faith would have perished utterly for it could not have survived the ghastly horror and sheer devastation of human life and the crushing sense of shame that followed after it was over'.[46] Just as vague religiosity was pastorally useless, natural religion did not begin to reflect the realities of the sinful human condition under stress: 'There is no real point of contact between a man and God apart from a Christian "a priori"'.[47] There was no doubt that Torrance's war experience had not only affected him deeply but confirmed the truth and the potency of his previous theological stance. 'The soldier does not want a mystic experience', he claimed. 'He desperately wants a Face and a Voice which he may know and trust. Symbol tells him nothing. It does not impart belief . . . Christianity must be a matter of clear belief, not aesthetics'.[48] Whereas Anglo-Catholicism, in Torrance's view, dealt in symbolism divorced from existential reality, the old liberalism of virtues and values placed a crushing burden on men's shoulders which virtually prevented them from knowing the Christ who was God: 'In the last resort God has no reality for the soul except in Jesus Christ. He alone covers the whole face and heart of God, so that there are no dark unknown spots in the Almighty which we need fear and dimly and mysteriously worship, for which Jesus does not wholly go bail'.[49] The only theology which was strong enough to refashion civilization was one which took nothing human for granted and found its integrating point in the sole victory of the God-man Christ: 'Christ himself, the Word, had to create the very capacity he needed for receiving him into his heart. When that happened, it was the

---

[44] John McConnachie, 'Reviews from the Scottish Church-Theology Society News Letter', *Crisis Christology* 3/2 (Winter 1945–46), 48–50 [48].

[45] T. F. Torrance, 'Down to bedrock', *Crisis Christology* 3/3 (Spring 1946), 30–2[30].

[46] Ibid., 30.

[47] Ibid., 31.

[48] Ibid., 32.

[49] Ibid., 30.

most rewarding moment in the padre's experience'.[50] For Torrance, as for those who had seen the Confessing Church challenge Hitler's tyranny before the war, theology was not a comfortable intellectual pastime but a matter of life and death.

Torrance had returned from active service to his parish responsibilities in Alyth, Perthshire, in July 1945 before taking up the ministry of the Beechgrove Parish Church, Aberdeen, in November 1947. It was from there that he and J. K. S. Reid established the *Scottish Journal of Theology* and acted as its joint editors.[51] The first editorial was both a celebration of victory and a call to arms. The Christian faith shines in its own light and is not dependent on any alien philosophy or scheme; it is centred on a gospel, a saving message of redemption through Christ, the crucified and risen Lord; it both presupposes and serves the church, a body ordained by God to witness to the truth of the Word, and that confidence, assertiveness and boldness are essential to its very existence: 'Theology cannot properly be the pursuit of the dilettante or the recluse or the scientific specialist; it can be practiced only by the active members of a living church'.[52] There was nothing halting in this statement. It was, in fact, a vibrant apologia for a revived biblical theology and a new era in the history of the church. As it happened *The Presbyter*, whose final issue appeared in October 1948, saw the new publication as a continuation of its own mission: 'The concerns of its sponsors are so very closely allied to our own', wrote its editor, the Congregationalist John Huxtable, 'that we can regard this new quarterly as a welcome and powerful reinforcement to the cause of Reformed theology'.[53]

The publication's Reformed credentials were apparent from the first. Along with J. K. S. Reid's treatment of the doctrine of election, George Hendry wrote on the doctrine of scripture quoting from Calvin and Luther while John McConnachie, who would pass away later that year, wrote on 'The uniqueness of the Word of God'.[54] The journal was not exclusively Barthian, or, indeed, entirely Scottish. During its first year the Aberdeen liberal theologian David Cairns was invited to write on the theology of

---

[50] Ibid., 31.

[51] For the establishment of the *Scottish Journal of Theology* see Alistair E. McGrath, *Thomas F. Torrance: an intellectual biography* (Edinburgh: T & T Clark, 1999), pp.128–9; Torrance's military experience and its significance are recounted on pp.69–77.

[52] T. F. Torrance and J. K. S. Reid, 'Editorial', *Scottish Journal of Theology* 1 (1948), 1–4 [2].

[53] John Huxtable, 'Editorial', *The Presbyter: journal of confessional and Catholic churchmanship* 6/3 (October 1948), 1.

[54] A précis had already appeared in *Crisis Christology* 5/3 (Spring 1948), 6–9; cf. John McConnachie, 'The uniqueness of the Word of God', *Scottish Journal of Theology* 1 (1948), 113–35.

Emil Brunner, Donald M. Baillie from St Andrews reviewed Barth's *Dog-matik im grundriss* (1948) and there was also a contribution from the Indian-based Anglican Stephen Neill: 'It would be quite ludicrous to suggest that the journal took an uncritically pro-Barth stance, or that it chose to devote its pages more or less entirely to or even predominantly to matters relating to Barth . . . It simply allowed Barth's perspective to be heard'.[55] Nevertheless, the writings of George S. Hendry, F. W. Camfield, G. D. Henderson as well as numerous essays and reviews by Torrance and Reid ensured that the *Scottish Journal of Theology* would be known as the means whereby the mature theology of Karl Barth would be disseminated not only in Scotland but far beyond.

Torrance's progress to New College, Edinburgh, where he would be appointed to the chair in church history in 1950 before succeeding G. T. Thomson as professor of Christian Dogmatics 2 years later, inaugurated what its supporters regarded as the triumph of a modern enlightened orthodoxy and its detractors as 'the time of the Barthian captivity'.[56] 'I must say I'm sorry that Torrance is being nominated for the systematic theology chair', wrote Donald Baillie in July 1952. 'New College will become even more conservative-ultra-Barthian than before'.[57] It would last beyond the 1950s and 1960s until Torrance's retirement in 1979. A man of forceful personality as well as huge strength of intellect and breadth of knowledge, he was both popular and effective as a teacher. The American evangelical scholar Carl F. H. Henry, who spent a sabbatical in Edinburgh during the early 1950s, remembered the admiration with which he was held: 'Whenever Torrance in the classroom attacked rationalistic Protestant modernism – which Barth in 1925 had already declared "dead" in Germany – students thumped their feet in approval'.[58] For Henry, whose religious tradition was blighted by a scholastic rationalism of its own, Torrance's whole approach, like that of Karl Barth, was doing untold harm to the evangelical faith. His studies in Edinburgh convinced him, if he needed convincing, that 'the Barthian erosion of scriptural authority in the Church of Scotland'[59] was calamitous, though fortunately the true faith was being preserved in the Free Church College next door to New College on the Mound. Whereas liberals faulted Torrance with being too orthodox and

[55] McGrath, *Thomas F. Torrance: an intellectual biography*, p.129.

[56] George Newlands, 'Divinity and Dogmatics', in David F. Wright and Gary D. Badcock, *Disruption to Diversity: Edinburgh Divinity 1846–1996* (Edinburgh: T & T Clark, 1996), pp.114–33 [127].

[57] George Newlands, *John and Donald Baillie: transatlantic theology* (Bern: Peter Lang, 2002), p.182.

[58] Carl F. H. Henry, *Confessions of a Theologian: an autobiography* (Waco, Texas: Word Books, 1986), p.134.

[59] Ibid., p.135.

scholastically minded, conservatives accused him of undermining the factual truth of God's inerrant Word. It would be the liberals, however, who would be most incensed, as Torrance's 1952 clash with a highly revered senior academic would show.

Torrance, Brand Blanshard and 'Reason and Belief'

Brand Blanchard (1892–1987), the Stirling Professor of Philosophy at Yale, was perhaps the most distinguished American philosopher of his generation. Neither a member of the American pragmatist school nor a devotee of linguistic analysis, he remained wedded to the somewhat Victorian absolute idealism in which he had been raised. In religious terms he was an unabashed modernist. Of the two modern Western philosophical traditions, the first of Hegel, Green, and Bradley which identified God with an impersonal absolute embracing all things on the level of the mind, and the other for which God was a personal being distinct from the world and its creator and redeemer, Blanchard held to the first. His mature belief was in 'a finite Deity limited in power but not in goodness. For God, so conceived, remains one person among others in an infinite universe, and is not himself the ultimate reality'.[60] Although he was the son and grandson of Congregational ministers, he had broken alike with Christian orthodoxy, the personhood of God and the concept of religious particularism as a young man. 'For us the ultimate reality in the universe is to be found in no part of it, however great, but only in the whole'.[61] Like Barth, Reinhold Niebuhr and Emil Brunner before him, he had been invited to deliver the Gifford Lectures, at St Andrews in 1952, and in so doing had challenged Barth and Brunner along with Luther and Kierkegaard in a forceful and pugnacious way. For Blanchard the concept of particular revelation was anathema. The only valid means of approaching deity, whatever the putative attributes of the Christian God, was through a natural theology of reason and ethics.

In his Gifford series entitled 'Reason and Belief', Blanchard mounted an extensive critique on confessional theology from the standpoint of absolute idealism and concluded that it was inherently irrational. Mentioning in passing J. H. Newman and his nineteenth century rejection of liberalism, he wrote: 'Even the young intellectuals of Oxford, we are told, began to go about murmuring "credo in Newmannum". We have something similar in today's outbreak of theological irrationalism'.[62] Because orthodox theology generally and Barthianism specifically put a premium on mystery, the

---

[60] Brand Blanshard, *Reason and Belief* (London: George Allen and Unwin, 1972), p.523.
[61] Ibid., p.524.
[62] Ibid., p.317.

American Hegelian had no option but to reject them outright. What was more he was clearly aggrieved by the new theologians' use of an alternative scheme of reality than the one which he believed was common to all enlightened thinkers.

> Philosophers for some thousands of years have been searching into creation, immortality, God, freedom, evil. They have not, perhaps, been notably successful, but they have closed many misleading trails and achieved, as they thought, some glimpses of the summit towards which they have been struggling. You now tell them that there is no road to it from where they stand, that all the trails they have been exploring wind up in swamps or deserts, and that they had therefore better give up their misguided effort.[63]

His knowledge of Barth was gleaned exclusively from a few portions of the *Romans* commentary in Hoskyns's 1933 translation, Barth's famous altercation with his fellow Swiss, *Nein! Antwort an Emil Brunner* (1934) and the pre-war Giffords *The Knowledge of God and the Service of God* (1938). He readily admitted that he had read nothing else. It was inevitable that there would be a response. It was equally predictable that it would come from New College's professor of church history, soon to become its professor of Christian dogmatics.

Torrance had not been present at the lectures but he responded to a report in the national daily *The Scotsman*.[64] The issue pivoted on the idea of a general rationality open to all and a specific rationality which was controlled by the claims of a revealed Word. 'Professor Blanchard considered that this attempt to save religious faith by making it irrational was disastrous', stated the report. 'The probable effect upon thoughtful men of asking that they believe the incredible would be the repudiation of faith altogether'.[65] Torrance, not unexpectedly, found this claim outrageous. In accusing the theology of revelation of irrationality, the American had 'perpetrated [an] antiquated blunder' due, in part, to his ignorance of Barth's mature works: 'It is a pitiful tragedy . . . that the American philosopher has not apparently peered beyond the egg-shells of the young Swiss thinker!'[66]

---

[63] Ibid., p.301.

[64] For the following I am indebted to an unpublished paper by Iain and Morag Torrance, 'A skirmish in the early reception of Karl Barth in Scotland: the exchange between Thomas F. Torrance and Brand Blanchard'.

[65] 'Theology in crisis', *The Scotsman*, 9 April 1952, 1; cf. Blanshard, *Reason and Belief*, pp.318–9.

[66] T. F. Torrance, 'Theology of Karl Barth', *The Scotsman*, 14 April 1952, 4.

Echoing the Catholic Hans Urs von Balthasar's recent assessment of Barth as a theologian of analogy,[67] Torrance insisted that Barth's thought was massively objective and that he had refuted all irrationalism not least the existentialism which was currently emanating from Bultmann's Marburg.

The philosopher's rejoinder was immediate. 'When Professor Torrance describes Barth as a defender of reason, he can only be using "reason" with a special meaning and a very different meaning from the philosophers', he claimed. Barth's God, 'the Wholly Other', patently defied definition according to all rational categories. 'If one claims to believe in reason, it should surely mean the reason used in common sense and science, for example the science of natural theology'.[68] It was quite obvious, therefore, that such a specific characterization of the concept of reason was disingenuous and perverse. In an early manifestation of what would become his familiar definition of theological reason, Torrance echoed the words of the Scottish philosopher John Macmurray, that 'reason is the capacity to behave in terms of the nature of the object, that is to say, to behave objectively'. It was not reason *per se* that was the culprit, but 'that autonomous, self-sufficient reason, reason turned in upon itself' which was at the root of the ills. What the natural theologians were guilty of was 'a diseased "rationalism" . . . the self-willed reason that chooses to go its own way and refuses to be determined by its object'.[69] In his own mind, it was Torrance and not the Gifford lecturer who was being truly scientific: 'What theology demands . . . is a ruthless scientific criticism of the activity of reason and of the reasoner himself to ensure that here in theological science he is behaving rationally, that is that his reason is conforming properly and obediently to the object given'.[70] Far from being 'the Wholly Other', Barth's God was the God of Christian revelation who had acted in history for humankind's redemption and bidden men and women to exercise obedient faith in him. Such a revelation was an offence to reason and demanded repentance and crucifixion of the self: 'If this is the real reason why Professor Blanshard calls Karl Barth's view of reason anti-rationalism', Torrance continued bluntly, 'then it is clear that the real issue does not lie between Blanshard and Barth, but between Blanshard and the Christian gospel'.[71]

It was hardly conceivable that the American would take this lying down. He repeated his contention that both Barth and Brunner were incontrovertibly irrationalist: 'Both have over and over again, and in the most

---

[67] Hans Urs von Balthasar, *Karl Barth: Darstellung und Deutung seiner Theologie* (Einsiedeln: Johannes Verlag, 1951).

[68] Brand Blanshard, 'Theology of Karl Barth', *The Scotsman*, 16 April 1952, 6.

[69] T. F. Torrance, 'Theology of Karl Barth', *The Scotsman*, 19 April 1952, 6.

[70] Ibid.

[71] Ibid.

explicit terms, denied that the standards of natural reason, the reason used by scientists and philosophers, are valid for the knowledge of God'.[72] Torrance's refashioning of the concept of reason to fit his own scheme was basically eccentric and self serving: 'To describe as "rational" a kind of knowledge that to our natural reason is not only unintelligible but self-contradictory, is to empty the word of all normal meaning',[73] he claimed. That being so, it was inevitable that there would be an unbridgeable divide between the so-called logic of faith and secular rationality and ordinary common sense: 'To offer the Barth-Brunner theology to philosophers as a rational account of things is to invite them to swarm down on you like devouring locusts. And Professor Torrance will agree that they may be a dreadful pest!'[74] The knockabout, however, was destined to continue. For Torrance it was a matter of incompatible axioms and two conflicting views of reality. 'Professor Blanshard sits so securely in his idealist parlour that real argument with him is hardly possible, except on his own idealist presuppositions',[75] he claimed. Christian theology had its own presuppositions and the theologian, like the humble believer, was obliged to adhere to the logic implicit in his own scheme. If this clashed with the conventions of a mundane rationality, so be it. As for the accusations of logical contradiction:

> That did not mean that [Barth] 'accepted both sides of a contradiction', as Professor Blanshard mistakenly assumes, but that [he] recognized the importance and depth of paradox in the human expression of truth and that [he] was prepared to say 'yes' and 'no' at crucial points of an issue where a scholastic distinction would falsify the truth and where a logical synthesis would only force an abortive unity against the facts.[76]

In fact Barth's 'massive mind' had reinvented the ground rules for the whole theological venture, and in so doing had freed Christian thought to be true to its own specific rationale.

Blanshard, however, was having none of it. 'What could irrationalism mean if not that the real is, to our reason, unintelligible and incoherent?'[77] For him Barthianism, and Torrances's take on it, was nothing less than

> the suicide of reason. A kind of knowledge which soars so high as to have left mere logic behind has simply evaporated as knowledge

---

[72] Brand Blanshard, 'Theology of Karl Barth', *The Scotsman*, 22 April 1952, 6.
[73] Ibid.
[74] Ibid.
[75] T. F. Torrance, 'Theology of Karl Barth', *The Scotsman*, 23 April 1952, 6.
[76] Ibid.
[77] Brand Blanshard, 'Theology of Karl Barth', *The Scotsman*, 28 April 1952, 6.

. . . Whoever says that reality does and must flout our reason is an irrationalist: Barth and Brunner plainly say this; they are irrationalists . . . Their theology, like that of Newman and Pascal, is built on despair of human reason. They hope by renouncing reason to save religion. It is a bad exchange. If you do not accept both, you will end with neither.[78]

For Blanshard it was inconceivable that the acceptance of critical reason would threaten the veracity and vitality of true religion. The bargain, however, meant that true religion would of necessity forfeit its nature as a medium of knowing an explicitly Christian God. Its characteristic dogmas including the miraculous, the incarnation, atonement and resurrection would have to be reinterpreted radically. For him Luther, Pascal, Kierkegaard, Newman, Brunner, Barth and now Torrance were irredeemably obscurantist. It was by any account a cavalier rejection of a whole strand of major Christian thought. And with that an extraordinary correspondence on the pages of a foremost national daily was brought to a close.

The English Baptists, Wales and Northern Ireland

Since its inception the Barthian movement in Britain had not been universally popular; in fact it was still incurring a vigorous backlash. E. L. Allen of King's College, Newcastle-upon-Tyne, was a particularly unsympathetic commentator on Barth's output and influence. 'It is one thing to say that God is to be seen in the light of Jesus Christ', he claimed, 'and another to use a particular Christological dogma as a principle from which the whole content of theology must in some way be deduced'.[79] Not only was Barth's Christological principle unbalanced but the Swiss's complex if naïve Biblicism was highly suspect: 'It may well be that we need a revival of systematic theology in the Protestant church, but we cannot be satisfied with one which is unwilling to recognize its obvious debt to new methods and new knowledge'.[80] Allen was contemptuous of Barth's 'ardent disciples', namely the contributors to *Reformation Old and New*, and decried their penchant for 'combining a resounding emphasis on the sovereignty of God and the nothingness of man with a naïve identification of one's own opinions with absolute truth'.[81] *Kirchliche Dogmatik* III/2, Barth's

[78] Ibid.
[79] E. L. Allen, 'The theology of Karl Barth', *The Contemporary Review* 172 (1947), 91–4 [94].
[80] Ibid.
[81] E. L. Allen, 'British theology and the great blight', in S. Stephen Spinks (ed.), *Religion in Britain since 1900* (London: Andrew Dakers, 1952), pp.182–97 [186].

Christological anthropology, was diffuse, speculative and ultimately unsatisfactory, while his assessment called forth a singularly unprophetic comment:
'Karl Barth's *Kirchliche Dogmatik* begun in 1927, has by now reached such
proportions as to make its complete translation into another language too
formidable a proposition to be entertained'.[82] An unrepentant liberal, he
could not wait for the Barthian phase in English (in his case) religious
history to pass. 'Neo-orthodoxy is not the revelation of a long forgotten
truth: it is a fashion which suits the time to which it belongs and will die
out as the time changes. Let its champions reflect that in fifty years time the
merest tyro in theology will be speaking of Barth and Brunner as they speak
today of Troeltsch and Harnack'.[83] The very stridency of his comments
reflected the fact that Barth's views were still gaining a considered hearing.
If that had not been the case for the most part within the Anglican or
Methodist Churches, among the Baptists or in Protestant Northern Ireland,
by the 1950s there were signs of change.

The news that Barth had been unhappy with the practice and theology of
infant baptism issuing a polemical tract *Kirchliche Lehre von der Taufe* in
1943 had not gone un-noticed. In it he had rejected the sacramental nature
of the ordinance and had pleaded for baptism as the believer's conscious
attestation to a salvation already wrought by Christ. Baptism should not be
a medium of grace but a witness to grace and as such administered only to
those who were conscious of its reality and meaning. This would mean a
break with both the convention of the Reformed Church and with the nearly
universal practice of Christendom. Barth well realized its radical significance: it would mean 'the end of the evangelical church within the Con-
stantinian *corpus christianum*'.[84] In 1948 Ernest A. Payne, tutor at Regent's
Park College, Oxford, and an ecumenically engaged English Baptist published his translation *The Teaching of the Church regarding Baptism* (1948).
Payne was a-typical of Baptists though representative of a younger generation of ministers in holding to a higher ecclesiology than was usual, a more
pronounced sacramentalism and a historical sense that went beyond the
stark Biblicism of much of his tradition. His volume *The Fellowship of
Believers* (1944) was, according to Alec Whitehouse, 'the Baptist version of
Church Order.'[85] Like the 'new Genevans', Payne was 'orthodox, scholarly

---

[82] E. L. Allen, 'Karl Barth on man', *The Expository Times* 60 (1948–49), 203–5 [203].
[83] E. L. Allen, 'The new orthodoxy and the contemporary mood', *The Congregational
Quarterly* 28 (1950), 143–50 [150].
[84] Karl Barth, *Kirchliche Lehre von der Taufe* (Zürich: Evangelischer Verlag, 1943),
p.40.
[85] W. A. Whitehouse, review of E. A. Payne, *The Fellowship of Believers: Baptist thought
and practice yesterday and today* (London: Kingsgate Press, 1944) in *The Presbyter* 3/3
(August 1945), 31.

and liturgically minded',[86] and represented the turn from individualism to churchmanship which was gaining ground at the time.[87] Although the tract drew fire from paedo-Baptists, Nathaniel Micklem and Daniel T. Jenkins included,[88] it contributed to the vigorous debate on ecclesiology and the renewal of churchmanship which had become such a marked character of the theological discourse during the post-war years. It also served to bring the Baptists within the orbit of mainstream Barthian thought, something that had ceased with the death of R. Birch Hoyle a decade earlier. Neville Clark, author of the pellucid *An Approach to the Theology of the Sacraments* (1956) who would become the English Baptists' leading liturgical scholar, would interpret the *Church Dogmatics* for his fellow denominationalists and correlate Barth's theology with his own insights and those of the biblical theology movement generally.[89]

In Wales the evangelical J. Ithel Jones, who would be called to the principalship of the Cardiff Baptist College, and Lewis E. Valentine, a senior Baptist minister and latterly president of the Welsh Baptist Union, propounded Barth's thoughts in a specifically Welsh language idiom and within their own milieu. Jones, whose family background was in the intense pietism of the 1904 revival, offered a highly penetrating assessment of Barth's thought in a series of essays in the Baptist quarterly *Seren Gomer* ('The Star of Gomer'). Having described the development of Protestant theology between Hume and Troeltsch, he explained the way in which the *Römerbrief*, through its concept of revelation, had revolutionized twentieth century theology and led to a positive reappraisal of virtually all the loci which had been championed by the Reformers. Jones's appraisal was informed by a first-hand knowledge of Barth's works including the second volume of the *Dogmatik*. It was Barth's activist doctrine of God which he found most

---

[86] D. W. Bebbington, *Evangelicalism in Modern Britain: a history from the 1780s to the 1980s* (London: Unwin Hyman, 1989), p.251.

[87] See Robert C. Walton (ed.), *The Gathered Community* (London: Carey Press, 1946); Ian M. Randall, *The English Baptists of the Twentieth Century* (Didcot: Baptist Historical Society, 2005), pp.219–21, 321–37.

[88] Nathaniel Micklem, 'Karl Barth on baptism', review of *The Teaching of the Church regarding Baptism* (London: SCM, 1948) in *The Presbyter* 5/2 (April 1948), 7–8; Daniel T. Jenkins, 'Is Barth a Baptist?', *The Ecumenical Review* 1 (1948–49), 463–4.

[89] Neville Clark, reviews of Karl Barth, *Church Dogmatics* IV/1 (Edinburgh: T & T Clark, 1956), *The Baptist Quarterly* 18 (1959–60), 40–2; idem. *Church Dogmatics* III/1 (Edinburgh: T & T Clark, 1958), *The Baptist Quarterly* 18 (1959–60), 175–6; idem. *Church Dogmatics* III/2 (Edinburgh: T & T Clark, 1960), *The Baptist Quarterly* 18 (1959–60), 373–5; for Clark's theological stance, see Don Black, 'The Cassock Club', *The Baptist Quarterly* 40 (2004), 436–9.

engaging: that God as the Holy Trinity was in his inmost essence act more than static being:

> In proceeding to deal with God's attributes, Barth re-emphasized that revelation was God's act and that it is better, therefore, to speak of God's 'reality' than his essence. God is subject, not object, and we cannot say 'God is' without realizing that God is active both in himself and in revealing himself. Both 'existence' and 'act' are present in the word 'reality'.[90]

Jones rejected the American Calvinist Van Til's scholastic critique of Barth as being forced and artificial and the criticism of his compatriot, the philosopher Hywel D. Lewis, as being conceptually misconstrued. An ethical critique of Barth based on common religious presuppositions was doomed to fail: 'Barth and the ethical philosophers are operating on two completely different planes'.[91] The genius of Barth was to have begun, continued and to have finished not with common ethical or philosophical concepts but with the unique nature of God's self-revelation in the Word. Despite its brevity, Ithel Jones's series of articles constituted perhaps the most judicious short assessment of Barth's work to appear in Britain during the early 1950s and showed the extent of the impact that his work was still having upon Nonconformist Wales: 'It was a feeling of release that so many of us had when we first came across the work of Karl Barth. Here at last was a theologian with sufficient gumption to call the church back to her proper task namely theology'.[92]

Lewis Valentine, who like the doyen of Welsh Barthians J. E. Daniel was a leading member of Plaid Cymru, the Welsh Nationalist Party, was especially indebted to Barth's work during the 1950s. In a powerful address to the annual assembly of the Baptist Union of Wales in 1954 in which he propounded a Barthian concept of God's gracious election of humankind in Christ, he described the minister's task:

> Through a healthy instinct people know that the politicians have little constructive to offer, and they know that it is through the pulpit that the eternal Word will find a voice, the Word that will free the captives, the Word that they must respond to with a 'Yes' or else perish. And this

---

[90] J. Ithel Jones, 'Diwinyddiaeth Karl Barth', ('The theology of Karl Barth'), *Seren Gomer* 42 (1951), 97–103, 130–138, *Seren Gomer* 43 (1952), 5–14.
[91] Jones, 'Diwinyddiaeth Karl Barth', 11.
[92] Ibid., 5.

is the miracle, that God through our words – that God takes a hold of our own Welsh words and turns them into a more stupendous miracle than that of Cana in Galilee – He turns them into the Word of God himself.[93]

In an astute assessment of the theological scene in Wales, R. Ifor Parry, whose critical volume on Barth was mentioned in the previous chapter, was nevertheless happy to credit the Swiss with the renewal of biblical theology which was registering throughout Europe at the time: 'The principal instigator of this change [from liberalism to Biblicism] is the movement known as "Crisis Theology" or "The New Traditionalism" which is chiefly connected with the name of Karl Barth'.[94] Its impact on Wales had been chiefly through the pulpit; indeed Barth's pupil, the Calvinistic Methodist Ivor Oswy Davies, had recently emphasized the same point in an essay of his own.[95] In an awesome address from that chair of the Union of Welsh Independents in 1952, J. D. Vernon Lewis issued a call for a renewed preaching of the Christ as the Lord of creation. 'Christ, according to the New Testament, is the mediator of the whole process of revelation in creation and in history', he claimed. 'He is the author of creation and the maker of all the worlds'.[96] It was not so much Barth's doctrine of the Word which lay behind this impassioned call to challenge modern scientific man with the claim of Christ but the creation doctrine of *Kirchliche Dogmatik* III: 'I very much doubt whether anyone can, in the end, refuse this gospel at all. It is at the root of all things, it is part of the texture and pattern of God's intentions on all levels, in nature and in spirit'.[97]

Barth's theology was also making its mark on biblical scholarship and exegesis. W. B. Griffiths who had served as tutor in Christian doctrine in the Presbyterian Board's college at Carmarthen, issued a sterling commentary on Paul's epistle to the Romans in 1954 which was patently influenced by Barth's own method of exegesis in the *Römerbrief*. The Apostle was

---

[93] Lewis E. Valentine, 'Pregethu' ('Preaching'), *Seren Gomer* 46 (1954), 76–83 [79]; for Valentine see D. Densil Morgan, *Cedyrn Canrif: Crefydd a Chymdeithas yng Nghymru'r Ugeinfed Ganrif* (Caerdydd: Gwasg Prifysgol Cymru, 2002), 68–104 and the biography by Arwel Vittle, *Valentine* (Tal-y-bont: Gwasg y Lolfa, 2006).

[94] R. Ifor Parry, 'Diwinyddiaeth yng Nghymru heddiw' ('Theology in Wales today'), *Yr Ymofynnydd* 54 (1954), 74–86.

[95] Ivor Oswy Davies, 'Fel hyn y dywed yr Arglwydd' ('Thus says the Lord'), *Y Drysorfa* 121 (1951), 149–53.

[96] J. D. Vernon Lewis, *Crist a'r Greadigaeth* ('Christ and the Creation') (Abertawe: Undeb yr Annibynwyr Cymraeg, 1952), p.6.

[97] Ibid., p.14.

portrayed as conveying a highly objective salvation in which Christ, God's elect, stood surety for the whole of humankind:

> In one way God's act in Jesus Christ is an objective act, wholly outside of man. To quote the hymn, it all happened 'without asking me'. But man cannot partake of that objective act without faith, which implies depending wholly on Jesus Christ and accepting God's way of making things right. This, however, is not a subjective inclination; it too partakes of God's objective and dynamic act, in which man, through faith, is placed within the ambit of God's righteous action.[98]

Although Griffiths was indebted to the work of Kierkegaard and P. T. Forsyth, Barth was the most formative influence on what was one of the most accomplished commentaries on Romans ever to have been written in Welsh. Like J. E. Daniel and Vernon Lewis, Griffiths was a Congregationalist. Along with J. Ithel Jones, Lewis Valentine and Ivor Oswy Davies, he was a highly effective preacher of the Word. In Wales it was the preachers more than the professors who were profiting from the Barthian renewal. 'The role of theology', stated Vernon Lewis in the Annual BBC Radio Lecture in 1954, 'is to deal with the content or message of preaching, and to the extent that is possible, to light the way for people today to comprehend that Christ's gospel is essential for their life'.[99] Karl Barth's great contribution had been to make that a valid possibility once more.

As this was happening in Wales, Ulster was not far behind. The link between the Church of Scotland and Irish Presbyterianism had always been strong, and 1951 saw the launch of the journal *Biblical Theology* along the lines of the now defunct *Presbyter* and sharing all the emphases of the *Scottish Journal of Theology*: a commitment to a catholic ecumenism, Reformed churchmanship, the World Council of Churches and the insights of the Barthian theology: 'The members of the editorial committee have, in varying degrees, consciously or unconsciously, been influenced by the work of the great reviver of Reformed Theology, as Le Cerf describes Karl Barth'.[100] Its mainspring was J. L. M. Haire, since 1944 professor of systematic theology at the Presbyterian College in Belfast, who had been a student contemporary of T. F. Torrance, J. K. S. Reid and Ian Henderson in Edinburgh and had studied with Barth at Basel. Haire was assisted by the biblical

---

[98] W. B. Griffiths, *Esboniad ar yr Epistol at y Rhufeiniaid* ('A Commentary on the Epistle to the Romans'), (Caernarfon: Calvinsitic Methodist Bookroom, 1954), p.41.

[99] J. D. Vernon Lewis, *Diwinyddiaeth a Phregethu Heddiw* ('Theology and Preaching Today'), (London: British Broadcasting Corporation, 1954), pp.32–3.

[100] 'Editorial', *Biblical Theology* 1/2 (1951), 3–4.

scholar Ernest Best and John Thompson, later to become his successor in the systematics chair and a doctoral student of Barth's in 1947–48. Though not 'a group of Barth's disciples bent on secure a following for him in the Irish churches',[101] it was obvious where the journal's sympathies lay. By the early 1950s the theology of Karl Barth had become an accepted and challenging reality within the British theological scene.

---

[101] 'Editorial', p.4.

10

BARTH RECEPTION DURING THE POST-WAR YEARS, 1948–56 (II)

Barth and the demythologizing controversy in Britain

In his correspondence with Brand Blanshard, T. F. Torrance had defended Barth against the accusations of irrationality which he admitted was a problem in continental theology, especially in the increasingly popular work of Rudolf Bultmann. 'Barth stands in Europe as the great propagandist against irrationalism', he wrote, 'and against existentialism which, particularly in the hands of a new school of interpreters headed by Professor Rudolf Bultmann of Marburg, is producing a radical reinterpretation of the Bible that we can only regard as a menace to the Christian gospel'.[1]

This radical reinterpretation was certainly gaining a following. Following his sojourns to Bonn during the summers of 1946 and 1947, Barth had returned to Basel keen to resume work on his major dogmatic project. *Kirchliche Dogmatik* III/2, on anthropology or humankind as creature was published in the summer of 1948 with *Kirchliche Dogmatik* III/3 on providence, nothingness and the angels following in the late spring of 1950. (*Kirchliche Dogmatik* III/4 on the ethics of creation would appear in summer 1951; this indicated a quite staggering productivity for a man who was approaching 65). It was just as Barth was writing on the existence and ministry of angels that 'the storm of the demythologizing controversy was beginning to break'.[2] His first mention of Bultmann's programme to demythologize the New Testament occurred in volume III/2 in the context of his treatment of 'Man in his Time': 'R. Bultmann "demythologizes" the

---

[1] T. F. Torrance, 'Theology of Karl Barth', *The Scotsman*, 14 April 1952, 4.
[2] Eberhart Busch, *Karl Barth: his life from letters and autobiographical texts* (London: SCM, 1976), p.365.

event of Easter by interpreting it as "the rise of faith in the risen Lord, since it was this faith which led to the apostolic preaching:" This will not do',[3] he claimed. The factual and historical aspect of the New Testament material was essential to the gospel itself and not something that could be detached from it. It was in June 1953, however, in the foreword to *Kirchliche Dogmatik* IV/1 on the doctrine of reconciliation, that he made his opposition to Bultmann's programme explicit:

> The present situation in theology . . . means that throughout I have found myself in an intensive, although for the most part quiet, debate with Rudolf Bultmann. His name is not mentioned often but his subject is always present . . . I respect the man, his mind and aim and achievements . . . [but] his hermeneutical suggestions can become binding on me only when I am convinced that by following them I would say what I wanted to say in a better and freer way. For the time being, I am not so convinced.[4]

It was among two of Barth's erstwhile Scottish followers that the demythologizing programme became known initially in Britain.

Ian Henderson (1910–69) and Ronald Gregor Smith (1913–68) had belonged to an exceptionally gifted generation of ministerial students who had studied at New College, Edinburgh, in the 1930s. 'Professor H. R. Mackintosh was at the height of his powering those years', Henderson reminisced. 'His lectures, packed with argument and delivered with great impressiveness, made an extraordinary profound impression on his hearers'.[5] After studying philosophy at Edinburgh under Norman Kemp Smith and divinity in New College, Henderson proceeded to Zürich in 1936 where he was taught by Emil Brunner and then to Basel and Karl Barth. It was he, along with his New College contemporary J. L. M. Haire, who acted as Barth's interpreters during his Gifford tours to Edinburgh in 1937 and 1938, both men taking responsibility for the translation of *The Knowledge of God and the Service of God* (1938). Deeply involved with T. F. Torrance and J. K. S. Reid in the founding of the Scottish Church Theology Society, he had been drawn to the reformation of modern Scottish theology and church life according to the Word of God.

Ordained into parish ministry at Fraserburgh, north east of Aberdeen in 1940, Henderson remained, nevertheless, indebted to the Scottish Enlightenment. According to his younger colleague John Macquarrie: 'A clue to the

---

[3] Karl Barth, *Kirchliche Dogmatik* III/2 (Zollikon-Zürich: Evangelischer Verlag, 1948), p.531.

[4] Karl Barth, *Kirchliche Dogmatik* III/2 (Zollikon-Zürich: Evangelischer Verlag, 1953), Vorwort.

[5] Ian Henderson, 'How it all began', *Crisis Christology* 3/1 (Fall 1945), 40–1 [40].

character of Henderson's theology may be found in his understanding of himself as a child of the Enlightenment and a foe of Romanticism'.[6] If Torrance belonged, by upbringing and conviction, to the Evangelical Party within the Scottish Church, Henderson was by inclination a 'Moderate'.[7] Although stirred by Barth's dogmatic principles and initially influenced by his work, 'There is something impressive about a theology so many-sided and so Christocentric'[8] he stated in a broadcast in 1951, nevertheless he drew away from Barth increasingly over the matter of applying the gospel to the modern mindset. His first book, *Can Two Walk Together?* (1948), an analysis of the possibility of a secular scheme of ethics unaffected by explicit dogmatic concerns, led to his appointment (against both Torrance and George S. Hendry) to the chair of systematic theology in the University of Glasgow in 1948. Joined in 1956 by Ronald Gregor Smith, who was called to the university's parallel chair of divinity, Glasgow would provide a counterpoint to New College as a centre for the dissemination of an existentialized, liberal and more secular theology, deeply influenced by Bultmann and others.[9] By the 1960s Barth would be in the process of being eclipsed, even in Scotland.

Henderson's slim volume *Myth in the New Testament* (1952) was the first full-length if brief English-language treatment of the demythologizing project. In four succinct chapters, he described the genesis of Bultmann's essay, read initially during the war to a minister's meeting of the German Confessing Church, he placed it in its background within the ontological thought of the Marburg philosopher Martin Heidegger, proceeded to analyse its content and concluded by asking whether modern Christianity can dispense with the category of myth or not. For Bultmann Christianity calls for radical decision, he claimed: 'Time and time again he sets aside doctrines which would protect the Christian from the necessity of coming to a decision',[10] while the encounter with the risen Christ in the preaching of the Word led to what was, in fact, authentic Spirit filled existence. Henderson was not shy to point to the programme's weaknesses: to what extent could

---

[6] John Macquarrie, 'A modern Scottish theologian' in *Thinking about God* (London: SCM, 1975), pp.204–12 [205].

[7] For the divergence between the evangelical 'Popular Party' and the 'Moderate Party', see A. L. Drummond and J. Bulloch, *The Scottish Church 1688–1843: the age of the Moderates* (Edinburgh: St Andrews Press, 1973).

[8] Ian Henderson, 'The Influence of Karl Barth', *The Listener*, 15 March 1951, 415–6 [416].

[9] George Newlands, 'Theologies at Glasgow in the twentieth century' in *Traces of Liberality: collected essays* (Bern: Peter Lang, 2006), pp.153–62 [159–60 esp.]; cf. idem., 'John Macquarrie in Scotland', in Robert Morgan (ed.), *In Search of Humanity and Deity: a celebration of John Macquarrie's theology* (London: SCM, 2006), pp.17–24.

[10] Ian Henderson, *Myth in the New Testament* (London: SCM, 1952), p.23.

the existential and divine elements of the New Testament be extricated from what was merely transitory, while modern myths such as those of Nazism or, more benignly, those of American material progress, showed that human reality functioned naturally within the sphere of the imagination. There was no doubt, however, that he sympathized fully with Bultmann's scheme and implied that Barth had not yet really begun to take the axioms of modernity seriously.

Ronald Gregor Smith

If Henderson had come under the spell of H. R. Mackintosh at New College, Ronald Gregor Smith's mentor had been the 'orthodox liberal' John Baillie[11] who had joined Mackintosh from Union Seminary in New York as Edinburgh's professor of divinity in 1934. At Baillie's instigation Smith had undertaken what would become the standard translation of the Jewish philosopher Martin Buber's *Ich und Du* as *I and Thou* (1937) and thereafter had spent a semester at Copenhagen studying the work of Kierkegaard. Already something of an existentialist, he was ordained into the ministry of the Church of Scotland, at Selkirk in the lowlands in 1939, and his earliest original work *Still Point* (1943), a sensitive reflection on the ministerial life, charts his inner experience at the time. 'True freedom is found only within orthodoxy',[12] he claimed; 'I am an incorrigible supernaturalist, a devotee of revelation'.[13] It was clear even at this juncture, however, that his interests were more speculative than dogmatic, and although he was involved in the Scottish Church Theology Society and published in *The Evangelical Quarterly*,[14] it was the subjective appropriation of religious truth rather than the objective claims of revelation which exercised his imagination. His disenchantment with orthodoxy would increase and he would soon write of his disengagement from 'the masquerade of dogmas': 'In discarding much of the accumulated dogmas of the church I am nearer than before to proper faith'.[15]

---

[11] Cf. David Fergusson, 'John Baillie: orthodox liberal', in idem. (ed.), *Christ, Church and Society: essays on John Baillie and Donald Baillie* (Edinburgh: T & T Clark, 1993), pp.123–53.

[12] Ronald Maxwell [pseudonym for R. Gregor Smith], *Still Point: an exercise in living* (London: Nesbit, 1943), p.23.

[13] Ibid., p.73.

[14] Ronald Gregor Smith, 'The canonical evidence for the doctrine of God the creator', *The Evangelical Quarterly* 14 (1942), 88–94; idem. 'The church and the churches', *The Evangelical Quarterly* 15 (1943), 32–9; idem. 'The Kingdom of God today', 269–78.

[15] Quoted in Keith W. Clements, *The Theology of Ronald Gregor Smith* (Leiden: Brill, 1986), p.40.

Like Ian Henderson, though, he was both impressed by Barth's personality when he met him, in Bonn in 1947, and was sufficiently engaged with his work to undertake an important translation of the Swiss's work, namely *Against the Stream: shorter post-war writings 1946–52* (1954). He had struck up a warm friendship with Barth, over 20 years his senior, during his time at Bonn where he had been engaged as an education officer under Allied Command following 2 years as a military chaplain, and could speak of 'the robust and merry character of Barth's faith as well as its unyielding strength'.[16] The bond between them tightened when Barth officiated at his wedding with a young German, Käthe Wittlake, in June 1947. Barth's impression, however, was that the Scotsman had 'a soul like an aspen leaf, full of good will, but much too refined for this world'.[17]

In a series of articles published concurrently with *Against the Stream*, Smith both explained Bultmann's mythologizing agenda and championed its claims. The German scholar had published his ground-breaking essay *Neues Testament und Mythologie* in 1941 and reissued it 7 years later in the symposium entitled *Kerygma und Mythos* (1948). The ensuing controversy, claimed Smith, 'marks one of the most important moments in theological thinking for generations'.[18] There was no doubt in Smith's mind that Bultmann's was the best interpretation of the gospel in the context of the modern, scientifically inclined world: 'I personally do not doubt that Bultmann's marks a major turning-point in the history of the impact of Christian thought on the world'.[19] Whereas modern human beings could no longer think in terms of a three-decker universe, a localized heaven and hell or the world as a stage for the interplay of angelic or demonic forces, they were still plagued by their finitude and longed for redemption, healing or release. In fact, even in New Testament times, it was not cosmology that was essential but anthropology, how those who heard the apostolic message responded to the divine claim on their lives. If, during pre-modern eras, that redemption had been couched in mythological terms centring on the miraculous incarnation, blood sacrifice and literal resurrection of a divine redeemer, a valid redemption was still available were it to be interpreted in suitable terms. According to Bultmann God was still active in Christ for human salvation, though Christ, of whom little historically could be known, had now become the means for actualizing an authentic self-realization through the preaching of the kerygma. 'The aim of demythologizing

---

[16] Ronald Gregor Smith, foreword to Karl Barth, *Against the Stream: shorter post-war writings 1946–52* (London: SCM, 1954), pp.7–11 [9].

[17] Busch, *Karl Barth: his life from letters*, p.338.

[18] Ronald Gregor Smith, 'What is demythologizing?', *Theology Today* 10 (1953–54), 34–44 [34].

[19] Ibid., 35; cf. idem., 'Some implications of demythologizing', *The Listener*, 12 February 1953, 259–60.

therefore, put briefly, is to understand the truth of scripture as a reality which meets our existence, and to express this reality in a way which can be understood by modern man'.[20]

Smith was well aware of Barth's response to this view. 'Karl Barth represents with all the weight of his personal authority the most massive opposition'[21] to this claim, he wrote.

> He sees in Bultmann's work an almost docetic loss of the actual historical *Christus-geschehen* ('Christ-event'); Jesus becomes a marginal figure to the act of decision made possible by the kerygma. Bultmann's theology is reduced to an anthropology, an understanding of being, which has lost the grand objectivity of God's action in Christ.[22]

The younger man was not convinced by Barth's response. Barth's whole theology was a vain attempt to resist the inevitable. Like Thomism which was currently fashionable in Roman Catholic circles, Barthianism was a throwback to the past. It could be effective for a time but its effectiveness was illusionary. 'When, as Barth . . . has done, you draw your theological weapons from this vast arsenal [of the historical faith as traditionally conceived], then you are tempted to think that the battle is won because your armaments are so huge'.[23] They will prove, alas, ultimately to be ineffective against the all-pervasive and normative presuppositions of a scientific world-view which reflects the ultimate reality of modernity. Barth's whole project was ill-conceived. As an evangelistic strategy it was posited on a mistake: 'Heaven help the man who tries to give his congregation undiluted Barth!'[24]

Ronald Gregor Smith's chief contribution to the demythologizing programme was his radical volume *The New Man: Christianity and man's coming of age* (1956). Published during the year of his appointment to the Glasgow divinity chair, he forwarded the thesis that the gospel of transcendence could no longer be posited in churchly terms, but that it must be relocated to the realm of the secular. Dietrich Bonhoeffer's *Letters and Papers from Prison* had recently appeared in English, and Smith was the first to champion the mischievous view, popularized by John Robinson in *Honest to God* (1963), that the German Lutheran was in fact an apostle of wholesale secularism. But it was with Bultmann that he was mostly concerned. 'Bultmann . . . is by no means a liberal who wants to get rid of

---

[20] Smith, 'What is demythologizing?', 37.
[21] Ronald Gregor Smith, 'Demythologizing', *The Ecumenical Review* 7 (1954–55), 100–3 [101].
[22] Ibid., 101.
[23] Smith, 'What is demythologizing?', 38.
[24] Ibid., 39.

eschatology', he claimed. 'On the contrary, he wishes to restate to Christian life an existentialist eschatology as a force striking out of our future into our present'.[25] The kerygma, stripped of its accoutrements in a primitive Jewish apocalyptic, remains the means whereby modern scientific men and women are challenged to live spiritually fulfilling and authentic lives:

> The guiding clue through the labyrinth seems to me to lie for our day in the hands of Bultmann, when he disentangles from the events [of history] an element of transcendence which is not . . . the transcendence of a primitive mythology of heaven and earth . . . [but] where the individual is invited to decide towards an objective possibility of grace.[26]

God, according to this interpretation, is revealed in the recurring moment of existential decision which constitutes the essence of the spiritual life. The pictorial mythology of the New Testament constitutes a barrier preventing modern sophisticated people from apprehending, or being apprehended by God. Eschatology does not imply a supra-historical end to history but the existence of creative and increasingly this-worldly possibilities within history. It is neither a spatial nor a temporal reality, rather it has to do with human consciousness in the here and now: 'The mythology of the second coming is intended to tell us something not about some ineffable cosmic conclusion, some supra-historical and therefore unhistorical end to history, but about the fullness of history itself'.[27] Smith's language was elusive and opaque and his style was at times obscure. It was no easy thing to extricate himself from the bonds of tradition and the idiom of apocalyptic to do full justice to his this-worldly theme. He remained, though, quietly confident. 'In the main this effort [at demythologizing] has not been acceptable in the churches . . . [but] with time and labour this pioneer effort will work its way into the tradition, but not yet, not easily'.[28]

The rapid displacement of the concept of the church in Smith's thought in favour of the sphere of the secular where God, once incarnate in Christ, had divested himself of particularity and personhood in order to become the creative life force or ground of being for unchurchly man, would soon become axiomatic. Smith pioneered the secular theology of the 1960s, popularized by Robinson's *Honest to God*, which robbed the gospel of

---

[25] Ronald Gregor Smith, *The New Man: Christianity and man's coming of age* (London: SCM, 1956), p.87.
[26] Ibid., p. 90.
[27] Ibid., pp. 91–2.
[28] Ibid., p. 95.

its historicity, helped destroy the SCM,[29] and led, in part, to the rapid de-Christianization of contemporary culture.[30]

> We must . . . say that the accounts of the empty tomb in the gospels, so far as they imply an 'objective' fact of resurrection, are mythologizing legends . . . So far as historicity is concerned, *historische* fact, it is necessary to be plain: we may freely say that the bones of Jesus lie somewhere in Palestine.[31]

It was an absurdly high price to pay for the ideal of relevance and a putative intellectual integrity. Was there any wonder that T. F. Torrance had said, as early as 1952, that this scheme was 'a menace to the Christian gospel'?

The eschatological note

Biblical eschatology as interpreted by the British Barthians was radically different from that proposed by the Bultmanian liberals of the Glasgow school. Like Ian Henderson and Gregor Smith, Alec Whitehouse and T. F. Torrance, who both published important articles on the matter in 1952 and 1953, agreed that the eschatological element in the New Testament was alien to the modern mindset and needed to be interpreted judiciously and intelligently but they were insistent that it should not be de-historicized or explained away as outmoded mythology in existential terms. For White-house, now teaching at Durham, the twin problems were a wooden literalism leading to incredulity and 'a species of *Entmythologisierung* which goes beyond any necessities imposed by the New Testament data'.[32] Whereas Smith had been insistent that in regards to eschatology both chronology and cosmology were beside the point, for Whitehouse neither element could be extricated from the truth of the doctrine itself. The Second Coming had to do with history, time and event:

> Its *telos*, lit up for us now by the advent of the *eschatos* and his current enactment of the *eschaton*, will not be achieved without events in which God and his people will be gloriously vindicated and creation

---

[29] See Robin Boyd, *The Witness of the Student Christian Movement: Church ahead of the Church* (London: SPCK, 2007), pp.98–120, 147–55.

[30] See Hugh McLeod, *The Religious Crisis of the 1960s* (Oxford: Oxford University Press, 2007), pp.83–92.

[31] Ronald Gregor Smith, *Secular Christianity* (London: Collins, 1966), pp.102–3.

[32] W. A. Whitehouse, 'The modern discussion of eschatology', in T. F. Torrance and J. K. S. Reid (eds), *Eschatology: Scottish Journal of Theology Occasional Papers* (Edinburgh: Oliver and Boyd, 1952), pp.63–89 [69].

will be renewed according to his original purpose. These events may therefore be confidently expected in the future, and their real futurity is not a source of embarrassment to the faith of the New Testament.[33]

The teleological aspect of the Christian faith as expressed in the apocalyptic language of the Bible may be uncomfortable for those with an Enlightenment or Darwinian world view, but it was essential nevertheless. It may be that 'its assumptions are a source of embarrassment to those who live with a modern scientific attitude',[34] but the Second Coming was, in reality, 'a factual event'.[35] Its continuity was of a piece with the first advent, the incarnation of Christ as the babe in Bethlehem. Such was the nature of the apostolic witness and as such it remains. 'It is not safe for the church to seek a statement of its message which is only *suggested* by the New Testament', he continued, 'and which for the sake of accommodation to the "modern mind" exhibits dilutions and accretions of which in fact biblical theology is intolerant'.[36]

T. F. Torrance was in total agreement. Bultmann's diminutions and Ronald Gregor Smith's abstractions were injurious to the truth. It had been a fault of modern theology since Schleiermacher 'to cut eschatology adrift from history',[37] just as a Platonized Western thought since the time of Augustine had majored on a-temporal immortality rather than a full-blooded concept of creation and the resurrection of the flesh: 'The New Testament looks towards a historic future and a redemption of the whole world, but from the angle of the fallen world and its history, that can only be expressed apocalyptically'.[38] Like Bultmann, Niebuhr and even C. H. Dodd with his 'realized eschatology', the early Barth, with 'a doctrine of timeless crisis, which was anti-evolutionary and non-teleological',[39] had demoted history to some ethereal plane. Whereas Barth in the *Kirchliche Dogmatik* had regained a full historicism, Bultmann had fled to the subjectivism of Heiddegar's existential philosophy: 'Its great fault lies in its failure to do justice to the event character of revelation which is essential to the fundamental history of faith'.[40] The crux of the matter for Torrance was the meaning of time.

---

[33] Ibid., 79.

[34] Ibid., 77.

[35] Ibid., 82.

[36] Ibid., 88.

[37] T. F. Torrance, 'The modern eschatological debate', *The Evangelical Quarterly* 25 (1953), 44–54, 94–106, 167–78, 224–32 [48].

[38] Ibid., 49.

[39] Ibid., 95.

[40] Ibid., 96; for Torrance's strictures on Bultmann and the mythology controversy in the context of his undergraduate teaching of systematic theology in New College during the 1950s onwards, see Robert T. Walker (ed.), Thomas T. Torrance, *Incarnation: the person and life of Christ* (Milton Keynes: Paternoster Press, 2008), pp.274–96.

Echoing the work of Oscar Cullmann, *Christ and Time* (1950) and John Marsh's *The Fullness of Time* (1952), Torrance was insistent that 'the Old Testament apocalyptic eschatology is rooted and grounded in history, and speaks proleptically of the Kingdom as a state in time'.[41] Christ arrived within time and inaugurated the Kingdom of God not on some abstract plane but within temporal bounds. The Kingdom, however, remains veiled within history and at the Second Coming history itself will partake of its fullness: 'What is still in the future is the full unveiling of a reality, but the reality itself is fully present here and now'.[42] For Torrance, it was in the sacrament of the Lord's Supper that the reality of Christ's saving incarnate presence becomes real for the church. It is within the church that faith 'becomes as it were sacramentally correlative to the life and passion of Jesus Christ'.[43] Despite the fact the church had never committed itself to a specific conception of time, both history and temporality were essential to the reality of God's ultimate revelation in Christ:

> When He comes He will come with the destiny of men and nations in his hands; He will come to fulfil his judgement upon all evil and to release history from the tragedy of guilt that no man can undo, and He will make all things new. He will come as the King of glory to take his power and reign over a renewed creation. That will be the Kingdom of peace to which there will be no end . . . *Even so, come, Lord Jesus.*[44]

For Torrance and his fellow Barthians, such language was realistic and not mythological.

Evangelicalism and British Barth reception

It could be supposed that, among mid-century British Protestants, it was the evangelicals who would potentially have been the most open to the perspectives of Karl Barth. The evangelical movement was biblical in orientation, theologically orthodox and depended on a strong message of redemption for its religious effectiveness. Barth, for his part, was known to have turned the tables on evolutionary modernism and to have propounded a theology of crisis through the cross while his trinitarianism and robust Christology, replete with doctrine of the virgin birth, were in tune with the evangelicals'

---

[41] Torrance, 'The modern eschatological debate', 100.

[42] Ibid., 101.

[43] Ibid., 173.; cf. T. F. Torrance, 'Eschatology and eucharist', in D. M. Baillie and John Marsh (eds), *Intercommunion* (London: SCM, 1955), pp.303–50.

[44] T. F. Torrance, *When Christ Comes and Comes Again* (London: Hodder and Stoughton, 1957), pp.20, 22.

concerns. Some Anglican evangelicals such as A. J. Macdonald had championed his cause a decade and a half earlier, while the broader and more liberal evangelicalism of Methodism's Arundel Chapman and the Congregationalists of 'Orthodox Dissent' had obvious affinities with the early Barth. In Scotland, apart from among the Baptists and the Brethren, there was no obvious divide between strong confessional orthodoxy and evangelical conviction.[45] H. R. Mackintosh, Daniel Lamont, G. T. Thomson, the church historian J. H. S. Burleigh, all of New College and the Church of Scotland, and the Free Church College theologian Donald Maclean, were perceived to be obvious evangelicals and deeply appreciative of the work of Karl Barth at the same time. This was also true of the post-war generation of whom T. F. Torrance would become the most pronounced exemplar.

That a rift developed between the liberal Protestantism which had come to characterize conventional Anglicanism and much of Nonconformity and a specifically evangelical faith, became obvious with the establishment of the Inter-Varsity Fellowship of Christian students in 1928.[46] Although the Student Christian Movement, as it was called from 1905, had emerged from the evangelistic volunteer bodies of the late Victorian era, by the 1920s it had broadened its scope to include both social concern and the liberalized idealism of Protestant modernism. While continuing to adhere to evangelism and the concept of Christian conversion, such doctrines as the unique deity of Christ and the atonement, human sinfulness and an authoritative scripture tended to be downplayed or interpreted in more liberal terms.[47] It remained, nevertheless, a missionary body and although intellectually open and conscious of the claims of biblical criticism and evolutionary biology, the SCM would continue as the main focus for student Christian commitment until the 1960s at least. It was the IVF, however, which would champion the cause of a doctrinally conservative evangelicalism during these decades.

Despite the apparent similarities between Barth's theology and that of the evangelical faith, conservative evangelicalism generally and the IVF in particular would become increasingly more truculent in their rejection of the theology of Karl Barth. Martyn Lloyd-Jones, who had left a Calvinistic Methodist charge in Aberavon, South Wales, in 1938, in order to assist the stately preacher G. Campbell Morgan in the Congregationalists' Westminster Chapel, London, was already allergic to Barth's thought and would use his considerable authority to curtail his influence within the conservative

---

[45] Cf. D. W. Bebbington, 'Evangelicalism in modern Scotland', *Scottish Bulletin of Evangelical Theology* 9 (1991), pp.4–12 [10–11 esp.].

[46] See Douglas Johnson, *Contending for the Faith: a history of the Evangelical movement in the universities and colleges* (Leicester: IVP, 1979); Geraint D. Fielder, *Lord of the Years: sixty years of student witness, the story of the Inter-Varsity Fellowship, 1928–88* (Leicester: IVP, 1988).

[47] See Boyd, *Church ahead of the Church*, pp.1–24.

constituency. The same was true of Douglas Johnson, the self-effacing but dedicated general secretary of the IVF and like Lloyd-Jones, by training a medical doctor. When evangelicalism was generally Arminian and lacking in doctrinal depth, both men contended for strong doctrine as interpreted by B. B. Warfield and J. Gresham Machen, the 'Old School' Calvinists of America's Princeton tradition.[48] The fact that Machen had clashed with his denomination, the Presbyterian Church in the United States, parted company acrimoniously with his academic institution, Princeton Theological Seminary, in 1929 and established the exclusively Calvinist Westminster Seminary in Philadelphia in the same year, somewhat endeared him to doctrinal conservatives as a supreme example of contending for the faith in the face of the liberal threat. When T. F. Torrance crossed swords spectacularly with Machen's disciple Cornelius Van Til on the question of Barth interpretation in *The Evangelical Quarterly* in 1947, the Scot became ever more suspect in conservative eyes. Not only was Torrance wholly committed to the World Council of Churches and the ecumenical endeavour, but also he was now seen to be championing Barth as a truly evangelical theologian against the 'heresies' of Calvinistic scholasticism.

Van Til's animus against Barth, and even more so against Princeton Seminary, had been patent since the mid-1930s[49] and had issued in an intemperate volume entitled *The New Modernism* (1946). By acrobatic contortions of awesome perversity, he attempted to prove that the theologies of Brunner and Barth were a Kantian projection of unregenerate human religiosity, that God, for Barth, possessed no objective existence, and that his works were not transcendent or supernatural in origin but a function of human autonomy. In assessing the Swiss theology, the author's method throughout was 'to foist his own interpretation upon the other in such a way as put the other into a fantastic position'.[50] By postulating the view that Barth was, in fact, a Kantian and that the whole of his theology was predicated on iron-clad philosophical presuppositions, even the written evidence of the *Kirchliche Dogmatik*, which Van Til quoted at length, was arrayed against him. 'One would like to commend to the American professor the famous words of Butler that everything is what it is and not another thing', wrote Torrance. 'There is no doubt, for example, that Barth's views in the *Church*

---

[48] Iain H. Murray, *D. Martyn Lloyd-Jones: the first forty years 1899–1939* (Edinburgh: Banner of Truth Trust, 1990), pp.190–1; Johnson, *Contending for the Faith*, p.243.

[49] See his articles 'Karl Barth on Scripture', *Presbyterian Guardian* 3 (1937), 137, 'Karl Barth on creation', 204, 'Karl Barth on historic Christianity', *Presbyterian Guardian* 4 (1937), 108, 'More Barthianism at Princeton', *Presbyterian Guardian* 5 (1938), 26–7, 'Changes in Barth's theology', 221 etc.

[50] T. F. Torrance, review of Cornelius Van Til, *The New Modernism: an appraisal of the theology of Barth and Brunner* (London: James Clarke, 1946), *The Evangelical Quarterly* 19 (1947), 144–9 [148].

Dogmatics are what they are, and not another thing'.[51] As it was, what Van Til did was to manipulate Barth's stated views to fit a preconceived non-biblical scheme: 'By means of this dialectical procedure added to his "lines of historical thinking", Dr Van Til actually makes Kierkegaard agree with Hegel, and Barth with Schleiermacher. But this is surely to argue like a Molotov!'[52] Torrance listed some of the assessor's most gratuitous distortions: that analogical concepts such as the fatherhood of God emptied God of objective personhood; that the creator, in Barth's humanistic scheme, is collapsed into the creature; that Barth's God only appears to be trinitarian but is, in fact, wholly bereft of ontological reality; that the concept of God's freedom implies that God can transform himself into the being of man; and that the Nicene nature of God's revelation in Christ, namely that in Christ God gives *himself* to mankind in the cause of human redemption, was an orthodox theological construct and not a philosophical ruse that God's essence is identical with his works: 'Then he goes on after twisting Barth round into a ridiculous position to make out that Barth thinks of God as spatial!'[53]

What really irked Torrance was the American's use of a philosophy, under the guise of evangelical orthodoxy, as a norm to judge theological truth: 'We must go on to ask what right Professor Van Til has to speak in the name of orthodoxy?'[54] Like his Anglican colleague T. H. L. Parker, the Scotsman had been immersing himself in the work of John Calvin and would soon publish a benchmark study of the Reformer's anthropology, *Calvin's Doctrine of Man* (1949). Just as his reading of Barth was at odds with the static propositionalism of conventional evangelicalism, his understanding of Calvin defied the strictures of scholasticism:

> It seems perfectly clear that the Calvinism with which Dr Van Til operates is not the Calvinism of John Calvin himself, but a spurious Calvinism amalgamated with the same Aristotelian logic that cursed the theology of the middle ages and the seventeenth century – only Dr Van Til's Calvinism is not so logical.[55]

The appeal to 'the old metaphysic', 'Christian theism' and, Van Til's favourite, 'orthodoxy', was deeply unevangelical: 'It is significant that not once in his criticism . . . has he appealed to scripture . . . Instead he has constantly appealed to . . . the theology or the philosophy of the natural man'.[56]

---

[51] Ibid., 145.
[52] Ibid., 145.
[53] Ibid., 146.
[54] Ibid., 148.
[55] Ibid., 148.
[56] Ibid., 148.

There was something grotesque about a hyper-Calvinism which was the result not of a reverent reading of scripture but of extrapolating general principles on the basis of bare logic and drawing conclusions concerning individuals' salvation: '[Any]one who reads his Bible must stand aghast at the crude doctrine that "the offence of the cross appears only . . . in the direct historic revelation of God's grace that may be given to some and not to others"'.[57] Despite glorying in its own soundness, this doctrine was in fact not only flawed but heretical. 'It seems perfectly clear', concluded Torrance,

> that Professor Van Til has yet to think clearly and humbly through the Pauline gospel of justification by faith alone, and to learn that he can deny the gospel of grace just as much by justifying himself through the works of his mind as through the works of his body – both are equally, according to the New Testament, works of the flesh.[58]

In all it was a stark indictment not only of the Westminster professor but of rigid scholasticism as a whole.

Torrance, Barthianism and the IVF

It was, alas, this very scholasticism allied with a frankly sectarian aversion to ecumenism which would gain the ascendancy among many conservative evangelicals during the succeeding decades. There were exceptions: the Evangelical Alliance would remain much more open to co-operation with less doctrinaire Christians, especially in the realm of evangelism, during the 1950s,[59] while many evangelicals at a local church level were hardly conscious of party-based positions favoured by their leaders. The IVF, however, and those influenced by Martyn Lloyd-Jones took an increasingly harsh line against any deviation from rigid orthodoxy. Some were not happy with this stance. In the same issue of *The Evangelical Quarterly* that T. F. Torrance had reviewed Van Til's book, F. F. Bruce, a founder member of the IVF's Biblical Research Committee (later to be renamed the Tyndale Fellowship), was insistent that its members should not be beholden to a scholastic doctrine of biblical inerrancy but free to draw their own conclusions on such matters as pentateuchical criticism, the composite nature of the Book of Isaiah and the dating of the Book of Daniel.[60] It was clear that his vision

[57] Ibid., 148.
[58] Ibid., 149.
[59] See Ian M. Randall and David Hilborn, *One Body in Christ: the history and significance of the Evangelical alliance* (Carlisle: Paternoster Press, 2001), pp.208–31.
[60] F. F. Bruce, 'The Tyndale Fellowship', *The Evangelical Quarterly* 19 (1947), 52–61.

of evangelicalism should be compatible with critical scholarship. (During his time as an undergraduate in Aberdeen during the 1930s Bruce had been an office-bearer in both the SCM and the IVF believing that the social witness of the one complemented the personal evangelism of the other.)[61] In 1950 Geoffrey Bromiley, then a young Anglican clergyman in Cumberland and like Bruce, a leader of the Tyndale Fellowship, insisted that Torrance, Van Til and the Dutch scholar G. C. Berkouwer should be invited, under the aegis of the fellowship, to debate Barth and evangelicalism. 'Why did I want a discussion of Barth?', he recalled. 'For all our disagreements on some of his reconstructions, [he] would be a valuable ally. For he had a fair grasp of the trinity, the incarnation, the virgin birth, the atonement, the resurrection, the authority and power of scripture and the church's primary mission. Did we really do any good by treating him as a foe, as Van Til had done?'[62] As it transpired, the meeting never took place while, among conservative evangelicals at least, the perception that Barth was indeed a foe was allowed to flourish.

By the late 1940s the formerly liberalized SCM had recovered much of its evangelical character and was being rapidly influenced by both the biblical theology movement with its emphasis on the unity, authority and inspiration of scripture,[63] and by the Augustinian neo-orthodoxy of Reinhold Niebuhr as well as by the theology of Karl Barth. For the SCM's leaders, who had always regretted the estrangement between their movement and the IVF, there seemed less reason than ever for the two to maintain an opposing witness. This was especially pressing since the SCM had been consumed by the growing ecumenical vision concerning the one-ness of the church according to the scriptural revelation and the serious nature of schism. In 1950 the aims of the movement were reformulated as prayer, bible study, evangelism, responsible churchmanship and social engagement, while its basis, 'to acknowledge and lead others to acknowledge God through Jesus Christ in the power of the Holy Spirit', and to call the student constituency 'to personal commitment to Jesus Christ as their Lord and saviour',[64] was made explicit. The IVF had more typically (though not exclusively) attracted Anglicans, Open Brethren and, in Scotland, established church Presbyterians

---

[61] F. F. Bruce, *In Retrospect: remembrance of things past* (Glasgow: Pickering & Inglis, 1980), pp.45–6.

[62] T. A. Noble, *Tyndale House and Fellowship: the first sixty years* (Leicester: IVP, 2006), p.64.

[63] E.g. Alan Richardson, *Preface to Bible Study* (London: SCM, 1943); H. Cunliffe-Jones, *The Authority of the Biblical Revelation* (London: James Clarke, 1945): George S. Hendry, 'The exposition of Holy Scripture', *Scottish Journal of Theology* 1 (1948), 29–47; Daniel T. Jenkins, 'Understanding the Bible', *Christian News-Letter*, supplement 330, 2 February 1949, 42–8.

[64] Boyd, *Church ahead of the Church*, p.81.

whereas virtually all of the 'new Genevans' from among the Congregationalists had been nurtured in the SCM. In the light of the theological renewal, a meeting between the two bodies was convened in March 1950, chaired by Nathaniel Micklem, to see whether a basis for co-operation could be achieved. Once more it was Martyn Lloyd-Jones and Douglas Johnson, accompanied by a younger colleague Oliver Barclay, who remained adamant that co-operation of any sort was out of the question. Lloyd-Jones's blunt response to Micklem's question 'If a person . . . accepted genuinely the Apostles' and Nicene Creed, would that be satisfactory?' was 'No, I would have to ask particular questions'.[65] For the minister of Westminster Chapel, the universal practice of undivided Christendom was an insufficient guarantee for the authenticity of a Christian profession: 'I disagree entirely with that because . . . the whole position of the heretics is bypassed'.[66] The implication was not only that the SCM tolerated heretics, but was a heretical body itself. The meeting concluded in deadlock while any anticipation of a greater measure of co-operation to say nothing of unity, were bleak.

As the 1950s progressed, evangelicals such as T. H. L. Parker, T. F. Torrance, his brother James (who had studied Calvin's theology with Barth in Basel and was a parish minister in Dundee) distanced themselves from the IVF, while others like J. I. Packer who were more enamoured of B. B. Warfield's theory of biblical inerrancy, came to the fore.[67] This new consensus reflected the attitudes of Martyn Lloyd-Jones and Douglas Johnson. Johnson had long warned of 'the pitfalls of Barthianism'[68] and insisted that the Swiss theology was incompatible with true evangelical faith: 'Barth was subtly but definitely sceptical of a historical view of Christ's resurrection, and his strong view of authority was nevertheless slippery and equivocal about the scriptures' objective inspiration'.[69] There were in fact evangelicals who doubted whether Barth or his followers were converted at all. This came to a head in Edinburgh where tensions between the IVF-affiliated Christian Union and its central executive became unbearable and a split ensued.

Relations between the university's Christian Union and its branch of the SCM had been cordial, and in 1951 a successful joint missionary conference had been held in New College where T. F. Torrance and the ecumenical leader Norman Goodall had been keynote speakers. This success led to the merging of the two bodies for practical purposes, much to the alarm of the IVF's central administrators (and some of the Edinburgh medical students,

---

[65] Ibid., p. 85.
[66] Ibid., p. 85.
[67] D. W. Bebbington, *Evangelicalism in Modern Britain: a history from the 1780s to the 1980s* (London: Unwin Hyman, 1989), pp.255–63; Alistair McGrath, *J. I. Packer: a biography* (London: Hodder and Stoughton, 1997), pp.79–96.
[68] Fielder, *Lord of the Years*, p.125.
[69] Ibid., p.144.

though not the theologians preparing for ministry) who censured the local officers forthwith. Neither the Christian Union nor the Edinburgh branch of the SCM envisaged disbanding. The ideal, rather, was to work in harmony as a joint body. The missive from the head office to abandon co-operation with those who did not adhere to the IVF's doctrinal basis was challenged forcefully by the Christian Union committee, not least that it was sectarian and foreign to the principles of the Protestant Reformers. This opposition was hardly appreciated, and in September 1953 the Edinburgh Christian Union was officially disaffiliated from the IVF. They were, according to the movement's historian, 'sadly strained times',[70] though neither Douglas Johnson nor Oliver Barclay mentions the matter in their respective assessments of the history of the IVF.[71] The Edinburgh Christian Union carried on regardless, neither did it forfeit the support of such senior members as James S. Stewart, professor of New Testament at New College, or Geoffrey Bromiley who had arrived in the city in 1951 to take up a position as rector of St Thomas' Episcopal Church. T. F. Torrance continued to proffer the Christian Union his wholesale support.

The growing divide

By the late 1950s Barthianism and evangelicalism had diverged sharply. Barth's British supporters held to a critical though orthodox doctrine of scripture and were staunchly committed to the ecumenical movement and its overwhelming concern with the unity of the church. They found sectarianism uncongenial and this level of doctrinal intransigence frankly bewildering. Even some who did not frequent British Council of Churches circles were also ostracized. In 1954 H. L. Ellison, by birth a Polish Jew who, following conversion had become an Old Testament scholar, was forced to resign from the faculty of the London Bible College after publishing work which was indebted to Karl Barth. In an essay entitled 'Some thoughts on inspiration' which appeared in *The Evangelical Quarterly*, Ellison, who had formerly been an Anglican cleric but was now a member of the Open Brethren, reminded his readers of the unexceptional truth that 'the Bible as a record is not in itself life-giving; it is not an agent of revelation; it is never more than an instrument, the instrument used by the Holy Spirit more than any other'.[72] It was not the book that engendered faith, but God the

---

[70] Ibid., p.145.

[71] Johnson, *Contending for the Faith*; Oliver Barclay, *Evangelicalism in Britain, 1935–95: a personal sketch* (Leicester: IVP, 1997); the most detailed assessment of the controversy is to be found in Boyd, *Church ahead of the Church*, pp.86–9.

[72] H. L. Ellison, 'Some thoughts on inspiration', *The Evangelical Quarterly* 26 (1954), 210–17.

Holy Spirit at work through the book, whereas God retained his sovereignty and Christ was made known through the written testimony. 'If we are prepared to say that the scriptures contain, are and become the Word of God, we occupy a position which seems to cover all the facts of revelation and spiritual experience'.[73] For the guardians of evangelical orthodoxy this was undiluted subjectivism that contravened blatantly the Princeton doctrine of the factual inerrancy of the text. The Bible could never *become* the Word of God; it *was* the Word of God plain and simple. The London Bible College's constituency overlapped with that of Westminster Chapel and the IVF. The minutes of the Board of Directors recorded that 'it was felt . . . by a number of friends, including Dr Martyn Lloyd-Jones, that this article was undermining the position of the college . . . The position had been explained to Mr Ellison who felt that it would be wise for him to resign'.[74] F. F. Bruce who as the editor of *The Evangelical Quarterly* had published Ellison's work, was mortified: '[It was] the most unpleasant experience I have had in my whole literary career . . . I was as flabbergasted by the sequel as he himself was, although it was infinitely more painful for him'.[75] Ellison's views were wholly in accord with those of Bruce and did not contravene, according to his interpretation, the doctrinal basis of the IVF. This, apparently, was not the view of the by now all-influential Lloyd-Jones. 'If anyone still asks what error [Ellison] was charged with, the answer (believe it or not) is – "Barthianism"', Bruce reminisced: 'Comment, as they say, would be superfluous'.[76]

The two doctrinal emphases which served to distance conservative evangelicalism from the theology of Barth's followers during the 1950s were the inerrancy of scripture and the concept of limited atonement, that Christ had died not for the whole of humanity but for the elect alone. Both would be advocated by the Anglican J. I. Packer, then emerging as a forceful leader within evangelicalism, and both would be challenged equally forcefully, by T. F. Torrance among others. Packer's popular *'Fundamentalism' and the Word of God* (1958) would become a benchmark for the evangelical understanding of scripture for a generation and more. According to Packer's biographer: 'The book can be seen as a distillation of the approaches to biblical authority developed at Princeton Theological Seminary, New Jersey, during the nineteenth century, and particularly through the writings of Charles Hodge and Benjamin B. Warfield'.[77] Torrance had already dissented from this view in a review of Warfield's essays *The Inspiration and Authority*

---

[73] Ibid., 213–4.

[74] Quoted in Ian M. Randall, *Educating Evangelicalism: the origins, development and impact of London Bible College* (Carlisle: Paternoster Press, 2000), p.86.

[75] Bruce, *In Retrospect*, p.187.

[76] Ibid., p.188.

[77] McGrath, *J. I. Packer: a biography*, p.85.

of the Bible (1954). He was careful to respect both the insight and the scholarship of the nineteenth century giant, but to dispute his method and conclusions. For Torrance the scholastic doctrine of biblical inerrancy – what Packer would refer to as 'infallibility' – was no longer tenable: 'It is clear that his whole doctrine of revelation and inspiration is bound up with a philosophical doctrine of predestination in which biblical eschatology is ousted for an unbiblical notion of rational causation'.[78] He saw a rationalism at work, paralleled by the Roman Catholic concept of the immaculate conception, designed to safeguard the Bible's divine content by downplaying its human aspect. Just as the Roman doctrine had been developed in order to safeguard the truth of Christ's birth from a virgin, so the Princeton concept of textual inerrancy attempted to uphold the Bible's divine authority by undercutting its patently human form:

> In Holy Scripture the Word of God is given to us . . . in the conditions and limitations of our fallen humanity, accommodated to our ignorance and weakness. In itself the Word of God is perfect. But even in Holy Scripture we see through a glass darkly . . . We have the Word only in conditions of imperfection and limitation, in eschatological suspension.[79]

It is clear that Torrance was endeavouring to allow for a legitimate use of biblical criticism on the basis of Barth's dynamic concept of the Word of God as elucidated in the *Kirchliche Dogmatik* I/1 and I/2: 'The miracle is that even now in spite of sin and imperfection and the limitations of a fallen humanity . . . we are given to hear the living voice of the Lord himself, and to see the light eternal'.[80] Warfield's theory, followed by Packer's, was to rule out *a priori* the conclusions of biblical scholarship were they to run counter to a rigid account of the inerrancy of the text. In effect, the biblical critic would not be at liberty to forward a concept of the composite nature of the Book of Isaiah or the non-Pauline authorship of Ephesians or the Pastoral Epistles however compelling the evidence may be: 'The basic error that lurks in the scholastic idea of verbal inspiration is that it amounts to an incarnation of the Holy Spirit'.[81] Inspiration did not imply deification, and reverent and believing biblical critics should be allowed the freedom to draw their conclusions in the light of compelling literary evidence: 'Revelation . . . even in the event of revelation remains a *mysterion* and will not yield its

---

[78] T. F. Torrance, review of Benjamin B. Warfield, *The Inspiration and Authority of the Bible* with an introduction by Cornelius Van Til (Philadelphia: Presbyterian and Reformed, 1954), in *Scottish Journal of Theology* 7 (1954), 104–8 [106].
[79] Ibid., 106
[80] Ibid., 106–7.
[81] Ibid., 107.

secret to analytic and logical investigation. We walk by faith and not by sight, not by the evidence of reason or by Platonic forms'.[82]

As well as popularizing Warfield's rationalistic Biblicism and making it a conservative norm, Packer was also credited with 'taking the lead in reviving the five-point Calvinism of [the synod of] Dort'.[83] Packer's doctoral research into English Puritanism at Oxford during the 1940s had led him to *The Death of Death in the Death of Christ* by John Owen, the seventeenth century Congregational divine. This postulated the view that Christ's sacrificial death had been sufficient and effective only for those who had been chosen by God from eternity. Atonement, therefore, was 'limited' and redemption 'particular' rather than 'general', or sufficient for all. 'Packer', according to his biographer, 'is noted as a leading and highly articulate defender of the doctrine of limited atonement, also known as "particular redemption"'.[84] The Calvinistic renewal of these decades impacted on the evangelical movement not via Nathaniel Micklem's and John Whale's 'new Genevans' but through a scholastic reading of post-Reformation Puritanism. This engendered controversy and a 1953 Tyndale House conference, chaired by Martyn Lloyd-Jones, brought these tensions to the surface in a painful way.

Even those who revered Calvin and stood within the Reformed tradition had long rejected the scholastic view of limited atonement, formalized by the Dutch Reformed Church's Synod of Dort in 1618, believing that scripture taught unequivocally that Christ's death had been for the whole of humankind. It was James Torrance, the younger brother of T. F. Torrance, who made the claim that the concept of unconditional election, which Calvin taught, did not imply a belief in limited atonement which was never apparent in the Reformer's work. This was challenged by John Murray, a colleague of Cornelius Van Til at Philadelphia's Westminster Theological Seminary, though he was unable to point out where, in the *Instiutio* or within Calvin's many biblical commentaries, that this was argued. Torrance, on the other hand, was unequivocal in his claim and could support his contention by detailed references to the Reformer's work. Packer, who was of the opinion that Calvinism was a self-contained theological system perfectly harmonious and logically coherent, sided with Murray. For him there were only two alternatives: either limited atonement or universalism: 'The arguments from history and exegesis having made no headway, recourse was made to logic'.[85] It was a fractious meeting which underlined the divide between churchly and scholastic Calvinism, and augured badly for the unity of evangelicalism during the coming years.

[82] Ibid., 107.
[83] Noble, *Tyndale House and Fellowship*, p.78.
[84] McGrath, *J. I. Packer: a biography*, p.55.
[85] Noble, *Tyndale House and Fellowship*, p.76.

T. F. Torrance had provided a masterly account of election in an early essay in *The Evangelical Quarterly* entitled 'Predestination in Christ'. It was clearly indebted to Barth's reformulation of Calvin's doctrine in an explicitly Christological direction. The fact of election was indubitably true as were the basic Reformed convictions concerning the sovereignty of God, invincible grace and unconditional salvation. Human beings, however, retained their genuine freedom when faced with the decision of the gospel: 'Election means that God has chosen us because He loves us, and that He loves us because He loves us . . . It is without the scope of human *arbitrium* altogether, and to bring in the philosophical concept of free-will is simply beside the mark'.[86] As for the stern assumption concerning reprobation, namely that God had chosen some for perdition, in Christ God had taken this upon himself, and however the enigma of eternal damnation were formulated, the biblical conviction that God so loved the *world* could no longer be compromised. Christ, as representative man, had freely taken *all* of humankind's sin upon himself and endured the divine wrath for the whole of human salvation. This was not universalism, Origen's concept of *apokatastasis* or the restoration of all things, but a clarified and non-speculative reading of what the New Testament actually taught. In a later controversy with John A. T. Robinson, Torrance expounded this conviction with unique force: 'Election is the love of God enacted and inserted into history in the life, death and resurrection of Jesus Christ',[87] he explained.

> The great fact of the gospel is . . . that God has actually chosen us in Jesus Christ in spite of our sin, and that in the death of Christ that election has become a *fait accompli*. It means too that God has chosen all men, in as much as Christ died for all men, and because that is once and for all no one can ever elude the election of his love.[88]

Rather than avoiding election, gospel proclamation presupposed the reality of election, not as a gloomy fatalism or celestial lottery, but because in Christ God had chosen to be gracious to all of humankind. As for the fate of the ungodly, Christ had died for the ungodly, therefore no-one could be beyond the scope of his love.

> The whole of the Bible stands aghast at this vast mystery of iniquity. It refuses to betray the love of God and the agony of Jesus by a doctrine of universalism, but on the other hand it refuses to teach the equally

---

[86] T. F. Torrance, 'Predestination in Christ', *The Evangelical Quarterly* 13 (1941), 108–41 [117].

[87] T. F. Torrance, 'Universalism or election?', *Scottish Journal of Theology* 2 (1949), 310–18 [315].

[88] Ibid., 315.

terrible doctrine that God's action is split into two by a double pre-destination. God's action remains for ever the one and indivisible action of love, and even the dark whirlpool of ultimate denial cannot alter that fact.[89]

Speculation as to individuals' fate of logical deductions on the basis of apparent response (or lack of response) to the gospel were inappropriate. What was luminously clear, on the basis of revelation, was God's costly and saving love to the whole of humankind.

There was no doubt as to the vitality of the personal faith of T. F. and James Torrance or Nathaniel Micklem, Daniel T. Jenkins and a host of others, or their commitment to the truths of evangelical religion, but such was the atmosphere of the late 1950s that the conservative evangelicals and the disciples of Karl Barth tended to go their separate ways. It was one of the tragedies of the period that the doctrinal renewal within the Pro-testant mainstream exemplified by *The Presbyter*, the early ecumenical movement, the 'new Genevans', *The Catholicity of Protestantism* and *The Scottish Journal of Theology* functioned largely apart from and not in tandem with British evangelicalism, and that the evangelical movement, at least in its Reformed guise, became sectarian, inflexible and harsh. It was an impoverishment from which no-one benefited at all.

[89] Ibid., 317.

11

BARTH RECEPTION IN BRITAIN DURING THE FINAL DECADE, 1956–68

The translation of the Church Dogmatics

'Karl Barth is incontestably the greatest figure in modern theology since Schleiermacher, occupying an honoured position among the great elite of the church – Augustine, Anselm, Aquinas, Luther and Calvin'.[1] So wrote Thomas F. Torrance in an article noting Barth's approaching seventieth birthday in 1956. It would be a key year not only for the theologian but also for the English-language reception of his work.

Since the war Barth had been a controversial and in some cases a reviled figure. His refusal to criticize eastern bloc communism had raised the ire not only of his own Swiss government but also of Emil Brunner and even more of the formerly radical Reinhold Niebuhr who had become a staunch defender of the liberal democracy of capitalist America. Still highly innovative in working out the implications of his doctrine of reconciliation, *Kirchliche Dogmatik* IV/2, the exaltation of Jesus as 'The Royal Man', was published in 1954, with IV/3 on the unity of the person, currently in progress; it would appear by Christmas 1958. His seventieth year was the occasion of tribute from the theological community with a United States-based symposium published by Hugh T. Kerr Jr. in Princeton's *Theology Today* and a more substantial British *Festschrift* edited by T. H. L. Parker entitled *Essays in Christology for Karl Barth*. Among the American congratulators were James D. Smart, Arthur C. Cochrane, Paul L. Lehmann, E. G. Homrighausen and John A. Mackay. Mackay, a highland Scot who as a missionary in Spain had been drawn to the thought of Miguel de Unamuno and thence to Kierkegaard, had spent a semester at Bonn studying with Barth in 1930: 'It was my

---

[1] T. F. Torrance, 'Karl Barth', *The Expository Times* 66 (1954–55), 205–9 [205].

good fortune to become intimately acquainted with Barth who was interested in a wayfaring Protestant evangelist from the Spanish-speaking world'.[2] Although exasperated by Barth's refusal to take the subjective aspect of the Christian life sufficiently seriously, he was pleased to know that the theme would be central in *Kirchliche Dogmatik* IV/3: 'It is apparent . . . that the erstwhile pastor of a Swiss Alpine village has written the most impressive and significant theological system since Aquinas and Calvin'.[3] The most substantial essays in the symposium came from the Canadian scholar Arthur Cochraine, then teaching at Dubuque in Iowa,[4] Paul L. Lehmann who had recently left Princeton for a chair at the Harvard Divinity School, and George S. Hendry who since 1949 had been Princeton Seminary's Charles Hodge Professor of Theology. Cochraine's 13-page description of *Kirchliche Dogmatik* 1V/2 was clear and workmanlike and Lehmann's essay on Barth's relation to the American neo-orthodox movement was informative and sympathetic,[5] but it was Hendry who produced the *tour de force*. With unerring accuracy he described and assessed the actualistic content of Barth's theology centring on his concept of election:

> The *Dogmatik* . . . is completely misunderstood by those who see in it merely a relapse into traditional orthodoxy or scholasticism. It is a gigantic experiment in a new form of theological thinking, and as the author has gained increasing assurance in its application, the patterns of traditional orthodoxy have been progressively transformed.[6]

Although there were signs that Hendry was distancing himself from the master, this was perhaps the most sophisticated and insightful summary treatment of Barth's scheme to appear in English to date.

Essays in Christology for Karl Barth was presented at a lavish occasion hosted by Geoffrey Fisher, the archbishop of Canterbury, at Lambeth Palace and coincided with Barth being invested with an LLD at Edinburgh. (He already had an Edinburgh DD along with honorary doctorates from the universities of Oxford, Aberdeen and Glasgow). It is instructive to make

---

[2] John A. Mackay, 'Bonn 1930 and after: a lyrical tribute to Karl Barth', *Theology Today* 13 (1956), 287–94 [288].

[3] Mackay, 'Karl Barth, a lyrical tribute', 291.

[4] Cochraine had translated Otto Weber's descriptive paraphrase of the *Dogmatik*, *Karl Barth's Kirchliche Dogmatik : ein einführender Bericht* (1952) a year later; see Otto Weber, *Karl Barth's Church Dogmatics: an introductory report on volumes I/1 to III/4* (Philadelphia: Westminster Press, 1953).

[5] Paul L. Lehmann, 'The changing course of a corrective theology', *Theology Today* 13 (1956), 332–57.

[6] George S. Hendry, 'The dogmatic form of Barth's theology', *Theology Today* 13 (1956), 300–14 [303].

a comparison between the contributors to *Reformation Old and New* (1946), the previous milestone in British Barth reception, and the later volume. Of the earlier contributors, F. W. Camfield and John McConnachie had died, while George S. Hendry was now resident in the United States. T. F. Torrance, Daniel T. Jenkins, W. A. Whitehouse wrote in both volumes, and were joined by the Church of Scotland's J. K. S. Reid, David Cairns, James Torrance and R. S. Wallace, and the Irish Presbyterian J. L. M. Haire. Anglicanism, which was represented in the earlier volume by the unexpected and un-Barthian H. A. Hodges, professor of philosophy at Reading, could now boast the presence of the evangelicals T. H. L. Parker and Geoffrey Bromiley and the catholic Anglican Donald MacKinnon, professor of philosophy at Aberdeen, a man equally at home both north and south of the border. Always something of a maverick, MacKinnon's youthful (and ferocious) tracts *God the Living and the True* (1940) and *The Church of God* (1940) had evidenced the disconcerting impact of Edwyn C. Hoskyns's dialectical Biblicism including his translation of the *Römerbrief* . Later to become Cambridge's Norris-Hulse professor of divinity, he remained the only senior Anglo-Catholic to continue to take seriously Barth's concerns.[7] The 'Geneva' tradition of English Congregationalism was reinforced by John Marsh, Nathaniel Micklem's successor as principal of Mansfield College, and Presbyterianism by the Durham New Testament scholar C. E. B. Cranfield. There were no Methodists, Baptists or (Daniel Jenkins apart) Welshmen involved. If the earlier volume bore the imprint of *The Presbyter*, the latter breathed the spirit of the *Scottish Journal of Theology*. It showed that influence of Barth was still at its strongest among the Scots and a section of the English Congregationalists. The volume's contributors were all well versed in Barth and, in the main, able to quote freely from the as yet untranslated *Kirchliche Dogmatik*. The book was accomplished, highly orthodox and characterized by the interests of the day: biblical theology, ecclesiology and ecumenism. 'Without being *ex officio* Barthians', wrote the editor (though in fact about a half of the contributors, including Parker himself, were) 'we recognize the importance of your work for our churches, and are happy to take the opportunity to thank you publicly'.[8]

In his piece in *Theology Today*, Princeton's Elmer G. Homrighausen had noted that 'Barth's theology is practically unknown except to those who have waded through his voluminous writings', and remained 'for most of

---

[7] See Richard Roberts, 'Theological rhetoric and moral passion in the light of MacKinnon's "Barth"', Kenneth Surin (ed.), *Christ, Ethics and Tragedy: essays in honour of Donald MacKinnon* (Cambridge: Cambridge University Press, 1989), pp.1–14.

[8] T. H. L. Parker, 'A Letter to Karl Barth', *Essays in Christology for Karl Barth* (London: Lutterworth Press, 1956), pp.9–10 [10].

us . . . a vast undiscovered country'.[9] The need was for a full, up-to-date translation of the whole of the Barthian corpus especially the *Kirchliche Dogmatik*. In fact, T. F. Torrance had already embarked on the task. The Edinburgh publisher T & T Clark, who had issued G. T. Thomson's rendering of *Church Dogmatics* I/1, 'The Doctrine of the Word of God', as far back as 1936, had committed themselves to the project and along with J. K. S. Reid, Torrance had assembled a team of translators, mostly parish-based Church of Scotland ministers.[10] Geoffrey Bromiley, who had graduated with a degree in modern languages from Cambridge in the 1930s and had completed doctoral studies on nineteenth-century German philosophical romanticism in Edinburgh a decade later, joined the team as the translator of the portion of *Kirchliche Dogmatik* II/2 on election. Following Reid's departure to take up the chair of theology in Leeds in 1956, Bromiley became associate editor of the project and, along with Torrance, would oversee the process in its entirety with T. H. L. Parker being employed to read the proofs. As it transpired, Bromiley would translate the later volumes, IV/1–3 virtually single-handedly, 'Parker also lightening the task with occasional humorous comments'.[11] Between 1956 and 1961 as much of the *Dogmatik* as was then available now appeared in a usable and linguistically correct English guise. There was no longer any cause for readers to depend on potted outlines or second-hand accounts. Barth's *magnum opus* was available to be read by all.

The decade of the secular

By 1960 Karl Barth's reputation in Britain had been secured. He was well known at least by name, while the churchly renewal which had impacted all of the mainline denominations had created a climate of opinion in which revelation, Christology and doctrinal seriousness were highly revered. Many who were still indebted to the older liberalism were less than enthusiastic. John Baillie, professor of divinity at New College, Edinburgh, had become progressively more uneasy as he witnessed his own brand of enlightened liberalism threatened, not least due to the influence of his younger colleague

---

[9] E. G. Homrighausen, 'Karl Barth reaches seventy', *Theology Today* 13 (1956), 407–11 [410].

[10] Harold Knight (1911–75), an Oxford graduate in Modern Languages and Theology, who was involved partially in translating six of the volumes, was an ordained Church of England schoolmaster living in Worcestershire. (I am indebted to Dr Clifford Anderson, curator of Special Collections at Princeton Theological Seminary, for this information).

[11] Geoffrey W. Bromiley, 'The Karl Barth experience', in Donald K. McKim (ed.), *How Karl Barth Changed my Mind* (Grand Rapids: Eerdmans, 1986), pp.65–78 [70].

Thomas F. Torrance. Well versed in the development of religion on two continents – after having studied in Germany before the Great War, he had taught both in Canada and at Union Seminary, New York, before returning to take up the Edinburgh chair in 1934 – Baillie recognized the significance of Barth's position. Liberalism, were it to survive, would have to adapt in the light of many of the Swiss theologian's most telling criticisms. But for him Barth's unbending supranaturalism, his refusal to countenance a natural theology and his downplaying of philosophy could only lead the church into a *cul-de-sac*. In 1956 he bewailed the fact that the Barthians 'are even more dogmatically entrenched in their new position than was the former generation in the old. This has something to do with the spirit of the age with its strong temptation to take refuge in totalitarian authority . . . It is a temper which I greatly regret, not least because it helps nourish the illusion of finality'.[12] Baillie predicted a reaction against Barth's views, and mentioned the increasing popularity of Bultmann's demythologizing, Paul Tillich's culture-sensitive ontology, and the radical insights of a young Lutheran theologian whom he had known a quarter-century earlier. 'Dietrich Bonhoeffer was my student in this seminary in 1930–31, and was then the most convinced disciple of Karl Barth that had appeared among us up to that time, and withal as stout an opponent of liberalism as had ever come my way'.[13] Bonhoeffer had taken a leading part in the German Church Struggle, and had paid for his opposition to Hitler with his life. Yet his posthumously published *Letters and Papers from Prison* (1952) had shown that he was moving in a radical direction, and suggests that Barth's 'positivism of revelation' would be unsustainable in a 'world come of age'.

The changes which Baillie foresaw and which become so noticeable during the 1960s had registered in a conference of the World Student Christian Federation at Strasbourg in July 1960 (the year of Baillie's death) when it became apparent that the axioms of the previous generation, God's authoritative revelation in Christ recorded in inspired scripture and mediated through the church, were no longer being taken for granted. 'The Life and Mission of the Church' conference had been organized by Wim Visser't Hooft, D. T. Miles and other stalwarts of the World Council of Churches who were deeply indebted to Barth's theology, in order to inspire a younger generation with the ecumenical ideals of the past and encourage them to take the vision forward. For the organizers it was a sobering experience. 'It must have been striking to everyone how much indifference there was to the theological issues and ecumenical achievements of an earlier generation', while the idea of gaining converts and forwarding the mission

---

[12] John Baillie, 'Some reflections on the changing theological scene', *Union Seminary Quarterly Review* 12 (1957), 3–9 [6].
[13] Ibid., 8.

and unity of the church as the Body of Christ was regarded scornfully as 'pious talk and Geneva ideology'.[14] It was becoming clear that the dynamic would be away from the church towards the world, and that the divine presence would be discerned not in religion as such but in radical social and political change.

The growing transformation of popular culture provided a context, a receptivity and a fillip for these changes. Following post-war austerity, Britain was becoming progressively more affluent. Employment had reached exceptionally high levels while working- and lower-middle class families were beginning to deem such objects as cars, washing machines, television sets and refrigerators not as luxuries but as necessities. Financial stability was accompanied by a progressive social liberalization. As the age of empire drew to a close – Nigeria gained its independence in 1960, Tanzania (Tanganika as it then was) in 1961, Uganda in 1962, Kenya in 1963 and Northern Rhodesia a year later – attitudes of deference would loosen and the establishment mentality would be challenged and openly mocked. The satire boom and the review 'Beyond the Fringe' gained huge popularity among the young, while it has been said that '[t]he breaking of taboos was a key theme of the early 1960s'.[15] The acquittal on obscenity charges of Penguin Books in October 1960 for having published, in unexpurgated form, D. H. Lawrence's sexually explicit novel *Lady Chatterley's Lover*, was emblematic of the times. Alterations in personal morality went hand in hand with idealism in public morality. 1958–61 was a high point in the Campaign for Nuclear Disarmament with the Labour Party Conference, also in 1960, declaring in favour of unilateral disarmament. By 1963 especially, the year of the assassination of John F. Kennedy and Martin Luther King's stirring Washington DC civil rights speech 'I Have a Dream', youth culture, along with the Beatles and James Bond, had triumphed. If younger people were not to be alienated from religion, it was thought that Christianity would have to adapt to the emancipatory and secularizing movements of a 'world come of age'.

The transference of the archbishopric of Canterbury from the traditionalist, institutionally minded Geoffrey Fisher in 1961 to the much more theologically creative Anglo-Catholic A. M. Ramsay marked the level of adjustment within the Church of England. Although Ramsay was patently orthodox and transparently godly, he would be more in tune with the challenges to the norms of establishment than his predecessor could ever have been. Doctrinal unrest was already fermenting in Cambridge where

---

[14] Quoted by Lesslie Newbigin, *Unfinished Agenda: an autobiography* (London: SPCK, 1985), p.175; cf. Risto Lehtonen, *Story of a Storm: The Ecumenical Student Movement in the turmoil of revolution, 1968–1973* (Grand Rapids: Eerdmans, 1998), pp.23–7.

[15] Hugh McLeod, *The Religious Crisis of the 1960s* (Oxford: Oxford University Press, 2007), p.69.

Alec Vidler, editor of *Theology*, dean of King's College and formerly a devotee of Reinhold Niebuhr and neo-orthodoxy (though never, explicitly, of Barth), was moving away from the hard-won consensus of the decades before. Since having arrived at Cambridge in 1956, Vidler had sensed that English theology had become stale and repetitive with theologians only interested in the minutiae of churchly things: episcopacy, baptismal practice, unity schemes and the like. They were complacent, he thought, about the more substantive matters of God and the nature of God's presence in the world.[16] He instigated the symposium *Soundings*, scheduled for 1960, the centenary of *Essays and Reviews*, the book that had jolted nineteenth-century Anglicanism out of its orthodox slumbers, though the current offering did not appear until 1962. For its authors the *status quo* could no longer be sustained: 'The man who has experienced and absorbed the effects of the scientific revolution – post-renaissance, post-Darwinian, post-Freudian man – . . . cannot go back, and ought not even if he could'.[17] Barth was hardly mentioned, nor the normative nature of the gospel as tradition-ally perceived. The absolute authority seemed now to be Bonhoeffer, at least his *Letters and Papers from Prison* which for many people were taking on something akin to canonical status. 'Many of the religious elements in historic Christianity . . . may thus be outgrown or survive chiefly as venera-ble archaisms or as fairy stories for children',[18] Vidler claimed. The abiding question was: 'What prospect is there that the Church of England may have a continuing mission in a society where the traditional forms of religion are being outgrown?'[19] There was no doubt, apparently, that this religious outgrowing or Western humanity's 'coming of age' was an established fact. A subsequent volume of essays, *Objections to Christian Belief* (1963) char-acterized the tenor of the time: 'I often find myself more in sympathy or *en rapport* with non-Christians who have . . . a large measure of agnosticism', wrote Vidler, 'than I do with Christians who are cocksure about their beliefs'.[20] Agnosticism was now seen to be more virtuous and authentic than to holding resolutely to the substance of the traditional faith.

This English trend culminated with John A. T. Robinson's explosive paperback *Honest to God* (1963). Another Cambridge academic, though currently engaged as suffragan bishop of Woolwich in the London diocese

---

[16] Alec Vidler, *Scenes from a Clerical Life* (London: Collins, 1977), p.177.

[17] Alec Vidler, 'Religion and the national church', in idem., *Soundings: essays in Christian understanding* (Cambridge: Cambridge University Press, 1962), pp.239–66 [254].

[18] Ibid.

[19] Ibid.

[20] Alec Vidler, 'Historical objections', in idem. (ed.), *Objections to Christian Belief* (London: Constable, 1963), pp.57–78 [77]; cf. Keith W. Clements, *Lovers of Discord: twentieth century theological controversies in England* (London: SPCK, 1988), pp.143–77.

of Southwark, 'Robinson', according to one historian, 'was a man for the sixties, apparently willing to demythologize almost anything of which modernity might conceivably be suspicious'.[21] In order to meet the needs of the day the church's God would have to be recast in terms of Tillich's 'Ground of Being', the gospel would need to be shorn of its mysterious elements after the fashion of Bultmann, and Christianity would have to exist in a religionless form because contemporary humanity had 'come of age'. Just as Glasgow under Ian Henderson, John Macquarrie (who would leave for Union Seminary, New York, in 1962) and Ronald Gregor Smith had become a centre for an increasingly radical secular theology in Scotland, in England Cambridge and its offshoot on the south bank of the Thames, had spearheaded the move towards disacralizing religion, discerning mission in worldly terms and making the church's explicit presence problematic if not wholly redundant. In Wales J. R. Jones, a philosopher at Swansea University and a Calvinistic Methodist elder, sparked a similar controversy with his comments on 'the crisis of meaninglessness'. He mocked Barthian 'salvation mongers' in 1964 and wondered, in the end, whether the Jesus of the New Testament gospels was in fact nothing but a dream.[22]

In the colleges and universities this move towards a secularized Christianity impacted on the SCM disastrously, though it allowed the evangelical IVF to flourish as never before: 'Through a somewhat slanted interpretation of Bonhoeffer by theologians like Paul van Buren [whose *Secular Meaning of the Gospel* had also been published in 1963] and John Robinson, and through a popularized version of Bultmann's "demythologizing", there developed a tendency to move away from the Bible and from church community of Word and sacrament'.[23] In fact both *Honest to God* and Ronald Gregor Smith's *Secular Christianity* (1966) pulled the carpet from beneath any recognizably Christian concept of God. Emptied of objective personhood, God could no longer act in any meaningful way in, with or for the world. There was no Holy Spirit to bring individuals into fellowship with the divine or make the gospel story transformatory for people's lives. Even liberal theologians came to realize what was being lost: 'John Mcintyre of New College, Edinburgh, no opponent of liberal thought, once described "man's coming of age" as a polite way of saying we don't believe in God

---

[21] Adrian Hastings, *A History of English Christianity, 1920–2000* (London: SCM, 2001), p.537.

[22] J. R. Jones, *Ac Onide* (Llandybïe: Christopher Davies, 1970), p.244; cf. Keith Robbins, *England, Ireland, Scotland, Wales: the Christian Church, 1900–2000* (Oxford: Oxford University Press, 2008), p.377.

[23] Robin Boyd, *The Witness of the Student Christian Movement: Church ahead of the Church* (London: SPCK, 2007), p.99.

anymore'.[24] In all, the secular theology of the 1960s was quite disastrous for the health, even for the continued existence of the Christian church.

Back in Basel Karl Barth was preparing to retire. Having been granted a dispensation by his university 5 years previously, in 1961, now aged 75, he finally vacated the chair that he had occupied since returning from Bonn in 1935. He was still at work on *Kirchliche Dogmatik* IV/4, the ethics of reconciliation, which would never be ultimately concluded, though the next few years would see the publication of a plethora of occasional papers[25] including two volumes of sermons.[26] It had been his practice to preach regularly to the inmates of the Basel prison, though old age dictated that this ministry should be relinquished. His 1956 lecture 'The Humanity of God' was given fresh impetus in Britain through its translation in 1961. In it he pointed out in a simple form what had been stated in a more complex fashion in the *Dogmatik* since the beginning, that God was not the 'Wholly Other' as he had been described in the *Römerbrief* 40 years before, but the sovereign Lord who had chosen in Christ to become a covenant partner with the whole human race.[27] There was some talk of his being succeeded by Thomas F. Torrance, indeed the New Testament scholar Oscar Cullmann, Barth's friend and colleague in Basel, contacted the Scotsman to enquire whether he would be attracted to the post.[28] In the event, Barth was replaced by a fellow Swiss, Heinrich Ott. The controversy which accompanied his succession meant that the older man was obliged to stay on for another session so that it was not until March 1962 that his employment was finally terminated. What followed was a joyous two-month visit to the United States where Marcus, his eldest son, held the New Testament chair in the Chicago Divinity School. As well as lecturing to capacity audiences at Chicago and Princeton, he visited Dubuque in Iowa, Richmond Virginia, San Francisco and New York where his presence created an extraordinary impression.[29] It was Barth's first, and only, visit to America, and it was obvious that his personality dispelled many preconceptions that his hosts had held. The two short lecture series that he delivered at Chicago and Princeton were published as *Evangelical Theology: an introduction* (1962).[30]

---

[24] George Newlands, 'Theologies at Glasgow in the twentieth century' in *Traces of Liberality: collected essays* (Bern: Peter Lang, 2006), pp.153–62 [159].

[25] Karl Barth (ed. H. Martin Rumscheidt), *Fragments Grave and Gay* (London: Collins, 1971).

[26] Karl Barth, *Deliverance to the Captives* (London: SCM, 1961); idem, *Call for God: new sermons from Basel Prison* (London: SCM, 1967).

[27] Karl Barth, *The Humanity of God* (London: Collins, 1961).

[28] Alister E. McGrath, *T. F. Torrance: an intellectual biography* (Edinburgh: T & T Clark, 1999), pp.102–3.

[29] The long article 'Witness to an ancient truth' in *Time* magazine, 20 April 1962, gives a vivid insight into the excitement engendered by the visit.

[30] George S. Hendry, 'Barth for beginners', *Theology Today* 19 (1962–63), 267–71.

Deprived of the stimulus of regular teaching, Barth found it difficult to return to the *Kirchliche Dogmatik*. Originally he had intended the project to include five volumes, and had planned the fifth, treating eschatology and the Holy Spirit. As it transpired each volume of the *Dogmatik* had increased in size, with Volume IV even in its incomplete state already quite gargantuan. At 75 he realized that it would never be completed, indeed the only portion henceforth to be published would be the 'fragment' of IV/4 on baptism – itself a substantial work of well over 200 pages – in 1967, a year before his death. Equally disconcerting was the decline in the health of Charlotte von Kirschbaum, known to the family as 'Aunt Lollo'. Originally a nurse, Lollo had become a member of Barth's circle during the mid-1920s and was employed as his researcher and secretary. It was not long before she joined the Barth household, much to the resentment of Nelly, his wife. Von Kirschbaum would remain Barth's assistant, confident and theological companion, and although she would be accepted by his colleagues, and apparently by his children, the shadow of impropriety would always hang over the relationship. In fact, the association was something of an enigma though there was no doubt that Lollo gave herself unstintingly to Barth as his fact-finder, researcher and general organizer throughout his career.[31] Following the onset of Alzheimer's disease, she was moved to a nursing home where Barth, and Nelly, would visit her weekly. She passed away in 1975, Nelly a year later, and all three eventually share the family grave in Basel's Hörnli cemetery. During his retirement Barth took great delight in his family, including his 14 grandchildren and 2 great-grandchildren, and it was obvious that a total reconciliation had by then occurred between Nelly and himself.

Although Barth was not by nature introspective, by the 1960s he had become increasingly disconcerted by the state of Protestant theology feeling that he had failed to stem the subjectivist tide: 'Tillich and the Bultmannites rampage on the platform along with problematic shades of Bonhoeffer. And poor Bishop Robinson in his *Honest to God* . . . has drawn off the froth from all this to put it on the market as the ultimate wisdom'.[32] Writing to Ronald Gregor Smith in June 1963 he stated:

> Can you not see that a choice has to be made today between an unimproved anthropological ontology and a consequent return to the darkest nineteenth century (*Honest to God* – O abyss of banality!) and

---

[31] See Renate Köbler, *In the Shadow of Karl Barth: Charlotte von Kirschbaum* (Louisville: John Knox Press, 1989); Suzanne Selinger, *Charlotte von Kirchbaum and Karl Barth: a study in biography and the history of theology* (University Park: University of Pennsylvania Press, 1998).

[32] Eberhart Busch, *Karl Barth: his life from letters and autobiographical texts* (London: SCM, 1976), p.465.

a seriously improved ordering of the relation between the object and the subject of theology, followed by . . . a spiritually enlightened and enlightening evangelical ecumenical proclamation.[33]

It is doubtful whether Smith took any heed. Ironically, one of the beacons of hope was the Second Vatican Council, called by Pope John XXIII in 1959 and in session between 1961 and 1964. For years some of his most appreciative and discerning critics had been Catholic theologians such as the French Jesuit Henri Boulliard and his fellow Swiss Hans Urs von Balthasar and latterly Hans Küng. Long encased in a rigid Thomist scholasticism, he now felt that Roman Catholic theology was finding its evangelical voice and rediscovering the Bible and God's sovereign Word. Witnessing the inner renewal of the Catholic Church was far more worthwhile than any notions of dialogue or even rapprochement with Protestantism as such.

British Barthianism during the mid-1960s

Secularity or not, there were those who felt a compulsion to continue to make Barth's emphases known. In 1960 T. H. L. Parker issued an essay in which he rehearsed all of Barth's strictures against natural theology with a pugnacity reminiscent of the debate with Brunner a quarter of a century earlier. Parker's aim, however, was clarity, not polemics.

> How is it . . . that Barth feels compelled to dispose with all natural theology and to begin, as he continues, with revelation and grace? The answer is, I believe, fundamentally simple. It is not that Barth has evolved a different doctrine of grace from his great Reformed predecessors . . . Rather, what he has done is to apply this doctrine more consistently and over a wider field than before.[34]

Revelation was *ipso facto* self-authenticating. The true God could never be presupposed, was never self-evident, could not be demonstrated through a rational deduction on the basis of neutral evidence, or even ventured upon in a leap of faith. All this would assume a capability on humankind's part to know something of God: 'The active partner . . . is man. He it is who moves toward his deity, searching him out, inquiring after him, coming upon him and knowing him. In all this the deity is passive and static, waiting to be found'.[35] But the logic of the gospel was different. The New Testament

---

[33] Karl Barth, *Letters, 1961–1981* (Edinburgh: T & T Clark, 1981), p.102.
[34] T. H. L. Parker, 'Barth on revelation', *Scottish Journal of Theology* 13 (1960), 366–82 [374].
[35] Ibid., 379.

bore witness to a God who had graciously forged a relationship with humankind through the incarnate life, costly atonement and glorious resurrection of Jesus Christ thus proving his existence and nature in the revelation of this very fact: 'Any attempt to establish the existence of God apart from his self-revelation in Jesus Christ is putting things in the wrong order. When God in Christ encounters man His existence is *ipso facto* shown and [thereby] authenticated'.[36] The fact that Parker had to labour the point as late as 1960 showed that despite everything, Barth's basic preconceptions had failed widely to register.

T. F. Torrance, whose pre-eminence as an interpreter of Barth was beginning to emerge, published two works in 1962 which sought to clarify the Swiss's contribution in the face of latent incomprehension on the one hand and mounting neglect on the other. His *Karl Barth: an introduction to his early theology, 1910–31* (1962) provided a clear if partisan appraisal of Barth's thought between his break with liberalism during the Great War and the commencement of the *Church Dogmatics*. Barth, he claimed, 'standing in the centre of the whole Christian tradition from the earliest times to the present, has given us a massive and formidable articulation of the substance of the Christian faith, and in so doing he has laid it more squarely than ever upon its solid foundation'.[37] The work displayed what would become Torrance's characteristic analysis: that Barth's theology was eminently objectivist and, like the work of Einstein, was in accord with all the standards of a strict scientific rationality. 'Theology', he claimed, 'is co-ordinated with the self-revelation of God and operates through repentant re-thinking of the preaching and teaching of the church under the critical and creative impact of the Word of God'.[38] What made his scheme rational and stringently scientific was the extent of its conformity with its proper object thus developing 'a mode of rationality in accordance with its nature and deriving appropriate critical criteria from the objective ground on which its knowledge actually rises'.[39] Torrance's fear, however, was that 'a reactionary movement of existentialist revolt',[40] namely Rudolf Bultmann and his school, was restoring the old liberalism from which Barth had struggled to free himself and the church, and was busy taking theology back to the tyranny of subjectivism and man-centredness: 'Behind this lies a horror for the notion of the being of God in space and time and therefore for the concrete act of God in the objective historical reality of Jesus Christ'.[41]

---

[36] Ibid., 381.
[37] T. F. Torrance, *Karl Barth: an introduction to his early theology, 1910–31* (London; SCM, 1962), p.206.
[38] Ibid., p.204.
[39] Ibid., p.204.
[40] Ibid., p.205.
[41] Ibid., p.206.

If demythologizing was felt by many to be the only way of making theology relevant and the mission of the church dynamic once more, for Torrance it was a blow at the heart of Christianity and little more than a method of self-redemption rooted in unbelief.

Torrance's second contribution was his detailed introduction to the early volume of essays *Die Theologie und die Kirche* (1928) translated as *Theology and Church* (1962): 'Karl Barth is the greatest theological genius that has appeared on the scene for centuries', he claimed, who 'has, in fact, so changed the whole landscape of theology, evangelical and Roman alike, that the other great theologians of modern times appear in comparison rather like jobbing gardeners'.[42] Whether such fulsome hyperbole served Barth's cause well was arguable: Torrance's reasoned and insightful account of Barth's development could be dismissed only too easily by his detractors as the blinkered enthusiasm of an overzealous devotee. There was little doubt, however, that Barth's genius could not ultimately be ignored:

> It will take generations to measure the significance of Barth's Herculean efforts in positive theology, but it is already clear that the whole of future theological thinking will have to reckon with what he has laid bare in the inner structure of catholic and evangelical doctrine, and with the central and dominant significance for all theological thinking he has uncovered in the grace of the Lord Jesus Christ.[43]

In 1964 Daniel T. Jenkins, newly returned from his 13 years as professor at the Chicago Divinity School (which he had combined with his ministry of the Congregational King's Weigh House in London's Mayfair) and now chaplain and reader in theology in the new University of Sussex, provided an interesting if somewhat journalistic account of Barth and his project. Although he still considered himself a Barthian, his early rather uncritical ardour had abated.

> The present writer is a part-time professor of theology, but he also has to preach to a congregation Sunday by Sunday and to spend much of his time alongside busy people much engaged in the day-to-day life of one of the world's great cities. He would like to say that he has found no theologian to be of more practical help than Karl Barth, in leading him and others to the knowledge and service of God revealed in Christ.[44]

---

[42] T. F. Torrance, 'Introduction' to Karl Barth, *Theology and Church: shorter writings 1920–8* (London: SCM, 1962), pp.7–54 [7].

[43] Ibid., p.49.

[44] Daniel T. Jenkins, 'Karl Barth', in Dean G. Peerman and Martin E. Marty, *A Handbook of Christian Theologians* (Cambridge: Lutterworth Press, 1964), pp.396–409 [409].

During the 1950s Jenkins had been drawn to religio-cultural issues and Christian apologetics, a task for which Barth had shown little appetite. Such works as *Believing in God* (1956), *Equality and Excellence* (1961) and *The Christian Belief in God* (1964) were more in keeping with the concerns of Emil Brunner and even Paul Tillich's method of correlation than with dogmatics as such, though his enlightened contribution to the secularization debate, *Beyond Religion* (1962), expounded sympathetically Barth's thesis 'The Revelation of God as the Abolition of Religion' in *Church Dogmatics* I/2.[45] His seven point précis of Barth's work in Martin E. Marty's *Handbook of Christian Theologians* (1964) though vigorous was superficial. Praising Barth for his humanity and industriousness: 'He is a brisk and vigorous man of bursting eloquence and lively humour, with a face of the greatest authority and distinction . . . a lover of Mozart [who] likes nothing so much after a hard day's work on his *Church Dogmatics* as a drink and a smoke and a visit to the cinema',[46] he listed his achievements in the fields of systematics, classical theology, churchmanship and ecumenical endeavour. The *Church Dogmatics*, he claimed, 'is the most massive and sustained theological enterprise of our time, rivalling the greatest systematic efforts of history . . . a great treasure house of theological truth, where fresh insights into familiar matters and into others which have been long neglected are constantly to be found'.[47] Jenkins, however, was critical of what he saw as Barth's verbosity and apparent negativity towards cultural forms – despite his teaching on incarnation and creation – and his continuing animus towards apologetics. That Jenkins found the key to Barth's work in a formal concept of God's freedom betrayed the fact that he was no longer fully in tune with the Swiss's material originality: 'Barth's overriding concern throughout the whole *Dogmatics* is so to state theological truth as to make clear the sovereignty and initiative of God in his revelation. That he largely succeeds in doing this is his decisive theological achievement'.[48] The full implications of Barth's Christological concentration, his activist doctrine of God and the breadth of his concept of reconciliation in *Church Dogmatics* IV are glossed over rather than expounded with any perceptiveness or depth. Though he never rejected Barthianism in the fashion of George S. Hendry and other earlier partisans, Jenkins did not really keep up with the essence of Barth's evolving thought.

The one British scholar who, along with Torrance, continued to show a highly insightful mastery of Barth's continuing work was the former

[45] Daniel T. Jenkins, *Beyond Religion: the truth and error of 'Religionless Christianity'* (London: SCM, 1962), pp.26–33.

[46] Jenkins, 'Karl Barth', p.396.

[47] Ibid., p.399.

[48] Ibid., pp.399–400.

German refugee Herbert Hirschwald. Following a hiatus of nearly 20 years, he produced a most solid, shrewd if unassuming assessment of Barth's achievement entitled *The Theology of Karl Barth: an introduction* (1964). Enticed out of silence by Nathaniel Micklem, now editor of Duckworth's series 'Studies in Theology', Herbert Hartwell (as he now was) had spent the post-war years as secretary of German affairs with the British Council of Churches Inter-Church Aid and Refugee Service, the forerunner of Christian Aid. He had, though, kept his theological weapons clean. Displaying the same broad knowledge and deep understanding of Barth's theology as in his Oxford dissertation of 1945, Hartwell's *Introduction* provided a series of interpretive keys to unlock the entire oeuvre. Although he did not withdraw his earlier contention that the concept of grace, linked inextricably to the person of Jesus Christ, was the governing principle of Barth's project, he listed a number of 'characteristic features' or motifs through which Barth carried out his work.

The Swiss, he claimed, always moved from the particular to the general, namely from the specific event of Jesus Christ as God's self-revelation to a more general understanding of application of theological truth: 'In a word he never theologizes *in abstracto* but always *in concreto*'.[49] Second, he always moved from reality to possibility. Neither God nor his revelation in Jesus Christ could ever be proved, they could only be assumed as having objectively occurred on the basis of the witness in Scripture: 'Throughout his entire work Barth takes great pains to impress upon the minds of those who study it the truth that it is only on the ground of the reality of revelation that its possibility too can and must be discussed'.[50] Revelation and the Word are always presupposed; only afterwards can we examine the mode and possibility of their having occurred. Third, '[Barth's] thought continually moves from thought to action',[51] meaning that all theological concepts include an active element whereby obedience to God's Word is presupposed in its very proclamation. Fourth, that Barth's work is massively objective: 'Objectivism', he explained, 'signifies no less but also no more than Barth's constant reference to, and dependence on, the objective fact of a reality outside of man which is neither of man's making nor at his disposal but . . . inescapably affects him and determines his destiny'.[52] This objectivism was at the root of Barth's early polemic against liberalism and his ongoing rejection of all humanized religiosity including the current propensity for existentialism and secular theology. Fifth there was what Hartwell described

---

[49] Herbert Hartwell, *The Theology of Karl Barth: an introduction* (London: Gerald Duckworth, 1964), p.23.

[50] Hartwell, *An Introduction*, p.25.

[51] Ibid., p.26.

[52] Ibid., p.27.

as 'historicism' which was linked inextricably to God's covenantal and creative will and humankind's active election in Christ: 'History in the sense used by Barth was already in the making when God decided in his eternal decree before the creation of the world . . . to elect man, all men, in Jesus Christ to be his partner in the covenant of grace which he then resolved to make with man in the God-man, Jesus Christ'.[53] The sixth and crowning theme was that of 'actualism': 'It is hardly possible to exaggerate the importance of this feature which . . . dominates every part of Barth's theology and exercises a decisive influence on the subject-matters dealt with therein'.[54] It was, in fact, 'the motive-force of his mode of thought'.[55]

> Actualism, as here understood, means that the essential elements of the Christian faith such as, for instance, the Word of God, the divine revelation, man's faith, love and hope, the church and the Christian life are represented as existing only *in actu* and, therefore, as being real and genuine only *in actu*.[56]

For Barth even being was act, whether faith, grace, the church or whatever. All theological virtues and realities, indeed God himself, existed as action and event. Being itself is constituted by God's perpetual act.

Hartwell's analytical scheme anticipated Eberhard Jüngel's explication of Barth's activist doctrine of God in *Gottes Sein ist im Werden* (1964) ('God's Being in Becoming') as well as George Hunsinger's widely used interpretive grid in *How to Read Karl Barth: the shape of his theology* (1991).[57] Although he was not wholly in accord with Barth especially on the matters of epistemology, the *analogia entis* and aspects of his Christology,[58] nevertheless he appreciated the scale of his achievement: 'Barth's theology represents a Copernican turn in the history of human thought about God, the universe and man, accomplishing such a complete change of the theological scene that it is not too much to say that a new theological epoch has been initiated by it'.[59] That such a sane, balanced and understated evaluator of Barth could write this was praise indeed. Neither was he unheeding of the

---

[53] Ibid., p.31.
[54] Ibid., p.32.
[55] Ibid., p.32.
[56] Ibid., p.33.
[57] Hunsinger's categories are 'actualism', 'particularism', 'objectivism', 'personalism', 'realism' and 'rationalism', see *How to Read Karl Barth: the shape of his theology* (Oxford: Oxford University Press, 1991). He expresses his indebtedness to Hartwell on pp.19–20.
[58] Hartwell, *An Introduction*, pp.184–8.
[59] Ibid., p.179.

demands of the current situation and the dangers in allowing Barth's massive contribution to be eclipsed:

> At this juncture in the history of human thought, disregarding God's self-revelation in Jesus Christ, once more the attempt is being made to conceive God in purely abstract formulas such as 'being itself' and 'the depth and ground of all being' or 'ultimate reality', it is of the utmost importance that Barth asks us to seek God nowhere else than in Jesus Christ.[60]

Tillich's sub-personal ontology, Robinson's popularizing abstractions and Ronald Gregor Smith's a-historical vagaries could do scant justice to either the reality of the gospel or the needs of contemporary society. Barth's mature theological message on the other hand was devoted to 'the proclamation of God's gracious, victorious and joyful Yes to his creation in Jesus Christ', Hartwell concluded, 'and it will be for this reason . . . that his theology will occupy a pre-eminent and lasting place in the history of Christian thought'.[61]

Barth celebrated his eightieth birthday on 10 May 1966 to much local and international acclaim. Although increasingly out of fashion with theologians, he was still being read avidly by pastors, Roman Catholics, and many lay people in the churches.[62] He was presented with *Service in Christ*, his third English language *Festschrift*, edited once more by T. H. L. Parker but assisted this time by James I. McCord, John A. Mackay's successor as president of Princeton Theological Seminary. This marked the fact that there was a growing unity between British reception of Barth's theology and that in the United States. A larger book than its predecessors, though in content rather tame and unadventurous by comparison, continuity was preserved in the guise of essays by Parker, Geoffrey Bromiley, T. F. Torrance, J. K. S. Reid, J. L. M. Haire and Donald MacKinnon. English Congregationalism was again represented by Alec Whitehouse (though not, surprisingly, by Daniel T. Jenkins) with an ecumenical input by A. M. Ramsay, John Coventry Smith S. J. and the Methodist Gordon Wakefield. Less surprising was the absence of an essay by George S. Hendry, who had grown increasingly impatient of Barth's apparent dogmatic certainties.[63] He was soon to feel that Barth's earlier theology had been 'pathological', that his Christological scheme was 'a Unitarianism of the second article [of the Creed]' and that his concept of creation, while providing the opportunity 'for a dazzling

---

[60] Ibid., p.182.
[61] Ibid., p.188.
[62] See Barth, *Letters, 1961–81*, passim.
[63] George S. Hendry, review of Busch, *Karl Barth: his life from letters* in *Theology Today* 34 (1977–8), 194–8.

display of exegetical pyrotechnics', shed virtually no light at all on the matter at hand.[64] The young man who, in the 1930s, had been young Scotland's premier champion of Barth's views had now become totally cynical and disenchanted.

Barth's contemporaries were by now moving from the scene. His philosopher brother Heinrich died in 1965 and Paul Tillich and Emil Brunner in 1966. Now in poor health, Barth was more or less confined to Basel. He busied himself with reading, correspondence and with welcoming the occasional caller. The streams of visitors of earlier years had now ceased though he did value the company of a new friend, the poet Carl Zuchmeier,[65] and the young Lutheran theologian Eberhart Jüngel who had been teaching in Zürich since late 1966. By now his long life was drawing to a close.

Karl Barth died peacefully on the morning of 10 December 1968, aged 83 and was buried on 13 December with a memorial service at the Basel Cathedral attended by dignitaries from church and state a day afterwards. There was no doubt that an epoch had drawn to a close and that a remarkable personality as well as a great theologian had passed on. In Britain, at least, the sense of grief was muted. 'Karl Barth was always something of an enigma to the English theological world',[66] wrote Daniel T. Jenkins, and was doubtful that he would ever be fully understood by those who knew nothing of the European scene. The tributes which followed in the American monthly *The Christian Century* were also low key.[67] Nothing comparable was published in Britain. Paul L. Lehmann, an American writing in the London-based journal *Religious Studies*, lamented 'a disquieting theological collapse' which had already occurred, while 'in Scotland a virulent "Barthian scholasticism" obstructs the freedom of God in his revelation to be God for man in the world, and enervates the faith and life of the churches'.[68] This was hardly the way that Torrance would have seen things. The fact was that '[i]n, with and under this "post-Barthian" disintegration of theological substance and sense of direction, a marked shift in the theological "centre of gravity" has occurred . . . In a world come of age, and with cybernetic intensity, it could be that theology is not even a *disciplina arcana* but, at best, a *disciplina antiquaria*'.[69] It would seem that, following his

---

[64] George S. Hendry, *Theology of Nature* (Philadelphia: Westminster Press, 1980), p.25 and passim.

[65] See Geoffrey W. Bromiley (ed.), *A Late Friendship: the letters of Karl Barth and Carl Zuckmeyer* (Grand Rapids: Eerdmans, 1982).

[66] Daniel T. Jenkins, 'Karl Barth', *Frontier* 12 (1969), 132–5 [132].

[67] The contributors were William Hordern, John Godsey, Avery Dulles and Robert McAfee Brown, *The Christian Century*, 26 March 1969, 402–13.

[68] Lehmann, 'Karl Barth and the future of theology', *Religious Studies* 6 (1970), 105–20 [105].

[69] Ibid., 106.

death, Barth's legacy was already fading to nothing. It was left to a poet to express not only wistfulness but confidence that a new appreciation would one day return. In his elegy 'On the Death of Karl Barth' the Cornish poet Jack Clemo wrote:

> ... He has not gone silenced in defeat:
> The suffocating swirl of heresy
> Confirms the law he taught us; we keep the glow,
> Knowing the season, the rhythm, the consummation.

> ...We touched His crag of paradox
> Through our tempestuous leader, now dead,
> Who ploughed from Safenwil to show us greatness
> In a God lonely, exiled, homeless in our sphere.
> Since his footfall breeds guilt, stirs dread
> Of a love fire-tongued, cleaving our sin,
> Retrieving the soul from racial evolution,
> Giving it grace to mortify,
> In deeps or shallows, all projections of the divine.[70]

Silence would once more give way to a renewed hearing of the Word.

---

[70] Jack Clemo, *The Echoing Tip* (London: Methuen, 1971).

POSTLUDE: BARTH IN
BRITAIN 1968–86

The 1970s was hardly a propitious decade for classical theology in either the academy or the church. Although the more faddish secular theology inspired by *Honest to God* had more or less played itself out, secularist presuppositions were taken for granted while a plethora of new, mainly egalitarian theologies – liberationist, feminist, pluralist, process and theologies of hope – were jostling to fill the void left by an earlier ecumenical Biblicism. In 1977 E. L. Mascall, former professor of historical theology at King's College, London, and one of the Church of England's most revered senior scholars, bewailed the lamentable nature of the situation: 'No sensitive observer will deny that at the present day both Christian theology and the Christian church are in a condition of crisis and indeed confusion'.[1] Within academic theology the tenor of the decade would be sceptical and revisionist just as the mood of previous decade had been secular. If *Honest to God* (1963) had been the emblematic text of the 1960s, the volume which encapsulated the temper of 1970s was John Hick's notorious symposium *The Myth of God Incarnate* (1977) which discarded the core Christian dogmas of trinity and incarnation as being outmoded, discredited, divisive and false. The doctrinal reductionism of Maurice Wiles, Regius Professor of Divinity at Oxford, Geoffrey Lampe who occupied the corresponding chair at Cambridge, as well Dennis Nineham, Don Cupitt and many others, dominated the theological discourse. In a word, scepticism and unbelief had become the accepted norm. It was hardly surprising that Karl Barth's legacy would be treated with either pity or with disdain.

The more dogged of Barth's disciples continued to work assiduously. The 1970s saw T. F. Torrance come into his own as a highly original as well as exceptionally learned dogmatician whose contribution to theological science would become even more marked during succeeding years. His *Theological Science* and *Space, Time and Resurrection* had appeared in 1969; *Theology in Reconciliation* was published in 1975 with *The Ground and Grammar of Theology* being released in 1980. T. H. L. Parker produced

---

[1] E. L. Mascall, *Theology and the Gospel of Christ: an essay in reorientation* (London: SPCK, 1977), p.15.

a brief but characteristically animated analytical sketch entitled simply
Karl Barth (1970) which served as the best English-language biographical
introduction prior to the appearance, in English, of Eberhard Busch's landmark *Karl Barth: his life and letters from autobiographical texts* (1976):
'It is difficult to think of a creative systematic theologian who has been his
superior', Parker claimed, 'or even his equal'.[2] The Swiss *Gesamtausgabe*
(Collected Works) had begun to appear in 1971 and by the end of the decade, portions of Barth's voluminous correspondence as well as many of his
earlier works, especially from the Göttingen and Münster periods, would
revolutionize scholarly perceptions making the case for a fundamental
continuity between Barth's break with liberalism around the time of the
Römerbrief and his substantive thought in the *Church Dogmatics*.[3] These
began to be translated around 1980 though Geoffrey Bromiley had already
rendered *Kirchliche Dogmatik* I/1 into English in 1975 providing a complete overhaul of G. T. Thomson's infelicitous and sometimes misleading
Doctrine of the Word of God (1936). Bromiley's version of *Church Dogmatics: index volume, with aids for the preacher* would appear in 1977.
A year earlier Eberhard Jüngel's *Gottes Sein ist im Werden* (1966), perhaps
the most perceptive analysis of Barth's doctrine of God, appeared as *The
Doctrine of the Trinity: God's Being is in Becoming*[4] while the Belfast
Presbyterian scholar John Thompson issued an elegant study entitled *Christ
in Perspective* in 1978.[5] Bromiley turned from translation to elucidation
in 1979 with his workmanlike *Introduction to the Theology of Karl Barth*,
a paragraph-by-paragraph summary of the *Church Dogmatics* in their
entirety,[6] while in 1981 Alec Whitehouse, the most discerning if not the
most vocal of Congregationalism's Barthian entourage, emerged from a
long literary exile with *The Authority of Grace: essays in response to Karl
Barth*. According to T. F. Torrance, Whitehouse was 'certainly one of the
ablest theological minds of our day' who 'set himself to think through
the far-reaching implications of Barth's thought for our understanding of
the physical world [according to] the seismic changes in the ontological
foundations of knowledge'.[7] Like Nathaniel Micklem, Daniel T. Jenkins,

---

[2] T. H. L. Parker, *Karl Barth* (Grand Rapids: Eerdmans, 1970), p.108.

[3] See Bruce L. McCormack, *Karl Barth's Critically Realistic Dialectical Theology: its
genesis and development 1909–36* (Oxford: Clarendon Press, 1995); John Webster,
Barth's Earlier Theology: four studies (London: T & T Clark International, 2005).

[4] Eberhart Jungel, *The Doctrine of the Trinity: God's Being is in Becoming* (Edinburgh:
Scottish Academic Press, 1976).

[5] John Thompson, *Christ in Perspective: Christological perceptives in the theology
of Karl Barth* (Edinburgh: St Andrew's Press, 1978).

[6] Geoffrey W. Bromiley, *Introduction to the Theology of Karl Barth* (Edinburgh:
T & T Clark, 1979).

[7] T. F. Torrance, 'Foreword', to W. A. Whitehouse, *The Authority of Grace: essays in
response to Karl Barth* (Edinburgh: T & T Clark, 1981).

Herbert Hartwell and the young Colin E. Gunton – whose *Becoming and Being: the Doctrine of God in Charles Hartshorne and Karl Barth* (1978) would prefigure a new and vital phase in English Barth reception – Whitehouse was by now a member of the United Reformed Church, the 1972 union of the Congregational Union of England and Wales with the Presbyterian Church of England. As chair of his denomination's theological commission, he had ensured that Barth's theology would characterize English Congregationalism's doctrinal stance as it entered into organic union with the Presbyterian Church.[8] During the 1970s however the convictions of these interpreters remained marginal and even obscure: the popular mainstream was decidedly reductionist in its assessment of the orthodox nature of the Christian faith.

The trend towards disregarding or downplaying Barth had begun long before his death. David Jenkins, who, as the Anglican bishop of Durham, would court controversy during the 1980s for challenging the received doctrines of the virgin birth and the physical resurrection of Christ, had reflected this trend in the mid-1960s with his useful *Guide to the Debate about God* (1966): 'I must bring the dreadful wrath of all Barthians down about my head and say that I do not myself believe that Karl Barth is of very much use to us in the heat of the present debate'.[9] As for Barth himself, the author had nothing but praise. He possessed such 'humanity, humour and serenity that I for one cannot doubt that he knows God and it is indeed God whom he knows'.[10] Although Jenkins showed a fair grasp of the essence of Barth's thought and had, evidently, read and pondered at least portions of the *Church Dogmatics*, he was far from being convinced that, in the context of the 1960s, Barth had anything particularly relevant to say: 'He restores autonomy to theology by putting it into splendid isolation'.[11] In the end, and despite much hedging, Jenkins accused Barth of a-historicism and irrationalism. In providing a brilliantly self-contained account of what it meant to be apprehended by the Christian God, Barth 'so isolates theology as not so much to make it incredible as to make it impossible for us to know whether it is incredible or not'.[12] In cognitive if not religious terms,

---

[8] See W. A. Whitehouse et al., *Christian Confidence: essays on a declaration of faith of the Congregational Church in England and Wales* (London: SPCK, 1970); for the creation of the United Reformed Church, see David Cornick, *Under God's Good Hand: a history of the traditions which have come together in the United Reformed Church in the United Kingdom* (London: URC, 1998), pp.173–83.

[9] David Jenkins, *Guide to the Debate about God* (London: Lutterworth Press, 1966), p.72.

[10] Ibid., p.73.

[11] Ibid., p.79.

[12] Ibid., p.81.

it inevitably led to scepticism and uncertainty. For Jenkins Barth's theology, though magnificent in its own way, could only lead to a dead end.

If David Jenkins (not to be confused with his near namesake Daniel Jenkins who in *Beyond Religion* (1962) had also contributed to the current 'debate about God') represented middle-of-the-road liberal Anglicanism, Colin Brown was a spokesman for evangelicalism. Brown, who would later join Geoffrey W. Bromiley on the faculty of Fuller Seminary in Pasadena, felt – unlike Bromiley – that Barth's thought was, on the whole, a declension from rather than a healthy corrective to traditional faith. By assuming that the Princeton-Warfield notion of inerrancy provided an adequate under-pinning for the doctrine of scriptural inspiration and that the historicity of the biblical Adam was an established fact, Brown's theology reflected conservative evangelicalism at its most staunch. He was especially critical of Barth's linking the doctrine of the covenant with the whole of humankind rather than with Christians as such, and was scathing as to the supposedly unscriptural basis for his doctrine of election: 'It is significant that Barth offers no biblical exegesis at this point to support his case'.[13] In fact, even a cursory reading of the small print sections of *Church Dogmatics* II/2, § 33, 'The Election of Jesus Christ', would prove that not to have been the case. 'We cannot remain true to the witness of the New Testament', Brown stated, 'and follow Barth in his christocentric programme . . . In saying this . . . we are not saying anything new'.[14] That, of course, was the whole point. In what was a sectionally influential study at the time, the author consistently judged Barth in the light of a conventional and rather wooden conservativism and never once allowed Barth to challenge the preconcep-tions of his inherited tradition. By the 1970s evangelicalism, already in the ascendant, would become the most vibrant force within the Church of England and a decade later would achieve a theological sophistication well beyond the worthy if unadventurous teachings of Colin Brown. By the time of the Barth centenary in 1986 even Anglicanism was beginning to interact positively, indeed highly intelligently, with the Swiss's thought, while the burgeoning scholarship of John Webster, Nigel Biggar, Trevor Hart and others would ensure that his theology would provide an invaluable resource for the renewal of evangelical theology within the Anglican Church.

In 1970 however, a progressively radical liberalism dominated Anglican thought. John Bowden, who would (ironically) serve Barth studies inesti-mably as the translator of Busch's landmark biography *Karl Barth: his life from letters and autobiographical texts*, encapsulated the general English view with his short study of the theologian in the SCM Centre book series.

---

[13] Colin Brown, *Karl Barth and the Christian Message* (Leicester: IVP, 1967), p.102.
[14] Ibid., p.152.

As an exercise in damning with faint praise it is unmatched. Barth was undoubtedly a genius who had squandered his immense talent in pursuing an abstraction: 'Barth's theology appears to be badly flawed. These flaws are becoming more obvious as time goes on'.[15] Barth, apparently, had three major insights which were problematic at the time and had proved insuperable since: his concept of God's greatness, his Christology and his Biblicism. 'Barth's insight into the majesty of God and his emphasis on the Word of God could, and unfortunately did, degenerate into a kind of theological triumphalism'.[16] Echoing Reinhold Niebuhr's grievance of two decades earlier, Barth had ensconced himself in an intellectual ivory tower and was impervious both to rational critique and to the realities of mundane life: 'Constant gazing into heaven may have dulled his perception of what was happening around him on earth'.[17] Given the inevitable preconditions of a scientific worldview his concept of God was unreal, his Christology uncritical and his idea of revelation was frankly unworkable:

> If knowledge of God is as Barth describes it, how can the Christian talk to his friend and persuade him to share his beliefs and concerns? He cannot point to any hints of God in experience, history, morality, for these are all ruled out of court. All that seems possible is to sit in silence and wait; and if nothing happens, atheism is a perfectly logical conclusion, on Barth's own premises.[18]

Even on the basis of *Church Dogmatics* I/1 this would have been a travesty. That Bowden could make this supposition after decades of scholarly discourse with the whole corpus of the *Dogmatics* freely available, was incredible though not, alas, untypical. Barth had never ruled out of court 'hints of God' in experience, history or morality. What he had denied, strenuously and relentlessly, was the validity of a natural *theology*, a means of knowing anything authoritative about God which was independent of and apart from God's unique revelation of himself in Jesus Christ. Something *had* happened, namely the being of God in his divine action. As God *had* spoken, in many and various ways and supremely in his Son, silence was not an option. On Barth's premises atheism, like sin, was patently irrational.

The basis for Bowden's critique of Barth's Christology was a typically reductionist essay by Dennis Nineham, warden of Keble College Oxford,

---

[15] John Bowden, *Karl Barth* (London: SCM, 1971), pp.116–7.
[16] Ibid., p.106.
[17] Ibid., p.14.
[18] Ibid., p.111.

'The use of the Bible in modern theology'[19] published in 1969. Barth's cardinal sin according to this view was to have eschewed the need for research into the historicity of the gospels. Barth's Christ was the kerygmatic Christ replete with resurrection and miracles whom he described 'entirely in metaphoric language'[20] and was only tangentially related to Jesus of Nazareth, the simple rabbi of Galilee. In Bowden and Nineham, liberal theology had, in fact, come full circle: theirs was the view that Nathaniel Micklem and Edwyn C. Hoskyns had challenged so forcefully in their debates with C. J. Cadoux and the Modern Churchman's Union 40 years previously. Yet for the renewed liberal consensus of the 1970s, Barth's Christ was historically an abstraction and a myth. Because of this 'Barth's influence has been noticeably negative', opined Bowden: 'It is difficult to point to any fruitful positive developments along the line which Barth himself initiated'.[21] It was this divide between a historic Jesus and the church's dogmatic Christ which created 'great obscurity at the heart of Karl Barth's thought which neither Barth nor his commentators have yet succeeded in lightening'.[22] It was left to the 1977 symposium *The Myth of God Incarnate* published under the imprimatur of the SCM Press, of which Bowden was managing director, to provide that light. Barth himself would be left to languish in darkness. 'It is striking that the name of Karl Barth is nowhere mentioned in this volume', wrote a commentator. 'For the authors the Barthian era apparently is no more than an interlude between the old and the new liberalism'.[23] During the 1970s, in mainstream British theology at least, this, more or less, was the case.

One of the first signs that the tide was turning occurred with a volume edited by S. W. Sykes, *Karl Barth: studies in his theological method* (1979). Very much an Anglican symposium edited by a subsequent bishop of Ely and including a perceptive early essay by Rowan Williams, later archbishop of Canterbury,[24] it demonstrated a close reading of the *Dogmatics* and a level of understanding seldom achieved in the past. It was a world away from the dismissiveness of David Jenkins, Bowden, Nineham and their friends. By Barth's centenary in 1986, disenchantment with the prevailing liberalism was registering forcefully and there was a growing appetite not only for a full-blooded trinitarianism exemplified by the popularity of

[19] Denis Nineham, 'The use of the Bible in modern theology', *Explorations in Theology* (London: SCM, 1977), pp.92–111 [103]; first published in the *Bulletin of the John Rylands Library* 52 (1969).

[20] Bowden, *Karl Barth* , p.112.

[21] Ibid., p.107.

[22] Ibid., p.113.

[23] Klaas Runia, *The Present-Day Christological Debate* (Leicester: IVP, 1984), p.85.

[24] R. D. Williams, 'Barth on the Triune God', S. W. Sykes, *Karl Barth: studies in his theological method* (Oxford: Clarendon Press, 1979), pp.147–93.

Jürgen Moltmann's *The Crucified God* (1974) and *The Trinity and the Kingdom of God* (1981), but a dawning appreciation of the massiveness, indeed genius, of Barth's project. 'Karl Barth', according to Donald McKim, 'was one of the theological giants of all times – not just of this century'.[25] His jubilant collection of testimonies, although international in scope, included contributions by such British stalwarts as T. F. Torrance, G. W. Bromiley and T. H. L. Parker as well as American scholars like Arthur Cochraine, Paul Lehmann, Paul Minear, Elizabeth Achtemeier, Martin E. Marty, Robert McAfee Brown and John Howard Yoder, all of whom seemed relieved to be allowed, at long last, to admit to Barth's greatness.

In a more British-based centenary study, the young evangelical scholar Alister McGrath, could state that '[i]t is currently fashionable, particularly within English theological circles to treat Barth with some derision',[26] yet both the volume to which he contributed and the occasion which caused it showed that was beginning to be no longer the case. *Reckoning with Barth* comprised the proceedings of the Barth symposium at Oxford in September 1986. Along with the old guard of Bromiley and Whitehouse, it included highly informed and deeply sympathetic essays by younger Anglicans such as McGrath, Nigel Biggar, John Webster and Rowan Williams, Colin E. Gunton from among the Reformed, along with the American ethicist Stanley Hauerwas. The fact that it emanated from Anglican Oxford, formerly so impervious to Barth's appeal, was in itself highly significant. If S. W. Sykes's corresponding volume, *Karl Barth: centenary essays* (1986), was more subdued in tone, it too marked the remarkable 'change of climate' that had occurred. One of the reasons, he claimed, was the success of Barth's 'utterly serious attempt to interpret Christian faith from the inside'.[27] Theologians were no longer cowed by secular philosophers and historians, and felt no compunction to justify their Christian convictions according to the norms of alien presuppositions. A more partisan collection, *Theology Beyond Christendom* (1986), edited by John Thompson, included substantial essays by Torrance, Bromiley, Whitehouse, J. K. S. Reid, Thomas Smail, Colin E. Gunton and others. Barth studies in Britain (and the United States) were achieving a level of seriousness and creative engagement hardly dreamed of even 10 years earlier. By 1986 the theology of Karl Barth was at last being accorded its due.

---

[25] Doanld K. McKim (ed.), *How Karl Barth Changed My Mind* (Grand Rapids: Eerdmans, 1986), p.ix.

[26] Alister McGrath, 'Barth on Jesus Christ, theology and church' in Nigel Biggar (ed.), *Reckoning with Barth: essays in commemoration of the centenary of Karl Barth's birth* (Oxford: Mowbray, 1986), pp.27–42 [42].

[27] S. W. Sykes (ed.), *Karl Barth: centenary essays* (Cambridge: Cambridge University Press), p.10.

The remarkable renaissance in English-language Barth studies which had occurred by the late-twentieth century is beyond the scope of this study.[28] A revival of interest at Princeton Theological Seminary which, despite a waning of commitment during the 1960s and 1970s, had always been in accord with Barth's basic impulses, linked with the work of Hans W. Frei at Yale, provided a focus for renewal which would combine scholarly acumen with creativity and inventiveness. Just as Frei had completed his researches on Barth's early theology, under the supervision of H. Richard Niebuhr, during the 1950s,[29] the Lutheran scholar Robert W. Jenson completed his doctoral studies, on Barth's doctrine of election, at Heidelberg at around the same time.[30] It was Jenson who provided the link between the American revival and that in Great Britain. Between 1966 and 1969 he functioned as tutor and dean of Lutheran students at Mansfield College, Oxford, itself an important centre of British Barth reception during former years. Oxford theology during the late 1960s was dominated by Anglican liberalism; both orthodoxy and Protestant Dissent were marginalized as never before. Nevertheless in 1966 Colin E. Gunton, a Mansfield student and ministerial candidate in the Congregational Church, embarked on research into Barth's doctrine of God under Jenson's supervision.[31] Although he would become a highly constructive theologian in his own right, Gunton did more than anyone to convince his generation not only of the magnitude of Barth's contribution but of the basic soundness of his method of doing theology.[32] Now championed by Gunton, Barth was seen to be a theologian of truly universal significance. 'Barth', according to Stephen Holmes, 'is the one person in the modern era who actually grasped what it is to do theology.

---

[28] Cf. Bruce L. McCormack, 'The Barth renaissance in America: an opinion', *Princeton Seminary Bulletin* 23 (2002), 337–40.

[29] Hans W. Frei, 'The Doctrine of Revelation in the thought of Karl Barth, 1909–22: the break with liberalism', PhD dissertation, Yale University, 1956; for Frei (1922–88) see George Hunsinger and William Placher (eds), Hans W. Frei, *Theology and Narrative: selected essays* (New York: Oxford University Press, 1993), introduction.

[30] Published as *Alpha and Omega: a study in the Theology of Karl Barth* (New York: Nelson, 1963); for Jenson see Carl E. Braaten in Colin E. Gunton (ed.), *Trinity, Time and Church: a response to the theology of Robert W. Jenson* (Grand Rapids: Eerdmans, 2000), pp.1–9.

[31] Jenson's own study on Barth's doctrine of God, *God after God: the God of the past and the future as seen in the work of Karl Barth* (Indianapolis: Boobs-Merrill, 1969), appeared at this time.

[32] See especially Colin E. Gunton, P. H. Brazier (ed.), *The Barth Lectures* (London: T & T Clark International, 2007); cf. Robert Pope, 'Colin Ewart Gunton (1941–2003): Christian theologian and preacher of the gospel', *Congregational History Society Magazine* 5/4 (2008), 250–63.

If the rest of us do theology after Barth, then that is only because he has shown us that it is possible, and what it looks like'.[33]

The story of the reception of Karl Barth's theology in Britain reflects not only the impact of his thought generally but illuminates the rich diversity of Christian thought within the nations of the British Isles during what was, despite all its tragedies and ambiguities, a fascinating century. If 'Barth's enormous contribution to theology, church and culture will take generations to assimilate and assess',[34] attention will need to be given to the different cultures in which assimilation occurred and the ongoing contexts in which all future assessment will progress.

---

[33] Stephen R. Holmes, 'Introduction to Colin Gunton', *Revelation and Reason: prologomena to Systematic Theology* (London: T & T Clark International, 2007), p.9.

[34] George Hunsinger, 'Karl Barth', in John Witte Jr. and Frank S. Alexander, *The Teachings of Modern Protestantism on Law, Politics and Human Nature* (New York: Columbia University Press, 2007), pp.155–209 [155].

BIBLIOGRAPHY

Books by Barth discussed in the text

Against the Stream: shorter post-war writings 1946–52 (London: SCM Press, 1954), trans. with introduction by Ronald Gregor Smith.

Anselm: Fides Quarens Intellectum (London: SCM Press, 1960), trans. Ian W. Robinson.

Call for God: new sermons from Basel prison (London: SCM Press, 1967), trans. A. T. Mackay.

Die christliche Dogmatik im Entwurf (München: Christian Kaiser Verlag, 1927).

Church Dogmatics (Edinburgh: T & T Clark, 1956–75), edited and trans. overseen by T. F. Torrance and Geoffrey W. Bromiley.

Church and State (London: SCM, 1939), trans. G. Ronald Howe.

Come, Holy Spirit, joint authored with E. Thurneysen (London: Hodder & Stoughton, 1934), trans. Elmer Homrighausen and George W. Richards.

Deliverance to the Captives (London: SCM Press, 1961), trans. M. Weiser.

The Doctrine of the Word of God (Edinburgh: T & T Clark, 1936), trans. with introduction by G. T. Thomson.

Dogmatics in Outline (London: SCM Press, 1949), trans. G. T. Thomson.

The Epistle to the Romans (Oxford: Oxford University Press, 1933), trans. Edwyn C. Hoskyns.

Ethics: lectures at Münster and Bonn (Edinburgh: T & T Clark, 1981), trans. Geoffrey W. Bromiley.

Fragments Grave and Gay (London: Collins, 1971), trans. Eric Mosbacher.

Gesamtausgabe, Vol. 5: *Offene Briefe 1909–35*, Diether Koch (ed.) (Zürich: Theologischer Verlag, 2001).

The Göttingen Dogmatics: instruction in the Christian religion (Edinburgh: T & T Clark, 1991), trans. Geoffrey W. Bromiley.

The Heidelberg Catechism for Today (Richmond: John Knox Press, 1964), trans. M. E. Bratcher.

The Holy Ghost and the Christian Life (London: Fredrick Muller, 1938), trans. R. Birch Hoyle.

The Humanity of God (London: Collins, 1961), trans. J. N. Thomas and Thomas Weiser.

Karl Barth: Brief des Jehres 1933 (Zürich: Theologischer Verlag, 2004), Eberhardt Busch et al (eds).

Die Kirchliche Dogmatik III/2 (Zollikon-Zürich: Evangelischer Verlag, 1948).

Die Kirchliche Dogmatik III/2 (Zollikon-Zürich: Evangelischer Verlag, 1953).

Kirchliche Lehre von der Taufe (Zürich: Evangelischer Verlag, 1943).

The Knowledge of God and the Service of God (London: Hodder and Stoughton, 1938), trans. Ian Henderson and J. L. M. Haire.

Letters, 1961–1981 (Edinburgh: T & T Clark, 1981), trans. Geoffrey W. Bromiley.

The Resurrection of the Dead (London: Hodder & Stoughton, 1933), trans. H. J. Stenning.

The Teaching of the Church Regarding Baptism (London: SCM, 1948), trans. E. A Payne.

Theological Existence Today! (London: Hodder and Stoughton, 1933), trans. R. Birch Hoyle.

Theology and the Church: shorter writings, 1920–28 (London: SCM Press, 1962), trans. Louise P. Smith with introduction by T. F. Torrance.

The Theology of Calvin (Grand Rapids: Eerdmans, 1995), trans. Geoffrey W. Bromiley.

The Theology of the Reformed Confessions (Louisville: John Knox Press, 2002), trans. Darryl and Judith Guder.

The Theology of Schleiermacher (Edinburgh: T & T Clark, 1982), trans. Geoffrey W. Bromiley.

Trouble and Promise in the Struggle of the Church in Germany (Oxford: Clarendon Press, 1938).

The Word of God and the Word of Man (New York: Harper and Row, 1928), trans. Douglas Horton.

Secondary sources

Allen, E. L.,'The theology of Karl Barth', *The Contemporary Review* 172 (1947), 91–4.

—'Karl Barth on man', *The Expository Times* 60 (1948–49), 203–5.

—'The new orthodoxy and the contemporary mood', *The Congregational Quarterly* 28 (1950), 143–50.

Althaus, Paul, 'The Kingdom of God and the Church', *Theology* 9 (1927), 290–2.

Anon, 'Conference of German and English Theologians', *Theology* 16 (1927), 247–95, 17 (1928), pp.183–260.

—'Professor Karl Barth in Scotland', *The British Weekly*, 26 June 1930, 257.

—'The significance of Karl Barth', *The British Weekly*, 7 May 1931, 1–2.

—'Congregational Union Centenary Meetings', *The Christian World*, 15 October, 1931, 5.

—'A turn to the right', *The Christian World*, 15 October, 1931, 10.

—'Karl Barth answers a question: how can churches abroad help the German Evangelical Church?', *The British Weekly*, 22 April 1937, 71.

—'Witness to an ancient truth', *Time* magazine, 20 April 1962, www.time/com/magazine/article/0919787355800.html.

Baillie, D. M. and Marsh, John (eds), *Intercommunion* (London: SCM, 1955).

Baillie, John, 'Some reflections on the changing theological scene', *Union Seminary Quarterly Review* 12 (1957), 3–9.

Baillie, John and Martin, Hugh (eds), *Revelation* (London: Faber and Faber, 1937).

Balthasar, Hans Urs von, *Karl Barth: Darstellung und Deutung seiner Theologie* (Einsiedeln: Johannes Verlag, 1951).

—*The Theology of Karl Barth* (San Francisco: Ignatius Press, 1991).

Barclay, Oliver, *Evangelicalism in Britain, 1935–95: a personal sketch* (Leicester: IVP, 1997).

Barnes, Kenneth C., *Nazism, Liberalism and Christianity: Protestant social thought in Germany and Great Britain, 1925–37* (Louisville: University of Kentucky Press, 1991).

Barnett, Victoria, *For the Soul of the People: Protestant protest against Hitler* (New York: Oxford University Press, 1992).

Barth, Karl, 'A preliminary reply to Dr Reinhold Niebuhr', *The Christian News-Letter*, supplement 326, 8 December 1948, 9–16.

Bebbington, D. W., *Evangelicalism in Modern Britain: a history from the 1730s to the 1980s* (London: Unwin Hyman, 1989).

—'Evangelicalism in modern Scotland', *Scottish Bulletin of Evangelical Theology* 9 (1991), 4–12.

—*Victorian Nonconformity* (Bangor, Gwynedd: Headstart History, 1992).

—'The evangelical conscience', *The Welsh Journal of Religious History* 2 (2007), 27–44.

Bell, G. K. A., *The Kingship of Christ: the story of the World Council of Churches* (London: Penguin, 1954).

Bell, G. K. A. and Deissmann, Adolf (eds), *Mysterium Christi: christological studies by British and German theologians* (London: Longmans Green & Co, 1930).

Bergen, Doris L., *Twisted Cross: the German Christian Movement and the Third Reich* (Chapel Hill: University of North Carolina Press, 1996).

Berkouwer, G. C., *The Triumph of Grace in the Theology of Karl Barth* (Grand Rapids: Eerdmans, 1956).

Betheune Baker, J. F., 'Jesus as both human and divine', *The Modern Churchman* 11 (1921), 287–301.

Beveridge, Craig and Turnbull, Ronnie, *Scotland after Enlightenment* (Edinburgh: Polygon, 1997).

Biggar, Nigel (ed.) *Reckoning with Barth: essays in commemoration of the centenary of Karl Barth's birth* (Oxford: Mowbray, 1989).

Binfield, Clyde, 'A learned and gifted Protestant minister: John Seldon Whale', *Journal of the United Reformed Church History Society* 6 (1998), 97–131.

Black, Don, 'The Cassock Club', *The Baptist Quarterly* 40 (2004), 436–9.

Blanshard, Brand, *Reason and Belief* (London: George Allen and Unwin, 1972).

Bocking, Ronald, 'Sydney Cave (1883–1953): missionary, principal, theologian', *Journal of the United Reformed Church History Society* 7/1 (2002), 36–44.

Boegner, Marc, *The Long Road to Unity* (London: Collins, 1970).

Bowden, John, *Karl Barth* (London: SCM, 1971).

Boyd, Robin, *The Witness of the Student Christian Movement: church ahead of the church* (London: SPCK, 2007).

Breeze, George E., 'Karl Barth: y dyn a'i genadwri', *Yr Eurgrawn* 127 (1935), 13–16, 63–6, 85–9, 144–8, 187–92, 247–51.

Brittain, F., *Bernard Lord Manning: a memoir* (Cambridge: Heffer's, 1942).

Bromiley, Geoffrey W., *Introduction to the Theology of Karl Barth* (Edinburgh: T & T Clark, 1979).

Bromiley, Geoffrey W. (ed.), *A Late Friendship: the letters of Karl Barth and Carl Zuckmeyer* (Grand Rapids: Eerdmans, 1982).

Brown, Callum G., *Religion and Society in Scotland since 1707* (Edinburgh: Edinburgh University Press, 1997).

Brown, Colin, *Karl Barth and the Christian Message* (Leicester: IVP, 1967).

Brown, Stewart J. 'The social vision of Scottish Presbyterianism and the union of 1929', *Records of the Scottish Church History Society* 24 (1990), 77–96.

—'"Outside the covenant": the Scottish Presbyterian churches and Irish immigration, 1922–38', *The Innes Review* 42 (1991), 19–46.

—'"A victory for God": the Scotish Presbyterian churches and the General Strike of 1926', *Journal of Ecclesiastical History* 42 (1991), 596–617.

—'"A solemn purification by fire": responses to the Great War in the Scottish Presbyterian churches, 1914–19', *Journal of Ecclesiastical History* 45 (1994), 82–104.

Bruce, F. F., 'The Tyndale Fellowship', *The Evangelical Quarterly* 19 (1947), 52–61.

—*In Retrospect: remembrance of things past* (Glasgow: Pickering & Inglis, 1980).

Brunner, Emil, *The Theology of Crisis* (New York: Scribners, 1929).

—*The Word and the World* (London: SCM Press, 1931).

Burleigh, J. H. S., *A Church History of Scotland* (Oxford: Oxford University Press, 1960).

Busch, Eberhart, *Karl Barth: his life from letters and autobiographical texts* (London: SCM, 1976).

Cadoux, C. J., 'A defence of Christian Modernism', *The Congregational Quarterly* 5 (1927), 164–72.

—Review of C. H. Dodd, *History and the Gospel*, *Mansfield College Magazine* 10 (1934–41), 588–92.

—'What is theology?', *The Presbyter* 2/10 (October 1944), 3–8.

Camfield, F. W., *Revelation and the Holy Spirit: an essay in Barthian theology* (London: Elliott Stock, 1933).

—'Barth's doctrine of God', *Theology* 46 (1943), 3–8.

Carlisle, J. C., 'The teaching of Karl Barth', *The Baptist Times* 7 August 1930, 568.

Cave, Sydney, 'Recent thought on the doctrine of the Person of Christ', *The Expository Times* 27 (1925–26), 247–53.

—'The teaching of Karl Barth and its influence on the churches', *The British Weekly*, 17 December, 1931, 243.

—Review of Karl Barth, *The Epistle to the Romans*, *Journal of Theological Study* 34 (1933), 412–6.

Chadwick, Owen, *Michael Ramsey: a life* (Oxford: Clarendon Press, 1990).

Chandler, Andrew, *Brethren in Adversity: Bishop George Bell, the Church of England and the crisis of German Protestantism, 1933–9* (Woodbridge: Boydell Press, 1997).

Chaning-Pearce, M., 'The theology of crisis', *The Hibbert Journal* 32 (1933–34), 161–74; 437–50.

—*The Terrible Crystal: studies in Kierkegaard and modern Christianity* (London: Keegan Paul, 1940).

—*Soren Kierkegaard: a study* (London: James Clark, 1945).

Chapman, J. Arundel, *The Theology of Karl Barth: a short introduction* (London: Epworth Press, 1931).

—*An Introduction to Schleiermacher* (London: Epworth Press, 1932).

—*Atonement and the Cross* (London: Epworth Press, 1933).

—*The Supernatural Life* (London, Epworth Press, 1934).

Cheyne, A. C., *The Transforming of the Kirk: Victorian Scotland's religious revolution* (Edinburgh: St Andrew's Press, 1983).

—*Studies in Scottish Church History* (Edinburgh: T. & T. Clark, 1999).

Church of Scotland, *Acts, Proceedings and Debates of the General Assembly* (Edinburgh: William Blackwood and Sons, 1934).

Clark, Neville, Review of Karl Barth, *Church Dogmatics* III/1 (Edinburgh: T & T Clark, 1958), *The Baptist Quarterly* 18 (1959–60), 175–6.

—Review of Karl Barth, *Church Dogmatics* III/2 (Edinburgh: T & T Clark, 1960), *The Baptist Quarterly* 18 (1959–60), 373–5.

—Review of Karl Barth, *Church Dogmatics* IV/1, *The Baptist Quarterly* 18 (1959–60), 40–2.

Clements, Keith W., *The Theology of Ronald Gregor Smith* (Leiden: Brill, 1986).

—*Lovers of Discord: twentieth century theological controversies in England* (London: SPCK, 1989).

—*Faith on the Frontier: a life of J. H. Oldham* (Edinburgh: T & T Clark, Geneva: WCC Publications, 1999).

—*Bonhoeffer in Britain* (London: Churches Together in Britain and Ireland, 2006).

Clemo, Jack, *The Echoing Tip* (London: Methuen, 1971).

Cochrain, Arthur C., 'The relation of Karl Barth to the historic creeds and standards of the Church', PhD dissertation, New College Edinburgh,1937.

—*The Church's Confession under Hitler* (Philadelphia: Westminster Press, 1962).

Conway, John S., *The Nazi Persecution of the Churches, 1933–45* (London: Weidenfield and Nicolson, 1968).

Cornick, David, *Under God's Good Hand: a history of the traditions which have come together in the United Reformed Church* (London: United Reformed Church, 1998).

Cowling, Maurice, *Religion and Public Doctrine in Modern England* (Cambridge: Cambridge University Press, 1980).

Cresswell, Amos and Tow, Max, *Dr Franz Hildebrandt: Mr Valiant-for Truth* (Leominster: Gracewing, 2000).

Cunliffe-Jones, H., *The Authority of the Biblical Revelation* (London: James Clarke, 1945).

—Review of F. W. Camfield, *Reformation Old and New*, *The Presbyter* 5/4 (October 1947), 24–7.

Currie, R., *Methodism Divided* (London: Faber and Faber, 1968).

Currie, R., Gilbert, Alan, Horsley, L., *Churches and Churchgoers: patterns of church growth in the British isles since 1700* (Oxford: Oxford University Press, 1977).

Daniel, J. E., 'Diwinyddiaeth Cymru', *Yr Efrydydd* 5 (1929), 118–22, 173–5, 197–203.

—'Gair Duw a Gair Dyn', *Yr Efrydydd* 5 (1929), 251–5.

—'Eglwys Crist yn hanfodol i Efengyl Crist', *Adroddiad Undeb Caernarfon* (Abertawe: Llyfrfa'r Annibynwyr, 1930), 107–11.

—*Dysgeidiaeth yr Apostol Paul* (Abertawe: Llyfrfa'r Annibynwyr, 1933).

—'Karl Barth', *Y Dysgedydd* 128 (1945), 7–10.

Davies, Horton, *Worship and Theology in England, vol. 3, The Ecumenical Century, 1900 to the Present* (Grand Rapids: Eerdmans, 1996).

Davies, Ivor Oswy, 'Adlais o'r Swistir', *Y Goleuad* 17 January 1934, 8–9.

—'Karl Barth: y dyn', *Y Goleuad* 24 November 1934, 2–3.

—'Mudiad Karl Barth', *Y Goleuad* 22 September 1937, 9–10.

—'Karl Barth', *Y Drysorfa* 112 (1942), 10–13, 44–9.

—Review of R. Ifor Parry, *Diwinyddiaeth Karl Barth*, *Y Traethodydd*, 3rd series 18 (1950), 92–4.

—'Fel hyn y dywed yr Arglwydd', *Y Drysorfa* 121 (1951), 149–53.

—'Schleiermacher in relation to the modern theological movement in Germany', Davies MSS, Bangor University Archive.

—'God in History', Davies MSS, Bangor University Archive.

Davies, Rupert E., George, A. Raymond and Rupp, E. Gordon (eds), *A History of the Methodist Church in Great Britain*, Vol. 3 (London: Epworth Press, 1983).

deCameron, Nigel M (ed.), *Dictionary of Scottish Church History and Theology* (Edinburgh: T & T Clark, 1993).

Demant, V. A., *The Religious Prospect* (London: Frederick Muller, 1939).

Dibelius, Otto, *In the Service of the Lord: the autobiography of Bishop Otto Dibelius* (London: Faber and Faber, 1964).

Dillistone, F. W., *Charles Raven: naturalist, historian, theologian* (London: Hodder and Stoughton, 1975).

—*C. H. Dodd, Interpreter of the New Testament* (London: Hodder and Stoughton, 1977).

Dodd, C. H., *The Apostolic Preaching and Its Developments* (London: Nisbet, 1937).

Drummond, Andrew L. and Bulloch, James, *The Scottish Church 1688–1843: The Age of the Moderates* (Edinburgh: St Andrews Press, 1973).

—*The Church in Late Victorian Scotland, 1874–1900* (Edinburgh: St. Andrew Press, 1978).

Duke, James O. and Streetman, Robert F. (eds), *Barth and Schleiermacher: beyond the impasse?* (Philadelphia: Fortress Press, 1988).

Edwards, D. Miall, 'Dr Thomas Rees of Bangor', *The Welsh Outlook* (1926), 182–5.

—*Bannau'r Ffydd* (Wrexham: Hughes and Son, 1929).

—'Yr Efengyl yn ôl Karl Barth', *Y Traethodydd* 84 (1929), 150–9.

Edwards, G. A. and Jones, J. Morgan, *Traethodau'r Deyrnas: Diwinyddiaeth yng Nghymru* (Wrexham: Hughes and Son, [1924]).

Ellison, H. L., 'Some thoughts on inspiration', *The Evangelical Quarterly* 26 (1954), 210–17.

Eriksen, Robert P.,'Theology in the Third Reich: the case of Gerhart Kittel', *Journal of Contemporary History* 12 (1977), 596–662.

—*Theologians under Hitler: Gerhart Kittel, Paul Althaus and Emanuel Hirsch* (New Haven: Yale University Press, 1985).

Evans, E. Keri, 'Cenadwri Karl Barth', *Yr Efengylydd* 16 (1931), 6–7.

—*My Spiritual Pilgrimage: from philosophy to faith* (London: James Clarke, 1961).

Evans, E. Keri and Huws, W. Pari, *Cofiant y Parchg David Adams* (Liverpool: Hughes and Sons, 1924).

Fairweather, A. M., *The Word as Truth: a critical examination of the Christian doctrine of revelation in Thomas Aquinas and Karl Barth* (London: Lutterworth Press, 1944).

Falk, Gerhart, *The Jew in Christian Theology: Martin Luther's anti-Jewish 'Von Schem Hamphoras'* (Jefferson NC: McFarland, 1992).

Farrar, Austin, Review of Karl Barth, *God in Action: theological addresses*, *Theology* 33 (1936), 373.

Fergusson, David (ed.), *Christ, Church and Society: essays on John Baillie and Donald Baillie* (Edinburgh: T & T Clark, 1993).

Ferguson, Ronald, *George MacLeod: founder of the Iona Community* (Glasgow: Collins, 1990).

Ferm, Veriglius (ed.), *Contemporary American Theology* (New York: Round Table Press, 1933).

Fielder, Geraint D., *Lord of the Years: sixty years of student witness, the story of the Inter-Varsity Fellowship, 1928–88* (Leicester: IVP, 1988).

Figgis, J. B., *The Countess of Huntingdon and her Connexion* (London: Marshall, [1892]).

Finke, Anne-Kathrin, *Karl Barth in Grossbritannien: rezeption und wirkungsgeschichte* (Neukirchen-Vluyn: Neukirchener Verlag, 1995).

Flew, R. Newton, *Jesus and his Church: a study of the idea of the Ecclesia in the New Testament* (London: Epworth Press, 1938).

Fox, Richard, *Reinhold Niebuhr: a biography* (New York: Pantheon Books, 1985).

Franks, R. F., 'The theological conference', *Mansfield College Magazine* 9 (1931–34), 88–90.

Frei, Hans W., 'The Doctrine of Revelation in the thought of Karl Barth, 1909–22: the break with liberalism', PhD dissertation, Yale University, 1956.

Frich, Heinrich, 'Christology in contemporary German theology', *Theology* 17 (1928), 193–200.

Garvie, A. E. 'Fifty years retrospect', *The Congregational Quarterly* 7 (1929), 18–25.

—*The Christian Belief in God* (London: Hodder and Stoughton, 1932).

Gavin, F.,'Contemporary religion in Germany', *Theology* 19 (1929), 272–82.

Glass, David, 'The Barthian idea of revelation', *The Baptist Quarterly* 6 (1932–33), 97–104.

Glover, T. R., *The Preaching of Christ* (London: Kingsgate Press, 1924).

—*Cambridge Retrospect* (Cambridge: Cambridge University Press, 1943).

Goodall, Norman, 'Nathaniel Micklem', *Journal of the United Reformed Church History Society* 1/10 (1977), 286–95.

Grant, John W., *Free Churchmanship in England, 1870–1940* (London: Independent Press, [1955]).

Grensted, L. W., *The Atonement in History and Modern Life* (London: SPCK, 1929).

Griffiths, Richard M., *Fellow Travellers of the Right: British enthusiasts for Nazi Germany, 1933–9* (London: Constable, 1980).

Griffiths, W. B., *Esboniad ar yr Epistol at y Rhufeiniaid* (Caernarfon: Llyfrfa'r Methodistiaid Calfinaidd, 1954).

Gunton, Colin E. (ed.), *Trinity, Time and Church: a response to the theology of Robert W. Jenson* (Grand Rapids: Eerdmans, 2000).

Gunton, Colin E. and P. H. Brazier (ed.), *The Barth Lectures* (London: T & T Clark International, 2007).

—*Revelation and Reason: prologomena to Systematic Theology* (London: T & T Clark International, 2007).

Gutteridge, Richards, *Open Thy Mouth for the Dumb: The German Evangelical Church and the Jews, 1879–1950* (Oxford: Blackwell, 1976).

Gutteridge, R. J. C., 'German Protestantism and the Hitler regime', *Theology* 27 (1933–34), 241–64.

Hall, Basil, 'The Presbyterian Church and its future', *The Presbyter* 5/1 (January 1947), 25–33.

Hampson, M. Daphne, 'The British response to the German Church Struggle, 1933–9', DPhil dissertation, Oxford University, 1973.

Hart, John W., *Karl Barth versus Emil Brunner: the formation and dissolution of a theological alliance, 1916–36* (New York: Peter Lang, 2001).

Harvey, G. L. H., 'Barthian and Modernism', *The Modern Churchman* 20 (1930–31), 586–95.

Hartwell, Herbert, *The Theology of Karl Barth: an introduction* (London: Gerald Duckworth, 1964).

Hastings, Adrian, *A History of English Christianity, 1920–2000* (London: SCM Press, 2001).

Hauerwas, Stanley, *With the Grain of the Universe: the church's witness and natural theology* (London: SCM Press, 2001).

Heath, Carl, *The Challenge of Karl Barth: a critical comment* (London: H. R. Allenson [1932]).

Henderson, Ian, 'How it all began', *Crisis Christology* 3/1 (Fall 1945), 40–1.

—'The Influence of Karl Barth', *The Listener* 15 March 1951, 415–6.

—*Myth in the New Testament* (London: SCM, 1952).

Henderson, John 'The controversy between Karl Barth and Emil Brunner concerning Natural Theology', PhD dissertation, New College Edinburgh, 1940.

Hendry, George S., *God the Creator* (London: Hodder and Stoughton, 1937).

—'The exposition of Holy Scripture', *Scottish Journal of Theology* 1 (1948), 29–47.

—'The dogmatic form of Barth's theology', *Theology Today* 13 (1956), 300–14.

—'Barth for beginners', *Theology Today* 19 (1962–63), 267–71.

—*Theology of Nature* (Philadelphia: Westminster Press, 1980).

Henry, Carl F. H., *Confessions of a Theologian: an autobiography* (Waco, Texas: Word Books, 1986).

Henson, H. Hensley, *Retrospect of an Unimportant Life*, Vols 1 & 2 (Oxford: Oxford University Press, 1942).

Hildebrandt, Franz, *Est: Das Lutherische Prinzip* (Göttingen: Vandenhoeck und Ruprecht, 1931).

—*This is the Message: a continental reply to Charles Raven* (London: Lutterworth Press, 1944).

Hirschwald, Herbert 'Karl Barth's conception of Grace and its place in his theology', DPhil dissertation, St Catherine's Society, Oxford, 1945.

—'The teaching of Karl Barth on the doctrine of the *imago Dei*', *The Presbyter* 5/4 (Winter 1947), 1–17.

Homrighausen, E. G., 'Karl Barth reaches seventy', *Theology Today* 13 (1956), 407–1.

Hopkins, Mark, *Nonconformity's Romantic Generation: Evangelical and Liberal theologies in Victorian England* (Milton Keynes: Paternoster Press, 2004).

Hordern, William, Godsey, John, Dulles, Avery and Brown, Robert McAfee, 'Karl Barth', *The Christian Century* 26 March 1969, 402–13.

Horton, R. F., 'Free Churchmen and the Modern Churchmen', *The Congregational Quarterly* 4 (1926), 167–171.

Hoskyns, Edwyn C.,'The other-worldly kingdom of God in the New Testament', *Theology* 9 (1927), 249–55.
—'Jesus Christ, Son of God, Saviour', *Theology* 17 (1928), 215–7.
—Review of Th. L. Haitjema, *Karl Barths 'Kritische Theologie'*, *Journal of Theological Studies* 29 (1928), 201–4.
—'Review', *Journal of Theological Studies* 33 (1932), 204–5.
—*Cambridge Sermons* (London: SPCK, 1938).
Hoskyns, Edwyn Clement and Davey, Noel, *Crucifixion–Resurrection: the pattern of the theology and ethics of the New Testament* (London: SPCK, 1981).
Hoyle, R. Birch, *The Teaching of Karl Barth: an exposition* (London: SCM Press, 1930).
—'Jesus', *The Congregational Quarterly* 9 (1931), 212–7.
—'Karl Barth and the Protestant revival', *The Churchman* 45 (1931), 113–23.
Hunsinger, George, *How to Read Karl Barth: the shape of his theology* (Oxford: Oxford University Press, 1991).
Hunsinger, George and Placher, William (eds), *Hans W. Frei, Theology and Narrative: selected essays* (New York: Oxford University Press, 1993).
Huxtable, John, 'Editorial', *The Presbyter* 6/3 (October 1948), 1.
Hylson-Smith, Kenneth, *Evangelicals in the Church of England, 1734–1984* (Edinburgh: T & T Clark, 1984).
Iain and Morag Torrance, 'A skirmish in the early reception of Karl Barth in Scotland: the exchange between Thomas F. Torrance and Brand Blanchard', unpublished paper, Princeton Theological Seminary.
Jasper, Ronald, *Arthur Cayley Headlam* (London: Faith Press, 1960).
Jenkins, Daniel T., 'Mr Demant and Karl Barth', *Theology* 39 (1939), 412–20.
—*Britain and the Future* (London: SCM, 1941).
—*The Nature of Catholicity* (London: Faber and Faber, 1942).
—'The transformation of theology in the twentieth century', *The Presbyter* 1/1 (January 1943), 4–7.
—'Questions about the Reformed Faith: do liberals understand it?', *The Presbyter* 1/4 (April 1943), 9–10, 13.
—*The Church Meeting and Democracy* (London: Independent Press, 1944).
—*Prayer and the Service of God* (London: Faber and Faber, 1944).
—'A theology of reconstruction: the place of the church', *The Presbyter* 2/1 (January 1944), 4–8.
—'Is an ecumenical theology emerging?', *The Presbyter* 2/10 (October 1944), 4–6.
—'A map of theology today', *The Christian News-Letter*, supplement 232, April 1945, 7–12.
—*The Place of a Faculty of Theology in the University of Today* (London: SCM, 1946).
—'Report on Wales', *The Christian News-Letter*, supplement 259, 1 May 1946, 5–12.
—*The Gift of Ministry* (London: Faber and Faber, 1947).
—Review of *Natural Theology: comprising 'Nature and Grace' by Professor Dr Emil Brunner and the reply 'No!' by Dr Karl Barth*, *The Presbyter* 5/2 (April 1947), 34–36.
—'Is Barth a Baptist?', *The Ecumenical Review* 1 (1948–49), 463–4.
—'Understanding the Bible', *Christian News-Letter*, supplement 330, 2 February 1949, 42–8.

293

—*Europe and America: their contribution to the world church* (Philadelphia: Westminster Press, 1951).

—*Beyond Religion: the truth and error of 'religionless Christianity'* (London: SCM, 1962).

—'Karl Barth', *Frontier* 12 (1969), 132–5.

—*The British: their identity and their religion* (London: SCM, 1975).

Jenkins, David, *Guide to the Debate about God* (London: Lutterworth Press, 1966).

Jenkins, J. Gwili, *Hanfod Duw a Pherson Crist* (Liverpool: Hugh Evans, 1931).

Jenson, Robert W., *Alpha and Omega: a study in the Theology of Karl Barth* (New York: Nelson, 1963).

—*God after God: the God of the past and the future as seen in the work of Karl Barth* (Indianapolis: Boobs-Merrill, 1969).

Johanson, Kurt I. (ed.), *The Word in this World: two sermons by Karl Barth* (Vancouver: Regent College, 2007).

Johnson, Dale A., *The Changing Shape of English Nonconformity, 1825–1925* (New York: Oxford University Press, 1999).

Johnson, Douglas, *Contending for the Faith: a history of the Evangelical movement in the universities and colleges* (Leicester: IVP, 1979).

Johnson, Mark D., *The Dissolution of Dissent, 1850–1918* (New York: Garland, 1987).

Jones, J. Ithel, 'Diwinyddiaeth Karl Barth', *Seren Gomer* 42 (1951), 97–103, 130–138, *Seren Gomer* 43 (1952), 5–14.

Jones, J. R., *Ac Onide* (Llandybïe: Christopher Davies, 1970).

Jones, Philip J., 'Theology in Wales during the last eighty years', *The Treasury* 15 (1927), 8–10, 43–5.

—'The new orthodoxy – a criticism', *The Welsh Outlook* 18 (1931), 180–3.

Jones, R. Tudur, *Congregationalism in England, 1662–1962* (London: Independent Press, 1962).

—*Yr Undeb: Hanes Undeb yr Annibynwyr Cymraeg, 1872–1972* (Abertawe: Gwasg John Penry, 1975).

Jones, R. Tudur and Pope, Robert (ed.), *Congregationalism in Wales* (Cardiff: University of Wales Press, 2004).

—*Faith and the Crisis of a Nation: Wales, 1890–1914* (Cardiff: University of Wales Press, 2004).

Jones, T. Ellis, 'Y Barthiaid', *Seren Gomer* 26 (1934), 100–10.

Jones, T. Ivon, 'Pregethu'r Gair yn ôl Karl Barth', *Y Traethodydd*, 2nd series 5 (1936), 18–27.

Jüngel, Eberhart, *The Doctrine of the Trinity: God's Being is in Becoming* Edinburgh: Scottish Academic Press, 1976).

Kaye, Elaine, *C. J. Cadoux: theologian, scholar and pacifist* (Edinburgh: Edinburgh University Press, 1988).

—*Mansfield College, Oxford: its origin, history and significance* (Oxford: Oxford University Press, 1996).

—*For the Work of the Ministry: a history of Northern College and its predecessors* (Edinburgh: T & T Clark, 1999).

Kegley, Charles (ed.), *The Theology of Emil Brunner* (New York: Macmillan, 1962).

Keller, Adolf, 'The theology of crisis', *The Expositor*, 9th series, 3 (1925), 164–75, 245–60.

—'The dialectical theology: a survey of the movement of Karl Barth and his friends', *The Congregational Quarterly* 6 (1928), 56–68.

—*Der Weg der dialectischen Theologie durch die kirchliche Welt* (München: Chr. Kaiser Verlag, 1931).

—*Karl Barth and Christian Unity: the influence of the Barthian movement upon the churches of the world* (London: Macmillan, 1933).

—*The Three Struggles of the Protestant Churches of Europe* (London: Free Church Council, 1934).

Keller, Adolf and Stewart, George *Protestant Europe: Its Crisis and Outlook* (London: Hodder and Stoughton, 1927).

Kent, John, *The Age of Disunity* (London: Epworth Press, 1966).

Knox, R. Buick, *Voices from the Past: a history of the English conference of the Presbyterian Church of Wales, 1889–1938* (Llandysul: Gomer Press, 1969).

Köbler, Renate, *In the Shadow of Karl Barth: Charlotte von Kirschbaum* (Louisville: John Knox Press, 1989).

Lehmann, Paul L., 'The changing course of a corrective theology', *Theology Today* 13 (1956), 332–57.

—'Karl Barth and the future of theology', *Religious Studies* 6 (1970), 105–20.

Lehtonen, Risto, *Story of a Storm: the Ecumenical Student Movement in the turmoil of revolution, 1968–1973* (Grand Rapids: Eerdmans, 1998).

Leitch, James W., *A Theology of Transition: H. R. Mackintosh as an approach to Karl Barth* (Edinburgh: T & T Clark, 1953).

Lewis, H. D., *Morals and the New Theology* (London: Victor Gollancz, 1947).

—*Gwybod am Dduw* (Caerdydd: Gwasg Prifysgol Cymru, 1952).

Lewis, J. D. Vernon 'Diwinyddiaeth Karl Barth', *Yr Efrydydd* 3 (1926–27), 254–8, 281–7.

—'Pregethu'r cyfandir: trosiad J. D. Vernon Lewis o bregeth Karl Barth', *Y Tyst*, 3 May 1928, 6–7.

—*Crist a'r Greadigaeth* (Abertawe: Undeb yr Annibynwyr Cymraeg, 1952).

—*Diwinyddiaeth a Phregethu Heddiw* (London: British Broadcasting Corporation, 1954).

Lilley, A. L., Review of Karl Barth, *The Knowledge of God and the Service of God*, in *The Journal of Theological Studies* 41 (1940), 212–4.

Lloyd-Jones, Martyn, *Crefydd Heddiw ac Yfory* (Llandybïe: Llyfrau'r Dryw, 1947).

Lofthouse, W. F.,'A theology of paradox', *The Contemporary Review* 132 (1927), 211–17.

—'Karl Barth and the Gospel', *London Quarterly and Holborn Review* 158 (1933), 28–37.

Macdonald, A. J., 'The message and theology of Barth and Brunner', *Theology* 24 (1932), 197–207, 252–8, 324–32.

—'Professor Karl Barth and the theology of crisis', *The Churchman* 46 (1932), 192–201.

—'Church and state in Germany', *The Nineteenth Century and After* 123 (1938), 338–50.

Mackay, John A., 'Bonn 1930 and after: a lyrical tribute to Karl Barth', *Theology Today* 13 (1956), 287–94.

Mackenzie, K. D., Review of F. W. Camfield, *Revelation and the Holy Spirit*, *Theology* 29 (1934), 55–6.

Mackintosh, Hugh Ross, 'The Swiss group', *The Expository Times* 26 (1924–5), 73–5.

—'Recent foreign theology', *The Expository Times* 27 (1925–26), pp.282–3.

—'Leaders of theological thought: Karl Barth', *The Expository Times* 29 (1927–28), 536–40.

—*Types of Modern Theology: Schleiermacher to Barth* (London: Nisbet, 1937).

Macquarrie, John, *Thinking about God* (London: SCM Press, 1975).

Major, H. D. A., *English Modernism: its origins, methods and aims* (Harvard: Harvard University Press, 1927).

Manning, Bernard Lord, 'Some characteristics of the Older Dissent, with some practical reflections', *The Congregational Quarterly* 5 (1927), 286–300.

—*Essays in Orthodox Dissent* (London: Independent Press, 1939).

Marsden, George, *Reforming Fundamentalism: Fuller Seminary and the New Evangelicalism* (Grand Rapids: Eerdmans, 1987).

Marsh, John (ed.), *Congregationalism Today* (London: Independent Press, 1942).

Marsh, John and Nuttall, Geoffrey F., 'The Congregational theological conference, 1937', *The Congregational Quarterly* 15 (1937), 498–505.

Mascall, E. L., *Theology and the Gospel of Christ: an essay in reorientation* (London: SPCK, 1977).

Mason, Rex, 'H. Wheeler Robinson revisited', *The Baptist Quarterly* 37 (1998), 213–26.

Maury, Pierre, *Predestination and Other Papers* (London: SCM, 1960).

Maxwell, Ronald [pseudonym for R. Gregor Smith], *Still Point: an exercise in living* (London: Nesbit, 1943).

McConnachie, John, 'The teaching of Karl Barth: a new positive movement in German theology', *The Hibbert Journal* 25 (1926–27), 385–400.

—*The Significance of Karl Barth* (London: Hodder and Stoughton, 1931).

—*The Barthian Theology and the Man of Today* (London: Hodder and Stoughton, 1933).

—'Natural religion or revelation?', *The Expository Times* 45 (1933–34), 441–7.

—'Karl Barth in Grossbritannien', *Reformierte Kirchenzeitung* 38 (1935), 259–61.

—'Karl Barth in Great Britain', *Union Seminary Review* 46 (1935), 302–7.

—'The Westminster confession of faith', *The Evangelical Quarterly* 16 (1944), 268–81.

—'Reviews from the Scottish Church-Theology Society News Letter', *Crisis Christology* 3/2 (Winter 1945–46), 48–50.

—'The uniqueness of the Word of God', *Scottish Journal of Theology* 1 (1948), 113–35.

McCormack, Bruce L., *Karl Barth's Critically Realistic Dialectical Theology: its genesis and development, 1909–36* (Oxford: Clarendon Press, 1995).

—'The Barth renaissance in America: an opinion', *Princeton Seminary Bulletin* 23 (2002), 337–40.

McGrath, Alistair, *J. I. Packer: a biography* (London: Hodder and Stoughton, 1997).

McGrath, Alister E. *T. F. Torrance: an intellectual biography* (Edinburgh: T & T Clark, 1999).

McKim, Donald K. (ed.), *How Karl Barth Changed My Mind* (Grand Rapids: Eerdmans, 1986).

McLeod, Hugh, *The Religious Crisis of the 1960s* (Oxford: Oxford University Press, 2007).

McPake, John Lewis, 'H. R. Mackintosh, T. F. Torrance and the reception of the theology of Karl Barth in Scotland', PhD dissertation, New College Edinburgh, 1994.

—'John McConnachie as the original advocate of Karl Barth in Scotland: the primacy of revelation', *Scottish Bulletin of Evangelical Theology* 14 (1996), 101–14.

Metzger, Bruce M., *Reminisces of an Octogenarian* (Peabody, Ma: Hendrickson, 1997).

Micklem, Nathaniel, *The Open Light: an enquiry into faith* (London: J. Clarke, 1919).

—*God's Freemen: a tract for the times* (London: J. Clarke, 1922).

—'Radicalism and Fundamentalism', *The Congregational Quarterly* 5 (1927), 327–34.

—'What is Christian experience?', *The Congregational Quarterly* 5 (1927), pp.549–55.

—'Jesus as prophet and teacher', *Theology* 17 (1928), 208–11.

—'The historical problem of the gospels', *Mansfield College Magazine* 9 (1931–34), 102–16.

—'A restatement of Christian thought', *The Christian World*, 9 March 1933, 7.

—'A restatement of Christian thought: a final letter', *The Christian World*, 8 June, 1933, 5.

—'The Holy Spirit and a new creed', *The Congregational Quarterly* 12 (1934), 545–57.

—(ed.), *Christian Worship: studies in its history and meaning* (Oxford: Oxford University Press, 1936).

—'The Genevan inheritance of Protestant Dissent', *The Hibbert Journal* 25 (1936), 115–31.

—'The faith by which the church lives', *International Review of Missions* 38 (1938), 321–32.

—'Theological issues in the German Church Conflict', *Christendom* 3 (1938), 250–9.

—'The religious situation in Great Britain', *Journal of Religion* 26 (1946), 44–8.

—'Karl Barth on baptism', Review of Karl Barth, *The Teaching of the Church regarding Baptism, The Presbyter* 5/2 (April 1948), 7–8.

—*The Box and the Puppets* (London: Geoffrey Bles, 1957).

—*The Place of Understanding* (London: Geoffrey Bles, 1963).

Miller, Alexander, 'Questions about the Reformed Faith: has it a social message?', *The Presbyter* 1/8 (August 1943), 9–11.

—'Editorial', *The Presbyter* 1/9 (September 1943), 3.

—'Theological counter-revolution', *The Presbyter* 2/1 (January 1944), 12–14.

—'Theology and lay responsibility', *The Christian News-Letter*, supplement 206, 19 April 1944, 5–12.

—'From a height in the Cairngorms: a theological survey of war-time Britain', *The Presbyter* 2/10 (October 1944), 4–7.

Morgan, D. Densil, *Barth* (Dinbych: Gwasg Gee, 1992).

—*Torri'r Seiliau Sicr: detholiad o ysgrifau J. E. Daniel* (Llandysul: Gwasg Gomer, 1993).

—*The Span of the Cross: Christian religion and society in Wales, 1914–2000* (Cardiff: University of Wales Press, 1999).

—*Cedyrn Canrif: Crefydd a Chymdeithas yng Nghymru'r Ugeinfed Ganrif* (Caerdydd: Gwasg Prifysgol Cymru, 2001).

—'Lewis Edwards (1809–87) and Welsh theology', *The Welsh Journal of Religious History* 3 (2008), 15–28.

—*Wales and the Word: historic perspectives on Welsh identity and religion* (Cardiff: University of Wales Press, 2008).

—*The SPCK Introduction to Karl Barth* (London: SPCK, 2010).

Morgan, Robert (ed.), *In Search of Humanity and Deity: a celebration of John Macquarrie's theology* (London: SCM, 2006).

Morris, Ivor Francis, 'The relation of the Word of God to the Doctrine of the Imago Dei in the Theology of Professor Karl Barth', PhD dissertation, New College Edinburgh, 1941.

Morrison, J. H., 'The Barthian school I: an appreciation', *The Expository Times* 43 (1931–32), 314–7.

Morton, T. Ralph, *The Iona Community: personal impressions of the early years* (Edinburgh: St Andrew's Press, 1977).

Mozley, J. K., *Some Tendencies in British Theology: from the publication of Lux Mundi to the present day* (London: SPCK, 1952).

Mozeley, J. K., 'What is christology?', *Theology* 17 (1928), 188–90.

—'The theology of Karl Barth', *The Review of the Churches* 9 (1929), 553–7.

—Review of Karl Barth, *The Epistle to the Romans*, *Theology* 29 (1934), 368–72.

Muir, Augustus, *John White* (London: Hodder and Stoughton, 1958).

Munson, James *The Nonconformists: in search of a lost culture* (London: SPCK, 1991).

Murray, Iain H., *The Life of Arthur W. Pink* (Edinburgh: Banner of Truth Trust, 1981).

—*D. Martyn Lloyd-Jones: the Fight of Faith, 1939–81* (Edinburgh: Banner of Truth Trust, 1990).

—(ed.), *D. Martyn Lloyd-Jones: letters 1919–81* (Edinburgh: Banner of Truth Trust, 1994).

Neale, E., 'A type of Congregational ministry: R. F. Horton (1855–1934) and Lyndhurst Road', *Journal of the United Reformed Church History Society* 5/4 (1997), 215–31.

Newbigin, Lesslie, *Unfinished Agenda: an autobiography* (London: SPCK, 1985).

Newlands, George, *John and Donald Baillie: transatlantic theology* (New York: Peter Lang, 2002).

—*Traces of Liberality: collected essays* (Bern: Peter Lang, 2006).

Niebuhr, Reinhold, 'We are men and not God', *The Christian News-Letter*, supplement 323, 27 October 1948, 11–16.

—'Answer to Karl Barth', *The Christian News-Letter*, supplement 332, 2 March 1949, 74–80.

Nineham, Denis, *Explorations in Theology* (London: SCM, 1977).

Noble, T. A., *Tyndale House and Fellowship: the first sixty years* (Leicester: IVP, 2006).

Norman, E. R., *Church and Society in England, 1770–1970* (Oxford: Clarendon Press, 1976).

Nye, Charles S., Review of Karl Barth, *The Epistle to the Romans*, *Church Quarterly Review* 117 (1933–4), 359–61.

Oldham, J. H., 'Karl Barth on the doctrine of creation', *The Christian News-Letter*, supplement 271, 16 October 1946, 6–16.

Parker, T. H. L., 'The approach to Calvin', *The Evangelical Quarterly* 16 (1944), 165–72.

—'Barth on revelation', *Scottish Journal of Theology* 13 (1960), 366–82.

—*Karl Barth* (Grand Rapids: Eerdmans, 1970).

Parker, T. H. L.(ed.), *Essays in Christology for Karl Barth* (London: Lutterworth Press, 1956).

Parry, R. Ifor, *Diwinyddiaeth Karl Barth: Traethawd Beirniadol* (Llandybïe: Llyfrau'r Dryw, 1949).

—'Diwinyddiaeth yng Nghymru heddiw', *Yr Ymofynnydd* 54 (1954), 74–86.

Payne, E. A., *Henry Wheeler Robinson: a memoir* (London: Nisbet, 1948).

—*The Baptist Union: a short history* (London: Carey Kingsgate Press, 1962).

Peerman, Dean G. and Marty, Martin E., *A Handbook of Christian Theologians* (Cambridge: Lutterworth Press, 1964).

Phillips, John, 'Barth's theology of crisis', *The Congregational Quarterly* 4 (1926), 322–30.

—'The Doctrine of the Word in relation to Holy Scripture as presented in the Theology of Karl Barth', BLitt dissertation, University of Oxford, 1930.

Pierard, Richard V., 'Why did Protestants welcome Hitler?', *Fides et Historia* 10 (1978), 8–29.

Pope, Robert, *Seeking God's Kingdom: the nonconformist social gospel in Wales, 1906–39* (Cardiff: University of Wales Press, 1999).

—*Codi Muriau Dinas Duw: Anghydffurfiaeth ac Anghydffurfwyr Cymru'r Ugeinfed Ganrif* (Bangor: Canolfan Uwchefrydiau Crefydd yng Nghymru, 2005).

—'Colin Ewart Gunton (1941–2003): Christian theologian and preacher of the gospel', *Congregational History Society Magazine* 5/4 (2008), 250–63.

Porteous, Norman W., 'The Barthian school II: the theology of Karl Barth', *The Expository Times* 43 (1931–32), 341–6.

—Review of Karl Barth, *The Epistle to the Romans*, *The Criterion* 13 (1933–34), 342–4.

Presbyterian Church of England, *Minutes of the General Assembly of the Presbyterian Church of England* (London: Presbyterian Church of England, 1934).

Price, E. J., Review of F. W. Camfield, *Revelation and the Holy Spirit*, *The Congregational Quarterly* 12 (1934), 107–8.

Ramsey, A. M., *From Gore to Temple: the development of Anglican theology between Lux Mundi and the Second World War, 1889–1945* (London: Longmans and Green, 1960).

Randall, Ian M.,'"Capturing Keswick": Baptists and the changing spirituality of the Keswick Convention in the 1920s', *The Baptist Quarterly* 36 (1996), 331–48.

—*Evangelical Experiences: a study in the spirituality of English Evangelicalism, 1918–39* (Carlisle: Paternoster Press, 1999).

—*Educating Evangelicalism: the origins, development and impact of London Bible College* (Carlisle: Paternoster Press, 2000).

—*The English Baptists of the Twentieth Century* (Didcot: Baptist History Society, 2005).

Randall, Ian and Hilborn, David, *One Body in Christ: the history and significance of the Evangelical Alliance* (Carlisle: Paternoster Press, 2001).

Rashdall, Hastings, 'Christ as Logos and as Son of God', *The Modern Churchman* 11 (1921), 278–86.

Raven, Charles E., 'Questions about the Reformed Faith: is the new expression of it valid?', *The Presbyter* 1/3 (March 1943), 8–9.

—*Science, Religion and the Future* (Cambridge: Cambridge University Press, 1943).

—*Good News of God: being eight letters . . . based upon Romans I–VIII* (London: Hodder and Stoughton, 1944).

Redman, Robert R. Jn., *Reformulating Reformed Theology: Jesus Christ in the theology of Hugh Ross Mackintosh* (Lanham, PA: University Press of America, 1997).

Reeves, Marjorie (ed.), *Christian Thinking and Social Order: conviction politics from the 1930s to the present day* (London: Cassell, 1999).

Reid, J. K. S., 'Ne taceretur', *Crisis Christology* 3/2 (Winter 1945–46), 32–4.

Richardson, Alan, *Preface to Bible Study* (London: SCM, 1943).

Riesen, R. A., 'Higher criticism in the Free Church fathers', *Records of the Scottish Church History Society* 20 (1979), 119–42.

Robbins, Keith, *History, Religion and Identity in Modern Britain* (London: Hambledon Press, 1993).

—*England, Ireland, Scotland, Wales: the Christian Church, 1900–2000* (Oxford: Oxford University Press, 2008).

Robbins, Keith (ed.), *Protestant Evangelicalism: Britain, Ireland, Germany and America, 1750–1950* (Oxford: Blackwells, 1990).

Roberts, John Wyn (ed.), *Sylfeini'r Ffydd Ddoe a Heddiw* (London: SCM, 1942).

Robinson, H. Wheeler, 'The place of baptism in Baptist churches today', *The Baptist Quarterly* 1 (1922–23), 212–18.

—*The Life and Faith of the Baptists* (London: Kingsgate Press, 1927).

Roggelin, Holger, *Franz Hildebrant: Ein lutherischer Dissenter im Kirchenkampf und Exil* (Göttingen: Vandenhoeck und Ruprecht, 1999).

Rouse, Ruth and Neill, Stephen C., *A History of the Ecumenical Movement, 1517–1948* (London: SPCK, 1967).

Routley, Erik, *The Story of Congregationalism* (London: Independent Press, 1961).

Rowse, Harold C., 'The Barthian challenge to Christian thought', *The Baptist Quarterly* 7 (1934–35), 254–63.

Rumscheidt, H. Martin, *Revelation and Theology: an analysis of the Barth–Harnack correspondence of 1923* (Cambridge: Cambridge University Press, 1972).

Rumscheidt, H. Martin (ed.), *Karl Barth in Re-View* (Pittsburg: Pickwick Press, 1981).

—(ed.), *The Way of Theology in Karl Barth: essays and comments* (Allison Park, PA: Pickwick Press, 1986).

Runia, Klaas, *The Present-Day Christological Debate* (Leicester: IVP, 1984).

BIBLIOGRAPHY

Rushbrooke, J. H. (ed.), *Fifth Baptist World Congress, Berlin August 4–10* (London: Baptist World Alliance, 1934).

Schad, Gustav (ed.), *Germany in the Third Reich* (Frankfurt, 1936).

Schmidt, Karl Ludwig, 'The other-worldly kingdom of God in Our Lord's teaching', *Theology* 9 (1927), 255–8.

Scholder, Klaus, *The Churches and the Third Reich, Vol 1, The Time of Illusions, 1918–34* (London: SCM, 1987).

—*The Churches and the Third Reich, Vol 2, Barmen and Rome, 1934* (London: SCM, 1988).

Schuster, Willy, 'Present day religious movements in Germany', *Church Quarterly Review* 103 (1926–27), 135–63.

Selden, William K., *Princeton Theological Seminary: a narrative history, 1812–1992* (Princeton: PTS, 1992).

Selinger, Suzanne, *Charlotte von Kirchbaum and Karl Barth: a study in biography and the history of theology* (University Park: University of Pennsylvania Press, 1998).

Sell, Alan P. F., *Defending and Declaring the Faith: some Scottish examples, 1860–1920* (Exeter: Paternoster Press, 1987).

—*Commemorations: studies in Christian thought and history* (Cardiff: University of Wales Press, 1993).

—*The Philosophy of Religion, 1875–1980* (Bristol: Thoemmes Press, 1996).

—*Nonconformist Theology in the Twentieth Century* (Milton Keynes: Paternoster, 2006).

Selwyn, E. G. 'The outlook for English theology', *Theology* 40 (1940), 6–14.

—(ed.), *Essays Catholic and Critical* (London: SPCK, 1926).

Simpson, P. Carnegie, *Recollections: mainly ecclesiastical but sometimes human* (London: Nisbet, 1943).

Smart (ed.), James D., *Revolutionary Theology in the Making: Barth–Thurneysen Correspondence, 1914–25* (London: Epworth Press, 1964).

Smith, Ronald Gregor, 'The canonical evidence for the doctrine of God the creator', *The Evangelical Quarterly* 14 (1942), 88–94.

—'The church and the churches', *The Evangelical Quarterly* 15 (1943), 32–39.

—'The Kingdom of God today', *The Evangelical Quarterly* 15 (1943), 269–78.

—'Some implications of demythologizing', *The Listener* 12 February 1953, 259–60.

—'What is demythologizing?', *Theology Today* 10 (1953–54), 34–44.

—'Demythologizing', *The Ecumenical Review* 7 (1954–55), 100–3.

—*The New Man: Christianity and man's coming of age* (London: SCM, 1956).

—*Secular Christianity* (London: Collins, 1966).

Spinks, S. Stephen (ed.), *Religion in Britain since 1900* (London: Andrew Dakers, 1952).

Stanley, Brian, 'Manliness and mission: Frank Lenwood and the London Missionary Society', *Journal of the United Reformed History Society* 5/8 (1996), 458–77.

Stephenson, Alan M. G. *The Rise and Decline of English Modernism* (London: SPCK, 1984).

Stewart, R. W., 'The theology of crisis: a criticism', *The Hibbert Journal* 32 (1933–34), 451–4.

Surin, Kenneth (ed.), *Christ, Ethics and Tragedy: essays in honour of Donald MacKinnon* (Cambridge: Cambridge University Press, 1989).

Sykes, S. W. (ed.), *Karl Barth: studies of his theological method* (Oxford: Oxford University Press, 1979).

—*Karl Barth: centenary essays* (Cambridge: Cambridge University Press, 1989).

Taylor, John and Binfield, Clyde (eds), *Who They Were in the Reformed Churches of England and Wales, 1901–2000* (Donington: United Reformed History Society, 2007).

Taylor, Vincent, 'The Barthian school 4: Rudolf Bultmann', *The Expository Times* 43 (1931–32), 485–90.

Thompson, John, *Christ in Perspective in the Theology of Karl Barth* (Edinburgh: St Andrew's Press, 1978).

Thompson, John (ed.), *Theology Beyond Christendom: essays on the centenary of the birth of Karl Barth* (Allison Park, Pa: Pickwick Publications, 1986).

Torrance, T. F., 'Predestination in Christ', *The Evangelical Quarterly* 13 (1941), 108–41.

—'Down to bedrock', *Crisis Christology* 3/3 (Spring 1946), 30–2.

—Review of Cornelius Van Til, *The New Modernism: An Appraisal of the Theology of Barth and Brunner*, *The Evangelical Quarterly* 19 (1947), 144–9.

—'Universalism or election?', *Scottish Journal of Theology* 2 (1949), 310–18.

—'Theology of Karl Barth', *The Scotsman*, 14 April 1952, 4.

—'The modern eschatological debate', *The Evangelical Quarterly* 25 (1953), 44–54, 94–106, 167–78, 224–32.

—Review of Benjamin B. Warfield, *The Inspiration and Authority of the Bible* with an introduction by Cornelius Van Til, *Scottish Journal of Theology* 7 (1954), 104–8.

—'Karl Barth', *The Expository Times* 66 (1954–55), 205–9.

—*When Christ Comes and Comes Again* (London: Hodder and Stoughton, 1957).

—*Karl Barth: an introduction to his early theology, 1910–31* (London; SCM, 1962).

Torrance, T. F. and Reid, J. K. S., 'Editorial', *Scottish Journal of Theology* 1 (1948), 1–4.

Torrance, T. F. and Reid, J. K. S. (eds), *Eschatology: Scottish Journal of Theology Occasional Papers* (Edinburgh: Oliver and Boyd, 1952).

Torrance, T. F. and Robert T. Walker (ed.), *Incarnation: the person and life of Christ* (Milton Keynes: Paternoster Press, 2008).

Travell, John, *Doctor of Souls: a biography of Dr Leslie D. Weatherhead* (Cambridge: Lutterworth Press, 1999).

Tribble , Harold W., 'The Doctrine of Sanctification in the Theology of Karl Barth', PhD dissertation, New College Edinburgh, 1937.

Vidler, Alec R., *Twentieth Century Defenders of the Faith* (London: SCM, 1965).

—*Scenes from a Clerical Life* (London: Collins, 1977).

Vidler, Alec (ed.), *Soundings: essays in Christian understanding* (Cambridge: Cambridge University Press, 1962).

—*Objections to Christian Belief* (London: Constable, 1963).

Visser't Hooft, W. A., *Memoirs* (London: SCM, 1973).

—*The Genesis and Formation of the World Council of Churches* (Geneva: WCC, 1982).

Vittle, Arwel, *Valentine* (Tal-y-bont: Gwasg y Lolfa, 2006).

Wakefield, Gordon S., *Methodist Devotion: the spiritual life in the Methodist tradition, 1791–1945* (London: Epworth Press, 1966).

—*Robert Newton Flew, 1886–1962* (London: Epworth Press, 1971).

Walton, Robert C. (ed.), *The Gathered Community* (London: Carey Press, 1946).

Webster, John, *Barth's Ethics of Reconciliation* (Cambridge: Cambridge University Press, 1995).

—*Barth's Moral Theology: human action in Barth's thought* (Edinburgh: T & T Clark, 1998).

—*Karl Barth's Early Theology* (London: Continuum, 2005).

Webster, John (ed.), *The Cambridge Companion to Karl Barth* (Cambridge: Cambridge University Press, 2000).

Whale, J. S., *What is a Living Church?* (London: Edinburgh House Press, 1937).

—*Christian Doctrine* (Cambridge: Cambridge University Press, 1942).

Whitehouse, A. W., *The Authority of Grace: essays in response to Karl Barth* (Edinburgh: T & T Clark, 1981).

Whitehouse, W. A. et al., *Christian Confidence: essays on a Declaration of Faith of the Congregational Church in England and Wales* (London: SPCK, 1970).

Wilkinson, Alan, *Dissent or Conform? war, peace and the English churches, 1900–45* (London: SCM Press, 1986).

Williams, D. D. (ed.), *Thomas Charles Edwards* (Liverpool: National Eisteddfod Society, 1921).

Williams, William, *Welsh Calvinistic Methodism: a historical sketch of the Presbyterian Church of Wales*, new edn. (Bridgend: Bryntirion Press, 1998).

Wilson, Roger C., *Frank Lenwood* (London: SCM, 1936).

Witte, John Jr. and Alexander, Frank S. *The Teachings of Modern Protestantism on Law, Politics and Human Nature* (New York: Columbia University Press, 2007).

Wolf, Ernst (ed.), *Theologische Aufsätze Karl Barth zum 50. Geburtstag* (München: Chr. Kaiser Verlag, 1936).

Wood, H. G., *Terrot Reavely Glover: a biography* (Cambridge: Cambridge University Press, 1953).

World Council of Churches, *The Universal Church in God's Design*, Vol. 1 (London: SCM, 1948).

—*Report of the Advisory Commission on the Main Theme of the Second Assembly: Christ, the Hope of the World* (New York: Harper and Brothers, 1954).

Wright, David F. and Badcock, Gary D., *Disruption to Diversity: Edinburgh Divinity 1846–1996* (Edinburgh: T & T Clark, 1996).

INDEX

INDEX

Lightning Source UK Ltd.
Milton Keynes UK
UKOW032210290612

195180UK00002B/4/P